Spring 5.0 Cookbook

Recipes to build, test, and run Spring applications efficiently

Sherwin John Calleja Tragura

BIRMINGHAM - MUMBAI

Spring 5.0 Cookbook

First published: September 2017

Production reference: 1250917

Published by Packt Publishing Ltd.
Livery Place
35 Livery Street
Birmingham
B3 2PB, UK.

ISBN 978-1-78712-831-6

www.packtpub.com

Credits

Author
Sherwin John Calleja Tragura

Copy Editor
Safis Editing

Reviewer
Glenn Base De Paula

Project Coordinator
Vaidehi Sawant

Commissioning Editor
Aaron Lazar

Proofreader
Safis Editing

Acquisition Editor
Sandeep Mishra

Indexer
Francy Puthiry

Content Development Editor
Zeeyan Pinheiro

Graphics
Abhinash Sahu

Technical Editor
Ketan Kamble

Production Coordinator
Nilesh Mohite

About the Author

Sherwin John Calleja Tragura started his career as a student assistant and a mathematics tutor during his college years at the University of the Philippines Los Baños, Laguna, Philippines. With meager resources, he graduated as a Department of Science and Technology (DOST) R.A. 7687 scholar under the Bachelor Of Computer Science degree. Immediately after graduation, he took up the offer to teach CMSC 150 (numerical and symbolic computation) at the Institute of Computer Science and completed his master's degree in computer science simultaneously. He became part of the International Rice Research Institute (IRRI) software team, which gave him the opportunity to use Struts, Spring, and RCP frameworks in many of its software projects.

Based on his experience at IRRI, he was given an opportunity to work as a Java analyst in various companies in Manila, such as ABSI, PHILAM- AIG, and Ayala Systems and Technology Inc. (ASTI). These companies have strengthened his skill set through training in Java and Java Enterprise platforms and some popular tools such as EMC Documentum, Alfresco Document, and Records Management System. He got his first career certification in the EMC Documentum Proven Associate course (E20-120).

After a few years, he decided to become an independent consultant and trainer, providing services mostly for Java-based projects, Alfresco, and Apache OFBiz requirements. He started his venture as a Java-JEE Bootcamp with 77Global and is currently a trainer at Software Laboratory Inc. (SLI), Alibata Business and Technology Services Inc. and Nityo Infotech, Philippines. He also conducts training and talks around the Philippines, for instance, in Cebu City and Tacloban City.

Sherwin has contributed as a technical reviewer to various books by Packt Publishing, including *Delphi Cookbook*, *Alfresco 3 Records Management*, *Alfresco Share*, and *Mastering Hibernate*. He owes everything to Packt Publishing with the unforgettable experience in the technical reviewing tasks, which have been an essential part of his career.

As an Oracle Certified Associate and Java SE 7 Programmer (1Z0-803), Sherwin will continue his mandate as a technical trainer, developer, architect, and designer to help the industry improve its standards in information technology. He will always be an epitome of honor, excellence, and service when it comes to software development and business intelligence.

About the Reviewer

Glenn De Paula is a product of the University of the Philippines Integrated School and is a computer science graduate of the country's most prestigious University of the Philippines. He has 12 years of industry experience, most of which he got working for the government's ICT institute and recently in the banking industry.

He uses Spring, Grails, and Javascript for his day-to-day activities. He has developed numerous Java web applications for the government and has also been the technical team lead for several projects. He currently manages Java developers assigned to different projects in one of the country's most reputable banks.

He is consistently involved in systems analysis and design, source code review, testing, implementation, training, and mentoring. He is currently learning NodeJS and Blockchain technologies in his free time.

I would like to thank the author of this book, the editors, and Packt Publishing for giving me the opportunity to review this great informative book.

I would also like to thank my managers and supervisors for mentoring me and trusting me with projects that helped improve my career.

Thank you very much to my family and friends for all their support. Especially, I thank my wife, Elaine, for all the love and patience.

www.PacktPub.com

For support files and downloads related to your book, please visit www.PacktPub.com.

Did you know that Packt offers eBook versions of every book published, with PDF and ePub files available? You can upgrade to the eBook version at www.PacktPub.com and as a print book customer, you are entitled to a discount on the eBook copy. Get in touch with us at service@packtpub.com for more details.

At www.PacktPub.com, you can also read a collection of free technical articles, sign up for a range of free newsletters and receive exclusive discounts and offers on Packt books and eBooks.

https://www.packtpub.com/mapt

Get the most in-demand software skills with Mapt. Mapt gives you full access to all Packt books and video courses, as well as industry-leading tools to help you plan your personal development and advance your career.

Why subscribe?

- Fully searchable across every book published by Packt
- Copy and paste, print, and bookmark content
- On demand and accessible via a web browser

Customer Feedback

Thanks for purchasing this Packt book. At Packt, quality is at the heart of our editorial process. To help us improve, please leave us an honest review on this book's Amazon page at `https://www.amazon.com/dp/1787128318`.

If you'd like to join our team of regular reviewers, you can e-mail us at `customerreviews@packtpub.com`. We award our regular reviewers with free eBooks and videos in exchange for their valuable feedback. Help us be relentless in improving our products!

Table of Contents

Preface

A *cookbook* is a definitive reference material that consists of several essential recipes on computer programming used for academic, professional, or personal workshops. This book is a large reference database of programming concepts, which aims to describe, highlight, and identify the general features of Spring Framework 5 and also its distinctive features and characteristics as the newest installment of Spring platforms.

The book is written for users who wants to build Spring 5 applications using its core Maven dependencies and for those who prefer to use Spring Boot as the mechanism for web development. It is divided into disciplines that are considered strengths of Spring 5 in which some are familiar concepts such as bean scopes, Model-View-Controller, aspect-object programming, `@Async` transactions, and Spring security concepts. There are also new theoretical frameworks that can only be found in this Spring version such as Reactor Core, WebFlux, cold and hot streams, and reactive web programming.

You will be guided on how to install the appropriate tools and plug-ins for Spring 5 to work properly. For those who are new to Spring framework, you will also be given a short discussion on its core principles through recipes that handle Dependency Injection and Inversion of Control and implementation of the `ApplicationContext` container. For experts, this book offers some recipes that illustrate how to implement reactive components such as reactive JPA, service layers, message-driven transactions, and WebSocket implementation.

When it comes to difficulty levels, there are parts that are for beginners and enthusiasts who want to learn Spring web development. But most chapters are intended for experienced Spring users who want to learn functional and reactive programming components of this newest Spring installment. This will provide a new paradigm to those who are seeking optimal and faster software performance with the help of the Stream API, `Publisher<T>`, `Flux<T>`, `@Async`, `Callable<T>`, and `HandlerFunction<T>`. These are just few concepts that this book will emphasize and expound through some robust and practical set of recipes.

What this book covers

Chapter 1, *Getting Started with Spring*, is the installation and configuration section of the book. It consists of recipes that enumerate the steps on how to install Java 1.8, Tomcat 9 with TLS, Eclipse STS 8.3, MySQL 5.7, and MongoDB 3.2. This will also provide a procedure on how to build a Maven project with Spring 5 dependencies and deploy it using the Tomcat Maven plugin.

Chapter 2, *Learning Dependency Injection (DI)*, covers the core concepts of Inversion of Control (IoC) design pattern. This chapter provides recipes on how to build ApplicationContext through XML-based configurations and the JavaConfig specification. You will also be guided on how to perform a @Bean injection and autowiring. Most importantly, this chapter will highlight the role of IoC in building Spring MVC web applications.

Chapter 3, *Implementing MVC Design Pattern*, highlights the construction of Spring 5 web applications based on its Spring WebMvc module. This will provide recipes that aim to implement the controller, service, and DAO layers with some supporting features such as view resolvers, message bundles, and JDBC connectivity.

Chapter 4, *Securing Spring MVC Application*, is all about Spring Security integration with Spring 5. The chapters that use Spring MVC will be applying Spring Security 4, while those that implement th Spring WebFlux module will be using Spring Security 5 with asynchronous and reactive transactions. Advance topics such as protection against **Cross-Site Request Forgery (CSRF)**, session fixation, and **cross-site scripting (XSS)** and **Clickjacking** will also be covered in some recipes.

Chapter 5, *Cross-Cutting the MVC*, contains recipes that discuss implement aspects, advices, and pointcuts. The aspect-object programming paradigm will be thoroughly discussed, focusing on how it will be used across the Spring 5 platform. Concepts such as improvised security, validating method parameters, monitoring @Controller request transactions, and interception will also be included in the recipes.

Chapter 6, *Functional Programming*, contains recipes that will layout the foundation of functional programming paradigm in Spring 5. This will showcase the Stream API of Java 1.8 and its threaded operations being applied to the service layer of the platform. Topics such as sequential and parallel streams will be covered here.

`Chapter 7`, *Reactive Programming*, focuses on Spring 5 integration with the Reactor Core module. The recipes of this chapter will apply `Publisher<T>` and `Subscriber<T>` from the reactive stream specification in order to generate reactive data streams with short-lived and continuous stream flows. Also included are implementations of asynchronous transactions using `@Async`, `Callable<T>`, and `DeferredResult<T>`. Apart from Reactor Core, this chapter will also include other reactive libraries such as RxJava 2.0 used in building the reactive service layer of Spring 5.

`Chapter 8`, *Reactive Web Applications*, is where we start using Reactor Core in building reactive web applications. This includes recipes that use `Publisher<T>`, `Flux<T>`, and `Mono<T>` in building the service and the `@Controller` layer. Some recipes also discuss how to implement `Callable<T>` and `DeferredResult<T>` response transactions. In this chapter, some view resolvers will be introduced to recognize reactive streams.

`Chapter 9`, *Spring Boot 2.0*, discusses how to build and deploy Spring MVC and Spring WebFlux projects using Spring Boot 2.0. It is only in this chapter that the functional and reactive web framework of Spring 5 will be completely implemented using the `HandlerFunction<T>` and `RouterFunction<T>` reactive components executed by the Reactor Netty server.

`Chapter 10`, *The Microservices*, applies the concept of functional and reactive web framework to microservices. This provides a set of recipes that will showcase the strength of Spring Boot 2.0 in building and consuming synchronous, asynchronous, and reactive services in a microservice. In the chapter, we will cover the procedure to implement a loosely-coupled microservices setup through the Eureka server or Docker.

`Chapter 11`, *Batch and Message-Driven Processes*, talks about how to implement a totally loosely-coupled microservices through message-driven transactions. There are also recipes that will discuss on how to implement background batch processes using Spring Batch and Spring Cloud Task.

`Chapter 12`, *Other Spring 5 Features*, is one of the most important chapters in this book because it showcases other reactive and non-reactive components of Spring 5 that are not mentioned in the previous chapter but are useful to professionals. In this chapter, there are recipes dedicated to how to enable Hibernate 5, WebSocket, and HazelCast caching. Also, there are others written to showcase the reactive features of Spring 5 such as Spring Data JPA, Spring Data MongoDB, and Kotlin.

`Chapter 13`, *Testing Spring 5 Components*, highlights the Spring TestContext framework and how it is utilized in testing synchronous, asynchronous, and reactive Spring components such as native and REST services, repositories, JPA transactions, controllers, and views.

What you need for this book

Firstly, this book is intended for readers who have a background at least in Java SDK programming. This book does not cover anything about how to start dealing with Java as a language. Secondly, each chapter contains recipes that can be developed using STS Eclipse 3.8 and can be executed using Apache Tomcat 9.x and the Reactor Netty server. The following are the required tools and libraries needed to perform the recipes in this book:

- Any machine with at least 4 GB of RAM
- Java 1.8
- STS Eclipse 3.8
- Apache Tomcat 9.x
- OpenSSL for Windows
- MySQL 5.7
- MongoDB 3.2
- RabbitMQ 3.6
- Erlang 9.0
- Apache Couchdb 2.1.0
- Docker Toolbox for Windows
- Google Chrome or Mozilla Firefox browser

Other versions of these requirements will not be covered in this book.

Who this book is for

This book is composed of two menus: core concepts and advance concepts. The core concepts found in the recipes of chapters 1 to 3 are recommended to Java programmers who have no background in Spring Framework but are willing to start their career with the Spring 5 platform. Also, enthusiasts who know OOP and MVC concepts can also deal with the first three chapters since these are just the same ideas and principles being implemented in Spring 4 and below.

The recipes covered in chapters 4 to 13 are for experienced Spring developers who want to learn how to integrate modules such as Spring Security, Spring WebFlux, Reactor Core, Spring Batch, Spring Cloud, and advance related libraries. Aspects, advices, pointcuts, and interceptors, for instance, can only be understood by readers who know where in the Spring platform to apply the cross-cutting procedure. It also takes a deep knowledge of Spring when it comes to implementing REST web services and how to consume them using client APIs. Since this book is more inclined to asynchronous and reactive programming concepts, this book will be challenging for someone who knows Spring Framework very well.

Sections

In this book, you will find several headings that appear frequently (Getting ready, How to do it, How it works, There's more, and See also).

To give clear instructions on how to complete a recipe, we use these sections as follows:

Getting ready

This section tells you what to expect in the recipe, and describes how to set up any software or any preliminary settings required for the recipe.

How to do it...

This section contains the steps required to follow the recipe.

How it works...

This section usually consists of a detailed explanation of what happened in the previous section.

There's more...

This section consists of additional information about the recipe in order to make the reader more knowledgeable about the recipe.

See also

This section provides helpful links to other useful information for the recipe.

Conventions

In this book, you will find a number of text styles that distinguish between different kinds of information. Here are some examples of these styles and an explanation of their meaning.

All recipes codes are written inside a numbered bullet and follow the following style:

```
public Set<String> getDistinctNames(){
    Function<Employee,String> allNames = (e) -> e.getFirstName();
    Set<String> setNames = employeeDaoImpl.getEmployees()
    .stream()
    .filter((a) -> a.getAge() > 25)
    .map(allNames)
    .collect(Collectors.toCollection(HashSet::new));
    return setNames;
}
```

Code words in text, HTML tags, database table names, folder names, filenames, file extensions, and pathnames are shown as follows: "Import `socketapps.js` inside `hotline.html` using the `<script>` tag"

A URL is written as follows: "Visit the site `https://www.mongodb.com/download-center#community` to download MongoDB under different operating system platforms. It also comes with SSL and no-SSL support."

Acronyms and **module names** may be shown in bold: "The **Hibernate 5** has no dedicated starter POM in Spring Boot 2.0, but it is by default contained in the Spring Data JPA starter POM."

Any command-line input or output is written as follows:

```
keytool -import -alias spring5server -file spring5packt.crt -keystore
"<Java1.8_folder>\Java1.8.112\jre\lib\security\cacerts" -storepass changeit
```

New terms and **important words** are shown in bold. Words that you see on the screen, for example, in menus or dialog boxes, appear in the text like this: "On the dashboard, look for **IDE EXTENSIONS** and click that button".

Important phrases, terminology, ideas, and *concepts* are written in this style: "MongoDB is an unstructured database so it has no concept of *relational models* such as database and table schema".

Warnings or important notes appear like this.

 Tips and tricks appear like this.

Reader feedback

Feedback from our readers is always welcome. Let us know what you think about this book-what you liked or disliked. Reader feedback is important for us as it helps us develop titles that you will really get the most out of. To send us general feedback, simply e-mail feedback@packtpub.com, and mention the book's title in the subject of your message. If there is a topic that you have expertise in and you are interested in either writing or contributing to a book, see our author guide at www.packtpub.com/authors.

Downloading the example code

You can download the example code files for this book from your account at http://www.packtpub.com. If you purchased this book elsewhere, you can visit http://www.packtpub.com/support and register to have the files e-mailed directly to you. You can download the code files by following these steps:

1. Log in or register to our website using your e-mail address and password.
2. Hover the mouse pointer on the **SUPPORT** tab at the top.
3. Click on **Code Downloads & Errata**.
4. Enter the name of the book in the **Search** box.
5. Select the book for which you're looking to download the code files.
6. Choose from the drop-down menu where you purchased this book from.
7. Click on **Code Download**.

Once the file is downloaded, please make sure that you unzip or extract the folder using the latest version of:

- WinRAR / 7-Zip for Windows
- Zipeg / iZip / UnRarX for Mac
- 7-Zip / PeaZip for Linux

The code bundle for the book is also hosted on GitHub at `https://github.com/PacktPublishing/Spring-5.0-Cookbook`. We also have other code bundles from our rich catalog of books and videos available at `https://github.com/PacktPublishing/`. Check them out!

Downloading the color images of this book

We also provide you with a PDF file that has color images of the screenshots/diagrams used in this book. The color images will help you better understand the changes in the output. You can download this file from `http://www.packtpub.com/sites/default/files/downloads/Spring5Cookbook.pdf`.

Errata

Although we have taken every care to ensure the accuracy of our content, mistakes do happen. If you find a mistake in one of our books-maybe a mistake in the text or the code- we would be grateful if you could report this to us. By doing so, you can save other readers from frustration and help us improve subsequent versions of this book. If you find any errata, please report them by visiting `http://www.packtpub.com/submit-errata`, selecting your book, clicking on the **Errata Submission Form** link, and entering the details of your errata. Once your errata are verified, your submission will be accepted and the errata will be uploaded to our website or added to any list of existing errata under the Errata section of that title. To view the previously submitted errata, go to `https://www.packtpub.com/books/content/support` and enter the name of the book in the search field. The required information will appear under the **Errata** section.

Piracy

Piracy of copyrighted material on the Internet is an ongoing problem across all media. At Packt, we take the protection of our copyright and licenses very seriously. If you come across any illegal copies of our works in any form on the Internet, please provide us with the location address or website name immediately so that we can pursue a remedy. Please contact us at `copyright@packtpub.com` with a link to the suspected pirated material. We appreciate your help in protecting our authors and our ability to bring you valuable content.

Questions

If you have a problem with any aspect of this book, you can contact us at `questions@packtpub.com`, and we will do our best to address the problem.

1
Getting Started with Spring

Spring 5.0 is the latest Spring Framework release that highlights **Functional Web Framework** and **Reactive Programming**. In this version, all the codes comply with the latest Java 1.8 syntax but the whole framework is designed to support the Java 1.9 **Java Development Kit** (**JDK**) in the near future. On the enterprise platform, the framework is supposed to use servlet 3.1 and 4.0 specifications and utilize HTTP/2 to run its applications.

This book will start with how to set up and configure the development environment given the necessary tools and plugins to run Spring 5.0 applications.

In this chapter, you will learn about the following:

- Installing Java Development Kit 1.8
- Installing Tomcat 9 and configuring HTTP/2
- Installing STS Eclipse 3.8 IDE
- Creating Eclipse projects using Maven
- Creating Spring STS Eclipse projects using Gradle
- Deploying Spring projects using Maven
- Deploying Spring projects using Gradle
- Installing the MySQL 5.7 database server
- Installing the MongoDB 3.2 database server

Installing Java Development Kit 1.8

The book will be using JDK 1.8, which has the support to run Spring 5.0. This version of Java supports @FunctionalInterface and lambda expressions, which are necessary concepts being showcased in this framework. A @FunctionalInterface is an interface with exactly one abstract method that may lead to its instantiation through lambda expressions. Lambda expressions are used to implement anonymous inner classes, avoiding too much bulk in the codes.

Moreover, JDK 1.8 has java.util.stream APIs that can work with collections and NIO 2.0, using stream operations such as filter, map, and reduce. These stream APIs work in sequential and parallel executions. In the area of concurrency, this JDK provides some very essential enhancements on ConcurrentHashMap for its forEach, forEachEntry, forEachKey, forEachValue, compute, merge, reduce, and search methods. Also some changes were done on the object creation of CompletableFuture and Executors.

Getting started

All Java JDK installers are downloaded from Oracle's site at http://www.oracle.com/technetwork/java/javase/downloads/index.html.

How to do it...

To download JDK 1.8, perform the following steps:

1. Visit the preceding Oracle's page for downloads.
2. On that page, click the **JDK Download** link. After the click, you will see the content page for JDK 1.8 installers as shown in the following image:

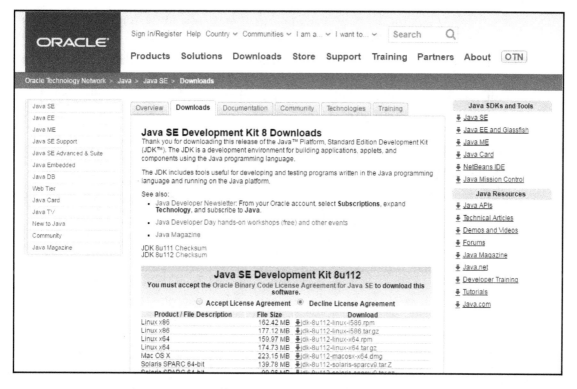

3. Select **Accept License Agreement** by clicking its radio button.

4. Start downloading the JDK depending on the operating system and architecture of your development machine. In the case of this book, we will be choosing the option `jdk-8u112-windows-x64` since the operating system used by this book will be 64-bit.

5. After saving the installer into the filesystem, run the installer and proceed with a series of installation wizards for JDK configuration with the inclusion of some JRE installation to your system.

6. This is optional but it is recommended you create an environment variable `JAVA_HOME` for your newly installed JDK 1.8.112. On Windows operating systems:

    1. Open the **System** section of the **Control Panel**.

    2. Select the **Advanced System Settings** link. Windows 10 will prompt you with a **User Account Control** dialog box if you are not an administrator.

    3. Create a system variable `JAVA_HOME` and assign the location of the JDK directory to it.

4. Look for the path system variable and append the following line: `%JAVA_HOME\%bin`.

7. Verify if all `classpath` settings are created correctly. On Windows, open a new command terminal and run the `javac -version` command. This command must be recognized as a valid command; otherwise, check your configuration details again.

How it works...

The installed JDK will be the core language interpreter of Spring 5.0 projects, whether or not they are deployed to a Tomcat 9.x application server through Maven or Gradle. To read more about JDK 1.8, the reference `http://www.oracle.com/technetwork/java/javase/8-whats-new-2157071.html` will provide you with some information about its highlights and will explain why it is popular nowadays in functional and reactive programming. More detailed concepts on functional programming will be discussed in `Chapter 6`, *Functional Programming*.

Installing Tomcat 9 and configuring HTTP/2

Since the focus of request and response connections in Spring 5.0 will be **HTTP/2**, this book will feature the use of HTTP/2 as the protocol for web communications. In HTTP1.1, each request sent to a server resource corresponds to only one response. If the server resources generated a longer processing time, then all other incoming requests are blocked. Unlike in HTTP/2, a single request-response transaction can contain multiple concurrently open streams to avoid starvation or deadlocks. On the other hand, HTTP/2 has superb performance when it comes to web browsing experience, notwithstanding the security it provides to the simple web applications and complex portals using SSL certificates. But what is appreciated in HTTP/2 is its backwards compatibility with HTTP/1.1, thus HTTP methods, status codes, and header fields can still be managed by `HttpServletRequest` and `HttpServletResponse` without any changes.

Getting started

Visit the download page of Apache Tomcat application server `https://tomcat.apache.org/download-native.cgi` and click the **Tomcat 9** link that will lead you to the download page.

How to do it...

The book will utilize Tomcat 9, which is the only Tomcat distribution that fully supports HTTP/2 without installing lots of third-party tools and modules. The following are the step-by-step details in setting up HTTP/2 in Tomcat 9:

1. Check if you have installed JDK 1.8 in your system. Tomcat 9 only runs with the latest JDK 1.8 without error logs.

2. If you have downloaded the zipped version, unzip the folder to the filesystem of the development machine. If you have the EXE or MSI version, double-click the installer and follow the installation wizards. The following details must be taken into consideration:

    1. You can retain the default server startup port (8005), HTTP connector port (8080), and AJP port (8009) or configure according to your own settings.

    2. Provide the `manager-gui` with the username as `packt` and its password as `packt`.

3. After the installation process, start the server and check whether the main page is loaded using the URL `http://localhost:8080/`.

4. If Tomcat 9 is running without errors, it is now time to configure HTTP/2 protocol. Since HTTP/2 uses **clear-text type** request transactions, it is required that we configure **Transport Layer Security** (**TLS**) to use HTTP/2 since many browsers such as Firefox and Chrome do not support clear text. For TLS to work, we need a certificate from **OpenSSL**. For Windows machines, you can get it from `https://slproweb.com/products/Win32OpenSSL.html`.

5. Install the OpenSSL (for example, `Win64OpenSSL-1_1_0c.exe`) by following the installation wizards. This will be used to generate our **certificate signing request** (**CSR**), SSL certificates, and private keys.

6. Create an environment variable `OPENSSL_HOME` for your operating system. Register it into the `$PATH` the `%OPENSSL_HOME%/bin`.

7. Generate your private key and SSL certificate by running the following command: `openssl req -newkey rsa:2048 -nodes -keyout spring5packt.key -x509 -days 3650 -out spring5packt.crt`.

8. In our setup, the file `spring5packt.key` is the private key and must be strictly unreachable to clients, but by the server only. The other file, `spring5packt.crt`, is the SSL certificate that we will be registering both in the **server keystore** and **JRE keystore**. This certificate is only valid for 10 years (3,650 days).

9. In *Step 8*, you will be asked to enter CSR information such as:

    ```
    Country name (two-letter code) [AU]:PH
    State or province name (full name) [Some-State]: Metro Manila
    Locality name (for example, city):Makati City
    Organization name (for example, company) [Internet Widgits
    Pty Ltd]:Packt Publishing
    Organizational unit name (for example, section): Spring 5.0
    Cookbook
    Common name (for example, server FQDN or your name):
    Alibata Business Solutions and Training Services
    E-mail address: sherwin.tragura@alibatabusiness.com
    ```

10. Generate a keystore that will be validated, both by your applications and server. JDK 1.8.112 provides `keytool.exe` that will be run to create keystores. Using the files in *Step 8*, run the following command:

    ```
    keytool -import -alias spring5server -file spring5packt.crt -
    keystore spring5server.keystore
    ```

11. If this is your first time, you will be asked to create a password of no less than six letters. Otherwise, you will be asked to enter your password. You will be asked if you want to trust the certificate. The message **Certificate reply was installed in keystore** means you have successfully done the process.

12. Java JRE must know the certificate in order to allow all the execution of your deployed Spring 5 applications. To register the created certificate into the JRE `cacerts`, run the following command:

    ```
    keytool -import -alias spring5server -file spring5packt.crt -
    keystore
    "<Java1.8_folder>\Java1.8.112\jre\lib\security\cacerts" -
    storepass changeit
    ```

13. The default password is `changeit`. You will be asked to confirm if the certificate is trusted and you just type *Y* or yes. The message **Certificate reply was installed in keystore** means you have successfully finished the process.

14. Copy the three files, namely `spring5packt.crt`, `spring5packt.key`, and `spring5server.keystore` to Tomcat's `conf` folder and JRE's `security` folder (`<installation_folder>\Java1.8.112\jre\lib\security`).

15. Open Tomcat's `conf\server.xml` and uncomment the `<Connector>` with port `8443`. Its final configuration must be:

    ```
    <Connector port="8443"
    protocol="org.apache.coyote.http11.Http11AprProtocol"
    ```

```
maxThreads="150" SSLEnabled="true">
    <UpgradeProtocol
    className="org.apache.coyote.http2.Http2Protocol"/>
    <SSLHostConfig honorCipherOrder="false">
        <Certificate certificateKeyFile="conf/spring5packt.key"
        certificateFile="conf/spring5packt.crt"
        keyAlias="spring5server" type="RSA" />
    </SSLHostConfig>
</Connector>
```

16. Save the `server.xml`.

17. Open `C:\Windows\System32\drivers\etc\hosts` file and add the following line at the end:

    ```
    127.0.0.1 spring5server
    ```

18. Restart the server. Validate the setup through running `https://localhost:8443`. At first your browser must fire a message; **Your connection is not secure**. Just click **Advanced** and accept the certificate:

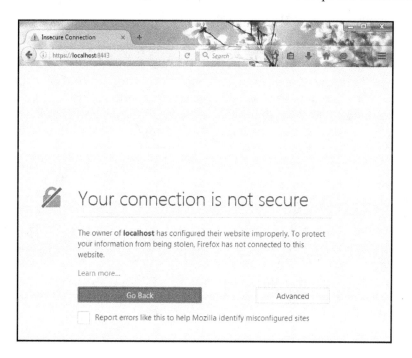

19. You will now be running HTTP/2.

How it works...

Java 1.8 and Java 1.9 together with Spring 5.0 support HTTP/2 for the advancement of the JEE servlet container. This improvement is part of their **JSR 369** specification which highlights the Servlet 4.0 specification. This Spring version is after Java 1.8's advance concurrency and stream support to run its functional and reactive modules. And since the core platform of Spring 5 is reactive, non-blocking and asynchronous, it needs **NIO 2.0** threads of Tomcat 9.x's HTTP/2 for its project execution.

Since enabling HTTP/2 requires configuring TLS, browsers such as Firefox and Chrome will be restricted a bit by this TLS when it comes to running applications. These client browsers do not support clear text TCP; thus there is a need for secured HTTP (or HTTPS) which is the only way these browsers can utilize HTTP/2. And since TLS is enabled, there is a need for a keystore certificate that must be recognized by the application servers and accepted by the browsers in order to execute the request URLs.

OpenSSL for Windows is chosen as our certificate generator in creating TLS certificates. The book will use a self-signed certificate only, which is the easiest and most appropriate method so far in order to secure Apache Tomcat 9. This method no longer needs the certificate to be signed by a **Certificate Authority (CA)**.

After generating the certificate, the certificate must be registered to both the keystore of the JRE and the custom keystore (for example, `spring5keystore.keystore`) of the application server. Keystores are used in the context of setting up the SSL connection in Java applications between client and server. They provide credentials, store private keys and certificates corresponding to the public keys of the applications and browsers. They are also required to access the secured server which usually triggers client authentication. The installed Java has its own keystore, which is `<installation_folder>\Java1.8.112\jre\lib\security\cacerts`. Always provide the official passwords in adding your certificates to these keystores. JRE has a default `changeit` password for its keystore.

The advantage of the TLS-enabled Tomcat 9 server is its support to **JSR-369**, which is the implementation of the Servlet 4.0 container. Moreover, the virtual hosting and multiple certificates are supported for a single connector, with each virtual host able to support multiple certificates. When the request-response transaction happens with HTTP/2, a session with multiple streams or threads of connections is created, as shown in the following code:

```
MetaData.Request metaData = new MetaData.Request("GET",
HttpScheme.HTTP, new HostPortHttpField("spring5server: 8443" +
server.getLocalport()), "/", HttpVersion.HTTP_2, new
HttpFields());
```

```
HeadersFrame headersFrame = new HeadersFrame(1, metaData, null,
true);
session.newStream(headersFrame, new Promise.Adapter<Stream>(),
new PrintingFramesHandler());
session.newStream(headersFrame, new Promise.Adapter<Stream>(),
new PrintingFramesHandler());
session.newStream(headersFrame, new Promise.Adapter<Stream>(),
new PrintingFramesHandler());
```

The whole concept of HTTP/2 transporting requests from client to server and responding back to its clients is depicted with the conceptual model as follows:

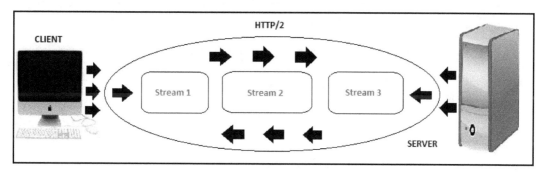

Installing STS Eclipse 3.8 IDE

All the recipes will be implemented using **Spring Tool Suite** (**STS**) Eclipse 3.8 which has the latest features that support JDK 1.8.

Getting started

Visit the site `https://spring.io/tools/sts/all` and download the STS 3.8 release for Windows, Linux, or macOS. In our case, we will be opting for the Windows version. It is also available in 32-bit or 64-bit operating systems.

How to do it...

To get STS Eclipse 3.8, perform the following steps:

1. After the download, unzip the file using WinZip or 7ZIP to your filesystem.

2. Update its VM usage to enhance performance through making the heap grow to a larger amount by adding the `-vmargs` command to the `eclipse.ini` file inside the installation folder, or by appending to the Eclipse shortcut's target property. Following the command are the following Java heap memory configurations:

```
-Xms512m
-Xmx1024m
```

3. Go to the installation folder `<installation_folder>\sts-bundle\sts-3.8.3.RELEASE` and run `STS.exe`.

4. Running `STS.exe` will result in launching your workspace launcher. Create an Eclipse workspace as shown as follows:

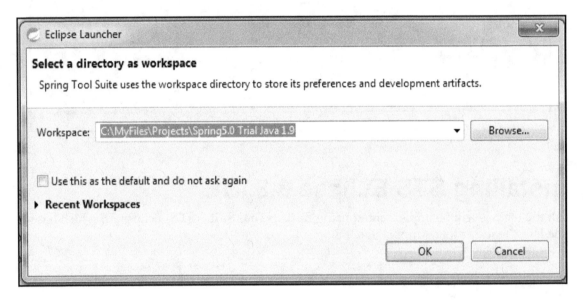

5. Then, you are now ready to create code snippets.

How it works...

STS Eclipse 3.8 is a customized all-in-one Eclipse-based distribution that provides support for Spring technologies such as Pivotal Cloud Foundry, Gradle, and Pivotal Server. Moreover, it is plugin-ready and contains language support, framework support, and runtime support for Java JDK 1.8 and Java EE 7.

The IDE has the following parts: *views, perspectives*, and the *option menus*. The *view* is the IDE's way of projecting its metadata or components graphically. Some views are **console**, **debug**, and **task list**, and **data management** views. The styling and the presence of the needed views depend on the type of *perspective* required for a particular project. A *perspective* is the logical arrangement of all these views. In our case, we have to choose a JEE perspective from the **Window** | **Perspective** | **Open Perspective** menu option to proceed with our programming.

But before we create our first project, always set the **Java Runtime Environment** to JDK's JRE. The JRE setting is located at **Windows** | **Preferences** and you need to **Add...** and choose the JDK's JRE as shown as follows:

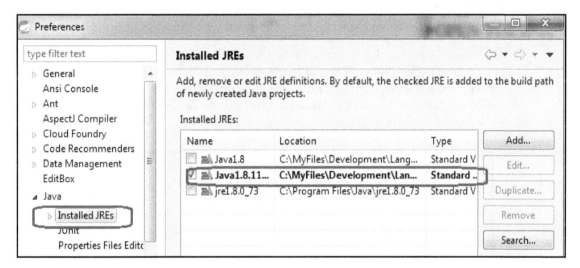

You are now ready to create your Maven and Gradle project for our recipes in the next chapters.

Creating Eclipse projects using Maven

One option for creating our Spring 5.0 projects is through Maven. The STS Eclipse 3.8 has built-in Maven plugins that will create Maven-ready Eclipse projects easily.

Getting started

Before creating the first Maven project, check first the JRE workspace configuration of your IDE. As noted in the previous recipe, the JRE of your Eclipse must be set to the JDK's JRE. Moreover, check the embedded version of Maven installed in STS Eclipse 3.8 through the **Windows** | **Preferences** panel. STS 3.8 will be using its embedded Maven 3.0 for the deployment operations. The list of Maven versions is available at `https://maven.apache.org/`.

How to do it...

Follow the steps to create Maven Projects for our succeeding code snippets as follows:

1. There are two ways that we can create a Maven project from scratch in STS. One option is to right-click the **Project Explorer** of the IDE in order to choose **New** | **Other...** from the pop-up window (or *Ctrl-N*). The other option is to click the **File menu** option then choose the **New** | **Other...** . Both of these operations will lead us to our **New** project wizard as shown as follows:

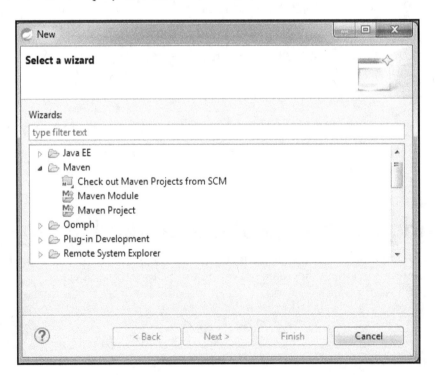

2. On the menu wizard, click the **Maven Module** and then the **Maven Project** option. The **New Maven project** wizard will pop-up anew. Just click **Create Simple Project (skip archetype selection)** to create a clean project from scratch:

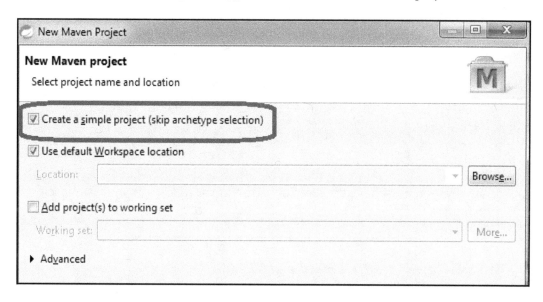

3. Afterwards, the next wizard will require you to fill out the necessary **Group Id** and **Artifact Id** for your project. In the following example, the **Group ID** is `org.packt.recipe.core` and the **Artifact Id** is, let us say, `ch01`. The next important field that needs to be filled is **Packaging** and it must be set to `war` in our case:

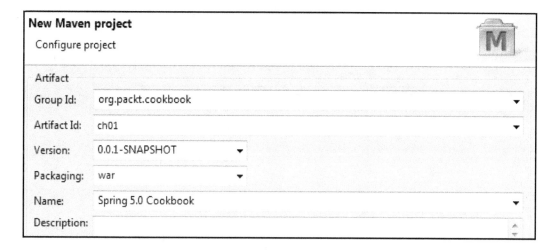

4. Click **Finish**. Look for the file `pom.xml` and insert below it the following lines to correct some Maven bugs:

```
<build>
  <finalName>ch01-spring5-cookbook</finalName>
  <plugins>
    <plugin>
      <artifactId>maven-war-plugin</artifactId>
      <version>2.3</version>
      <configuration>
        <failOnMissingWebXml>false</failOnMissingWebXml>
      </configuration>
    </plugin>
  </plugins>
</build>
```

5. Finally, you must have the directory structure as follows in your own project explorer:

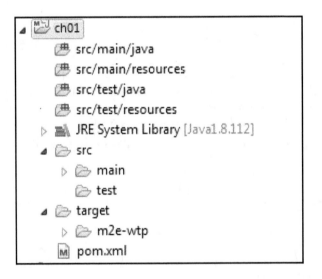

How it works...

Apache Maven is already a built-in plugin in Eclipse and helps developers manage projects and use some build tools to clean, install, and deploy Eclipse projects. It has the main configuration file which is called the **Project Object Model (POM)** file.

POM is the fundamental unit of work in Maven that contains information and configuration details about the project. Some core information in POM is `<modelVersion>`, which currently must be set to `4.0.0`, `<groupId>`, that identifies the project uniquely together with `<projectId>` and `<versionId>` across all projects in the Maven repository, `<artifactId>`, which is the name of the WAR file without the version, and `<packaging>`, which is WAR.

Later in this book, we will be adding `<properties>` and `<dependencies>` and `<plugins>` for our Spring 5.0 code recipes in our `pom.xml` file.

Creating Spring STS Eclipse projects using Gradle

Another option in building Spring 5.0 projects is through the use of **Gradle**. STS Eclipse includes Gradle as one of its tooling and project management tools. In our case, we will be installing an STS Eclipse module extension in the easiest way in order to fully use Gradle.

Getting started

Install the Gradle module extension in our STS Eclipse 3.8 in order to clean, build, and deploy projects in Gradle. Perform the following steps:

1. Click the **Dashboard** toolbar option of your Eclipse. After clicking, you will be opening the main dashboard of the IDE:

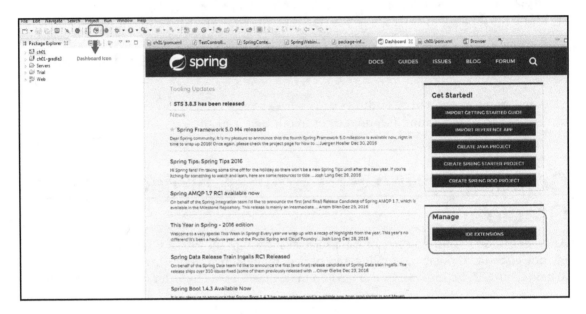

2. On the dashboard, look for **IDE EXTENSIONS** and click that button. A new window showing all the available Eclipse STS extensions will pop up. Click on **Gradle (STS Legacy) Support** and install it:

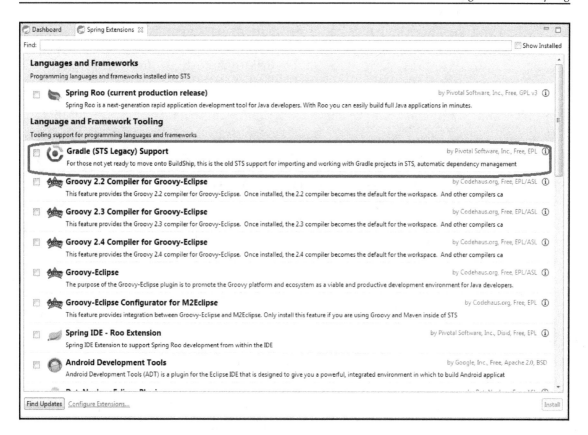

3. The next steps will just be similar to installing new Eclipse plugins. Just click the **Install** button and follow the installation wizard. Eclipse needs to be restarted after a successful installation.

4. If you want to change the Gradle distribution, you can replace the Eclipse embedded Gradle installation with some new version at `https://gradle.org/gradle-download/`. Or you can shift to Eclipse Buildship with Gradle Plugin if some of the files are not supported by the installed Gradle plugin:

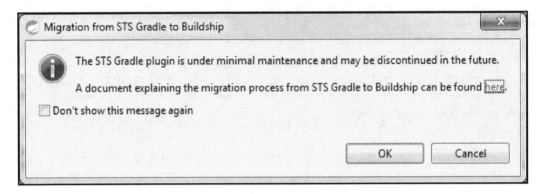

How to do it...

After installing the Gradle STS extension, perform the following steps to install the Spring Gradle project:

1. After installing, you are ready to create a Gradle project for Spring development. Go to the **New project wizard** (*Ctrl-N*) of STS Eclipse and create a Gradle project.

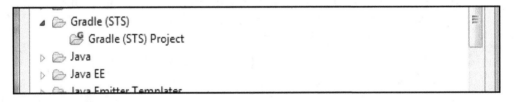

2. On the **Gradle Project wizard**, assign a name for your project and choose **Java Quickstart** for the **Sample project** option. Click **Finish** and it will take a while to create, build, clean, and install your Gradle STS project.

3. Delete unnecessary project files. Right-click on the project and click on **Gradle (STS) | Refresh all**.

4. Open the `build.gradle` and overwrite the existing configuration with this:

```
apply plugin: 'eclipse'
apply plugin: "war"

sourceCompatibility = 1.8
version = '1.0'

war {
    baseName = 'ch02-gradle'
    version = '1.0'
}

sourceCompatibility = 1.8

repositories {
    mavenCentral()
    jcenter()
}
```

5. Right-click on the project and click **Gradle (STS)** | **Tasks Quick Launcher** to run the **Gradle Task Launcher**. Using the launcher, **clean** and **build** the project for the first time:

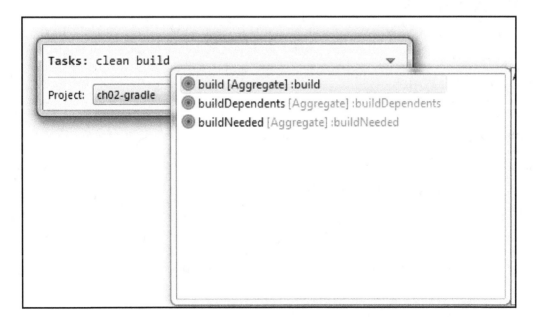

6. Finally, at this point, you have created your Spring Gradle project which will look like this:

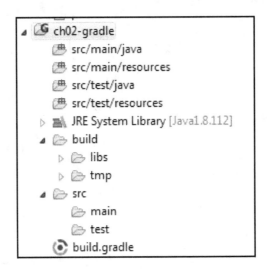

How it works...

The most important configuration file in a Gradle project is the `build.gradle`. First, we have to add `apply plugin: 'java'` to tell Gradle that Java is the core language in building the scripts, testing the codes, executing compiled objects, creating Javadoc, and deploying JAR or WAR files. Since all project management and tooling depends on STS Eclipse, there is a need to add `apply plugin: 'eclipse'` in order to tell Gradle that all descriptors are Eclipse-specific and can be integrated and executed with Eclipse core and extension plugins. A by-product of its project installation and execution are the Eclipse folders such as `.project`, and `.classpath`. And since this is a web development project, we need to `apply plugin: 'war'` to indicate that the deployment is at WAR mode. Later on we will be adding some plugins needed in the development of our recipes.

In the properties section, the configuration must tell Gradle the version of the JDK through the `sourceCompatibility` property. Another property is the version of the WAR or project deployment, which is at first set to 1.0. Since the mode of deployment is the web, Java must know the name and the version of the WAR file to be generated.

On the repositories section, the configuration must define where to find the dependencies, which are at **JCenter** and **MavenCentral**.

Deploying Spring projects using Maven

Our application server is Tomcat 9 and we will be using HTTP/2 to execute all Spring 5.0 projects at port `8443` with some certificates stored in the server's keystore.

Getting started

At this point, the Tomcat 9 server must be running at `https://localhost:8843/` in all browsers. Using OpenSSL, certificates are already installed in JRE's keystore and our server's keystore. Moreover, you have already successfully created your STS Maven project in order for us to configure your POM file.

How to do it...

Open the POM file of your Maven project and add the following details:

1. There is no available working Maven plugin for Tomcat 9 so we need to use the latest stable version, which is `tomcat7-maven-plugin`. Add the following Maven plugin details for Tomcat 7 deployment under the `<plugins>` section of the `<build>`:

```
<plugin>
  <groupId>org.apache.tomcat.maven</groupId>
  <artifactId>tomcat7-maven-plugin</artifactId>
  <version>2.2</version>
  <configuration>
    <url>https://spring5server:8443/manager/text</url>
    <path>/ch01</path>
    <keystoreFile>C:MyFilesDevelopmentServersTomcat9.0
    confspring5server.keystore</keystoreFile>
    <keystorePass>packt@@</keystorePass>
    <update>true</update>
    <username>packt</username>
    <password>packt</password>
  </configuration>
</plugin>
```

2. Right-click on the project and click on **Run As** | **Maven Build...** and execute the following goal: `clean install tomcat7:deploy`

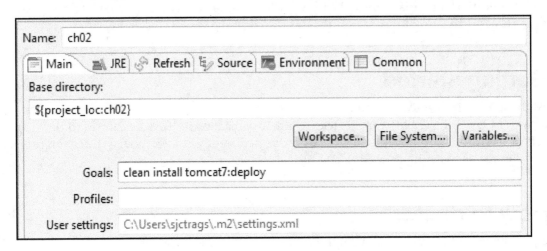

3. Everything is successful if the console outputs this Maven log:

```
[INFO] Deploying war to https://spring5server:8443/ch02
Uploading: https://spring5server:8443/manager/text/deploy?path=%2Fch02&update=true
Uploaded: https://spring5server:8443/manager/text/deploy?path=%2Fch02&update=true (2 KB)

[INFO] tomcatManager status code:200, ReasonPhrase:
[INFO] OK - Deployed application at context path /ch02
[INFO] ------------------------------------------------------------------------
[INFO] BUILD SUCCESS
[INFO] ------------------------------------------------------------------------
[INFO] Total time: 3.222 s
[INFO] Finished at: 2017-01-06T00:12:32+08:00
[INFO] Final Memory: 18M/202M
[INFO] ------------------------------------------------------------------------
```

How it works...

The configuration detail starts with the `<url>` that sets Tomcat's plain-text-based administration interface used by Maven to invoke commands of the server. Maven needs to access the administration panel to allow the copy of the WAR file to the `webapps`. Since we will be using the TLS-enabled connector, we will be using the secured-HTTP together with the registered hostname in the keystore which is `spring5server`.

The tag `<path>` sets the context root of the project and must have a forward slash while the `<username>` and `<password>` refer to the credentials of the administrator having the roles `manager-gui` and `manager-script`.

The most important configuration details are `<keystoreFile>` and `<keystorePass>`. `<keystoreFile>` makes reference to the keystore of Tomcat that contains the TLS certificate. `<keystorePass>` provides the password used by `<keystoreFile>` in registering certificates. Together with these credentials, we have to be sure that the certificate has been added to the JRE's keystore which is `<installation_folder>\Java1.8.112\jre\lib\security\cacerts`.

`<update>` is required to undeploy all existing WAR files that already exist in the `webapps`. Sometimes the deployment does not work without this forced update.

Deploying Spring projects using Gradle

If the project is written in Gradle, there will be some modification to be done in our `gradle.build` configuration details.

Getting started

Validate that your Tomcat with TLS-enabled connection is working by running `https://localhost:8080/` on any browser. Also, check if your STS Gradle project is clean and updated.

How to do it...

1. Open the `gradle.build` file and add the `buildScript()` function that accepts a closure containing all libraries needed to be referenced in `classpath`. At this step, we need to import `gradle-tomcat-plugin` under the group `com.bmuschko`:

```
buildscript {
    repositories {
        jcenter()
    }
    dependencies {
        classpath 'com.bmuschko:gradle-tomcat-plugin:2.0'
    }
}
```

2. Add the following libraries to the `classpath`:

```
apply plugin: 'com.bmuschko.tomcat'
apply plugin: 'com.bmuschko.tomcat-base'
```

3. (Optional) Add the following Tomcat 9.0 libraries that enable Gradle to run embedded Tomcat through the `tomcatRun()` and `tomatRunWar()` functions:

```
dependencies {
    def tomcatVersion = '9.0.0.M9'
    tomcat "org.apache.tomcat.embed:tomcat-embed
    core:${tomcatVersion}",
    "org.apache.tomcat.embed:tomcat-embed-logging-
    juli:${tomcatVersion}"
    tomcat("org.apache.tomcat.embed:tomcat-embed-
    jasper:${tomcatVersion}") {
        exclude group: 'org.eclipse.jdt.core.compiler',
            module: 'ecj'
    }
}
```

4. (Optional) Configure Tomcat 9 details through the `tomcat()` function:

```
tomcat {
    httpsPort = 8443
    enableSSL = true
    users {
        user {
            username = 'packt'
            password = 'packt'
```

```
        roles = ['manager-gui', 'manager-script']
    }
}
}
```

5. To deploy the project into the installed Tomcat 9, create a Gradle task `deploy` that copies the WAR file to the `/webapp` folder:

```
task deploy (dependsOn: war){
    copy {
        from "build/libs"
        into
        "C:\MyFiles\Development\Servers\Tomcat 9.0\webapps"
        include "*.war"
    }
}
```

6. You can now run `deploy` in the Gradle Task Launcher.

```
[sts] ------------------------------------------------------
[sts] Starting Gradle build for the following tasks:
[sts]       deploy
[sts] ------------------------------------------------------
:compileJava UP-TO-DATE
:processResources UP-TO-DATE
:classes UP-TO-DATE
:war UP-TO-DATE
:deploy UP-TO-DATE

BUILD SUCCESSFUL

Total time: 0.67 secs
```

How it works...

When it comes to building projects with conflicting versions of libraries, Gradle is one of those build tools that can satisfy any structure and state of project deployment and management. Since it is not written in XML, Gradle can provide logic in building `classpath` and project dependencies.

Gradle is efficient when it comes to incremental builds where the current and previous changes in deployment files are monitored. And when it comes to different repositories, Gradle can monitor changes of artifacts through effective repository-aware caches. In general, Gradle is advanced when it comes to repository management and project deployment than Maven.

Gradle is written in Groovy; thus, the build scripts are declarative, readable, and straightforward and can provide developers with easier conventions and philosophy of deployment.

First, Gradle must build the needed `classpath` libraries that are the main dependencies to the deployment, which happen to be `com.bmuschko:gradle-tomcat-plugin:2.0`. After building the external library, import the following plugins: `com.bmuschko.tomcat` and `com.bmuschko.tomcat-base`. Inject a closure to the `tomcat()` function that details all the needed configuration before the deployment. The custom Gradle task `deploy` takes all the configuration loaded by the `tomcat()` and `war()` functions. Running `deploy` in **Gradle (STS)** | **Gradle Task Launcher** will copy the WAR file found in `build/libs` to the Tomcat instance.

Installing the MySQL 5.7 database server

The book will be covering some concepts on how Spring 5.0 handles data persistence involving relational database management systems. MySQL 5.7 will be the database server that will be used to create, store, update, and delete records of data.

Getting started

Visit the site `http://dev.mysql.com/downloads/mysql/` to download the preferred community server for your projects. MySQL server is available in any operating system platform.

How to do it...

1. On the download page, choose the **General Available (GA) Releases** tab.
2. Choose the desired platform through the **Select Platform** dropdown. The book will be using the MySQL server for Windows.
3. Once the Windows platform is chosen, there are other options available for download under the **Other Downloads** link. Choose the **Windows (x86, 32-bit) Windows MSI installer** for easy installation.
4. Afterwards, just click **No thanks, just start my downloads!** to download the installer immediately.
5. After downloading the installer (for example, `mysql-installer-community-5.7.17.0.msi`), click the file and start the following wizards.
6. Choose **Developer Default** as our server type.
7. Install all the connectors.
8. Use port `3306` and set the password to `packt`.
9. After installing the MySQL server, proceed with installing the **Samples and Examples scripts**.
10. After finishing the installation, create `MySQL_HOME` in your `classpath` and expose `<installation_folder>MySQLMySQL Server 5.7bin` commands.
11. At this point, you are now ready to install the server for database transactions.

How it works...

To deal with SQL transactions, we can us the CLI of MySQL or the given GUI-based **MySQL Workbench**:

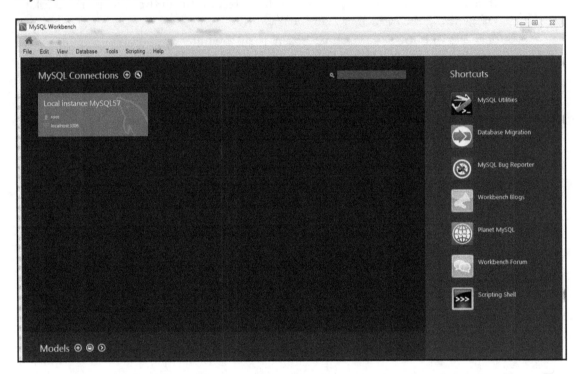

Installing the MongoDB 3.2 database server

Spring 5.0 has the capability to perform data transactions with **NoSQL** databases where schema design is not fixed and the data involved is so complex wherein its read-write operations are defined by graph theory. The **MongoDB 3.2** server will highlight some **NoSQL** and document-based data transactions with Spring 5.0 using the raw implementation and its **Spring Data** module.

Getting started

Visit the site `https://www.mongodb.com/download-center#community` to download MongoDB under different operating system platforms. It also comes with SSL and no-SSL support.

How to do it...

1. After downloading the installer (for example, `mongodb-win32-x86_64-2008plus-ssl-3.2.0-signed.msi`), follow the installation wizards:

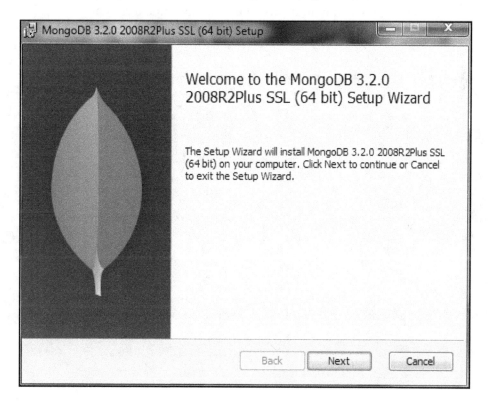

2. After the installation, create the `MONGODB_HOME` system variable in your `classpath` and expose the `<installation_folder>MongoDbServer3.2bin` commands.

3. Since MongoDB requires a data directory to store all data, create a default data directory path, `/data/db`, at the root level (for example, `C:dataadb`).

4. You are now ready to start the MongoDb server.

How it works...

The MongoDB server will be running with the default port `27017`. In order to run the server, we type the `mongod` command using the command-line terminal:

And then we open another terminal to open the server for the no-SQL transactions through the `mongo` command:

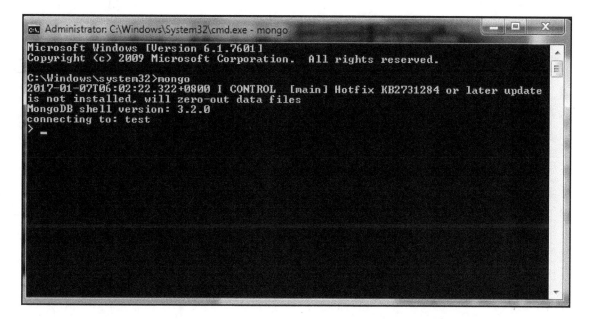

Learning Dependency Injection (DI)

2

After a series of installations and configurations, this chapter will begin the discussion on how Spring Framework 5.0 works from its core. The recipes here will define the characteristics of Spring 5.0 as a framework. We will connect the dots starting from where the objects are created up to the layers where the series of data transactions, services and controllers are interconnected.

In this chapter, you will learn about the following:

- Implementing a Spring container using XML
- Implementing a Spring container using JavaConfig
- Managing beans in an XML-based container
- Managing the beans in a JavaConfig container
- Creating Singleton and Prototype beans
- Defining eager and lazy spring beans
- Creating an inner bean
- Injecting Collections and Properties
- Creating a Spring MVC using an XML-based approach
- Creating a Spring MVC using the JavaConfig approach
- Generating multiple ApplicationContexts
- Using ResourceBundleMessageSource for Views

Implementing a Spring container using XML

Let us begin with the creation of the **Spring Web Project** using the Maven plugin of our STS Eclipse 8.3. This web project will be implementing our first Spring 5.0 container using the XML-based technique. This is the most conventional but robust way of creating a Spring container.

The container is where the objects are created, managed, wired together with their dependencies, and monitored from their initialization up to their destruction. This recipe will mainly highlight how to create an XML-based Spring container.

Getting started

Create a Maven project ready for development using the STS Eclipse 8.3. Be sure you have installed the correct JRE. Let us name the project ch02-xml.

How to do it...

After creating the project, certain Maven errors will be encountered just like in Chapter 1, *Getting Started with Spring*. Bug-fix the Maven issues in our ch02-xml project in order to use the XML-based Spring 5.0 container by performing the following steps:

1. Open pom.xml for the project and add the following properties, which contain the Spring build version and servlet container to utilize.

```
<properties>
  <spring.version>5.0.0.BUILD-SNAPSHOT</spring.version>
  <servlet.api.version>3.1.0</servlet.api.version>
</properties>
```

2. Add also the following Spring 5 dependencies in pom.xml, which are essential in providing us with the interfaces and classes to build our Spring container:

```
<dependencies>
  <dependency>
    <groupId>org.springframework</groupId>
    <artifactId>spring-context</artifactId>
    <version>${spring.version}</version>
  </dependency>
  <dependency>
    <groupId>org.springframework</groupId>
    <artifactId>spring-core</artifactId>
```

```
        <version>${spring.version}</version>
      </dependency>
      <dependency>
        <groupId>org.springframework</groupId>
        <artifactId>spring-beans</artifactId>
        <version>${spring.version}</version>
      </dependency>
    </dependencies>
```

3. It is required to add the following repositories in `pom.xml` where all the Spring 5.0 dependencies in *Step 2* will be downloaded through Maven:

```
<repositories>
  <repository>
  <id>spring-snapshots</id>
  <name>Spring Snapshots</name>
  <url>https://repo.spring.io/libs-snapshot</url>
  <snapshots><enabled>true</enabled></snapshots>
  </repository>
</repositories>
```

4. Then add the Maven plugin for deployment in `pom.xml` but be sure to recognize `web.xml` as the deployment descriptor. This can be done by enabling `<failOnMissingWebXml>` or just deleting the `<configuration>` tag as follows:

```
<plugin>
  <artifactId>maven-war-plugin</artifactId>
  <version>2.3</version>
  </plugin>
<plugin>
```

5. Add the rest of the Tomcat Maven plugin for deployment in `pom.xml`, as explained in `Chapter 1`, *Getting Started with Spring.*

6. After the Maven configuration details, check if there is a `WEB-INF` folder inside `src\main\webapp`. If there isn't, create one. This is mandatory for this project since we will be using a deployment descriptor (or `web.xml`).

7. Inside the `WEB-INF` folder, create a deployment descriptor or drop a `web.xml` template inside the `src\main\webapp\WEB-INF` directory.

8. Then create an XML-based Spring container named `ch02-beans.xml` inside the `ch02-xml\src\main\java\` directory. The configuration file must contain the following namespaces and tags:

```xml
<?xml version="1.0" encoding="UTF-8"?>
<beans xmlns="http://www.springframework.org/schema/beans"
xmlns:xsi="http://www.w3.org/2001/XMLSchema-instance"
xmlns:context="http://www.springframework.org/schema/context"
xsi:schemaLocation="http://www.springframework.org/schema/beans
http://www.springframework.org/schema/beans/spring-beans.xsd
http://www.springframework.org/schema/context
http://www.springframework.org/schema/context/spring-context.xs
d">
</beans>
```

 You can generate this file using the STS Eclipse Wizard (*Ctrl-N*) and under the module `Spring`à`Spring` *Bean Configuration File* option.

9. Save all the files. Then `clean` and `build` the Maven project. Do not deploy yet because this is just a standalone project at the moment.

How it works...

This project just imported three major Spring 5.0 libraries, **Spring-Core**, **Spring-Beans**, and **Spring-Context**, because the major classes and interfaces for creating the container are found in these libraries. This shows that Spring, unlike other frameworks, does not need the entire load of libraries just to set up the initial platform. Spring can be perceived as a huge enterprise framework nowadays but internally it is still lightweight.

The basic container that manages objects in Spring is provided by the `org.springframework.beans.factory.BeanFactory` interface and can only be found in the Spring-Beans module. Once additional features are needed such as message resource handling, AOP capabilities, application-specific contexts, and the listener implementation, the sub-interface of `BeanFactory`, namely the `org.springframework.context.ApplicationContext` interface, is then used. This `ApplicationContext`, found in Spring-Context modules, is the one that provides an enterprise-specific container for all its applications because it encompasses a larger scope of Spring components than its `BeanFactory` interface.

The container created, `ch02-beans.xml`, an `ApplicationContext`, is an XML-based configuration that contains XSD schemas from the three main libraries imported. These schemas have tag libraries and bean properties, which are essential in managing the whole framework. But beware of runtime errors once libraries are removed from the dependencies because using these tags is equivalent to using the APIs.

The final Spring Maven project directory structure should look like this:

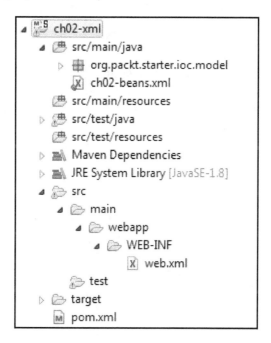

Implementing a Spring container using JavaConfig

Another option for implementing the Spring 5.0 container is through the use of **Spring** `JavaConfig`. This is a technique that uses pure Java classes in configuring the framework's container. This solution eliminates the use of bulky and tedious XML metadata and also provides a type-safe and refactoring-free approach in configuring entities or collections of objects into the container. This recipe will showcase how to create the container using `JavaConfig` in a `web.xml-less` approach.

Getting started

Create another Maven project using the methodology in Chapter 1, *Getting Started with Spring,* and name the project ch02-xml. This STS Eclipse project will be using a Java class approach including its deployment descriptor.

How to do it...

Let us now apply the JavaConfig specification in building the Spring context definition:

1. To get rid of the usual Maven bugs, immediately open the pom.xml of ch02-jc and add <properties>, <dependencies>, and <repositories>, equivalent to what was added in the *Implementing the Spring Container using XML* recipe.

2. Since the time Servlet 3.0 specification was implemented, servlet containers can now support projects without using web.xml. This is done by implementing the handler abstract class called org.springframework.web.WebApplicationInitializer to programmatically configure ServletContext. Create a SpringWebInitializer class and override its onStartup() method without any implementation yet:

```
public class SpringWebInitializer implements
   WebApplicationInitializer {
     @Override
     public void onStartup(ServletContext container) throws
         ServletException {
       }
}
```

3. The lines in *Step 2* will generate some runtime errors until you add the following Maven dependency:

```
<dependency>
  <groupId>org.springframework</groupId>
  <artifactId>spring-web</artifactId>
  <version>${spring.version}</version>
</dependency>
```

4. In `pom.xml`, disable the `<failOnMissingWebXml>` and add the same Tomcat Maven plugin for the deployment used in Chapter 1, *Getting Started with Spring*.

5. Now, create a class named `BeanConfig`, the `ApplicationContext` definition, with a class-level annotation `@Configuration`. The class must be inside the `org.packt.starter.ioc.context` package and must be an empty class at the moment:

```
@Configuration
public class BeanConfig {    }
```

6. Save all the files and `clean` and `build` the Maven project.

How it works...

The Maven project `ch02-xml` makes use of both `JavaConfig` and `ServletContainerInitializer`, meaning there will be no XML configuration from servlet to Spring 5.0 containers. The `BeanConfig` class is the `ApplicationContext` of the project and has an annotation `@Configuration`, indicating that the class is used by `JavaConfig` as a source of bean definitions. This is handy when creating an XML-based configuration with lots of metadata.

The project `ch02-xml` introduces the API `org.springframework.web.WebApplicationInitializer`, which serves as a handler of `org.springframework.web.SpringServletContainerInitializer`, the framework's implementation class to the servlet's `ServletContainerInitializer`. The class `SpringServletContainerInitializer` is designed to receive notification from `WebApplicationInitializer` through its method `startup(ServletContext)`. The class `ServletContext` is a JEE container that manages filters, servlets, and listeners. Once this servlet container acknowledges the *no-web.xml* status provided by `SpringServletContainerInitialize`, an option not to use `web.xml` is acceptable.

On Maven's part, the plugin for deployment must be notified that the project will not use `web.xml`. This is done through setting the `<failOnMissingWebXml>` to `false` inside its `<configuration>` tag.

The final Spring Web Project directory structure must look like the following structure:

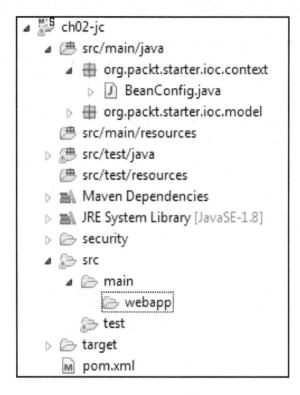

Managing beans in an XML-based container

Frameworks become a popular because of the principle behind the architecture they built from. Each framework is built from different design patterns that manage the creation and behavior of the objects they manage. This recipe will detail how Spring 5.0 manages objects of the applications and how it shares a set of methods and functions across the platform.

Getting started

The two Maven projects previously created will be utilized to illustrate how Spring 5.0 loads objects into the *heap*. We will also be utilizing the `ApplicationContext` rather than the `BeanFactory` container in preparation for the next recipes involving more Spring components.

How to do it...

With `ch02-xml`, let us demonstrate how Spring loads objects using the XML-based `ApplicationContext` container:

1. Create a package `org.packt.starter.ioc.model`, where our model classes will be placed. Our model classes will be typical **Plain Old Java Objects (POJO)**, for which the Spring 5.0 architecture is known.

2. Inside the newly created package, create the classes `Employee` and `Department`, which contain the following blueprints:

```
public class Employee {
    private String firstName;
    private String lastName;
    private Date birthdate;
    private Integer age;
    private Double salary;
    private String position;
    private Department dept;
    public Employee(){
        System.out.println(" an employee is created.");
    }

    public Employee(String firstName, String lastName, Date
            birthdate, Integer age, Double salary, String
position,
            Department dept) {
        his.firstName = firstName;
        his.lastName = lastName;
        his.birthdate = birthdate;
        his.age = age;
        his.salary = salary;
        his.position = position;
        his.dept = dept;
        System.out.println(" an employee is created.");
        }
        // getters and setters
```

```
   }

public class Department {
    private Integer deptNo;
    private String deptName;
    public Department() {
        System.out.println("a department is created.");
    }
    // getters and setters
}
```

3. Afterwards, open the `ApplicationContext` implemented as `ch02-beans.xml`.
   Register using the `<bean>` tag our first set of `Employee` and `Department` objects
   as follows:

```
<bean id="empRec1" class="org.packt.starter.ioc.model.Employee"
/>
<bean id="dept1" class="org.packt.starter.ioc.model.Department"
/>
```

4. The beans in *Step 3* contain private instance variables that have *zeroes* and `null`
   default values. To update them, our classes have mutators or setter methods that
   can be used to avoid the `NullPointerException` that is always encountered
   whenever empty objects undergo transactions. In Spring, calling these setters is
   tantamount to injecting data into the `<bean>`, similarly to how the following
   objects are created:

```
<bean id="empRec2"
class="org.packt.starter.ioc.model.Employee">
  <property name="firstName"><value>Juan</value></property>
  <property name="lastName"><value>Luna</value></property>
  <property name="age"><value>70</value></property>
  <property name="birthdate">
    <value>October 28, 1945</value>
  </property>
  <property name="position">
    <value>historian</value>
  </property>
  <property name="salary"><value>150000</value></property>
  <property name="dept"><ref bean="dept2"/></property>
</bean>
<bean id="dept2"
class="org.packt.starter.ioc.model.Department">
  <property name="deptNo"><value>13456</value></property>
  <property name="deptName">
    <value>History Department</value>
```

```
    </property>
</bean>
```

5. A `<property>` tag is equivalent to a setter definition accepting an actual value or an object reference. The `name` attribute defines the name of the setter minus the prefix set with the conversion to its camel-case notation. The `value` attribute or the `<value>` tag both pertain to supported Spring-type values (for example, `int`, `double`, `float`, `Boolean`, `Spring`). The `ref` attribute or `<ref>` provides a reference to another loaded `<bean>` in the container. Another way of writing the bean object `empRec2` is through the use of `ref` and `value` attributes such as the following:

```
<bean id="empRec3"
class="org.packt.starter.ioc.model.Employee">
    <property name="firstName" value="Jose"/>
    <property name="lastName" value="Rizal"/>
    <property name="age" value="101"/>
    <property name="birthdate" value="June 19, 1950"/>
    <property name="position" value="scriber"/>
    <property name="salary" value="90000"/>
    <property name="dept" ref="dept3"/>
</bean>
<bean id="dept3"
class="org.packt.starter.ioc.model.Department">
    <property name="deptNo" value="56748"/>
    <property name="deptName" value="Communication Department" />
</bean>
```

6. Another way of updating the private instance variables of model objects is to make use of constructors. Actual Spring data and object references can be inserted to the `<bean>` through the `<contructor-arg>` metadata:

```
<bean id="empRec5"
class="org.packt.starter.ioc.model.Employee">
    <constructor-arg><value>Poly</value></constructor-arg>
    <constructor-arg><value>Mabini</value></constructor-arg>
    <constructor-arg><value>August 10, 1948</value></constructor-
arg>
    <constructor-arg><value>67</value></constructor-arg>
    <constructor-arg><value>45000</value></constructor-arg>
    <constructor-arg><value>Linguist</value></constructor-arg>
    <constructor-arg><ref bean="dept3"></ref></constructor-arg>
</bean>
```

7. After all the modifications, save `ch02-beans.xml`. Create a `TestBeans` class inside `org.packt.starter.ioc.model.test` of the `src\test\java` directory. This class will load the XML configuration resource to the `ApplicationContext` container through `org.springframework.context.support.ClassPathXmlApplicationContext` and will fetch all the objects created through its `getBean()` method:

```
public class TestBeans {
    public static void main(String args[]){
        ApplicationContext context = new
                ClassPathXmlApplicationContext("ch02-beans.xml");
        System.out.println("application context loaded.");
        System.out.println("****The empRec1 bean****");
        Employee empRec1 = (Employee)
context.getBean("empRec1");
        System.out.println("****The empRec2*****");
        Employee empRec2 = (Employee)
context.getBean("empRec2");
        Department dept2 = empRec2.getDept();
        System.out.println("First Name: " +
                        empRec2.getFirstName());
        System.out.println("Last Name: " +
empRec2.getLastName());
        System.out.println("Birthdate: " +
                        empRec2.getBirthdate());
        System.out.println("Salary: " + empRec2.getSalary());
        System.out.println("Dept. Name: " +
dept2.getDeptName());
        System.out.println("****The empRec5 bean****");
        Employee empRec5 = context.getBean("empRec5",
                        Employee.class);
        Department dept3 = empRec5.getDept();
        System.out.println("First Name: " +
                        empRec5.getFirstName());
        System.out.println("Last Name: " +
empRec5.getLastName());
        System.out.println("Dept. Name: " +
dept3.getDeptName());
    }
}
```

8. The expected output after running the `main()` thread will be:

```
an employee is created.
an employee is created.
a department is created.
an employee is created.
```

```
a department is created.
an employee is created.
a department is created.
application context loaded.
*********The empRec1 bean ***************
*********The empRec2 bean ***************
First Name: Juan
Last Name: Luna
Birthdate: Sun Oct 28 00:00:00 CST 1945
Salary: 150000.0
Dept. Name: History Department
*********The empRec5 bean ***************
First Name: Poly
Last Name: Mabini
Dept. Name: Communication Department
```

How it works...

The principle behind creating <bean> objects in the container is called the *Inversion of Control* design pattern. In order to use objects, their dependencies and also their behaviors, these must be placed within the framework *per se*. After registering them in the container, Spring will just take care of their instantiation and their availability to other objects. Developer can just *fetch* them if they want to include them in their software modules, as shown in the following diagram:

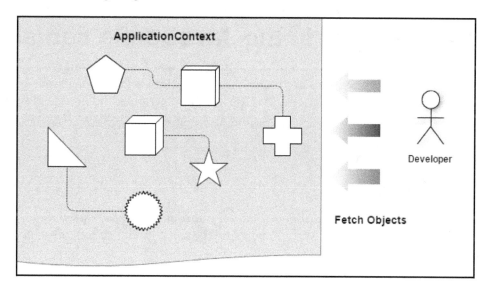

The IoC design pattern can be synonymous with the Hollywood Principle (*Don't call us, we'll call you!*), which is a popular line in most object-oriented programming languages. The framework does not care whether the developer needs the objects or not because the lifespan of the objects lies on the framework's rules.

In the case of setting new values or updating values of an object's private variables, **IoC** has an implementation that can be used for "injecting" new actual values or object references to <bean> and it is popularly known as the **Dependency Injection** (**DI**) design pattern. This principle exposes all the <bean> to the public through its setter methods or the constructors. Injecting Spring values and object references to the method signature using the <property> tag without knowing its implementation is called the **Method Injection** type of DI. On the other hand, if we create the bean with initialized values injected to its constructor through <constructor-arg>, it is known as **Constructor Injection**.

To create the ApplicationContext container, we need to instantiate ClassPathXmlApplicationContext or FileSystemApplicationContext, depending on the location of the XML definition file. Since the file is found in ch02-xml\src\main\java\, ClassPathXmlApplicationContext implementation is the best option because everything in src is compiled and deployed to the classes folder of the web project ch02-xml\WEB-INF. This proves that the ApplicationContext is an object too, bearing all those XML metadata. It has several overloaded getBean() methods used to fetch all the objects loaded with it.

Managing beans in the JavaConfig container

The JavaConfig approach provides an easier, straightforward and programmatical way of loading beans to the container. This approach uses annotations and classes to manage the lifespan of the objects, the dependencies, and the injection of values and objects to setters and constructors. The next recipe showcases how to construct and utilize a Java-based ApplicationContext container.

Getting started

Let us create and use the ch02-jc project to create our first annotation-based ApplicationContext container. We will be using the same model classes presented in the recent recipe.

How to do it...

Let us create beans inside a **JavaConfig**'s context definition class:

1. Inside the `ch02-jc\src\main\java` directory, create a package:
   `org.packt.starter.ioc.model`. Implement the same `Employee` and
   `Department` model classes as in the previous recipe, *Managing the beans in a
   XML-based container* recipe. Open `BeanConfig` context definition class and inject
   these newly created `Employee` and `Department` beans in the container:

   ```
   @Configuration
   public class BeanConfig {
           @Bean(name="empRec1")
           public Employee getEmpRecord1(){
               Employee empRec1 = new Employee();
               return empRec1;
           }

           @Bean(name="dept1")
           public Department getDept1(){
               Department dept1 = new Department();
               return dept1;
           }

   }
   ```

2. To pass actual values and object references to the beans, we programmatically
   use the setters as one of the approaches for dependency injection. Add the
   following modifications to `BeanConfig`:

   ```
   @Bean(name="empRec2")
   public Employee getEmpRecord2(){
       Employee empRec2 = new Employee();
       empRec2.setFirstName("Juan");
       empRec2.setLastName("Luna");
       empRec2.setAge(50);
       empRec2.setBirthdate(new Date(45,9,30));
       empRec2.setPosition("historian");
       empRec2.setSalary(100000.00);
       empRec2.setDept(getDept2());
       return empRec2;
   }

   @Bean(name="dept2")
   public Department getDept2(){
       Department dept2 = new Department();
       dept2.setDeptNo(13456);
   ```

```
        dept2.setDeptName("History Department");
        return dept2;
    }
```

3. Another approach is to use the overloaded constructor for the dependency injection. Add the following modifications to `BeanConfig`:

```
@Bean(name="empRec3")
public Employee getEmpRecord3(Department dept2){
    Employee empRec1 = new Employee("Jose","Rizal",
 new Date(50,5, 19), 101, 90000.00, "scriber", getDept3());
    return empRec1;
}
```

```
@Bean(name="dept3")
public Department getDept3(){
    Department dept3 = new Department(56748,
"Communication Department");
    return dept3;
}
```

4. Inside the package `org.packt.starter.ioc.model.test` in `src\test\java`, create a `TestBeans` class that will instantiate the `ApplicationContext` container using `org.springframework.context.annotation.AnnotationConfigApplicationContext` and will fetch all the beans using the familiar method `getBean()`:

```
public class TestBeans {
    public static void main(String[] args) {
        AnnotationConfigApplicationContext context =
                new AnnotationConfigApplicationContext();
        context.register(BeanConfig.class);
        System.out.println("--Result by
        Setter based Dependency Injection--");
        context.refresh();
        Employee empRec1 = (Employee)
                    context.getBean("empRec1");
        //refer to sources
        context.registerShutdownHook();
    }
}
```

Before invoking the `getBean()` overloads, pass the first `BeanConfig` definition to `AnnotationConfigApplicationContext` through `context.register()`. Then call `context.refresh()` to load all the registered beans to the container since we do not have the `ApplicationServer` yet to trigger the container loading. Finally, all objects are ready to be fetched. After all the method invocation, manually close the container through `registerShutdownHook()`.

How it works...

The `@Bean` annotation is equivalent to `<bean/>` in the XML-based `ApplicationContext` definition. It is method-level and must be attached to functions inside `@Configuration` classes. Without it, the method will be considered as a typical function and might give some container errors.

The recipe advices developers to use the `name` attribute of `@Bean` in order to monitor and specify the bean `id` of the containers without compromising the Java coding standard for the function signature. Without this attribute, the container will consider the method name as the bean `id` just as shown in the following example:

```
@Bean
public Employee empRec4(){
    Employee empRec4 = new Employee("Diego","Silang",
    new Date(65,11, 15), 55, 85000.00, "guitarist", dept4());
    return empRec4;
}
@Bean
public Department dept4(){
    Department dept4 = new Department(11223, "Music Department");
     return dept4;
}
```

With effect from Spring 3.0, the `ApplicationContext` can be instantiated through `AnnotationConfigApplicationContext` when the `JavaConfig` approach is used. It is XML-free since it only accepts classes that are annotated with `@Configuration`, `@Component`, and **JSR-330** annotations such as `@Inject`, `@Named`, and `@Singleton`. The class is very versatile in that it also recognizes DI metadata such as `@Autowired`, `@Resource`, or `@Inject` and considers them as part of the `ApplicationContext` definition.

Creating Singleton and Prototype beans

Creating beans to the containers is not enough for any project specification using the Spring framework. It is always necessary to determine the lifespan of the beans through bean scopes. The following recipe will determine how to optimize a container by creating Singleton and Prototypes beans.

Getting started

The scope of the beans characterizes how many of their instances will be used by the application. It categorizes also the purpose of each bean as to why it is loaded to the Spring container. There are four scopes that can be associated with Spring beans but only two of them will be discussed in this chapter as part of the core platform.

How to do it...

This recipe will be using both ch02-xml and the ch02-jc project in declaring which beans are considered Singleton and Prototype. We will explore and identify the effects of applying either of the two scopes to the container:

1. Open the project ch02-xml and locate the XML definition file in the ch02-xml\src\main\java directory. Let us convert empRec1 to a Singleton bean by setting the value of its scope attribute to *Singleton*:

   ```
   <bean id="empRec1" class="org.packt.starter.ioc.model.Employee"
       scope="Singleton" />
   ```

 By default, all loaded beans in the container are *Singleton*.

2. Convert the bean empRec2 to a Prototype one with its scope attribute set to *Prototype*:

   ```
   <bean id="empRec2" class="org.packt.starter.ioc.model.Employee"
       scope="Prototype">
       // refer to sources
   </bean>
   ```

3. Let us focus now on project `ch02-jc` and open its context `BeanConfig` definition. Convert the scope of `empRec1` to a *Singleton* bean by applying the Spring-based annotation `@Scope` with a value *Singleton*:

```
@Bean(name="empRec1")
@Scope("Singleton")
public Employee getEmpRecord1(){
        Employee empRec1 = new Employee();
        return empRec1;
}
```

 By default, all loaded beans, even without the `@Scope` annotation, are *Singleton*.

4. Make the scope of `empRec2` a *Prototype* by applying the same annotation `@Scope` with the value *Prototype*:

```
@Bean(name="empRec2")
@Scope("Prototype")
public Employee getEmpRecord2(){
        // refer to sources
        return empRec2;
}
```

5. Lastly, create a test class `TestScopes` for each project that will be used to fetch the preceding objects many times. Observe the number of instances the container creates per scoped bean. Use the object's `hashCode()` method to determine the identity of each instance:

```
public class TestScopes {

    public static void main(String[] args) {
        AnnotationConfigApplicationContext context =
new AnnotationConfigApplicationContext();
        context.register(BeanConfig.class);
        System.out.println("application context loaded.");
        context.refresh();
        System.out.println("*********The empRec1 bean ******");
        Employee empRec1A = (Employee)
context.getBean("empRec1");
        System.out.println("instance A: " +
empRec1A.hashCode());
        Employee empRec1B = (Employee)
context.getBean("empRec1");
```

```
        System.out.println("instance B: " +empRec1B.hashCode());
        System.out.println("*********The empRec2 bean
**********");
        Employee empRec2A = (Employee)
context.getBean("empRec2");
        System.out.println("instance A: " +
empRec2A.hashCode());
        Employee empRec2B = (Employee)
context.getBean("empRec2");
        System.out.println("instance B: " +
empRec2B.hashCode());
        context.registerShutdownHook();
    }
}
```

6. Running the test class will give us a result that will prove that a Singleton bean is only created once in its lifetime during the entire application execution while Prototype beans are always instantiated every time the application fetches them from the container:

```
*********The empRec1 bean ***************
instance A: 1691875296
instance B: 1691875296
*********The empRec2 bean ***************
instance A: 667346055
instance B: 1225197672
```

How it works...

Most of the time, developers prefer to load Singleton objects because they consume memory efficiently rather than having several Prototype objects across the platform.

When it comes to the post-processing clean up, Spring will not have a hard time managing the resources used by *Singleton* since the entire application uses only one bean object during its request-response transactions. In the case of *Prototype* beans, the container must implement a post-processor that will clean up all the garbage and some bulk of resources consumed by the series of instantiations every fetch.

Defining eager and lazy spring beans

At this point, it is clear already how beans are instantiated inside Spring 5.0 containers. The practical definition of *Inversion of Control* and *Dependency Injection* design patterns has been established too. Two approaches to implementing a container have been illustrated with the previous recipes. This time we will provide a recipe on how to decide what form of instantiation the beans must undergo in a container.

Getting started

We need both ch02-xml and ch02-jc in this recipe since the bean loading strategy depends on what type of ApplicationContext container is being used. There are two bean loading strategies in the Spring 5.0 framework namely *eager* and *lazy loading*.

How to do it...

Let us illustrate the eager and lazy loading of beans in a context definition using these steps:

1. In the case of the XML-based ApplicationContext, eager loading means all the beans in the definition will be loaded and initialized aggressively in the heap memory during start-up (for example, pre-instantiating). To opt for this type of initialization, each <bean> has an attribute lazy-init, which must be set to false. Open ch02-beans.xml in the project ch02-xml and add the following bean:

```
<bean id="empRec6" class="org.packt.starter.ioc.model.Employee"
  lazy-init="false">
  <constructor-arg><value>Diego</value></constructor-arg>
  <constructor-arg><value>Silang</value></constructor-arg>
  <constructor-arg>
    <value>December 16, 1965</value>
  </constructor-arg>
  <constructor-arg><value>55</value></constructor-arg>
  <constructor-arg><value>87000</value></constructor-arg>
  <constructor-arg><value>Guitarist</value></constructor-arg>
  <constructor-arg><ref bean="dept4"></ref></constructor-arg>
</bean>
```

By default, all Spring beans load in eager mode since `lazy-init="auto"` also means `lazy-init="false"`. Also, all *Singleton* beans use eager loading automatically.

2. In the case of the `JavaConfig` approach, by default `@Bean` loads aggressively and we do not have a special annotation or metadata for eager initialization.
3. The other option of bean loading happens only during the fetching stage (for example, the use of the `getBean()` method) and this is called **lazy** loading. In the XML-based container, we set the `lazy-init` attribute of a `<bean>` to `true` to implement lazy bean loading. Using the same class models in Step 1, apply the necessary changes as follows:

```
<bean id="empRec6" class="org.packt.starter.ioc.model.Employee"
  lazy-init="true">
    // refer to sources
</bean>
```

 All *Prototype* beans use the lazy loading mode.

4. For `JavaConfig`, Spring has a method-level annotation `@Lazy`, which can be applied to `@Bean` objects to perform lazy loading:

```
@Lazy
@Bean
public Employee empRec4(Department dept2){
    Employee empRec4 = new Employee("Diego","Silang",
new Date(65,11, 15), 55, 85000.00, "guitarist", dept4());
    return empRec4;
}
```

 Setting `@Lazy(value=false)` makes the loading mode eager.

How it works...

Consider running the `TestBeans` for either of the `ch02-xml` or `ch02-jc` projects. When all beans load eagerly, the result of the execution looks like this:

```
an employee is created.
an employee is created.
a department is created.
a department is created.
an employee is created.
a department is created.
an employee is created.
a department is created.
*********The empRec1 bean **************
*********The empRec2 bean **************
First Name: Juan
Last Name: Luna
Birthdate: Tue Oct 30 00:00:00 CST 1945
Salary: 100000.0
Dept. Name: History Department
*********The empRec3 bean **************
First Name: Jose
Last Name: Rizal
Birthdate: Mon Jun 19 00:00:00 CDT 1950
Salary: 90000.0
Dept. Name: Communication Department
*********The empRec4 bean **************
First Name: Diego
Last Name: Silang
Birthdate: Wed Dec 15 00:00:00 CST 1965
Salary: 85000.0
Dept. Name: Music Department
```

The preceding result shows us that all `Employee` and `Department` objects are created prior to their fetching stage. But once `@Lazy` or `lazy-init="true"` is applied to `empRec4`, for instance, there will be a change in the result:

```
an employee is created.
an employee is created.
a department is created.
a department is created.
an employee is created.
a department is created.
a department is created.
*********The empRec1 bean **************
*********The empRec2 bean **************
First Name: Juan
```

```
Last Name: Luna
Birthdate: Tue Oct 30 00:00:00 CST 1945
Salary: 100000.0
Dept. Name: History Department
*********The empRec3 bean ***************
First Name: Jose
Last Name: Rizal
Birthdate: Mon Jun 19 00:00:00 CDT 1950
Salary: 90000.0
Dept. Name: Communication Department
*********The empRec4 bean ***************
an employee is created.
First Name: Diego
Last Name: Silang
Birthdate: Wed Dec 15 00:00:00 CST 1965
Salary: 85000.0
Dept. Name: Music Department
```

The bean `empRec4` was not pre-instantiated, rather its `ApplicationContext` loads and instantiates the object right after the `getBean()` method is invoked.

Whether to apply the eager or lazy mode on beans depends on the project requirement or specification. Usually, the eager bean loading method is applied to objects that need to be loaded at start-up due to faster request demands from its client applications. Or, some beans do not really consume more JVM space; thus, loading them at the container level will not compromise the project performance. There are also objects that are tightly wired to some other objects in the container and loading in lazy mode will cause a series of dependency errors and runtime exceptions.

On bean objects that consume many resources, which may cause performance issues during application start-up, it is advisable to apply the lazy loading method.

Creating an inner bean

When there are beans that can only be called once by some certain top-level beans, it will be easier to manage the `ApplicationContext` definition if we allow these objects to be inner beans. This recipe will show you how to create inner beans to some objects that exclusively use them.

Getting started

Both the `ch02-xml` and `ch02-xml` projects can be utilized separately on this recipe since each container creates inner beans differently.

How to do it...

Perform the following to create inner beans:

1. In the `ch02-xml`, inject an `Employee` object, applying method injection for the actual values:

```
<bean id="empRec4"
class="org.packt.starter.ioc.model.Employee">
  <property name="firstName" value="Gabriela"/>
  <property name="lastName" value="Silang"/>
  <property name="age" value="67"/>
  <property name="birthdate" value="June 19, 1950"/>
  <property name="position" value="writer"/>
  <property name="salary" value="897000"/>
</bean>
```

2. Let us wire a `Department` object to the `empRec4` object. Instead of using `<ref/>` to wire any `Department` object in the container, one option is to use a feature similar to an anonymous inner class and that is `inner beans`. The usual `<bean>` metadata is still used to create inner beans but without the `id` and `class` attributes. Also, an inner bean does not need a scope attribute because it is bounded within the scope of its top-level object. The following is the full-blown `empRec4` bean with a `Department` object created as an inner bean:

```
<bean id="empRec4"
class="org.packt.starter.ioc.model.Employee">
  <property name="firstName" value="Gabriela"/>
  <property name="lastName" value="Silang"/>
  <property name="age" value="67"/>
  <property name="birthdate" value="June 19, 1950"/>
  <property name="position" value="writer"/>
  <property name="salary" value="897000"/>
  <property name="dept">
    <bean class="org.packt.starter.ioc.model.Department"
    scope="Prototype">
      <property name="deptNo" value="48574"/>
      <property name="deptName" value="Humanities Department"/>
    </bean>
```

```
            </property>
        </bean>
```

3. In the case of the ch02-jc project, the JavaConfig approach allows the creation of an anonymous inner class at the argument body of the setter method. To create an Employee bean with an inner bean Department, add the following snippet in the BeanConfig definition:

```
@Bean(name="empRec5")
public Employee getEmpRecord5(){
    Employee empRec5 = new Employee();
    empRec5.setFirstName("Gabriela");
    empRec5.setLastName("Silang");
    empRec5.setAge(67);
    empRec5.setBirthdate(new Date(50,5,19));
    empRec5.setPosition("writer");
    empRec5.setSalary(89700.00);
    empRec5.setDept(new Department(){
        String deptName = "Communication Department";
        Integer deptNo = 232456;
        @Override
        public String getDeptName() {
            // TODO Auto-generated method stub
            return deptName;
        }
        @Override
        public Integer getDeptNo() {
            // TODO Auto-generated method stub
            return deptNo;
        }
        @Override
        public void setDeptName(String deptName) {
            his.deptName = deptName;
        }
        @Override
        public void setDeptNo(Integer deptNo) {
            his.deptNo = deptNo;
        }
    });
    return empRec5;
}
```

How it works...

The Spring IoC design pattern permits the creation of beans that look similar to anonymous beans for the purpose of injecting a lone bean object to a top-level one. Since inner beans are bounded within the scope of the top-level objects, their id and scope are no longer accessible outside the enclosing bean, generally anywhere in the container; thus, they are not considered mandatory <bean> attributes at this point.

The scope of an inner bean is by default *Prototype*. Changing it will be ignored by the container.

In JavaConfig containers, implementing inner beans is typically similar to creating an anonymous inner class instance at the method call level. But creating inner beans in Spring, generally, does not imply that the classes involved should be anonymous inner classes by specification. The Department classes are still loaded and initialized in some area of the container as top-level beans. Since the empRec5 object has exclusive access to a certain "Communication Department", the instance of the Department object per se was created immediately as an inner bean component of empRec5.

Injecting Collections and Properties

Spring containers allow injection of List, Set, Map, or Properties objects to other Spring-defined beans through <property> tags. The following recipe will distinguish between XML-based and JavaConfig context definitions when it comes to implementing *type-safe injection*.

Getting started

Reopen ch02-xml and ch02-jc for this recipe. We will be injecting a few POJO objects to both of the containers in our projects.

How to do it...

Perform the following steps to auto-wire Collections and Properties components:

1. For both of the projects involved in the preceding recipes, create the following model classes inside their own package `org.packt.starter.ioc.model`:

```
public class ListEmployees {
    private List<Employee> listEmps;
    private List<String> listEmpNames;

// getters and setters
}
public class SetDepartments {
    private Set<Department> setDepts;
    private Set<String> deptNames;

// getters and setters
}
public class MapEmpTasks {
    private Map<String, Employee> mapEmpTask;
private Map<String,String> mapEmpMgr;

// getters and setters
}

public class PropertiesAudition {
    private Properties auditionAddress;
private Properties auditonRequirement;

// getters and setters
}
```

2. Each model class must contain `Collections` and `Properties` instance objects with their respective *setter methods* to be used later for *method dependency injection*.

3. In `ch02-xml`, use the `<list>` tag to inject required object references and actual values to `setListEmps()` and `setListEmpNames()`.Within the `<list>` tag is a series of `<value>` and `<ref>` metadata, where `<value>` holds the typical Spring-supported types such as `string`, `int`, `double` and other primitive types while `<ref>` holds references to other beans:

```
<bean id="listEmployees"
    class="org.packt.starter.ioc.model.ListEmployees">
        <property name="listEmps">
            <list>
                <ref bean="empRec2"/>
```

```
            <ref bean="empRec3"/>
            <ref bean="empRec4"/>
        </list>
    </property>
    <property name="listEmpNames">
        <list>
            <value>Juan</value>
            <value>Jose</value>
        </list>
    </property>
</bean>
```

4. Let us use the `<set>` tag to inject `Department` objects to `setDepts()` and *department names* to `deptNames()` for the `SetDepartments` bean. Just like `<list>`, the `<set>` metadata contains a number of `<value>` or `<ref>` tags:

```
<bean id="setDepartments"
    class="org.packt.starter.ioc.model.SetDepartments">
        <property name="setDepts">
            <set>
                <ref bean="dept2"/>
                <ref bean="dept3"/>
                <ref bean="dept4"/>
            </set>
        </property>
        <property name="deptNames">
            <set>
                <value>Music</value>
                <value>Arts</value>
            </set>
        </property>
</bean>
```

5. Inject Map objects to any bean properties in the Spring container using the `<map>` tag and add within it a series of `<entry>` metadata containing the key and value of an `Entry`. The following code injects tasks (key) to `Employee` records (Object value) and `managers` (String value):

```
<bean id="mapEmpTasks"
    class="org.packt.starter.ioc.model.MapEmpTasks">
        <property name="mapEmpTask">
            <map>
                <entry key="expository">
                    <ref bean="empRec2"/>
                </entry>
                <entry key="feature" value-ref="empRec3"/>
            </map>
```

```
            </property>
            <property name="mapEmpMgr">
                <map>
                    <entry key="expository">
                        <value>Joan Arkos</value>
                    </entry>
                    <entry key="feature" value="Billy Jean"/>
                </map>
            </property>
        </bean>
```

6. `Properties` objects are used to store configuration details and information for initialization instance and class variables, database connections, or e-mail transactions. This recipe has a custom model, `PropertiesAudition`, which simply provides information for an audition request. To inject a `Properties` object to the Spring container, we use the `<props>` tag with a series of `<value>` or `<prop>` metadata that holds the *key* and *value* of a property. Add the following code, which injects entries to the properties of `PropertiesAudition`:

```
<bean id="auditionInfo"
    class="org.packt.starter.ioc.model.PropertiesAudition">
        <property name="auditionAddress">
            <value>
                    country=Philippines
                    city=Makati
                    building=Rufino Tower 2
                    zipcode=1233
            </value>
        </property>
        <property name="auditionRequirement">
            <props>
                <prop key="document">curriculum vitae</prop>
                <prop key="picture">2x2 recent picture</prop>
                <prop key="time">8:00 AM</prop>
            </props>
        </property>
    </bean>
```

7. In our `ch02-jc` project, use the simple and straightforward `JavaConfig` way of using the `@Bean` annotation as shown by the following injection:

```
@Bean
public ListEmployees listEmployees(){
    ListEmployees listEmps = new ListEmployees();
    List<Employee> empRecs = new ArrayList<>();
    // refer to sources
```

```
        listEmps.setListEmps(empRecs);
        List<String> empNames = new ArrayList<>();
        // refer to sources
        listEmps.setListEmpNames(empNames);
        return listEmps;
    }
    @Bean
    public SetDepartments setDepartments(){
        SetDepartments setDepts = new SetDepartments();
        Set<Department> deptRecs = new HashSet<>();
        // refer to sources
        setDepts.setSetDepts(deptRecs);
        Set<String> deptNames = new HashSet<>();
        // refer to sources
        setDepts.setDeptNames(deptNames);
        return setDepts;
    }
    @Bean
    public MapEmpTasks mapEmpTasks(){
        MapEmpTasks mapTasks = new MapEmpTasks();
        Map<String,Employee> empTasks = new HashMap<>();
        // refer to sources
        mapTasks.setMapEmpTask(empTasks);
        Map<String, String> mgrTasks = new HashMap<>();
        // refer to sources
        mapTasks.setMapEmpMgr(mgrTasks);
        return mapTasks;
    }
    @Bean
    public PropertiesAudition auditionInfo(){
        PropertiesAudition auditionInfo = new PropertiesAudition();
        Properties addressProps = new Properties();
        // refer to sources
        auditionInfo.setAuditionAddress(addressProps);
        Properties reqtProps = new Properties();
        // refer to sources
        auditionInfo.setAuditionRequirement(reqtProps);
        return auditionInfo;
    }
```

8. Create a test class, `TestInjectData`, which retrieves all the bean models with the data injected using the `getBean()` method.

How it works...

Injecting Collections and Properties data to either of the container types is pretty straightforward. For the XML-based `ApplicationContext`, developers must be cautious with the use of generics. If the Collections of data is needed to be type-specific, injection is streamlined to use only one type throughout the process either setting `<value>` as the `wrapper` or `string` object type or listing all `<ref>` object references to one type. Mixing both metadata requires us to drop Generics on our model classes; otherwise a `ClassCastException` will be thrown, which will cause a container loading error. The same exception is also encountered when the model class requires the collection of `employee` objects in one of its setters but then accidentally a lone `department` bean has been `<ref>` mapped to it.

In general, XML-based `ApplicationContext` is not type-safe and type-sensitive as to what types of collection the model classes need. Unlike in `JavaConfig`, the `@Bean` objects are created programmatically; the needed Generic types are recognized by the container during bean creation and initialization.

Creating a Spring MVC using an XML-based approach

It is now time to apply all the previous recipes to create a working Spring MVC setup. Applying *Inversion of Control* and *Dependency Injection*, our main goal now is to build a working baseline project with an XML-based container running on top of the Servlet container of our Tomcat 9 application server. This recipe will feature MVC components of Spring 5.0 and explain how this MVC works together with the servlet components.

Getting started

Create a new project `ch02-web.xml` using STS Eclipse 8.3. Configure the Maven and deployment descriptor as per the recipe, *Implementing the Spring Container using XML*. Once all configuration errors are bug-fixed, perform the following steps to create a Spring MVC backbone.

How to do it...

Let us build a simple web application using the Spring MVC concept:

1. Open `web.xml` and register the main servlet handler of our Spring MVC application, which is
    `org.springframework.web.servlet.DispatcherServlet`.

    ```xml
    <servlet>
      <servlet-name>ch02</servlet-name>
      <servlet-class>
        org.springframework.web.servlet.DispatcherServlet
      </servlet-class>
      <load-on-startup>1</load-on-startup>
    </servlet>
    <servlet-mapping>
      <servlet-name>ch02</servlet-name>
      <url-pattern>*.html</url-pattern>
    </servlet-mapping>
    ```

     Be cautious with the `<url-pattern>` in `web.xml` because it is where `DispatcherServlet` picks the correct format for its request URLs. The pattern `*.html` means the main servlet will recognize all URL paths with a view extension of `.html`.

2. In the previous recipes, the XML bean definition file was created on the Classpath level. It is an option to import this file or just move the file to `WEB-INF` and name it `ch02-servlet.xml`. Additional modules such as *Spring Web*, *Spring WebMvc*, *Spring Tx*, and *Spring AOP* must be included with their dependencies:

    ```xml
    <?xml version="1.0" encoding="UTF-8"?>
    <beans xmlns="http://www.springframework.org/schema/beans"
        xmlns:xsi="http://www.w3.org/2001/XMLSchema-instance"
    xmlns:context="http://www.springframework.org/schema/context"
        xmlns:mvc="http://www.springframework.org/schema/mvc"
    xsi:schemaLocation="http://www.springframework.org/schema/beans
    http://www.springframework.org/schema/beans/spring-beans.xsd
    http://www.springframework.org/schema/context
      http://www.springframework.org/schema/context
    /spring-context.xsd
        http://www.springframework.org/schema/mvc
          http://www.springframework.org/schema/mvc/spring-mvc.xsd">
    </beans>
    ```

3. This `ch02-servlet.xml` file will be the first *servlet-specific context* or root context definition of the `DispatchServlet`. This servlet needs this context to instantiate `WebApplicationContext`, which is Spring's root `ApplicationContext`, which manages *controllers, view resolvers, resource bundle message configurators,* and other MVC-specific requirements. To successfully create `WebApplicationContext`, the `DispatcherServlet` must first specify the location of the XML file through its `contextConfigLocation` parameter:

```
<servlet>
  <servlet-name>ch02</servlet-name>
  <servlet-class>
    org.springframework.web.servlet.DispatcherServlet
  </servlet-class>
  <init-param>
    <param-name>contextConfigLocation</param-name>
    <param-value>/WEB-INF/ch02-servlet.xml</param-value>
  </init-param>
</servlet>
<servlet-mapping>
  <servlet-name>ch02</servlet-name>
  <url-pattern>*.html</url-pattern>
</servlet-mapping>
```

If the XML is named using the pattern `<servlet-name>-servlet.xml`, there is no need to configure `contextConfigLocation`, thus, *Step 1* is enough.

4. Save all files. Deploy the project using the Maven goals presented in `Chapter 1`, *Getting Started with Spring*. Observe if there are any container errors. If none, let us proceed with building the view layer of the application using the `WebApplicationContext`. First, inject the two most popular view resolvers of the MVC application, namely the `org.springframework.web.servlet.view.InternalResourceViewResolver` and `org.springframework.web.servlet.view.ResourceBundleViewResolver`. Open the `ch02-servlet.xml` and add the following details:

```
<bean id="viewResolverA" class="org.springframework.web.servlet.view.InternalResourceViewResolver">
      <property name="prefix" value="/WEB-INF/jsp/"/>
      <property name="suffix" value=".jsp"/>
      <property name="order" value="1"/>
</bean>
```

```
<bean id="viewResolverB" class="org.springframework.web.servlet
.view.ResourceBundleViewResolver">
        <property name="basename" value="config.views"/>
        <property name="order" value="0"/>
</bean>
```

5. In order for `InternalResourceViewResolver` to work, create its lookup `WEB_INF\jsp` directory, which is the static location of all its JSP pages.

6. For `ResourceBundleViewResolver` to function, create its `view.properties` inside the `src\main\resources\config` directory. All view names are required to be declared here and each must have two specific configuration details, which are the `<view-name>.(class)` and `<view-name>.url`. The `<view-name>.(class)` refers to the view type (for example, JSP, Tiles, JSON) of the rendition page while the `<view-name>.url` contains the context root path of the physical view page. Leave the file empty.

7. The views, models, and transactions will be nothing without the `@Controller`. Create the first controller, `MainController`, inside the package `org.packt.starter.ioc.controller`. The class must contain a set of *handler methods* that directly deals with the request and response of the client. Each method has URL mapping through the method-level `@RequestMapping` annotation. Let us create a handler that outputs page-generated content (in the String type) on the page using `@ResponseBody`:

```
@Controller
public class MainController {
        @ResponseBody
        @RequestMapping("/main.html")
        public String pageGenerate(){
        String content = "<html>"
                + "" + "<head><title>Ch02 MVC Web</title></head>"
                + "" + "<body>This is Spring MVC Web!</body>"
                + "" + "</html>"
                + "";
        return content;
    }
}
```

8. In order for the `DispatcherServlet` to recognize all the MVC components and annotations of the project, add the following important lines in the root context `ch02-servlet.xml`:

```
<context:component-scan base-package="org.packt.starter.ioc"/>
<mvc:annotation-driven />
```

9. The chosen *root or core directory* of the `Classpath` is `org.packt.starter.ioc` where all other sub-directories contain the MVC layers and components such as the controllers, services, repository, and model classes. Save all the files. Deploy the project. If there are no errors, open any browser and run `https://localhost:8443/ch02/main.html`. The output must be similar to the following:

10. Let us add more handlers by adding the following methods to our `MainController`:

```
@RequestMapping("/intro.html")
public String introPage(){
        return "intro";
}
@RequestMapping("/welcome.html")
public String welcomePage(){
        return "welcome";
}
```

11. The `welcomePage()` request handler requires a view name *welcome* from `InternalResourceViewResolver`. Add a JSP file named `welcome.jsp` in the `WEB-INF\jsp` directory:

```
<%@ page language="java" contentType="text/html;
charset=ISO-8859-1" pageEncoding="ISO-8859-1"%>
<!DOCTYPE html PUBLIC "-//W3C//DTD HTML 4.01 Transitional//EN"
"http://www.w3.org/TR/html4/loose.dtd">
<html>
<head>
<meta http-equiv="Content-Type" content="text/html;
charset=ISO-8859-1">
<title>Insert title here</title>
</head>
<body>
        <h1>Welcome!</h1>
    <em>-- from InternalResourceViewResolver</em>
</body>
</html>
```

12. The other handler, `introPage()`, calls a view name *intro* from `ResourceBundleViewResolver`. Add a JSP file named `intro_page.jsp` in the `WEB-INF\page` directory. The page must contain the following content:

```
<%@ page language="java" contentType="text/html;
charset=ISO-8859-1" pageEncoding="ISO-8859-1"%>
<!DOCTYPE html PUBLIC "-//W3C//DTD HTML 4.01 Transitional//EN"
"http://www.w3.org/TR/html4/loose.dtd">
<html>
<head>
<meta http-equiv="Content-Type" content="text/html;
charset=ISO-8859-1">
<title>Insert title here</title>
</head>
<body>
    <h1>Introduction to Spring MVC Web</h1>
    <em>-- from ResourceBundleViewResolver</em>
</body>
</html>
```

13. To recognize the *logical view names*, open `views.properties` and add the following details of the view name `intro`:

```
intro.(class)=org.springframework.web.servlet.view.JstlView
intro.url=/page/intro_page.jsp
```

14. Save all the files. Deploy the project and check the Maven console to see whether there are errors. If there are none, open any browser and run `https://localhost:8443/ch02/welcome.html` and expect a result like this:

15. Run `https://localhost:8443/ch02/intro.html` seperately and expect the following result:

How it works...

The `DispatcherServlet` is always declared as a typical `<servlet>` in any Tomcat servlet container. But more than a servlet, `DispatcherServlet` is the core servlet handler of any Spring MVC application which controls request dispatch processing and responses for each web transaction. It has a `WebApplicationContext` that manages `@Controllers`, `@RequestMapping`, and view resolvers for every **HTTP/2** transaction.

To enable `WebApplicationContext`, `DispatcherServlet` must have a lookup configuration document known as the XML-based Spring definition file, which needs to be loaded to the servlet container also. In this project, `ch02-servlet.xml` serves as the root context definition file, which is just a typical `ApplicationContext` definition from our previous recipes.

As the project progresses, many custom and extension servlets (for example, `WSServlet`, `ServletContainer`) will be added to Tomcat's servlet container. In order to initially load `DispatcherServlet` among all the others, we indicate `<load-on-startup>` to have a value of the rest of the servlets; they must have values greater than *1* to prioritize the loading of our main servlet.

The next step in the configuration is the creation of the view resolver beans. The `InternalResourceViewResolver` is the easiest to set up but the most unreliable to use. It requires physical view pages to be compiled inside `WEB-INF` and must only use one technology, JSP. Also, it requires that the filenames of the JSP pages should be the same with the view name redirected by the `@Controller`. And whenever you inject more than one view resolver, `InternalResourceViewResolver` is always called first because it is one of the default configurations of `DispatcherServlet`. Since we have injected `MessageResourceViewResolver` also, the former must be executed last by setting its priority `<order>` property to 1 while `MessageResourceViewResolver` must have 0, the highest priority order level. The `MessageResourceViewResolver` needs the `views.properties` configuration to work.

After the view layer, `@Controllers` and its `@RequestMapping` handlers must be created to manage the request and response transactions. Avoid duplicate URL path names and view names must be valid ones.

To enable the use of annotations inside classes, `<mvc:annotation-driven />` must appear in the context definition. It tells `WebApplicationContext` that there are classes that utilize both Spring-proprietary and JSR-330 annotations essential for the application. Lastly, to tell `WebApplicationContext` what classes use these annotated features on object auto-wiring, the `Classpath` root package must be declared in `<context:component-scan base-package="org.packt.starter.ioc"/>` metadata.

Creating a Spring MVC using the JavaConfig approach

After creating the Spring MVC backbone using the XML-based `ApplicationContext`, this recipe will highlight the `JavaConfig` equivalent of the same baseline project.

Getting started

Create a `web.xml-less` Spring web project using the processes established in the *Implementing a Spring container recipe using JavaConfig*. Configure appropriately and correctly the `pom.xml` file so that the project will no longer use `web.xml`. Deploy the blank project first and verify if there are errors before doing this recipe.

How to do it...

Perform the following to build a simple Spring MVC project using the **JavaConfig** specification:

1. Create the `JavaConfig` root context through implementing the abstract class `org.springframework.web.servlet.config.annotation.WebMvcConfigu rerAdapter`. It has the `@Configuration` annotation and contains methods that can be overridden to manage validators, view resolvers, controllers, interceptors, and other MVC-specific components needed to be injected to the container. Let us name the implementation class `SpringDispatcherConfig` and place it inside the `org.packt.starter.ioc.dispatcher` package:

```
@Configuration
public class SpringDispatcherConfig extends
        WebMvcConfigurerAdapter{ }
```

2. Let us now configure the `DispatcherServlet`. The implementation of `WebApplicationInitializer` permits us to programmatically create, configure, and register the `DispatcherServlet` to the servlet container through `org.springframework.web.context.support.AnnotationConfigWebAppl icationContext`. It only needs the root context to successfully register it to the `ServletContext`. Modify our `SpringWebInitializer` by overriding the `onStartup()` method where `ServletContext` is available for programmatical servlet registration:

```
@Configuration
public class SpringWebinitializer implements
    WebApplicationInitializer {
    @Override
    public void onStartup(ServletContext container)
throws ServletException {
        addDispatcherContext(container);
    }
    private void addDispatcherContext(ServletContext
container) {
        // Create the dispatcher servlet's ROOT context
        AnnotationConfigWebApplicationContext dispatcherContext
=
            new AnnotationConfigWebApplicationContext();
    dispatcherContext.register(SpringDispatcherConfig.class);
        // Declare  <servlet> and <servlet-mapping> for the
        // DispatcherServlet
        ServletRegistration.Dynamic dispatcher =
            container.addServlet("ch02-servlet",
```

```
                new DispatcherServlet(dispatcherContext));
        dispatcher.addMapping("*.html");
        dispatcher.setLoadOnStartup(1);
    }
}
```

3. Save all the files. Then `build` and `deploy` the project and verify if errors are encountered. If none, add the following view resolvers to our root context `SpringDispatcherConfig` to manage our views later:

```
@Bean
    public InternalResourceViewResolver jspViewResolver() {
        InternalResourceViewResolver viewResolverA =
new InternalResourceViewResolver();
        viewResolverA.setPrefix("/WEB-INF/jsp/");
        viewResolverA.setSuffix(".jsp");
        viewResolverA.setOrder(1);
        return viewResolverA;
    }
    @Bean
    public ResourceBundleViewResolver bundleViewResolver(){
        ResourceBundleViewResolver viewResolverB =
new ResourceBundleViewResolver();
        viewResolverB.setBasename("config.views");
        viewResolverB.setOrder(0);
        return viewResolverB;
}
```

4. Create the same `views.properties`, JSP pages, and just as we did in the previous recipe:

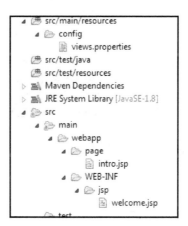

5. To close this `JavaConfig` project setup, apply class-level annotations `@EnableWebMvc` and `@ComponentScan` to our `SpringDispatcherConfig` root context definition class to finally recognize all the classes and interfaces in each package as a valid Spring `@Component` ready for auto-wiring:

```
@EnableWebMvc
@ComponentScan(basePackages="org.packt.starter.ioc")
@Configuration
public class SpringDispatcherConfig extends
    WebMvcConfigurerAdapter{
    @Bean
     public InternalResourceViewResolver jspViewResolver() {
         InternalResourceViewResolver viewResolverA =
new InternalResourceViewResolver();
         viewResolverA.setPrefix("/WEB-INF/jsp/");
         viewResolverA.setSuffix(".jsp");
         viewResolverA.setOrder(1);
         return viewResolverA;

    }
    @Bean
    public ResourceBundleViewResolver bundleViewResolver(){
        ResourceBundleViewResolver viewResolverB =
new ResourceBundleViewResolver();
        viewResolverB.setBasename("config.views");
        viewResolverB.setOrder(0);
        return viewResolverB;
    }
}
```

6. Save all files. Then `build` and `deploy` the project.

How it works...

The overall flow of the project setup is similar to what has been done in the XML-based Spring MVC project configuration. The only difference is the presence of several configuration classes that can be categorized according to the set of beans they manage and inject. The core configuration class is always given to the root context class, such as the `SpringDispatcherConfig`, because of its role to register the `DispatcherServlet` to the servlet container.

The `JavaConfig` specification has provided the `@Configuration` annotation to all context definition classes to establish the MVC backbone of the application, which makes it easier than implementing `org.springframework.web.servlet.config.annotation.WebMvcConfigurationSupport`.

On the other hand, the `setLoadOnStartup()` method tells the servlet container about the loading time of the `DispatcherServlet`, which is by convention set to *1*, meaning it must be loaded first.

After a successful `DispatcherServlet` registration, a `WebApplicationContext` object is created, waiting for a bean injection from the view resolvers and other MVC-specific components.

On the `InternalResourceViewResolver` and `MessageResourceViewResolver` configuration, the `JavaConfig` approach only requires these beans to use the `@Bean` annotation during its injections. The rest of the rules on creating *physical view pages* with their corresponding *logical view names* are just the same as with the XML-based approach.

In order for the MVC application to finally work, the root context class `SpringDispatcherConfig` must recognize all these `JavaConfig` components and `JSR-330` annotations through the use of the `@EnableWebMvc` annotation. And to recognize all MVC components, `SpringDispatcherConfig` must declare the `@ComponentScan` annotation with the list of packages including the main root package of the application.

Generating multiple ApplicationContexts

The root `ApplicationContext` is only used for Spring-specific dependency injection such as creating and loading interceptors, message handling resources, and view resolvers. It is not recommended to contain middle-tier models, services, data sources, and web services configuration because it might affect the runtime performance of the `DispatcherServlet` registration and loading. This recipe will provide a solution on how to organize beans per layer or module to avoid a convoluted bean injection setup.

Getting started

This recipe needs both the `ch02-web-xml` and `ch02-web-jc` projects to illustrate how to provide additional definition files so that the first root context will not get bloated with non-Spring beans.

How to do it...

Adding more `ApplicationContext` definition files might require some changes to be made on the servlet and Spring containers. Follow the given steps:

1. In the `ch02-web-xml` project, it is recommended to create another XML definition file for application-related model objects such as `Employee` and `Department`. Using STS Eclipse or a template, define `beans-context.xml` and save the file in the directory where the root context is located:

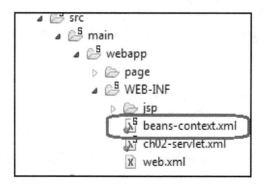

2. Open `beans-context.xml`, together with the required XSD schemas and metadata including all the `Employee`- and `Department`-related bean objects created in the previous recipes:

```xml
<?xml version="1.0" encoding="UTF-8"?>
<beans xmlns="http://www.springframework.org/schema/beans"
    xmlns:xsi="http://www.w3.org/2001/XMLSchema-instance"
  xmlns:context="http://www.springframework.org/schema/context"
    xmlns:mvc="http://www.springframework.org/schema/mvc"
  xsi:schemaLocation="http://www.springframework.org/schema/beans
  http://www.springframework.org/schema/beans/spring-beans.xsd
    http://www.springframework.org/schema/context
     http://www.springframework.org/schema/context/
  spring-context.xsd
  http://www.springframework.org/schema/mvc
   http://www.springframework.org/schema/mvc/spring-mvc.xsd">

    <bean id="empRec1"
      class="org.packt.starter.ioc.model.Employee" />
    <bean id="empRec2"
        class="org.packt.starter.ioc.model.Employee">
        // refer to sources
    </bean>
```

```
<bean id="empRec3"
    class="org.packt.starter.ioc.model.Employee">
    // refer to sources
    </bean>
    // refer to sources
</beans>
```

3. All `ApplicationsContexts` are considered child-contexts of `WebApplicationContext`. The listener `org.springframework.web.context.ContextLoaderListener` is responsible for the initialization of both root and child Spring containers with the help of the `DispatcherServlet`. Thus, register `ContextLoaderListener` together with the `ApplicationContext` beans-context.xml in the `ServletContext` by adding the following configuration in web.xml:

```
<context-param>
        <param-name>contextConfigLocation</param-name>
        <param-value>/WEB-INF/beans-context.xml</param-value>
</context-param>
<listener>
    <listener-class>
org.springframework.web.context.ContextLoaderListener
</listener-class>
</listener>
```

4. The context parameter `contextConfigLocation` may look familiar and it is still the placeholder for all the context files needed to be loaded to the servlet container. If there are other context files, we can accommodate them in `contextConfigLocation` as:

```
<context-param>
    <param-name>contextConfigLocation</param-name>
    <param-value>/WEB-INF/beans-context.xml
                 /WEB-INF/xxx-context.xml
                 /WEB-INF/yyy-context.xml
    </param-value>
</context-param>
```

5. The next changes must be reflected inside the root definition file. Since `WebApplicationContext` is the parent of `ApplicationContextbeans-context.xml`, it recognize all the loaded beans of its child. We attach the `ApplicationContext` definition to the root context ch02-servlet.xml through `<import>` metadata invoked by the root context itself:

```
<import resource="beans-context.xml"/>
```

6. To test whether `beans-context.xml` is considered a valid child
   `ApplicationContext`, create a `BeanController` and fetch all objects through
   `@Autowired`, `@Inject`, and `@Resource` as follows:

```
@Controller
public class BeanController {

@Autowired
@Qualifier(value="empRec2")
private Employee empRecs;

@Inject
private Department dept2;

@Resource(name="listEmployees")
private ListEmployees listEmps;


}
```

7. For `@Inject` to work properly, attach the following Maven dependencies for
   JSR-330 to `pom.xml`:

```
<dependency>
  <groupId>javax.inject</groupId>
  <artifactId>javax.inject</artifactId>
  <version>1</version>
</dependency>
```

8. To further validate the correctness of our context configuration, create a
   `@Component` class `DataService` in the `org.packt.starter.ioc.model`
   package:

```
@Component
public class DataService {
   public String getTitle(){
      return "Spring 5.0 Cookbook";
   }
}
```

9. Let us `@Autowire` the `DataService` in `BeanController`. If the controller can
   successfully fetch `DataService` then we can say that our
   `WebApplicationContext` is still functional after the configuration:

```
@Autowired
private DataService dataService;
```

10. At this point, we introduce `org.springframework.ui.Model` and `org.springframework.ui.ModelMap`, which are both responsible for transporting our model objects to different views for rendering. Add the following handler methods to our `BeanController` to complete our MVC code snippet:

```
@RequestMapping("/list_emps.html")
    public String showEmployee(ModelMap model){
        model.addAttribute("firstName", empRecs.getFirstName());
        model.addAttribute("title", dataService.getTitle());
        return "list-employees";
    }
@RequestMapping("/show_dept.html")
    public String showDepartment(Model model){
        model.addAttribute("deptNo", dept2.getDeptNo());
        return "show-dept";
    }
@RequestMapping("/view_emps.html")
    public String viewEmps(Model model){
        model.addAttribute("empList", listEmps.getListEmps());
        return "view-emps";
    }
```

11. In `ch02-web-jc`, not many changes need to be done because the only way to add a child `ApplicationContext` is to create a definition similar to our `SpringDispatcherConfig`, only with a different component package to scan. Create the child context class `SpringContextConfig` with the inclusion of all the `@Beans` created previously:

```
@Configuration
@EnableWebMvc
@ComponentScan(basePackages = "org.packt.starter.ioc.model")
public class SpringContextConfig {
    @Bean(name="empRec1")
    public Employee getEmpRecord1(){
        Employee empRec1 = new Employee();
        return empRec1;
    }

    @Bean(name="empRec2")
    public Employee getEmpRecord2(){
        // refer to sources
        return empRec2;
    }
    @Bean(name="empRec3")
    public Employee getEmpRecord3(){
```

```
                    // refer to sources
                    return empRec3;
                }
                @Lazy
                @Bean
                public Employee empRec4(){
                    // refer to sources
                    return empRec4;
                }
            }
```

12. Perform *Steps 4* to *7* for the rest of the JavaConfig project.
13. Build and deploy both the projects. Test both the projects and run all the URLs.

How it works...

WebApplicationContext (ch02-servlet.xml) and ApplicationContext (beans-context.xml) have the same XML definition components. They exhibit the same principle of bean injection and also implement the same bean initialization and loading. The only difference is that the root context is needed by DispatcherServlet during its creation while the child contexts are optionally created once additional application layers are added to the MVC application.

Loaded beans in ApplicationContext containers are fetched by MVC components such as controllers and services using the @Autowired, @Inject, or @Resource annotations. Among the three, @Autowired is the only Spring-based annotation used to fetch and inject the bean objects of our container to any Spring component. The injected variable type and name must be coherent with the loaded bean id and class type. If we declare the bean as `<bean id="empRec1" class="org.packt.starter.ioc.model.Employee" />`, we inject this bean to a controller or service as:

```
@Autowired
private Employee empRec1;
```

And if there is a need to change the variable name against the bean id, we use the @Qualifier annotation to fix the ambiguities:

```
@Autowired
@Qualifier(value="empRec1")
private Employee employee;
```

The `@Qualifer(value="")` is a Spring-proprietary annotation used to resolve conflicts and ambiguities on variable and bean naming syntax. What is unique about `@Autowired` is its non-strictness side when it comes to injection. Once `@Autowired(required=false)` is set, there will be no `org.springframework.beans.factory.NoSuchBeanDefinitionException` when ambiguities happen. Rather, it will just map the injected variable to the `null` value.

On the other hand, the non-Spring annotations `@Inject` and `@Resource` can also be used to resolve dependency injection. If the developer wants a strict approach in injecting beans to a component, `@Inject` is the best choice since it will throw an `org.springframework.beans.factory.NoSuchBeanDefinitionException` when the beans do not exist in the container. To resolve the variable name and bean `id` ambiguities, it is paired with another `JSR-330` annotation, `@Named(value="")`, which works similar to `@Qualifier`.

On the other hand, `@Resource` is the oldest annotation among the three and is part of `JSR-250`, which is part of the standard annotations for Java and JEE. It has its own way of searching and fetching the object from the container. Using `@Resource`, the search starts by checking the injected variable name against all bean `id`s, followed by their types and their `@Qualifier` if and only if the search by name failed. Both `@Autowired` and `@Inject` search all beans by first checking the injected variable type against the bean types, `@Qualifier` against the bean `id`, and finally, by its name with the bean `id`.

In addition to auto-wiring, Spring uses its `@Component` annotation to create Spring-managed beans without the need for XML for registering. We can inject these beans to any component using the preceding three annotations.

One of the most important parts of this recipe is the introduction of the model layer, which transports our injected beans from the `@Controller` to their respective views. There are three known Spring APIs that are used widely on this layer and these are `ModelAndView`, `ModelMap`, and `Model`. The recipe only highlighted the current classes, `ModelMap` and `Model`. The only difference between the two is the number of helper methods they contain. `Model` is an interface with only four `addAttribute(...)` methods and a `mergeAttribute()` while `ModelMap` is an implementation of `ModelMap` with some additional `Map`-related methods. `ModelAndView` is been in the Spring framework for a long time and is used to contain both a `ModelMap` and its view object. When to use any of these three depends on the requirement of the response. If the response needs to perform *redirection* using the `RedirectView` API, the `ModelAndView` is appropriate to use.

Using ResourceBundleMessageSource for Views

As far as possible, all `@Bean` of a Spring MVC project must be managed by its context definition classes. The labels, content headings, and tab title of the view pages, which the majority of developers take for granted, must not be hardcoded but declared also as Spring-managed components.

Getting started

This recipe will manage lighter features of an application such as error names, labels, header names, and titles using the `ApplicationContext`.

How to do it...

Let us add view labels and titles to the previous projects `ch02-web-xml` and `ch02-web-jc`, through the following steps:

1. In `ch02-web-xml`, create a `messages_en_US.properties` file in the `src\main\resources\config` directory.
2. A configuration file is composed of a code and message pair. The *key* is called the lookup of the message and also called the *code* of the message. Open `messages_en_US.properties` and add the following label to be used later in our title bar:

    ```
    title=Creating View Titles
    ```

3. Add another message, but this time it needs arguments at runtime. This resulting label will be used as a content page header:

    ```
    content_header=Goodbye! {0}. Last of Chapter {1}.
    ```

4. Declare the
   `org.springframework.context.support.ReloadableResourceBundleMessageSource` API, which is responsible for loading, reading, and caching messages to the container. This object must be loaded by `WebApplicationContext`, containing the location of `messages_en_US.properties`, the encoding type of the messages, the compliance of the key lookup mechanism to its message values, and the number of seconds it loads and caches the bundle of String messages to the container:

```
<bean id="messageSource"
    class="org.springframework.context.support
.ReloadableResourceBundleMessageSource">
        <property name="basename"
          value="classpath:config/messages_en_US"/>
        <property name="defaultEncoding" value="UTF-8" />
        <property name="useCodeAsDefaultMessage" value="true"/>
        <property name="cacheSeconds" value="1"/>
</bean>
```

5. Open any view pages, let us say the `view_emps.jsp`, and add the Spring Taglib directive `<%@ taglib prefix="spring" uri="http://www.springframework.org/tags"%>`. We need this Taglib to read all the messages from the properties file.

6. Using the Spring Taglib, we use the `<spring:message>` tag to access the keys of all the needed labels and titles from `messages_en_US.properties`. To retrieve the title message and content header, use the following:

```
<head>
<meta http-equiv="Content-Type" content="text/html;
charset=ISO-8859-1">
<title><spring:message code="title"  /></title>
</head>
<h1>
<spring:message code="content_header" arguments="Spring
Fanatics,2" />
</h1>
```

7. In `ch02-web-jc`, create the same `messages_en_US.properties` in its own `src\main\resources\config` directory. The bundle contains the same `title` and `content_header` codes with their values. The same Spring Taglib is declared in `show_emps.jsp` and the same `<spring:bind>` techniques are used for reading both keys. The only difference is its JavaConfig way of loading the `ReloadableResourceBundleMessageSource` bean to `SpringDispatcherConfig`:

```
@Bean
public MessageSource messageSource() {
    ReloadableResourceBundleMessageSource messageSource =
new ReloadableResourceBundleMessageSource();
 messageSource.setBasenames("classpath:config/messages_en_US");
    messageSource.setUseCodeAsDefaultMessage(true);
    messageSource.setDefaultEncoding("UTF");
    messageSource.setCacheSeconds(1);
    return messageSource;
}
```

8. Build and deploy both projects. Open a browser and run `https://localhost:8443/ch02/view_emps.html` and `https://localhost:8443/ch02jc/view_emps.html` one at a time.

How it works...

`WebApplicationContext` can also be used to load specific String messages for rendering purposes, Internationalization (*i18N*), and error messages. There are two types of Spring component responsible for loading message bundles to the container and these are `ResourceBundleMessageSource` and `ReloadableResourceBundleMessageSource`. The former, one of the oldest Spring APIs, contains synchronized helper methods while the latter is the current implementation that contains advanced features such as caching.

Just like `InternalResourceViewResolver`, `MessageSource` beans are automatically defined by `DispatcherServlet` searching it through the bean id `messageSource`. So if the bean id is different, the message bundle will never be retrieved by `<spring:bind>`, which will give you an error:

```
javax.servlet.jsp.JspTagException: No message found under code 'title' for
locale 'en_US'
```

The entire message bundle is stored in a property file and each entry is a code/message pair where the code is the typical key used to fetch its corresponding message. Some message values are simple `String` but some might look like our `content_header`:

```
content_header=Goodbye! {0}. Last of Chapter {1}
```

Here `{0}` and `{1}` are called placeholders. Placeholders are expressions that wait for an argument at runtime through the `argument` attribute of `<spring:bind>`.

3
Implementing MVC Design Patterns

A rigorous set of recipes on how to kick off Spring 5.0 projects verified that the core platform is still composed of almost the same APIs found in its previous version. Even though Spring 5.0 promotes the new functional and reactive web framework, it still upholds the traditional annotations and web APIs such as `@Controller`, `@RequestMapping`, `@Bean`, the `ApplicationContext` interface, and many other old features such JSR-330 annotations.

Now, we focus on how the basic MVC components are written if Spring 5.0 is used. We will observe the differences and similarities between Spring 5.0 and the other versions especially when creating data sources, the Data Access Object (DAO) layer, service layers, validation, and other types of request handling.

In this chapter, you will learn the following:

- Creating a simple @Controller
- Creating a simple @Controller with method-level URL mapping
- Designing a simple form @Controller
- Creating a multi-action @Controller
- Form validation and parameter type conversion
- Creating request- and session-scoped beans
- Implementing page redirection and Flash-scoped beans
- Creating database connection pooling
- Implementing the DAO layer using the Spring JDBC Framework
- Creating a service layer in an MVC application

Creating the simple @Controller

Let us start with a recipe that will provide us with different strategies for how to implement Spring 5.0 @Controller classes. These are just typical non-reactive and non-functional features of Spring 5.0, which can be useful in the later chapters.

Getting started

Using the recipes in Chapter 1, *Getting Started with Spring* and Chapter 2, *Learning Dependency Injection (DI)*, create and set up another Maven project for Spring web development and name it ch03. The project will be using the JavaConfig specification in generating the ApplicationContext. Also, this web.xml-less project will demonstrate how to optimize @Controller classes based on the number of request handlers needed and the nature of the request and response transactions.

How to do it...

In order to create our first controllers, do the following steps:

1. Locate pom.xml inside the ch03 folder and configure it to include the entire Spring 5.0 core, Spring Web MVC module, servlet and JSP APIs, JTSL, and standard taglib dependencies:

```xml
<properties>
  <spring.version>5.0.0.BUILD-SNAPSHOT</spring.version>
  <servlet.api.version>3.1.0</servlet.api.version>
</properties>
<dependencies>
  <dependency>
    <groupId>org.springframework</groupId>
    <artifactId>spring-context</artifactId>
    <version>${spring.version}</version>
  </dependency>
  <dependency>
    <groupId>org.springframework</groupId>
    <artifactId>spring-core</artifactId>
    <version>${spring.version}</version>
  </dependency>

  <dependency>
    <groupId>org.springframework</groupId>
    <artifactId>spring-beans</artifactId>
```

```
        <version>${spring.version}</version>
    </dependency>

    <dependency>
        <groupId>org.springframework</groupId>
        <artifactId>spring-web</artifactId>
        <version>${spring.version}</version>
    </dependency>

    <dependency>
        <groupId>org.springframework</groupId>
        <artifactId>spring-webmvc</artifactId>
        <version>${spring.version}</version>
    </dependency>
    <dependency>
        <groupId>javax.servlet</groupId>
        <artifactId>javax.servlet-api</artifactId>
        <version>${servlet.api.version}</version>
        <scope>provided</scope>
    </dependency>

    <dependency>
        <groupId>javax.servlet.jsp</groupId>
        <artifactId>javax.servlet.jsp-api</artifactId>
        <version>2.3.1</version>
        <scope>provided</scope>
    </dependency>

    <dependency>
        <groupId>javax.servlet</groupId>
        <artifactId>jstl</artifactId>
        <version>1.2</version>
    </dependency>
    <dependency>
        <groupId>taglibs</groupId>
        <artifactId>standard</artifactId>
        <version>1.1.2</version>
    </dependency>

    // refer to sources

</dependencies>
```

2. Since this project complies with the `JavaConfig` specification, create the usual `SpringWebInitializer` to enable MVC configuration and auto-detect all the annotations used by the internal components. Configure `@ComponentScan` to recognize the **base-package** `org.packt.dissect.mvc`.

3. Configure also the root `ApplicationContext` and the `SpringDispatcherConfig` to auto-detect the `@Controller` annotations contained in the package `org.packt.dissect.mvc.controller` through the `@ComponentScan`.

4. Now, create the first type of controller, which is the `SimpleController`. A simple controller is used to take control of every incoming request using only one URL. The centralized top-level URL setting filters the incoming request and easily identifies the type of HTTP method and headers essential in managing those requests. Let us name this controller `SimpleController`, having this implementation:

```
@Controller
@RequestMapping("/simple.html")
public class SimpleController {
  @RequestMapping(method=RequestMethod.GET)
  public String processGetReq(Model model){
    String transactionType = "Simple GET Transaction";
    model.addAttribute("transactionType", transactionType);
    return "get";
  }
  @RequestMapping(method=RequestMethod.POST)
  public String processPostReq(Model model){
    String transactionType = "Simple POST Transaction";
    model.addAttribute("transactionType", transactionType);
    return "post";
  }
}
```

On the other hand, this `SimpleController` illustrates how to call two handler methods sharing only one URL, but of different HTTP methods.

5. From the preceding code, create the views `get` and `post` using `ResourceBundleViewResolver`. Create and open `src\main\resources\config\views.properties` and add the following mappings:

```
post.(class)=org.springframework.web.servlet.view.JstlView
post.url=/page/post_view.jsp
```

```
get.(class)=org.springframework.web.servlet.view.JstlView
get.url=/page/get_view.jsp
```

6. Using `ReloadableResourceBundleMessageSource`, create and open `src\main\resources\config\messages_en_US.properties` and add the following label mappings:

```
#Title Labels
post_title=POST VIEW
get_title=GET VIEW
```

7. After changing the properties file, create the physical view `src\main\webapp\page\post_view.jsp` for the POST transaction using the following template:

```
<%@ page language="java" contentType="text/html;
charset=ISO-8859-1" pageEncoding="ISO-8859-1"%>
<%@ taglib prefix="spring"
uri="http://www.springframework.org/tags" %>
<!DOCTYPE html PUBLIC "-//W3C//DTD HTML 4.01 Transitional//EN"
"http://www.w3.org/TR/html4/loose.dtd">
<html>
<head>
<meta http-equiv="Content-Type" content="text/html;
charset=ISO-8859-1">
<title><spring:message code="post_title" /></title>
</head>
<body>
    <h1>${ transactionType }</h1>
</body>
</html>
```

8. For the GET transaction, create `src\main\webapp\page\get_view.jsp`, having the following script:

```
<%@ page language="java" contentType="text/html;
charset=ISO-8859-1"  pageEncoding="ISO-8859-1"%>
<%@ taglib prefix="spring"
uri="http://www.springframework.org/tags" %>
<!DOCTYPE html PUBLIC "-//W3C//DTD HTML 4.01 Transitional//EN"
"http://www.w3.org/TR/html4/loose.dtd">
<html>
<head>
<meta http-equiv="Content-Type" content="text/html;
charset=ISO-8859-1">
<title><spring:message code="get_title" /></title>
</head>
```

```
<body>
    <h1>${ transactionType }</h1>
</body>
</html>
```

9. To execute the handler methods, create a facade controller like this `SimpleTestController`, as shown here:

```
@Controller
@RequestMapping("/simplecontroller.html")
public class SimpleTestController {
  @RequestMapping(method=RequestMethod.GET)
  public String viewTransactions(){
    return "simple_list";
  }
}
```

10. Implement a physical page for the `simple_list` view of the previous controller. Name it as `src\main\webapp\page\get_view.jsp`, with the following script:

```
<%@ page language="java" contentType="text/html;
charset=ISO-8859-1" pageEncoding="ISO-8859-1"%>
<%@ taglib prefix="spring"
  uri="http://www.springframework.org/tags" %>
<!DOCTYPE html PUBLIC "-//W3C//DTD HTML 4.01 Transitional//EN"
  "http://www.w3.org/TR/html4/loose.dtd">
<html>
<head>
<meta http-equiv="Content-Type" content="text/html;
charset=ISO-8859-1">
<title><spring:message code="simple_facade" /></title>
</head>
<body>
<a href="${pageContext.request.contextPath}/simple.html">
  GET Transaction</a>
<br/>
<form action="${pageContext.request.contextPath}
    /simple.html" method="post" >
<input type="submit" value="POST Transaction" />
</form>
</body>
</html>
```

The ${pageContext.request.contextPath} is an **EL** expression that retrieves the context path of the deployed web application. This is recommended instead of hardcoding the context.

11. Configure the messageSource and viewResolver to include the preceding added components.
12. Save all files. clean, build, and deploy the project to your Tomcat 9 application server using our Maven deployment library. Open a browser and run https://localhost:8443/ch03/simplecontroller.html:

How it works...

Because of the @ComponentScan of the WebApplicationContext, all classes having @Controller will be detected by DispatcherServlet and recognized as controllers during bootstrap. Afterwards, the servlet will search for the controller's URL through the @RequestMapping annotations. In the implementation of our simple controller, the mapping of the URL is done only at the class level. This URL will be invoked by user requests and will eventually tell the servlet what controller to execute. Since there is no other URL mapping in the controller's blueprint, the DispatcherServlet will stop the search and continue identifying the HTTP methods sent by the request to each request handler's @RequestMapping attribute method.

When the client invoked https://localhost:8443/ch03/simple.html through a GET transaction (that is, the hyperlink triggers a GET request), the handler method processGetReq() will be executed by the servlet since it is mapped to RequestMethod.GET. But when a POST form transaction is invoked, the processPostReq() method will be chosen by the DispatcherServlet because it is mapped to the POST method.

Creating a simple @Controller with method-level URL mapping

The previous recipe centralizes on the URL mapping by having a class-level @RequestMapping annotation. This time the goal is to illustrate how a simple @Controller manages handler methods with each having both the HTTP method and request URL settings.

Getting started

Utilize the same Eclipse STS project ch03 to implement our @Controller and its components. This recipe focuses on other ways of dealing with @Controller and @RequestMapping with the inclusion of using other HTTP methods such as DELETE and PUT. In relation to the PUT method, the recipe will discuss file uploading at the side.

How to do it...

To perform different ways of URL mapping to types of HTTP request handlers, follow these steps:

1. Since ch03 is a working project already, let us add a simple controller, SimplePatternsController, with three handler methods handling GET and POST transactions inside the org.packt.dissect.mvc.controller package. This simple controller has both the class-level and method-level @RequestMapping annotations, through which the request URLs will be determined based on the class level going down to the URL of its respective handler methods:

```
@Controller
@RequestMapping("/simple")
public class SimplePatternsController {

  @RequestMapping(value="/form_upload_get.html",
    method=RequestMethod.GET)
  public String uploadFileFormGet(Model model) {
    FileUploadForm fileUploadForm = new FileUploadForm();
    model.addAttribute("fileUploadForm", fileUploadForm);
     return "put_form";
  }
  @RequestMapping(value="/form_upload_post.html",
```

```
        method=RequestMethod.POST)
    public String uploadFileFormPost(Model model) {
      FileUploadForm fileUploadForm = new FileUploadForm();
      model.addAttribute("fileUploadForm", fileUploadForm);
       return "put_form";
    }
    @RequestMapping(value="/patterns.html",
      method=RequestMethod.GET)
    public String uploadFileForm() {
      return "simple_patterns";
    }
  }
```

The handler method `uploadFileFormGet()` calls the form view for file uploading with the GET transaction mode, while `uploadFileFormPost()` calls the same form component using the POST method. On the other hand, the method `uploadFileForm()` is mapped to `/patterns.html` to serve as the entry point or facade of the application.

2. The facade page will simply consist of a typical form for the POST method option and hyperlink for the GET method preference. The user can click either of the components to call the upload page:

```
<%@ page language="java" contentType="text/html;
charset=ISO-8859-1"
    pageEncoding="ISO-8859-1"%>
<%@ taglib prefix="spring"
   uri="http://www.springframework.org/tags"%>
<!DOCTYPE html>
<html>
<head>
<meta http-equiv="Content-Type" content="text/html;
charset=ISO-8859-1">
<title><spring:message code="simple_patterns_facade" />
</title>
</head>
<body>
   <a href="${pageContext.request.contextPath}/simple/
        form_upload_get.html">GET Transaction</a>
   <br/>
   <form action="${pageContext.request.contextPath}/simple/
            form_upload_post.html" method="post">
     <input type="submit" value="POST Transaction" />
   </form>
</body>
</html>
```

3. The `put_form` view, called by either the POST or GET options of the facade page, serves as the form page where the user is asked to upload a file. Clicking its submit button will generate a PUT request:

```jsp
<%@ page language="java" contentType="text/html;
charset=ISO-8859-1" pageEncoding="ISO-8859-1"%>
<%@ taglib prefix="c" uri="http://java.sun.com/jsp/jstl/core"%>
<%@ taglib prefix="spring"
uri="http://www.springframework.org/tags" %>
<%@ taglib prefix="form"
uri="http://www.springframework.org/tags/form"%>
<!DOCTYPE html>
<html>
<head>
<meta http-equiv="Content-Type" content="text/html;
charset=ISO-8859-1">
<title><spring:message code="put_title" /></title>
</head>
<body>
<form:form  modelAttribute="uploadFileForm"
   action="${pageContext.request.contextPath}
   /simple/upload.html" enctype="multipart/form-data"
   method="PUT">
    <input type="file" name="file"/>
    <input type="submit" value="Submit"/>
</form:form>
</body>
</html>
```

4. The Spring Form tag library will be used to introduce data binding-aware tags and model form objects to the MVC application and, most of all, will give support and fast delegation to the PUT transactions. After clicking the submit button, the `put_form` request will be redirected to the method `SimplePatternsController`, mapped to `RequestMethod.PUT`. Implement this method as `uploadFileSubmit()`:

```java
@RequestMapping(value="/upload.html",
method={RequestMethod.PUT, RequestMethod.POST})
public String uploadFileSubmit(Model model,
  @ModelAttribute("fileUploadForm") FileUploadForm
    fileUploadForm, HttpServletRequest req) {
    String fileName =
      fileUploadForm.getFile().getOriginalFilename();
    model.addAttribute("transactionType", transactionType);
    model.addAttribute("fileName", fileName);
     return "put_result";
```

```
}
```

In order for the `PUT` transaction to be successfully recognized by the `DispatcherServlet`, `RequesMethod.POST` must also be included in `@RequestMapping`.

5. The `put_result` view is implemented by the JSP page below.

```
<%@ page language="java" contentType="text/html;
charset=ISO-8859-1" pageEncoding="ISO-8859-1"%>
<%@ taglib prefix="c" uri="http://java.sun.com/jsp/jstl/core"%>
<%@ taglib prefix="spring"
uri="http://www.springframework.org/tags" %>
<!DOCTYPE >
<html>
<head>
<meta http-equiv="Content-Type" content="text/html;
charset=ISO-8859-1">
<title><spring:message code="put_title" /></title>
</head>
  <body>
    <h1>${ transactionType }</h1>
    <em> ${ fileName } </em>
  </body>
</html>
```

6. Now, create another handler method, invoking the `DELETE` request transaction:

```
@RequestMapping(value="/delete.html",
  method={RequestMethod.DELETE, RequestMethod.GET})
public String deleteEvent(Model model){
    String transactionType = "Simple DELETE Transaction";
    model.addAttribute("transactionType", transactionType);
    return "delete";
}
```

In order for the `DELETE` transaction to pass through the `DispatcherServlet`, `RequesMethod.GET` must also be included in `@RequestMapping`.

7. Configuring PUT and DELETE transactions to work in Tomcat 9 is not as easy as their implementation because almost all of the browsers only support POST, GET, and HEAD methods. Using methods other than these will result in HTTP status 405 Request method not supported. There are few solutions which can be helpful in fixing this problem, and these are:

- Using the framework's org.springframework.web.filter.HiddenHttpMethodFilter, which can auto-generate a _method hidden parameter needed by the framework in the conversion and recognition of PUT and DELETE request modes as valid HTTP methods. We have to add HiddenHttpMethodFilter into our SpringWebInitializer and utilize the Spring Form tag library. This filter will not work without the <form:form> tag component. The following is the FilerRegistration for the HiddenHttpMethodFilter:

```
@EnableWebMvc
@ComponentScan(basePackages="org.packt.dissect.mvc")
@Configuration
public class SpringWebInitializer implements
    WebApplicationInitializer {

  // refer to sources

   private void addDispatcherContext(ServletContext
container) {
      // refer to sources
      FilterRegistration.Dynamic filter =
         container.addFilter("hiddenmethodfilter",
new HiddenHttpMethodFilter());
            filter.addMappingForServletNames(null,
true, "/*");
    }
  }
```

- Customize the `org.apache.catalina.filters.CorsFilter` and override its `cors.allowed.methods` property. Most application servers do not support other HTTP methods except `GET`, `POST`, `HEAD`, and `OPTIONS`. In Tomcat 9, an appropriate solution is to add the `CorsFilter` into the servlet container `SpringWebInitializer`, with the addition of `PUT` and `DELETE` on its `cors.allowed.methods`:

```
private void addDispatcherContext(ServletContext container) {
   // refer to sources

   FilterRegistration.Dynamic corsFilter =
   container.addFilter("corsFilter", new CorsFilter());
   corsFilter.setInitParameter(
   "cors.allowed.methods","GET, POST, HEAD,
   OPTIONS, PUT, DELETE");
   corsFilter.addMappingForUrlPatterns(null,
   true, "/*");
}
```

- `CorsFilter` is not inherent to Spring APIs but to Tomcat 9 libraries; thus, we need to include the following Maven dependency, given the provided scope:

```
<dependency>
   <groupId>org.apache.tomcat</groupId>
   <artifactId>tomcat-catalina</artifactId>
   <version>9.0.0.M15</version>
   <scope>provided</scope>
</dependency>
```

The provided scope means that the JAR files from `tomcat-catalina` are needed for compilation but not for packaging because of the assumption that it is already provided by the environment.

8. On the file uploading transaction, the `put_form` in *Step 3* uses the Spring Form tag library to map all request data to a `modelAttribute` named `fileUploadForm`. This `modelAttribute` refers to a form model object or a form backing object that persists all request data for every user transaction. The `fileUploadForm` is typically a POJO and is written as:

```
public class FileUploadForm {
   private MultipartFile file;
      // getter and setter
}
```

In Spring, the uploaded file must be wrapped by an object called `org.springframework.web.multipart.MultipartFile`, given that the request comes from multipart/form-data. The `MultipartFile` wraps file contents that come either from memory or temporary disks.

9. For the `PUT` transaction to work, the multipart request needs to inject `org.springframework.web.multipart.commons.CommonsMultipartResolver` to the `WebApplicationContext` and add `org.springframework.web.multipart.support.MultipartFilter` to the servlet container. Open the root context definition `SpringDispatcherConfig` and add the following snippet to the `CommonsMultipartResolver` settings:

```
@Bean(name = "multipartResolver")
public CommonsMultipartResolver getResolver() throws
IOException{
        CommonsMultipartResolver resolver =
          new CommonsMultipartResolver();
        resolver.setMaxUploadSizePerFile(5242880);
        resolver.setMaxUploadSize(52428807);
        resolver.setDefaultEncoding("UTF-8");
        return resolver;
}
```

Given the preceding details, the `CommonsMultipartResolver` only accepts files with `UTF-8` content-encoding of size 52428807 KB or 5 MB of either single or multiple file uploads. The bean name must be `multipartResolver`.

10. For the filter, open `SpringWebInitializer` and register the `MultipartFilter` snippet in the `addDispatcherContext()` method:

```
FilterRegistration.Dynamic multipartFilter =
container.addFilter("multipartFilter", new MultipartFilter());
multipartFilter.addMappingForUrlPatterns(null, true, "/*");
```

11. To wrap up, add the following dependencies for the file uploading `PUT` request transaction:

```
<dependency>
    <groupId>commons-net</groupId>
    <artifactId>commons-net</artifactId>
    <version>3.3</version>
</dependency>
<dependency>
    <groupId>commons-fileupload</groupId>
    <artifactId>commons-fileupload</artifactId>
```

```
        <version>1.3.1</version>
    </dependency>
    <dependency>
        <groupId>commons-io</groupId>
        <artifactId>commons-io</artifactId>
        <version>2.2</version>
    </dependency>
```

12. Save all files. `clean`, `build`, and `deploy` ch03. Run the facade handler `uploadFileForm()` by calling the class-level URL first (`/simple`) and then append it to its own URL (`/patterns.html`). This rule is also true when executing the rest of the handler methods.

How it works...

The main target of this recipe is how to create a simple controller with `@RequestMapping` used to assign URLs to both the controller and its request handlers. Then, it is followed by topics on how to the use of `RequestMethod.PUT` and `RequestMethod.DELETE` with topics on file uploading as a `PUT` request transaction.

To start, the use of `@RequestMapping` is not limited to the `@Controller` level when we deal with URL mapping. The annotation `@RequestMapping("/simple")`, for instance, is attached on top of the `@Controller` declaration, which means that all the handling methods are called relative to the given path `/simple`. The other `@RequestMapping("/upload.html")` found on the method `uploadFileSubmit()` indicates that this request transaction is executed whenever the end of the URL matches

`/upload.html` or `/ch03/simple/upload.html`.

In the other part of the recipe, the use of HTTP methods other than GET and POST are always given in any application server, especially if the specification does not fit with GET or POST alone. Spring 5.0 supports HEAD, GET, POST, DELETE, PATCH, TRACE, and OPTIONS request methods that can be used anytime depending on the nature of the transaction. As with file uploading, the PUT transaction is always associated with file processing, such as sending and updating files to the file storage. Likewise, the PUT method can also be used in handlers that update database records. There is also the inclusion of the DELETE transaction in our controller, which may be used to focus on database record deletion or file removal from a repository. In cases like REST services, the DELETE transaction may require a URL request parameter which indicates which component will be deleted. Using the DELETE method in form handling has one problem and that is HTML forms support only GET, POST, or HEAD, which makes this <form> snippet:

```
<form action="${pageContext.request.contextPath}/simple/
      upload.html"
  enctype="multipart/form-data" method="PUT">
    <input type="file"name="file"/>
    <input type="submit" value="Submit"/>
</form>
```

This is capable of triggering **HTTP Status 405**:

HTTP Status 405 - Request method 'GET' not supported

type	Status report
message	Request method 'GET' not supported
description	The specified HTTP method is not allowed for the requested resource.

Apache Tomcat/9.0.0.M15

To fix this problem, we need the Spring Form tag library to bind the <form> to the Spring framework, and an inclusion of HiddenHttpMethodFilter in our servlet container:

```
<form:form  modelAttribute="uploadFileForm"
  action="/ch03/simple/upload.html" enctype="multipart/form-data"
  method="PUT">
      <input type="file"name="file"/>
      <input type="submit" value="Submit"/>
</form:form>
```

The preceding resulting component, `<form:form>`, will give us auto-generated HTML with a _method parameter having PUT as a value:

```
<form id="uploadFileForm" action="/ch03/simple/upload.html"
  method="post" enctype="multipart/form-data">
  <input type="hidden" name="_method" value="PUT"/>
        <input type="file" name="file"/>
        <input type="submit" value="Submit"/>
</form>
```

But examining the preceding code, there is only one unexpected `<form>` attribute that showed up, and that is the `method="POST"`. This means that the filter `HiddenHttpMethodFilter` forwards the request to the `DispatcherServlet` as a POST transaction first before it reaches the method handler bearing the PUT method. Because of this internal filter processing, the handler method, `uploadFileSubmit()`, must not only map to the PUT request method type but also to POST:

```
@RequestMapping(value="/upload.html",
method={RequestMethod.PUT, RequestMethod.POST})
public String uploadFileSubmit(Model model,
    @ModelAttribute("fileUploadForm") FileUploadForm
      fileUploadForm, HttpServletRequest req) { }
```

Otherwise, it will give you the same **HTTP Status 405** error. On the other hand, the DELETE request is forwarded as GET first to the `DispatcherServlet` before it reaches the controller as a DELETE transaction.

Another solution that can be useful in recognizing PUT and DELETE is to configure the `CorsFilter` of Apache Tomcat 9 by overriding its `cors.allowed.methods` property, which is a comma-separated list of HTTP methods, which, by default, only includes GET, POST, HEAD, and OPTIONS.

Designing a simple form @Controller

This concept is related to the creation of the file uploading transaction in the previous recipe, but the concept here is leaning towards general form handling transactions.

Getting started

The same `ch03` project will be used to implement a simple form controller. The recipe will still revolve around controllers and request handlers, with emphasis on creating form backing objects and Spring Form tag libraries.

How to do it...

To implement form handling using Spring 5, perform the following steps:

1. Let us first implement the model object that will contain all request data during form transactions. The `form_page` handles all the HTML components that will receive all request parameters from the client. To organize these numerous parameters during the request dispatch, it will be ideal if we create a form model or form backing object to persist all this data. This strategy can avoid a convoluted declaration of request parameters at the `@Controller` level. So, before creating the physical view and the `@Controller`, write this POJO first, containing all the data and its properties:

   ```
   public class EmployeeForm {
      private String firstName;
      private String lastName;
      private String position;

      // getters and setters
   }
   ```

2. Then, create a `@Controller` named `FormController` inside the `org.packt.dissect.mvc.controller` package. A form controller is similar to a simple one because of its use of class-level `@RequestMapping` configuration for the URL. The only difference is that a form controller must only contain two methods: the GET handler, to serve the form views, and the POST handler to perform the operations after the form submission. Both of these handlers must not have URL mapping. The following is our `FormController`:

   ```
   @Controller
   @RequestMapping("/employee_form.html")
   public class FormController {
     @RequestMapping(method=RequestMethod.GET)
     public String initForm(Model model){
     EmployeeForm employeeForm = new EmployeeForm();
       model.addAttribute("employeeForm", employeeForm);
       return "form_page";
   ```

```
    }
    @RequestMapping(method=RequestMethod.POST)
    public String submitForm(Model model,
        @ModelAttribute("employeeForm") EmployeeForm
            employeeForm){
        model.addAttribute("employeeForm", employeeForm);
        return "success_page";
    }
}
```

The `initForm()` loads the `form_page` view and initializes the `EmployeeForm` form backing object for the form's `modelAttribute` mapping. The `submitForm()` is executed after the form submission receives the form backing object that is persisted with the form data. Moreover, this method is implemented to pass the unaltered form object as a request attribute to the `success_page` view using the `Model` interface.

3. Next, create the `form_page` as `src/main/webapp/page/employee_form.jsp`, which will contain the binding of the `EmployeeForm` form model to the HTML form components. This binding mechanism requires the use of the Spring Form tag library, again declared at the directive level of our JSP page together with the core Spring tag library for static texts and labels, and JSTL for common JSP supplementary support:

```jsp
<%@ taglib prefix="c" uri="http://java.sun.com/jsp/jstl/core"%>
<%@ taglib prefix="spring"
uri="http://www.springframework.org/tags" %>
<%@ taglib prefix="form"
uri="http://www.springframework.org/tags/form"%>
<!DOCTYPE html PUBLIC "-//W3C//DTD HTML 4.01 Transitional//EN"
    "http://www.w3.org/TR/html4/loose.dtd">
<html>
<head>
<title><spring:message code="employee_form" /></title>
</head>
<body>
    <h1><spring:message code="employee_form" /></h1>
    <form:form  modelAttribute="employeeForm" method="post">
        <spring:message code="fnameLbl" />
            <form:input path="firstName"/><br/>
        <spring:message code="lnameLbl" />
            <form:input path="lastName"/><br/>
        <spring:message code="posLbl" />
            <form:input path="position"/><br/>
        <input type="submit" value="Add Employee"/>
    </form:form>
```

```
</body>
</html>
```

To use the Spring Form tag library, we use the prefix `form` to access all its data binding-aware tags, to be used for accessing the setters of each component of the model attribute `EmployeeForm`. The first tag, `<form:form>`, renders the HTML `<form>` and enables the binding of request parameters to its inner tags. The `<form:input>` tag renders the HTML `<input>` tag with access to the model attributes with a default empty value. The `<spring:message>` just accesses the labels and header titles from the message bundle.

4. The last view to create is the `success_pagesrc/main/webapp/page/employee_profile.jsp`, which contains the rendition of all the properties of the `modelAttribute` using the JSP's expression language and `JSTL`:

```
<%@ taglib prefix="c" uri="http://java.sun.com/jsp/jstl/core"%>
<%@ taglib prefix="spring"
uri="http://www.springframework.org/tags" %>
<%@ taglib prefix="form"
uri="http://www.springframework.org/tags/form"%>
<!DOCTYPE html PUBLIC "-//W3C//DTD HTML 4.01 Transitional//EN"
  "http://www.w3.org/TR/html4/loose.dtd">
<html>
<head>
<title><spring:message code="employee_profile" /></title>
</head>
<body>
  <h1><spring:message code="employee_profile" /></h1>
  <table>
      <tr>
         <th>First Name</th>
         <th>Last Name</th>
         <th>Position</th>
      </tr>
       <tr>
        <td><c:out value='${ employeeForm.firstName }'/></td>
        <td><c:out value='${ employeeForm.lastName }' /></td>
        <td><c:out value='${ employeeForm.position }' /></td>
      </tr>
  </table>
</body>
</html>
```

5. Update the `views.properties` by adding the following mappings:

```
form_page.(class)=org.springframework.web.servlet.view.JstlView
form_page.url=/page/employee_form.jsp

success_page.(class)=org.springframework.web.servlet.view.JstlV
iew
success_page.url=/page/employee_profile.jsp
```

6. Also, update the message bundle to have proper header titles and labels.
7. Save all files. `clean`, `install`, and `deploy` the project. Open a browser and run `https://localhost:8443/ch03/employee_form.html`:

How it works...

The simple form controller contains only one URL mapping and it is confined at the class-level `@RequestMapping` annotation. It only consists of two handler methods: the `initForm()`, which is the GET handler method, and the `submitForm()`, the POST handler. Request handlers such as `initForm()` prepare the form view for form loading, while the `submitForm()` processes all the incoming request data, validates them against form rules, and generates the needed response by forwarding all results to the success view.

The usual way of retrieving request parameters is to use the `getParameter()` method of `HttpServletRequest`, but the only problem here is when the number of request data increases, which makes validation and type-checking difficult to manage. Spring devised an organized way of managing request data and that is to store it in a model object such as the `EmployeeForm`. Using the Spring Form tag library, we bind all the parameter data to the properties of the POJO model through the `modelAttribute` of the `<form:form>` tag. After clicking the submit button, this model object is passed on to the `submitForm()` in the form of an object parameter using the `@ModelAttribute` annotation. These model objects are synonymous to the term *form backing objects*. Depending on the intention, the `submitForm()` either calls its own `success_page` or just redirects to the `form_page`, especially when form validation is implemented to avoid SQL injection and **Denial of Attack (DoA)** problems.

Creating a multi-action @Controller

The implementation of the multi-action controller has evolved from extending the class `org.springframework.web.servlet.mvc.multiaction.MultiActionController` up to the modern day use of the `@Controller` annotation. This recipe will show you how to easily create a multi-action controller using `JavaConfig`.

Getting started

We will be adding a multi-action controller to the same project, `ch03`. This is another option to manage all the request handlers.

How to do it...

To create a multi-action controller in the Spring 5.0 platform, follow these steps:

1. Let us start this recipe with a multi-action controller named `MultiActionController` with all its handler methods mapped to their respective URLs, similar to a hub of independent services:

```
@Controller
public class MultiActionController {

    @RequestMapping(value={"/send/*", "/list/*"},
        method=RequestMethod.GET)
    public String defaultMethod(){
```

```
      return "default_msg";
    }
    @RequestMapping(value="/send/message_get.html",
       method=RequestMethod.GET)
    public String sendGetMessage(Model model){
      String message = "Multi-action GET URL Mapping";
      model.addAttribute("message", message);
      return "get_msg";
    }
    @RequestMapping(value="/send/message_post.html",
       method=RequestMethod.POST)
    public String sendPostMessage(Model model){
      String message = "Multi-action Post URL Mapping";
      model.addAttribute("message", message);
        return "post_msg";
    }
    @RequestMapping(value="/list/multilist.html",
       method=RequestMethod.GET)
    public String viewTransactions(){
        return "multi_list";
    }
}
```

2. The preceding three handler methods are typical request transactions mapped to their respective URL and HTTP methods. The handler `defaultMethod()` is quite unique because its action will be triggered whenever a request URL that starts with a context path `/send` or `/list` has been executed but happens to be non-existent. This method serves as the *callback feature* of the multi-action controller whenever the URL invoked does not exist.

3. Next, create the simple views `default_msg`, `get_msg` and `post_msg`, all having their own set of message bundle labels and JSTL tags for rendering.

4. Moreover, create a `multi_list` page that will serve as a facade for GET and POST transactions:

```
<%@ taglib prefix="spring"
uri="http://www.springframework.org/tags" %>
<!DOCTYPE html PUBLIC "-//W3C//DTD HTML 4.01 Transitional//EN"
"http://www.w3.org/TR/html4/loose.dtd">
<html>
<head>
<meta http-equiv="Content-Type" content="text/html;
 charset=ISO-8859-1">
<title><spring:message code="multi_facade" /></title>
</head>
<body>
    <a href="/ch03/send/message_get.html">GET Transaction</a>
```

```
            <br/>
            <form action="/ch03/send/message_post.html" method="post"
    >
                <input type="submit" value="POST Transaction" />
            </form>
        </body>
        </html>
```

5. Update both `views.properties` and `messages_en_US.properties` for the changes in the view configuration and resource bundle messages, respectively.

6. Then `clean`, `build`, and `deploy` the project. Call each request handler independently.

How it works...

Creating a multi-action controller is quite easy and simple because each handler method has its own `@RequestMapping` setup. Each method can be mapped to any HTTP method without having conflict with the others. The only problem is the high possibility of creating ambiguous URL mappings once the list of handlers increases in number. To solve this case, it is mandatory to create a default method such as `defaultMethod()` to filter an ambiguous and erroneous URL of the `@Controller`. The asterisk (*) means all the possible patterns of the path excluding those URLs declared. Just be cautious with the use of `@RequestMapping("/*")` since it will filter all possible URLs of the `WebApplicationContext`.

Form validation and parameter type conversion

The advantage of using form backing objects in implementing request parameter handling is attributed to the ease of applying form input rules and validation to the incoming request data. Moreover, type conversion of some request parameters that are non-string can be done using property editors included in the framework.

Getting started

Open again the Eclipse STS `ch03` project and perform the following steps for implementing the validator and input type conversion mechanism on simple form controllers without using any client-side scripts and services.

How to do it...

To apply form validation and input type conversion, do the following procedures:

1. The validation process will progress after modifying the `EmployeeForm` form model of the previous recipe to contain three more request data, namely the `email`, `age`, and `birthday` of the employee:

```
public class EmployeeForm {
    private String firstName;
    private String lastName;
    private String position;

    // additional information
    private Integer age;
    private Date birthday;
    private String email;

    // getters and setters
}
```

 Primitive types are not recommended in declaring form model properties because form validation and type conversion works easily with object types. Thus, wrapper classes must be used instead of their primitive counterparts.

2. The most straightforward and easiest way to apply the validator is to use the JSR-303/349 and Hibernate Validator annotations. These are two different external libraries which need to be included in our `pom.xml`. To access the JSR-303/349 bean annotations, this Maven library must be listed:

```
<dependency>
    <groupId>javax.validation</groupId>
    <artifactId>validation-api</artifactId>
    <version>1.1.0.Final</version>
</dependency>
```

Whereas, to utilize some Hibernate 5.x annotations for form model validation, we need this Maven dependency:

```
<dependency>
    <groupId>org.hibernate</groupId>
    <artifactId>hibernate-validator</artifactId>
    <version>5.0.1.Final</version>
</dependency>
```

Spring MVC projects must only choose either of the two libraries, but not both, to avoid confusion. But for the sake of this recipe, `ch03` will be mixing annotations from both.

3. To apply the two rules, modify `EmployeeForm` by adding the following annotations:

```
public class EmployeeForm {
    @Size(min=2, max=30)
    private String firstName;
    @Size(min=2, max=30)
    private String lastName;
    @NotNull
    @Size(min=5, max=100)
    private String position;
    @NotNull
    @Min(0) @Max(100)
    private Integer age;
    @NotNull
    @Past
    private Date birthday;
    @Email(message="Must be email formatted.")
    @NotEmpty
    private String email;

    // getters and setters
}
```

`@Size`, `@NotNull`, `@Min`, `@Max`, and `@Past` are rule-defining annotations of JSR-303/349, while `@NotEmpty` and `@Email` are both under the Hibernate Validation annotation group.

4. Next, create a bundle of error messages that will be displayed every time a violation on the rules is encountered. There are three ways to link an error message to each data rule:

- By creating an `errors.properties` file to be referenced by our `ReloadableResourceBundleMessageSource`. This file contains a list of code/message pairs wherein the code part is written using the `{annotation-name}.{modelAttribute}.{property-name}` pattern. In the case of `firstName`, the entry for its error message must be:

```
Size.employeeForm.firstName=Employee First Name should be
between {2} and {1} characters long inclusive
```

- In the preceding code {2} and {1} are placeholders for the maximum and minimum range values, respectively.
- By writing a code/message entry in `errors.properties`, where the message is immediately mapped to the annotation name:

```
Past=Date should be Past
NotEmpty=Email Address must not be null
```

- By assigning a hardcoded value to the message attribute of some annotations. The preceding email property has an annotation `@Email` whose error message is hardcoded within its bound:

```
@Email(message="Must be email formatted.")
@NotEmpty
private String email;
```

- Before proceeding, modify the `@Bean` configuration of the `ReloadableResourceBundleMessage` to include the `errors.properties` in its reference. This is done by replacing the property `basename` with `basenames`:

```
@Bean
public MessageSource messageSource() {

        ReloadableResourceBundleMessageSource messageSource =
          new ReloadableResourceBundleMessageSource();
        messageSource.setBasenames(
               "classpath:config/messages_en_US",
               "classpath:config/errors");
         // refer to sources
        return messageSource;
}
```

5. Create an empty `SpringContextConfig` that will define some of the `@Bean` needed for form validation and type checking. This definition class must scan and recognize all these classes from their respective packages.

```
@Configuration
@EnableWebMvc
@ComponentScan(basePackages = "org.packt.dissect.mvc,
org.packt.dissect.mvc.controller,
org.packt.dissect.mvc.validator")
public class SpringContextConfig { }
```

6. In order for the `ApplicationContext` to recognize all these external annotations, the `org.springframework.validation.beanvalidation.LocalValidatorFac toryBean` must be injected to the container. Once configured, `LocalValidatorFactoryBean`, Spring's central API for JSR-303/349 support can now explicitly validate any annotated form backing objects. Just add this `@Bean` to our `SpringContextConfig` definition and the rest will be taken care of by the `@Controller`:

```
@Bean
public LocalValidatorFactoryBean validator(){
    return new LocalValidatorFactoryBean();
}
```

7. After its injection, `@Autowire` the `LocalValidatorFactoryBean` into the `FormController` to `validate()` the `employeeForm` parameter of `submitForm()`.To capture all the error messages encountered during validation, add the `BindingResult` object in the parameter list. `BindingResult` has helper methods such as `hasErrors()`, which are essential in detecting registered errors during the validation process. Now, the new `submitForm()` must be written this way:

```
@Controller
@RequestMapping("/employee_form.html")
public class FormController {
  @Autowired
  private LocalValidatorFactoryBean validator;
  @RequestMapping(method=RequestMethod.POST)
  public String submitForm(Model model,
    @ModelAttribute("employeeForm") EmployeeForm
        employeeForm, BindingResult result ){

    model.addAttribute("employeeForm", employeeForm);
    validator.validate(employeeForm, result);
    if(result.hasErrors()){
      return "form_page";
    }
    return "success_page";
  }
}
```

In Spring 5.0, using `@Valid` of JSR-303/349 to auto-detect and execute bean annotations does not work anymore, unlike in Spring 3.0 and lower. The `validate()` method of `LocalValidatorFactoryBean` is the only feasible way to explicitly read `EmployeeForm`, execute all the annotations, validate all the request data that complies with the rules, and register all errors in `BindingResult`.

8. Given the changes in `submitForm()`, it is designed, that when `hashErrors()` encounters some non-compliance to the rules, it will re-load the `form_page` displaying all the registered error messages. The Spring Form tag library has a `<form:errors>` tag which displays all error messages linked to each property of the `modelAttribute`. At this point, modify the `form_page` view to include the `<form:errors>` tags:

```
<form:form modelAttribute="employeeForm" method="post">
        <spring:message code="fnameLbl" />
            <form:input path="firstName"/>  
            <form:errors path="firstName"/><br/>
        <spring:message code="lnameLbl" />
            <form:input path="lastName"/>  
            <form:errors path="lastName"/><br/>
        <spring:message code="posLbl" />
            <form:input path="position"/>  
            <form:errors path="position"/><br/>
        <hr/>
        <em>Added Information</em><br/>
        <spring:message code="ageLbl" />
            <form:input path="age"/>  
            <form:errors path="age"/><br/>
        <spring:message code="bdayLbl" />
            <form:input path="birthday"/>  
            <form:errors path="birthday"/><br/>
        <spring:message code="emailLbl" />
            <form:input path="email"/>  
            <form:errors path="email"/><br/>
        <input type="submit" value="Add Employee"/><br>
    </form:form>
```

9. Save all files. Then `clean`, `install`, and `deploy` ch03 into the Tomcat 9 container. Execute and test `https://localhost:8443/ch03/employee_form.html` to check if our annotations are working appropriately:

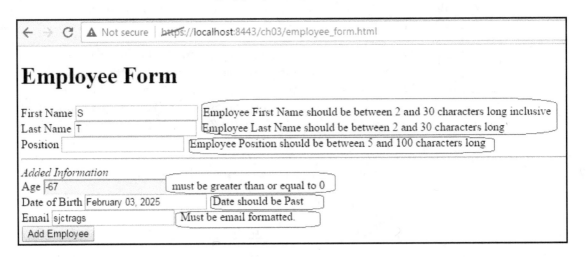

10. There are data rules that are so complex to handle an annotation and can only be implemented through programming. The Spring framework supports highly customized validation through its `org.springframework.validation.Validator` interface. Once implemented, this validator requires two methods to implement, and these are `supports()` and `validate()`. The `supports()` method checks and verifies the `@ModelAttribute` to be validated, whereas `validate()` performs the custom validation process. Create a new package, `org.packt.dissect.mvc.validator`, to store our `EmployeeValidator`:

```java
public class EmployeeValidator implements Validator{

    @Override
    public boolean supports(Class<?> clazz) {
      return clazz.equals(EmployeeForm.class);
    }

    @Override
    public void validate(Object model, Errors errors) {
      EmployeeForm empForm = (EmployeeForm) model;
      ValidationUtils.rejectIfEmptyOrWhitespace(errors,
        "firstName", "empty.firstName");
      ValidationUtils.rejectIfEmptyOrWhitespace(errors,
```

```
        "lastName", "empty.lastName");
    if(empForm.getAge() < 0) errors.rejectValue("age",
      "negative.age");
    if(empForm.getAge() > 65) errors.rejectValue("age",
      "retirable.age");
    if(empForm.getBirthday().before(new Date(50,0,1)))
      errors.rejectValue("birthday", "old.birthday");
    Date now = new Date();
    if(empForm.getBirthday().getYear() == now.getYear()
        || empForm.getBirthday().after(new Date(99,0,1)))
     errors.rejectValue("birthday", "underage.birthday");
  }
}
```

11. Inject `EmployeeValidator` into the `SpringContextConfig` container using the `JavaConfig` specification:

```
@Bean
public Validator employeeValidator(){
    return new EmployeeValidator();
}
```

12. The bean `employeeValidator` must be `@Autowired` into the `FormController` to be registered in a `@InitBinder` method. The main purpose of the `initBinder()` method is to bind the `@ModelAttribute` to validators through the `WebDataBinder` object:

```
@Controller
@RequestMapping("/employee_form.html")
public class FormController {
  @Autowired
  private Validator employeeValidator;
  // refer to sources
  @InitBinder("employeeForm")
  public void initBinder(WebDataBinder binder){
    binder.setValidator(employeeValidator);
  }
}
```

13. To let the Spring framework know that the `EmployeeForm` can now be validated using `EmployeeValidator`, the `@Validated` annotation of Spring must be added before the `employeeForm` parameter of `submitForm()`:

```
@RequestMapping(method=RequestMethod.POST)
public String submitForm(Model model,
    @ModelAttribute("employeeForm") @Validated EmployeeForm
        employeeForm, BindingResult result ){

  model.addAttribute("employeeForm", employeeForm);
  validator.validate(employeeForm, result);
  if(result.hasErrors()){
      return "form_page";
  }
  return "success_page";
}
```

14. Save all files. Then `clean`, `compile`, and `deploy` the project. Run and test `https://localhost:8443/ch03/employee_form.html`, again but focus on the `EmployeeValidator` rules:

15. The whole recipe will not be complete without a type conversion mechanism for incoming request data. Spring validation has a limitation and that is to convert request parameters to their qualified `modelAttribute` types. **Employee Form**, **Age** and **Date of Birth** are examples of data that will throw an exception once saved into the database or processed in a mathematical formula, because they remain as strings at this point. To fix the bug, create custom editors named `AgeEditor` and `DateEditor` inside a new package, `org.packt.dissect.mvc.editor`:

```java
public class AgeEditor extends PropertyEditorSupport{
  @Override
  public void setAsText(String text) throws
      IllegalArgumentException {

    try{
      int age = Integer.parseInt(text);
      setValue(age);
    }catch(NumberFormatException e){
        setValue(0);
    }
  }
  @Override
  public String getAsText() {
    return  "0";
  }
}

public class DateEditor extends PropertyEditorSupport{
  @Override
  public void setAsText(String text) throws
        IllegalArgumentException {

    SimpleDateFormat sdf =
      new SimpleDateFormat("MMMM dd, yyyy");
    try {
      Date dateParam = sdf.parse(text);
      setValue(dateParam);
    } catch (ParseException e) {
      setValue(new Date());
    }
  }
  @Override
  public String getAsText() {
    SimpleDateFormat sdf =
      new SimpleDateFormat("MMMM dd, yyyy");
    String bdayFmt = sdf.format(new Date());
```

```
                    return bdayFmt;
        }
    }
```

16. Just like validators, these custom editors must be added into the `@InitBinder` through its `WebDataBinder` to serve the main objective, type conversion. `AgeEditor` will convert the age parameter into `Integer` after clicking the submit button, while `DateEditor`, on the other hand, will manage the conversion of all request parameters to be saved as `java.util.Date` types. Modify the existing `initBinder()` method to bind all these custom editors to `employeeForm`:

```
@InitBinder("employeeForm")
  public void initBinder(WebDataBinder binder){

    binder.setValidator(employeeValidator);
    binder.registerCustomEditor(Date.class, new DateEditor());
  binder.registerCustomEditor(Integer.class, "age",new
AgeEditor());
}
```

17. Update the `success_page` views to include all the changes in the `modelAttribute` properties. This view will also introduce JSTL tags `<fmt>` for formatting rendered data:

```
<%@ taglib prefix="c" uri="http://java.sun.com/jsp/jstl/core"%>
<%@ taglib prefix="spring"
uri="http://www.springframework.org/tags" %>
<%@ taglib prefix="form"
uri="http://www.springframework.org/tags/form"%>
<%@ taglib prefix="fmt" uri="http://java.sun.com/jsp/jstl/fmt"
%>
<!DOCTYPE html PUBLIC "-//W3C//DTD HTML 4.01 Transitional//EN"
"http://www.w3.org/TR/html4/loose.dtd">
<html>
<head>
<meta http-equiv="Content-Type" content="text/html;
charset=ISO-8859-1">
<title><spring:message code="employee_profile" /></title>
</head>
<body>
  <h1><spring:message code="employee_profile" /></h1>
  <table>
      <tr>
          // refer to sources
      </tr>
       <tr>
```

```
      <td><c:out value='${ employeeForm.firstName }'/></td>
      <td><c:out value='${ employeeForm.lastName }' /></td>
      <td><c:out value='${ employeeForm.position }' /></td>
      <td><c:out value='${ employeeForm.age }' /></td>
      <td><fmt:formatDate value="${employeeForm.birthday}"
 type="date" /></td>
      <td><c:out value='${ employeeForm.email }' /></td>
    </tr>
  </table>
 </body>
</html>
```

18. Save all files of `ch03`. Then `clean`, `build`, and `deploy` it.

How it works...

This recipe just elaborated on how to build two of the most important layers of Spring MVC applications: the validator and type conversion engine components. Once installed and properly configured, these two components are the first ones to intercept the incoming request parameters, which are all strings by object type.

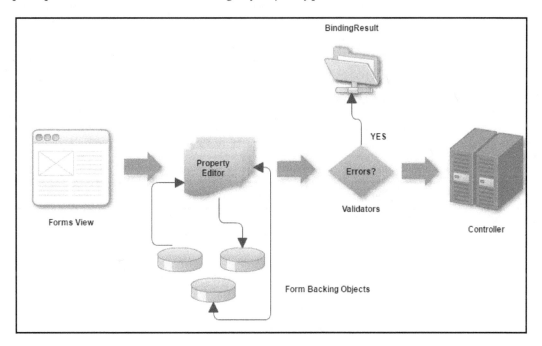

Before the `modelAttribute` reaches the controller, `PropertyEditors`, whether built-in or custom, convert first the textual request data to their respective object types during `<form:form>` binding. A `PropertyEditor` is a JavaBeans API, famous in the Spring framework for converting `modelAttribute` property values to and from string values. Its `setAsText()` converts the parameters to the desired type, while its `getAsText()` method initializes the form through the `modelAttribute` once the form is loaded.

Each built-in `PropertyEdior` manages the conversion per valid Spring type, while `CustomPropertyEditor` handles one or more conversions of complex or custom types. Although there is a built-in `PropertyEditor` for `Number` (for example, `Long`, `Short`, `Integer`), initializing the form components is always an exception. Thus, a custom `CustomPropertyEditor` such as `AgeEditor` is implemented to initialize the `<form:input path="age"/>` to zero after form loading to avoid `@Controller` exceptions during data processing or service calls. Likewise, the `DateEditor` is implemented to handle a successful conversion of any request parameters that are needed to be `java.util.Date` type, such as the `birthday` property of `EmployeeForm`.

After the type conversion of all the request data, validators will come into the picture in the form of JSR 303/349 and Hibernate Validation annotations, in Spring's Validator framework. The JSR 303/349 Bean Validation offers some popular annotations that can be attached to each `modelAttribute` property for the purpose of maintaining data integrity. The following are the annotations applied to `EmployeeForm`:

JSR 303/349 Validation Rules	Description
`@Size`	Sets the minimum and maximum length of the `String` property.
`@Max`	Sets the `Integer` property not greater than the specified value.
`@Min`	Sets the `Integer` property not lower than the specified value.
`@NotNull`	Sets the `Object` property not to be `NULL`.
`@Past`	Sets the `Date` property not to be futuristic.

Hibernate 5.x also has validation constraints that can be applied to form backing objects through its own set of annotations. `EmployeeForm` used `@NotEmpty` to apply a non-nullity constraint to emails. Also, it has an annotation, `@Email`, which has a built-in regular expression for correcting the email address format.

Most of the time, validation constraints are complex in nature and must be crafted through logic. Spring has an `org.springframework.validation.Validator` interface that can be implemented to apply form backing objects to custom integrity rules. The implementation also carries with it the use of utility class `org.springframework.validation.ValidationUtils`, which contains generic constraints such as `rejectIfEmpty()` or `rejectIfEmptyOrWhitespace`. All violations are monitored and registered by Spring in the `BindingResult` object. We enable `BindingResult` in our `submitForm()` to check if there are validation errors encountered, and this can be retrieved for display in some views.

The tandem of `PropertyEditor` and `Validator` will not work without the creation of the `@InitBinder` method of the controller. The general role of `@InitBinder` is to alter the normal course of parameter `modelAttribute` binding. It initializes the `WebDataBinder` object so that it can use `addValidators()` or `setValidator()` to apply integrity rules on the `modelAttribute` and `registerCustomerEditor()` methods to configure custom `PropertyEditors`.

Creating request- and session-scoped beans

Chapter 2, *Learning Dependency Injection (DI)*, discussed a recipe about configuring the lifespan of a bean inside the `ApplicationContext` container based on fetching or `getBean()`. These are the long-lived singleton and prototype beans. Now, we will discuss configuring the lifespan or scope of some beans which are bounded within MVC web transactions. This recipe will discuss creating short-lived beans that only last during request dispatch and session handling.

Getting started

Open the same `ch03` project we have created previously and perform the following steps.

How to do it...

To create and differentiate session- and request-based beans, follow these steps:

1. This recipe needs some custom models that can be injected into the container: either request-scoped or session-scoped beans. First, let us create a model `SalaryGrade` in the `org.packt.dissect.mvc.model.data` package. This model must be injected as a `@Bean` into the `ApplicationContext` through the annotation `@Component`:

   ```
   @Scope(value=WebApplicationContext.SCOPE_REQUEST,
       proxyMode=ScopedProxyMode.TARGET_CLASS)
   @Component
   public class SalaryGrade {
     private String grade;
     private Double rate;
     private Date date;

     public SalaryGrade() {
        date = new Date();
     }
     // getters and setters
   }
   ```

   This bean is registered as a `request-scoped` bean, and since this type of bean is short-lived and can only be used within a request dispatch process, we configure it as a `proxy` object. Thus, the `proxyMode=ScopedProxyMode.TARGET_CLASS` is found in `@Scope`.

2. Next, create another model object, `Education`, inside the same package. This must also be injected as a `@Bean` component:

   ```
   @Scope(value=WebApplicationContext.SCOPE_SESSION,
       proxyMode=ScopedProxyMode.TARGET_CLASS)
   @Component
   public class Education {
     private String degree;
     private String institution;
     private String major;
     private Date date;
     public Education() {
        date = new Date();
     }
     // getters and setters
   }
   ```

This bean is registered as a `session-scoped` bean and since this type of bean is short-lived and can only be used in session-based transactions, we configure it as a `web-aware` or `proxy` object. Thus, the `proxyMode=ScopedProxyMode.TARGET_CLASS` setting in `@Scope`.

3. Check if `@ComponentScan` of `SpringContextConfig` recognizes `SalaryGrade` and `Employee` beans from the package in which they are placed. If these beans are not properly injected into the container, an `org.springframework.beans.factory.NoSuchBeanDefinitionException` is encountered, creating a `HTTP 404 error status`.

4. Create a controller class named `BeansScopeController` that fetches `Employee` and `SalaryGrade` beans from the container. This controller also populates both objects and passes them through request dispatch and page redirection:

```
@Controller
public class BeanScopeController {
  @Autowired
  private SalaryGrade salaryGrade;
  @Autowired
  private Education education;
  @RequestMapping(value="/salgrade.html",
    method=RequestMethod.GET)
  public String processRequestBeans(Model model){
    salaryGrade.setGrade("SG-45");
    salaryGrade.setRate(50000.00);
    education.setDegree("BS Operations Research");
    education.setMajor("Linear Algebra");
    education.setInstitution("University of the Philippines
        Los Banos");
    model.addAttribute("salaryGrade", salaryGrade);
    model.addAttribute("education", education);
    return "req_beans";
  }
}
```

The preceding `@Controller` purposely included the `Date` property in the `@Bean` to monitor the instantiation of the objects after a request dispatch and session handling process.

5. Create another controller that will implement the page redirection once a hyperlink is clicked at the view level:

```
@Controller
public class RedirectBeanController {
  @Autowired
  private SalaryGrade salaryGrade;
  @Autowired
  private Education education;
  @RequestMapping(value="/salgrade_proceed.html",
    method=RequestMethod.GET)
  public String processRequestBeansRedirect(Model model){

    model.addAttribute("salaryGrade", salaryGrade);
    model.addAttribute("education", education);
    return "req_proceed";
  }
}
```

6. Afterwards, create the views `req_beans` and `req_proceed` from the preceding controllers. Just have a stub template to monitor the instance of the two objects with different scopes:

```
<html>
<head>
</head>
<body>
   <h1>Request Object Created:
       ${salaryGrade.instantiatedDate }</h1>
   <h1>Object Id: ${ salGradeId }</h1>
   <table>
     <tr>
        <th>Grade Level </th>
        <th>Grade Rate</th>
     </tr>
     <tr>
       <td>${ salaryGrade.grade }</td>
       <td>${ salaryGrade.rate }</td>
     </tr>
   </table>
   <br/>
   <h1>Session Object Created:
       ${ education.instantiatedDate }</h1>
   <h1>Object Id: ${ educationId }</h1>
   <table>
     <tr>
        <th>Course </th>
```

```
        <th>Major</th>
        <th>University/College</th>
      </tr>
      <tr>
        <td>${ education.degree }</td>
        <td>${ education.major }</td>
        <td>${ education.institution }</td>
      </tr>
    </table>
    <br>
  </body>
</html>
```

7. Save all files. Then `clean`, `build`, and `deploy` the updated `ch03` project.

8. Open a new browser and execute `processRequestBeans()` through the URL `https://localhost:8443/ch03/salgrade.html`:

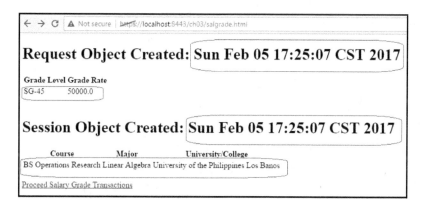

9. To check whether there are changes, click the hyperlink **Proceed Salary Grade Transactions**:

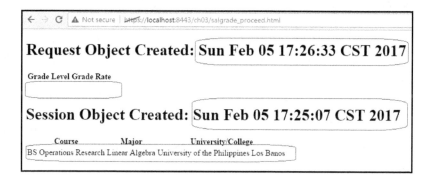

How it works...

Session-scoped and request-scoped objects are only allowed by Spring to exist in a web-aware Spring ApplicationContext container. If these objects are to be fetched in an AnnotationConfigApplicationContext or ClassPathXmlApplicationContext container, an IllegalStateException will be thrown.

In the case of a request-scoped bean, the validity of its life cycle depends on the duration of each request dispatch. This mode of transaction starts when the client accesses the handler method and ends when the views have received all transported objects from the request handler. Once the HTTP request cycle is completed, all request-scoped beans are destroyed.

Session-scoped beans live longer than request-scoped beans because all their properties are coterminous with a specific HTTP session in the application.

The SalaryGrade bean is injected as a WebApplicationContext.SCOPE_REQUEST bean and must always be proxyMode=ScopedProxyMode.TARGET_CLASS to avoid IllegalStateException. In XML-based containers, the injection can be done as:

```
<bean id="salaryGrade"
 class="org.packt.dissect.mvc.model.data.SalaryGrade"
 scope="request">
      <aop:scoped-proxy/>
</bean>
```

In the case of the Education bean, it is injected as WebApplicationContext.SCOPE_SESSION with proxyMode=ScopedProxyMode.TARGET_CLASS also. The XML equivalent of this injection is:

```
<bean id="education"
   class=" org.packt.dissect.mvc.model.data.Education"
   scope="session">
      <aop:scoped-proxy/>
</bean>
```

These two beans will be searched and injected into the BeanScopeController through the @Autowired annotation. This controller will first dispatch these objects to req_beans for rendition. Now, a hyperlink in req_beans will redirect all these beans to a separate view which is already the request dispatch transaction. From the image in *Step 7*, it is shown that the request-scoped SalaryGrade was instantiated a few seconds after clicking the hyperlink, whereas the session-scoped Education maintains its values and properties for the entire process.

Note that in order to use the session scope, you have to be using a web-aware Spring application context, such as `WebApplicationContext`. Otherwise, there's no way for the scoped proxy to reference a current session.

Lastly, do not be confused between `@SessionAttributes` and session-scoped beans because the former creates objects in the session, while the latter only uses the session as the basis of its object life cycle and nothing else.

Implementing page redirection and Flash-scoped beans

Creating lots of session-scoped beans causes some performance and security issues and is not always recommended in small-scale and simple applications. Most often than not, using request-scoped objects is still the best way to manage data among request transactions. But as shown in the previous recipe, it would be a lot easier to share data if session-scoped beans are used, especially when there are several redirections. Another solution to avoid sessions sharing data among request handlers will be illustrated by this recipe.

Getting started

Open again ch03 for some additional features of `@Controller` when it comes to page redirection. This recipe will focus on other methods of redirection than the usual HTML `<form>` submission and `<a>` hyperlink page jump.

How to do it...

To implement page redirection with Flash-scoped objects, apply these steps:

1. To start our experiment on implementing page redirection, let us create a controller that loads a login form, processes the `username` and `password`, and then redirects to another form controller through Spring's old way of page navigation, that is, through `RedirectView`:

```
@Controller
public class RedirectPageController {
  @RequestMapping(value="/login.html",
      method=RequestMethod.GET)
  public String login(){
```

```
    return "login";
}
@RequestMapping(value="/jump_page.html",
  method=RequestMethod.POST)
public RedirectView sendRedirection(RedirectAttributes
  atts, @RequestParam("username") String username,
      @RequestParam("password") String password){

    atts.addFlashAttribute("username", username);
    atts.addFlashAttribute("password", password);
    atts.addAttribute("request", "loginForm");
    return new RedirectView("/redirectviewOld.html",true);
}

@RequestMapping(value="/redirectviewOld.html",
  method=RequestMethod.GET)
public String resultPageOld(Model model ){
    return "result_page";
}
}
```

The handler method uses
`org.springframework.web.servlet.mvc.support.RedirectAttributes`
to convert `username` and `password` parameters to Flash-scoped objects. Flash-scoped objects are capable of holding their values until the next redirected view is processed. Likewise, they can also pass typical request-scoped objects to success views.

2. Create the `login` form view with typical HTML *textboxes* and *submit* buttons:

```
<%@ page language="java" contentType="text/html;
charset=ISO-8859-1" pageEncoding="ISO-8859-1"%>
<%@ taglib prefix="spring"
uri="http://www.springframework.org/tags" %>
<!DOCTYPE html PUBLIC "-//W3C//DTD HTML 4.01 Transitional//EN"
"http://www.w3.org/TR/html4/loose.dtd">
<html>
<head>
<meta http-equiv="Content-Type"
content="text/html;charset=ISO-8859-1">
<title><spring:message code="login_title" /></title>
</head>
<body>
  <form action="/ch03/jump_page.html" method="POST">
    <spring:message code="userLbl" />  
    <input type="text" name="username" /><br/>
    <spring:message code="passwordLbl" />  
```

```
<input type="text" name="password" /><br/>
<input type="submit" value="Login" />
</form>
</body>
</html>
```

3. Create the redirected page that will show on screen both the `username` and `password` Flash-scoped objects and a request-scoped one:

```
<%@ page language="java"
contentType="text/html;charset=ISO-8859-1"
pageEncoding="ISO-8859-1"%>
<!DOCTYPE html PUBLIC "-//W3C//DTD HTML 4.01 Transitional//EN"
"http://www.w3.org/TR/html4/loose.dtd">
<html>
<head>
<meta http-equiv="Content-Type" content="text/html;
charset=ISO-8859-1">
<title>Insert title here</title>
</head>
<body>
    User Name: ${ username } <br/>
    Password: ${ password } <br/>
    Requested by: ${ loginForm }
</body>
</html>
```

4. Update the `views.properties` and `messages_en_US.properties` for all the updates on the views and the view's message bundles.

5. Save all files and `deploy` the project. Open a browser and execute `https://localhost:8443/ch03/login.html`. Observe how the two Flash-scoped and a request-scoped data behave when in this form:

6. This submits to another form controller using page redirection:

7. Add the following request handlers that use a modern technique of implementing page redirection through the shorthand keyword `redirect`:

```
@RequestMapping(value="/new_jump.html",
method=RequestMethod.GET)
public ModelAndView sendRedirectionModel(ModelMap atts){
    atts.addAttribute("pageId_flash", "12345");
    return new ModelAndView(
        "redirect:/redirectviewNew.html",atts);
}
@RequestMapping(value="/redirectviewNew.html",
    method=RequestMethod.GET)
public String resultPageNew(Model model,
    @ModelAttribute("pageId_flash") String flash){
    model.addAttribute("pageId_flash", flash);
    return "new_result_page";
}
```

There are three conditions expected to be met when using the prefix `redirect`, and one is the absence of `RedirectAttributes` for Flash-scoped object generation. Also, this technique is best paired with `ModelAndView` with regard to the transporting of objects to views. And lastly, the redirected handler method must have `@ModelAttribute` to fetch all objects passed by the originator request from which the redirection started.

8. Save all files. Then `clean`, `build`, and `deploy` the project. Run `https://localhost:8443/ch03 /new_jump.html` on a browser and expect this output:

How it works...

Redirection is essential in designing the navigation paths of a system. One page can jump from another through form transactions and hyperlinks. Internally, Spring has two ways of implementing redirection. The old way is to use `RedirectView` in a handler method. Once a method returns `RedirectView`, it technically invokes `HttpServletResponse.sendRedirection()`, which performs the actual navigation process. The modern implementation is through the use of the `redirect` keyword, which requires a handler to return only the `ModelAndView` object for passing request objects and executing the views. In short, there is no longer a built-in Flash-scoped object but an improvised one. Thus, it is a requirement that the redirected handler uses `@ModelAttribute` to catch those improvised Flash-scoped objects.

There is always one problem when implementing navigation and that is the passing of objects from the originator to the redirected page. Request-scoped objects will give us NULL since they are non-existent already after the request dispatch. The redirection always happens after the request dispatch; otherwise, if it interrupts the request-response handshake, `IllegalStateException` will be thrown. Using `RedirectView`, we can use `RedirectAttributes` to generate and store Flash-scoped objects which can persist during navigations. The `RedirectAttributes` has an `addFlashAttribute()` method for Flash-scoped objects and `addAttribute()` for the usual request-scoped attributes.

On the other hand, using the modern way of implementation requires us to use the workaround of `ModelAndView` to pass all objects during redirection and `@ModelAttribute` for the counterpart handler to fetch all this data.

Session handling is not the ultimate solution in sharing objects from one page to another. Sessions can slow down runtime performance, especially if they are loaded with huge objects such as collections of JDBC objects for their entire production. Creating or simulating Flash-scoped is the recommended solution whenever there are navigations all over the software specification.

Creating database connection pooling

We have created recipes that give us tips and tricks on how to construct and manage the `ApplicationContext` containers with injected beans, implement and design HTTP request transactions through different types of `@Controllers`, manage types of scoped-beans, implement views for request dispatch and redirection, and apply the concept of Inverse of Control and Dependency Injection principles. Now, it is time to introduce the integration of the MVC application to some database vendors such as MySQL 5.7. Our main goal is to define, identify, and create the necessary database connection pooling for a Spring MVC project.

Getting started

Create a new Eclipse web project, `ch03-jdbc`, and configure its `pom.xml` to make the project `web.xml-less`. Add the previous Maven dependencies and also implement the same `SpringWebInitializer` and root context `SpringDispatcherConfig` for the initialization of our `ServletContext`. Moreover, set up the same `SpringContextConfig` for the application-related `@Bean`. Our package is still `org.packt.dissect.mvc.context`.

How to do it...

Using the MySQL server configured in Chapter 1, *Getting Started with Spring*, let us now scrutinize some popular connection pool libraries that can be used to perform JDBC transactions:

1. The first few steps will be devoted to the listing of needed Maven libraries for Spring 5.0, especially Spring JDBC dependency and MySQL 5.7 connector. With regard to its connection, add this current MySQL-Java connector to the Maven dependencies:

```
<dependency>
    <groupId>mysql</groupId>
    <artifactId>mysql-connector-java</artifactId>
    <version>5.1.40</version>
</dependency>
```

2. Next, we will be doing some comparative analysis on which database JDBC resource pooling best fits with our applications. Consider the following third-party libraries to be included in our Maven repository:

```xml
<!-- Apache DBCP Connection Pooling -->
<dependency>
  <groupId>org.apache.commons</groupId>
  <artifactId>commons-dbcp2</artifactId>
  <version>2.1.1</version>
</dependency>
<!-- C3P0 -->
<dependency>
  <groupId>com.mchange</groupId>
  <artifactId>c3p0</artifactId>
  <version>0.9.5.2</version>
</dependency>
<!-- Tomcat JDBC Connection Pooling -->
<dependency>
  <groupId>org.apache.tomcat</groupId>
  <artifactId>tomcat-jdbc</artifactId>
  <version>9.0.0.M15</version>
</dependency>
<!-- Hikari Connection Pooling -->
<dependency>
  <groupId>com.zaxxer</groupId>
  <artifactId>HikariCP</artifactId>
  <version>2.5.1</version>
</dependency>
```

3. At this point, let us use the Spring Test Framework to validate the capability of each JDBC `resource` pooling library by creating a test SQL script for MySQL's world schema. To enable Spring Test, add the following Maven dependencies in the test scope:

```xml
<dependency>
  <groupId>org.springframework</groupId>
  <artifactId>spring-test</artifactId>
  <version>${spring.version}</version>
  <scope>test</scope>
</dependency>
<dependency>
  <groupId>junit</groupId>
  <artifactId>junit</artifactId>
  <version>4.12</version>
  <scope>test</scope>
  <exclusions>
    <exclusion>
```

```
            <groupId>org.hamcrest</groupId>
            <artifactId>hamcrest-core</artifactId>
          </exclusion>
        </exclusions>
      </dependency>
      <dependency>
        <groupId>org.hamcrest</groupId>
        <artifactId>hamcrest-library</artifactId>
        <version>1.3</version>
        <scope>test</scope>
      </dependency>
```

4. Create a property file, `src\main\resources\config\jdbc.properties`, containing the necessary details for database connectivity:

```
jdbc.driverClassName=com.mysql.jdbc.Driver
jdbc.url=jdbc:mysql://localhost:3306/world?autoReconnect=true
&useSSL=true&serverSslCert=classpath:config/spring5packt.crt
jdbc.username=root
jdbc.password=spring5mysql
```

 To avoid a warning such as **WARNING: Establishing SSL connection without server's identity verification is not recommended**, we include the `spring5packt.crt` to the URL connection detail of the MySQL instance.

5. In order for Spring components to read all the properties in `jdbc.properties`, inject into the web context root container the `org.springframework.context.support.PropertySourcesPlaceholderC onfigurer` class and make reference to `jdbc.properties` through `@PropertySource`:

```
@EnableWebMvc
@ComponentScan(basePackages="org.packt.dissect.mvc")
@PropertySource("classpath:config/jdbc.properties")
@Configuration
public class SpringDispatcherConfig extends
    WebMvcConfigurerAdapter{

    // refer to sources
    @Bean
    public static PropertySourcesPlaceholderConfigurer
      propertyConfig() {
      return new PropertySourcesPlaceholderConfigurer();
    }
}
```

6. Include also all the JavaScript, CSS, images, and all other *static resources* inside SpringDispatcherConfig by overriding its method addResourceHandlers(). Also include some web-related configurations like caching:

```
import
org.springframework.web.servlet.config.annotation.ResourceHandl
erRegistry;
// refer to sources
@Override
    public void addResourceHandlers(ResourceHandlerRegistry
registry) {
        registry
            .addResourceHandler("/css/**")
            .addResourceLocations("/js/**")
            .setCachePeriod(31556926);
    }
```

7. Now, create a new JavaConfig context named SpringDbConfig, which contains all @Bean related to database connectivity. The first injection is the creation of the java.sql.DataSource which implements the Connection object per user access. The DataSource needs to retrieve the JDBC details in @PropertySource("classpath:config/jdbc.properties") through the Enviornment class, which throws PropertyVetoException when used:

```
@Configuration
@EnableWebMvc
@ComponentScan(basePackages =
        "org.packt.dissect.mvc.model.data")
public class SpringDbConfig {

    @Autowired
    private Environment environment;

    @Bean
    public DataSource dataSource() throws
        PropertyVetoException { }
```

8. Implement the first DataSource using Spring's built-in DataSource implementation, the org.springframework.jdbc.datasource.DriverManagerDataSource:

```
@Configuration
@EnableWebMvc
@ComponentScan(basePackages =
```

```
"org.packt.dissect.mvc.model.data")
public class SpringDbConfig {

    @Autowired
    private Environment environment;

    @Bean
    public DataSource dataSource() throws
        PropertyVetoException {
      DriverManagerDataSource dataSource =
        new DriverManagerDataSource();
      dataSource.setDriverClassName(environment
.getProperty("jdbc.driverClassName"));
        dataSource.setUrl(environment.getProperty("jdbc.url"));
        dataSource.setUsername(environment
.getProperty("jdbc.username"));
        dataSource.setPassword(environment
.getProperty("jdbc.password"));
        return dataSource;
    }
```

9. To measure the performance of each JDBC connection pooling, let's use Metrics API `DropWizard` to report the statistics of resource pooling running time, given 1,000 simulated users accessing the database. Add the following Maven dependencies in order to use this library.

```
<dependency>
    <groupId>com.codahale.metrics</groupId>
    <artifactId>metrics-core</artifactId>
    <version>3.0.2</version>
</dependency>
```

10. Create a test class `TestDbPool` in `src\test\java`, with `ConsoleReporter`, `MetricRegsitry`, and `Timer` for the performance testing:

```
@RunWith(SpringJUnit4ClassRunner.class)
@WebAppConfiguration
@ContextConfiguration(classes = {SpringDbConfig.class,
        SpringDispatcherConfig.class})
public class TestDbPool {
    @Autowired
    private DataSource dataSource;
    private static final int MAX_ITERATIONS = 1000;
    private ConsoleReporter logReporter;
    private Timer timer;
    @Before
    public void init() {
```

```
MetricRegistry metricRegistry = new MetricRegistry();
this.logReporter = ConsoleReporter
        .forRegistry(metricRegistry)
        .build();
logReporter.start(1, TimeUnit.MINUTES);
timer = metricRegistry.timer("connection");
}
@Test
public void testOpenCloseConnections() throws
    SQLException {

    for (int i = 0; i < MAX_ITERATIONS; i++) {
        Context context = timer.time();
        Connection conn = dataSource.getConnection();
        Statement stmt = conn.createStatement();
        stmt.executeQuery("select * from city");
        conn.close();
        context.stop();
    }
    logReporter.report();
}
}
```

The `@ContextConfiguration(classes = {SpringDbConfig.class, SpringDispatcherConfig.class})` indicates that all the `@Bean` will be fetched during testing from the `SpringDbConfig` and `SpringDispatcherConfig` containers.

11. Execute `TestDbPool` using the Eclipse STS JUnit plugin:

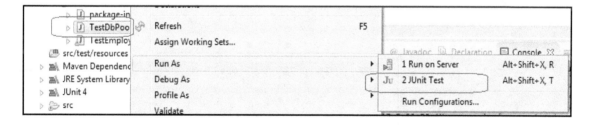

12. Check the statistics shown on the console view:

```
------ Timers -----------------connection
count = 1000
mean rate = 140.19 calls/second
1-minute rate = 128.20 calls/second
5-minute rate = 128.20 calls/second
15-minute rate = 128.20 calls/second
min = 5.36 milliseconds
max = 839.60 milliseconds
mean = 7.10 milliseconds
stddev = 26.44 milliseconds
median = 5.91 milliseconds
75% <= 6.24 milliseconds
95% <= 7.24 milliseconds
98% <= 8.81 milliseconds
99% <= 17.81 milliseconds
99.9% <= 838.81 milliseconds
```

13. Apply the test to the following third-party database connection pooling implementations and examine the results:

```
/*
    BasicDataSource dataSource = new BasicDataSource();
    dataSource.setDriverClassName(environment
.getProperty("jdbc.driverClassName"));
    dataSource.setUrl(environment
.getProperty("jdbc.url"));
    dataSource.setUsername(environment
.getProperty("jdbc.username"));
    dataSource.setPassword(environment
.getProperty("jdbc.password"));
    dataSource.setMaxTotal(100);
    */
/*
    ComboPooledDataSource dataSource =
new ComboPooledDataSource();
    dataSource.setDriverClass(environment
.getProperty("jdbc.driverClassName"));
    dataSource.setJdbcUrl(environment
.getProperty("jdbc.url"));
    dataSource.setUser(environment
.getProperty("jdbc.username"));
    dataSource.setPassword(environment
.getProperty("jdbc.password"));
    dataSource.setMaxPoolSize(100);
        */
/*
```

```
     org.apache.tomcat.jdbc.pool.DataSource dataSource =
new org.apache.tomcat.jdbc.pool.DataSource();
     PoolProperties props = new PoolProperties();
     props.setUrl(environment.getProperty("jdbc.url"));
     props.setDriverClassName(environment
.getProperty("jdbc.driverClassName"));
     props.setUsername(environment
.getProperty("jdbc.username"));
     props.setPassword(environment
.getProperty("jdbc.password"));
     props.setMaxActive(100);
     dataSource.setPoolProperties(props);
      */
     HikariDataSource dataSource = new HikariDataSource();
     dataSource.setMaximumPoolSize(100);
     dataSource.setDriverClassName(environment
.getProperty("jdbc.driverClassName"));
     dataSource.setJdbcUrl(environment
.getProperty("jdbc.url"));
     dataSource.setUsername(environment
.getProperty("jdbc.username"));
     dataSource.setPassword(environment
.getProperty("jdbc.password"));
     dataSource.setMaximumPoolSize(100);
```

 Uncomment only one data connection pooling before running the test methods in step 9.

How it works...

Before a Spring MVC application implements Java database transactions, a DataSource must be injected first into the ApplicationContext. This object creates a java.sql.Connection object per user who wants to access a database instance, given the username and password of the server, JDBC URL of the database schema, and the driver class name of the JDBC connector for some database transactions.

The immediate way to implement `DataSource` is to instantiate the `DriverManagerDataSource` of the Spring JDBC framework. The only problem with this class is the absence of connection pooling capabilities which slows down the performance of the applications once there is more than one user involved in accessing the database schema. It may even cause an `OutofMemoryError` which causes the Tomcat server to crash:

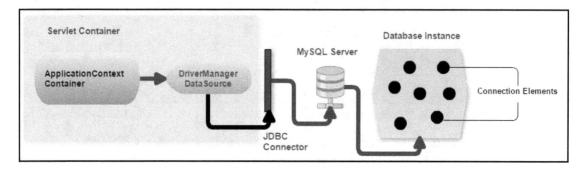

This degradation is due to the fact that `DriverManagerDataSource` will create another `Connection` object when another user is added. For the enterprise application, it is recommended to use third-party JDBC connection pooling that provides a cached logical connection pool rather than instantiating additional `Connection` objects for the additional user connectivity:

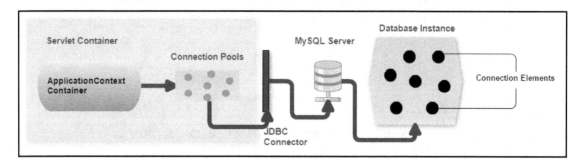

Based on our unit testing using the Metrics API, `HikariCP` provides us the best case performance, given 1,000 users. After executing the test cases, we will roughly arrive at the following statistics:

Connection Pooling Implementation	Mean call rate (call/second)	Max time elapsed per call (millisec)	Min time elapsed per call (millisec)	Mean time elapsed per call (millisec)
`DriverManagerDataSource` (Spring)	140.19	839.60	5.36	7.10
`BasicDataSource` (DBCP2)	194.82	739.04	4.01	5.06
`ComboPooledDataSource` (C3P0)	208.28	547.79	3.92	4.78
Tomcat's `DataSource`	111.89	1847.79	3.92	8.92
`HikariDataSource` (HikariCP)	215.08	437.33	3.89	4.63

To wrap up this recipe, it is always a protocol not to hardcode the database details during `DataSource` injection. Use the `jdbc.properties` file to store all the credentials in order to avoid messing up once changes happens. Just declare `PropertySourcesPlaceholderConfigurer` into the container and apply `@PropertySource` to the context's `@Configuration` definition to make reference to the `jdbc.properties`. Aside from establishing reference, the `@PropertySource` will classify all details as Spring environment variables, thus `org.springframework.core.env.Environment` can now be used to fetch the key values of `jdbc.properties`. Before deploying to the production server, it is recommended to configure JNDI or transaction listeners to register JDBC properties.

Implementing the DAO layer using the Spring JDBC Framework

After identifying the appropriate `DataSource` implementation, we are now ready to establish the database transactions in our Spring MVC application.

Getting Started

Open again the ch03-jdbc project and verify if MySQL 5.7 is updated and working fine. Also, check again if the DataSource implementation is appropriate for your application.

How to do it...

It is always the best practice to design the database and table schemas using an ERD model. After finalizing our schema designs, follow these steps to build our DAO layer:

1. Let us open a MySQL workbench or a command line terminal, log in using the username root and password spring5mysql, and create the following schema definition of the hrs database:

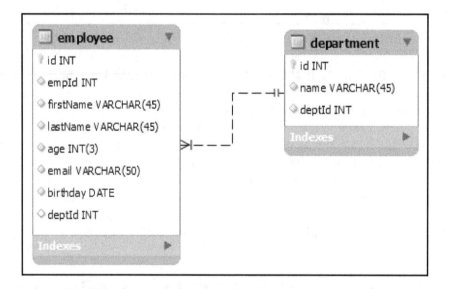

2. Since we will be dealing with database models, create a package, org.packt.dissect.mvc.model.data, that will contain data models representing the schema of the preceding tables. Given the two tables, create the Employee and Department data models found here:

```
public class Department {

    private Integer id;
    private Integer deptId;
    private String name;
```

```
// getters and setters
}

public class Employee {

    private Integer id;
    private Integer empId;
    private String firstName;
    private String lastName;
    private Integer age;
    private String email;
    private Date birthday;
    private Integer deptId;

// getters and setters
}
```

 Data models must be different from the form backing objects or form models created in the previous recipe. Although it seems the two layers are similar because both are POJOs, we do not allow misrepresentation of data and data integrity errors during validation and type checking.

3. We need to update the URL details of our `jdbc.properties` since we will be accessing our newly created schema, `hrs`:

```
jdbc.driverClassName=com.mysql.jdbc.Driver
jdbc.url=jdbc:mysql://localhost:3306/hrs?autoReconnect=true
&useSSL=true&serverSslCert=classpath:config/spring5packt.crt
jdbc.username=root
jdbc.password=spring5mysql
```

4. Now, inject `org.springframework.jdbc.core.simple.SimpleJdbcInsert` in the `SpringDbConfig` context. This Spring JDBC API manages the JDBC transactions:

```
@Bean
public SimpleJdbcInsert jdbcInsert()
  throws PropertyVetoException {
    return new SimpleJdbcInsert(dataSource());
}
```

5. This implementation for the data access template and callback fits with Spring 5.0 because of its multithreading characteristics, while using the low-level `JdbcTemplate`. `SimpleJdbcInsert` is easier to configure than `JdbcTemplate` and can easily work with database configurations without so many unnecessary metadata. Now, create the **Data Access Object (DAO)** layer, which uses the two data models in exposing the database transactions. This layer is composed of interfaces (such as `DepartmentDao`), which are used to fetch their implementations (such as `DepartmentDaoImpl`) once needed by the `@Controller` in saving, retrieving, updating, and deleting records. The following is the `Department` interface and its implementation class `DepartmentDaoImpl`:

```
package org.packt.dissect.mvc.dao;

public interface DepartmentDao {
  public List<Department> getDepartments();
  public Department getDepartmentData(Integer id);
  public void addDepartmentBySJI(Department dept);
  public void addDepartmentByJT(Department dept);
  public void updateDepartment(Department dept);
  public void delDepartment(Integer deptId);
}

package org.packt.dissect.mvc.dao.impl;

@Repository
public class DepartmentDaoImpl implements DepartmentDao{
  @Autowired
  private SimpleJdbcInsert jdbcInsert;

  @Override
  public List<Department> getDepartments() {
    String sql = "SELECT * FROM department";
    List<Department> depts =
       jdbcInsert.getJdbcTemplate().query(sql,
       new RowMapper<Department>() {

      @Override
      public Department mapRow(ResultSet rs,
        int rowNum) throws SQLException {

        Department dept = new Department();
        dept.setId(rs.getInt("id"));
        dept.setDeptId(rs.getInt("deptId"));
        dept.setName(rs.getString("name"));
        return dept;
```

```
      }
    });
    return depts;
  }
  // refer to sources·
}
```

All DAO implementation classes must have a `@Repository` annotation which tells Spring that these classes are valid `@Bean` and classified persistence layer classes, triggering some special exceptions and code translators at runtime.

The DAO method `addDepartmentBySJI()` uses `SimpleJdbcInsert` to add records to the table `department`, while `addDepartmentByJT()` does the same but with `JdbcInsert`.

6. Create a `TestDepartmentDao` class in `src\test\java` to perform initial testing without injecting them yet to the `@Controller` for request-response transactions:

```
@RunWith(SpringJUnit4ClassRunner.class)
@WebAppConfiguration
@ContextConfiguration(classes = { SpringDbConfig.class,
    SpringDispatcherConfig.class })
public class TestDepartmentDao {

  @Autowired
  private DepartmentDao departmentDaoImpl;
  @Test
  public void testDetachedDepartment(){
    Department rec = new Department();
    rec.setDeptId(9999);
    rec.setName("Security Department");
    departmentDaoImpl.addDepartmentBySJI(rec);
  }
  @Test
  public void testPopulateDepartment(){
    Department rec1 = new Department();
    rec1.setDeptId(1);
    rec1.setName("Engineering Department");
    Department rec2 = new Department();
    rec2.setDeptId(2);
    rec2.setName("Human Resources Department");
    // refer to sources
    departmentDaoImpl.addDepartmentByJT(rec1);
    departmentDaoImpl.addDepartmentByJT(rec2);

    // refer to sources
```

```
      }
   // refer to sources
   }
```

7. Repeat the preceding processes for `EmployeeDao`.

8. Save all files and be ready to connect our DAO layer to the `@Controller`.

How it works...

The DAO layer serves as the data persistency layer of the MVC application. All objects in this layer must have `@Repository` applied since these objects are injected into the container with a special translator and exception, such as `DataAccessException`:

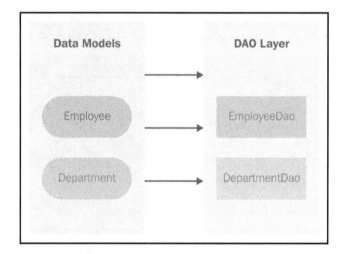

After designing and constructing the database and tables schemas, Spring must ready its data model objects, which are normally POJO, to hold property values during CRUD transactions. To utilize these models, Spring has a built-in Spring JDBC module which is the ultimate provider of APIs for data access templates actions and `callback` handlers.

This recipe introduces the multithreaded `SimpleJdbcInsert` to simplify the configuration details needed in saving objects to the database. The rule is just to provide the table name and a map containing the column names and the column values, to be inserted without using too many placeholders (?) for mapping. The only problems is that you can only set its table name once before every `execute()`, otherwise, this exception will be thrown:

```
☰ Failure Trace
ᴶ⁰ org.springframework.dao.InvalidDataAccessApiUsageException: Configuration can't be altered once the class has been compiled or used
☰ at org.springframework.jdbc.core.simple.AbstractJdbcInsert.checkIfConfigurationModificationIsAllowed(AbstractJdbcInsert.java:323)
☰ at org.springframework.jdbc.core.simple.AbstractJdbcInsert.setTableName(AbstractJdbcInsert.java:126)
☰ at org.springframework.jdbc.core.simple.SimpleJdbcInsert.withTableName(SimpleJdbcInsert.java:74)
☰ at org.packt.dissect.mvc.dao.impl.DepartmentDaoImpl.addDepartmentBySJI(DepartmentDaoImpl.java:59)
```

In the background, this API still uses the low-level `JdbcTemplate` for its SQL executions; thus, the performance of `SimpleJdbcInsert` must be almost the same as `JdbcTemplate` when it comes to single-table record transactions. `SimpleJdbcInsert` can easily be fetched from the container while `JdbcTemplate` can only be derived from `SimpleJdbcInsert` through its factory method, or as an injected `@Bean` to be `@Autowired` by the DAO classes.

`JdbcTemplate` and `SimpleJdbcInsert` will not work without the implementation of the `java.sql.DataSource`. There are five implementations featured in this recipe which are popularly used nowadays, but each has its own disadvantages and advantages. The `DriverManagerDataSource` has no database connection pooling, so every user access corresponds to one instance of the `Connection` object. Connection pooling is very important in an enterprise application because it gives a threshold whenever there is connection traffic. It provides a set of logical connection objects that can be used to virtualize the user connection instead of creating another set and separate instances of `Connection` objects. Deciding on the appropriate `DataSource` implementation can help the MVC application minimize the overhead caused by the DAO layer at runtime.

To successfully implement the JDBC connection to our MySQL 5.7 server, the MySQL connector class named `com.mysql.jdbc.Driver` needs to be part of the Maven dependencies of the project. This class will communicate with the `DataSource` and verifies the `username`, `password`, and URL details of the database instance in order to successfully establish a connection.

After implementing all the required DAO classes, inject them into `SpringDbConfig` through the `@Repository` annotation to be `@Autowired` by services.

Creating a service layer in an MVC application

If the DAO layer manages the persistence of data, given the data models and Spring JDBC's `JdbcTemplate` and `SimpleJdbcInsert`, the service layer, on the other hand, exposes all DAO transactions through its own set of interfaces and implementations. This recipe will close the whole chapter regarding how to assemble a Spring MVC application.

Getting started

This last recipe requires us to use `ch03-jdbc` to implement a service layer which contains native services for `EmployeeDao` and `DepartmentDao` transactions.

How to do it...

For `@Controllers` to execute some DAO transactions and business-related logic, add the service layer by following these steps:

1. After ensuring that the DAO layer is ready for use, add two more packages to contain our service interfaces and implementation. All interfaces must be in `org.packt.dissect.mvc.service` and their implementation must be saved inside `org.packt.dissect.mvc.service.impl`.

2. Create the following interfaces that will be used to fetch the service implementations at the controller layer. These will just expose `read` and `add` record transactions:

```
public interface DepartmentService {
  public List<Department> readDepartments();
  public void addDepartment(Department dept);
}

public interface EmployeeService {
  public List<Employee> readEmployees();
  public void addEmployeee(Employee emp);
}
```

3. Then, create the service implementations of the interfaces in *Step 2*. The other purpose of these services is to add more logic on the records being retrieved, or manipulate some details before adding, viewing, and deleting them as shown here:

```
@Service
public class DepartmentServiceImpl implements
    DepartmentService {
  @Autowired
  private DepartmentDao departmentDaoImpl;

  @Override
  public List<Department> readDepartments() {
      return departmentDaoImpl.getDepartments();
  }

  @Override
  public void addDepartment(DepartmentForm dept) {

    Department deptData = new Department();
    deptData.setDeptId(dept.getDeptId());
    deptData.setName(dept.getName());
    departmentDaoImpl.addDepartmentBySJI(deptData);
  }
}

@Service
public class EmployeeServiceImpl implements
    EmployeeService {
  @Autowired
  private EmployeeDao employeeDaoImpl;

  @Override
  public List<Employee> readEmployees() {
      return employeeDaoImpl.getEmployees();
  }

  @Override
  public void addEmployeee(EmployeeForm empForm) {
    Employee emp = new Employee();
    emp.setDeptId(empForm.getEmpId());
    emp.setFirstName(empForm.getFirstName());
    emp.setLastName(empForm.getLastName());
    emp.setAge(empForm.getAge());
    emp.setBirthday(empForm.getBirthday());
    emp.setEmail(empForm.getEmail());
    emp.setDeptId(empForm.getDeptId());
```

```
        employeeDaoImpl.addEmployeeBySJI(emp);
    }
}
```

All service implementations must be injected into the container through the annotation @Service. Although this annotation classifies a class to be a service, it has no special background event yet when compared to @Repository.

 The service layer manages the form models (such as EmployeeForm) because there are model attributes containing all the request data after form submission. DAO layer manages, on the other hand, the data models (such as Employee) created by the service layer.

4. Afterwards, create a controller called DepartmentController that will complete the whole MVC application with database connection in the background. This controller will invoke a form asking for department information needed to be saved into the hrs database schema, and from there will generate a view for all the records:

```
@Controller
public class DepartmentController {
  @Autowired
  private DepartmentService departmentServiceImpl;
   @RequestMapping("/deptform.html")
  public String initForm(Model model){

    DepartmentForm departmentForm = new DepartmentForm();
    model.addAttribute("departmentForm", departmentForm);
     return "dept_form";
  }
  @RequestMapping(value="/deptform.html",
    method=RequestMethod.POST)
  public String submitForm(Model model,
    @ModelAttribute("departmentForm")
        DepartmentForm departmentForm){

    departmentServiceImpl.addDepartment(departmentForm);
    model.addAttribute("departments",
     departmentServiceImpl.readDepartments());
    return "dept_result";
  }
}
```

5. Create the views indicated by the `@Controller` and update the `views.properties` and `message_en_US.properties`.

6. Save all files. Then `clean`, `install`, and `deploy` the project.

How it works...

To complete our dissection, the service layer must be at the scene to provide further algorithms, manipulations, and operations on the data sent to and from the DAO and the client. It is recommended that the DAO and service layer must work together to build a loosely-coupled architecture:

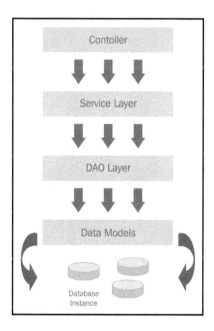

Services usually handle form models to retrieve the necessary request data needed to undergo database processing through the help of DAO classes, structured or unstructured data conversion and file processing, FTP data transmission, and rendition for business intelligence. All sorts of algorithms that help link DAO classes to the controllers are all placed inside the service layer. Avoid implementing CRUD transactions in any service class because these database-linked processes are placed in the DAO layer.

4

Securing Spring MVC
Applications

Securing the application is one of the most delicate procedures because of so many vulnerabilities that need to be considered, such as poor user authentication, unreliable authorization processes, lack of logging mechanisms, and fail-top-open error handling. At the application level, Spring offers a configurable and customizable security framework that can easily enable login authentication and authorization procedures for protection against session fixation, **cross-site scripting** (**XSS**) attacks, clickjacking, denial of service attacks, session fixation attacks, and cross-site request forgery (CSRF).

Spring Security 4.2.2 also provides an easy way to build **Access Control List** (**ACL**) comprising of users, roles, and permissions that will be the basis of user authorization. Users and roles have options to be created in-memory or through the database storage. Their restrictions, which are based on roles, are applicable to request handlers, view pages, and service methods, which shows how flexible and configurable its architecture is.

On the other hand, Spring Security has several ways to manage the user details for screening and validation purposes. It also has wide support for password encryption with or without salt or hash functions.

This chapter will provide a series of recipes related to how to install, configure, and extend Spring Security 4.2.2 for Spring 5.0 MVC applications.

In this chapter, we will cover the following topics:

- Configuring Spring Security 4.2.2
- Mapping sessions to channels and ports
- Customizing the authentication process
- Implementing authentication filters, login success, and failure handlers

- Creating user details
- Generating encrypted passwords
- Applying Security to MVC methods
- Creating roles and permissions from the database
- Managing and storing sessions
- Solving Cross-Site Request Forgery (CSRF) and session fixation attacks
- Solving Cross-Site Scripting (XSS) and clickjacking attacks
- Creating interceptors for login data validation

Configuring Spring Security 4.2.2

This chapter will start with a recipe that will integrate **Spring Security 4.2.2** with Spring-based applications. This recipe will enumerate all the steps needed to set up and configure Spring Security 4.2.2 with Spring 5.0 MVC applications.

Getting started

Create an STS Eclipse Maven project, `ch04`, and make it a `web.xml-less` one. Update the `pom.xml` by including the previous *Maven WAR files, Maven Compiler*, and *Tomcat 7 Maven Deployment* plugins. Also, include the *Spring 5.0, Servlet 3.1, JSP 2.3, JUnit 4.x*, and other dependencies needed to compile and run the application. The core package for this chapter is `org.packt.secured.mvc`.

How to do it...

This recipe will provide proof that Spring 5 can work with the current Spring Security 4.2.2 without encountering any conflicts:

1. To integrate the Spring Security 4.2.2 framework, include the following Maven dependencies into the Maven repository:

```
<dependency>
  <groupId>org.springframework.security</groupId>
  <artifactId>spring-security-web</artifactId>
  <version>4.2.2.BUILD-SNAPSHOT</version>
</dependency>
<dependency>
  <groupId>org.springframework.security</groupId>
```

```
    <artifactId>spring-security-config</artifactId>
    <version>4.2.2.BUILD-SNAPSHOT</version>
</dependency>
<dependency>
    <groupId>org.springframework.security</groupId>
    <artifactId>spring-security-taglibs</artifactId>
    <version>4.2.2.BUILD-SNAPSHOT</version>
</dependency>
```

2. Reuse the `SpringWebInitializer`, `SpringDispatcherConfig`,
   `SpringDbConfig`, and `SpringContextConfig`. Set their `@ComponentScan` base
   packages to `org.packt.secured.mvc`. The following is the final directory
   structure with these three main `@Configuration` files:

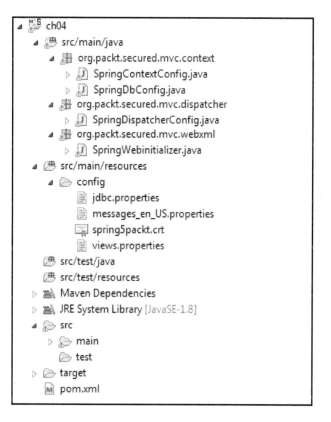

Be sure to have an empty `SpringContextConfig` context definition.

3. Now, create another context definition which will implement the security model consisting of the Spring Security 4.2.2 APIs. Let us start with the creation of `AppSecurityConfig` inside `org.packt.secured.mvc.core`, which lists all the basic security rules for our MVC application:

```
@Configuration
@EnableWebSecurity
public class AppSecurityConfig extends
    WebSecurityConfigurerAdapter {
    @Override
    protected void configure(AuthenticationManagerBuilder auth)
throws Exception {
        auth.inMemoryAuthentication()
            .withUser("sjctrags").password("sjctrags")
            .roles("USER");
    }
    @Override
    protected void configure(HttpSecurity http) throws Exception
{
        http
            .authorizeRequests()
            .antMatchers("/login*").permitAll()
            .anyRequest().authenticated()
            .and()
            .formLogin()
            .loginPage("/login.html")
            .defaultSuccessUrl("/deptform.html")
            .failureUrl("/login.html?error=true")
            .and().logout().logoutUrl("/logout.html")
            .logoutSuccessUrl("/after_logout.html");
          http.csrf().disable();
    }
    @Override
    public void configure(WebSecurity web) throws Exception
    {
      web
        .ignoring()
            .antMatchers("/resources/**")
            .antMatchers("/css/**")
            .antMatchers("/js/**")
            .antMatchers("/image/**");
    }
}
```

The difference between the Spring MVC context definition and the Spring Security one is the presence of `@EnableWebSecurity` in the latter. This annotation enables security in the application through the creation of a servlet named `springSecurityFilterChain`, which is responsible for all the core and extra security features. To complete the `@Configuration`, the class must extend `org.springframework.security.config.annotation.web.configuration.WebSecurityConfigurerAdapter` to override the needed security-related methods.

Do not use `@EnableWebMVCSecurity` anymore since it has been considered as deprecated by Spring Security 4.x.

4. To apply `AppSecurityConfig`, import this context to our application context `SpringContextConfig` through the `@Import` annotation:

```
@Import(value = { AppSecurityConfig.class })
@Configuration
@EnableWebMvc
@ComponentScan(basePackages = "org.packt.secured.mvc")
public class SpringContextConfig {   }
```

This annotation is the same with the `<import>` tag used when augmenting two or more XML-based definitions.

5. Then, create `SpringSecurityInitializer` inside the package `org.packt.secured.mvc.core` that will register the `delegatingFilterproxy` filter to be used by the `springSecurityFilterChain` previously created. So far, this strategy is the one working when compared to the direct `Filter.Registration` of the `ServletContext`:

```
public class SpringSecurityInitializer extends
    AbstractSecurityWebApplicationInitializer {  }
```

Leave this class empty.

6. At this point, it is time to implement our MVC application starting with the model objects. Reuse `Department` and `Employee` from the `ch03-jdbc` project. Drop these files inside `org.packt.secured.mvc.model.data`.

7. Reuse also our form backing objects from `ch03-jdbc`, namely `DepartmentForm` and `EmployeeForm`. Place them inside the package `org.packt.secured.mvc.model.data.form`.

8. For the DAO layer, let us consider implementing a new `DepartmentDao`, which contains the following method signatures:

```
public interface DepartmentDao {
    public List<Department> getDepartments();
    public Department getDepartmentData(Integer id);
    public void addDepartmentBySJI(Department dept);
    public void addDepartmentByJT(Department dept);
    public void updateDepartment(Department dept);
    public void delDepartment(Integer deptId);
}
```

9. Place this in the `org.packt.secured.mvc.dao` package.

10. Implement `DepartmentDaoImpl` by using `SimpleJdbcInsert` and `JdbcTemplate` from `ch03-jdbc`, and place them in the `org.packt.secured.mvc.dao.impl` package. Be cautious with the use of `SimpleJdbcInsert`'s `addDepartmentBySJI()`, which gives the `HTTP status 500` during successive calls to the `jdbcInsert.withTableName("department")` line.

11. Implement a new `DepartmentController` which contains create, delete, update record, and query database transactions after a successful login:

```
@Controller
public class DepartmentController {
  @Autowired
  private DepartmentService departmentServiceImpl;
  @RequestMapping("/deptform.html")
  public String initForm(Model model) {

    DepartmentForm departmentForm = new DepartmentForm();
    model.addAttribute("departmentForm", departmentForm);
    return "dept_form";
  }
  @RequestMapping(value={"/deptform.html"},
          method=RequestMethod.POST)
  public String submitForm(Model model,
    @ModelAttribute("departmentForm") DepartmentForm
                departmentForm) {
```

```
            departmentServiceImpl.addDepartment(departmentForm);
            model.addAttribute("departments",
              departmentServiceImpl.readDepartments());
            return "dept_result";
        }
        @RequestMapping("/deldept.html/{deptId}")
        public String deleteRecord(Model model,
            @PathVariable("deptId") Integer deptId){
          departmentServiceImpl.removeDepartment(deptId);
          model.addAttribute("departments",
            departmentServiceImpl.readDepartments());
          return "dept_result";
        }
        @RequestMapping("/updatedept.html/{id}")
        public String updateRecord(Model model,
          @PathVariable("id") Integer id){

          Department dept = departmentServiceImpl.getDeptId(id);
          DepartmentForm departmentForm = new DepartmentForm();
          departmentForm.setDeptId(dept.getDeptId());
          departmentForm.setName(dept.getName());
          model.addAttribute("departmentForm", departmentForm);
          return "dept_form";
        }
    @RequestMapping(value=/updatedept.html/{id}",
        method=RequestMethod.POST)
    public String updateRecordSubmit(Model model,
      @ModelAttribute("departmentForm") DepartmentForm
      departmentForm, @PathVariable("id") Integer id ){

        departmentServiceImpl.updateDepartment(
          departmentForm, id);
        model.addAttribute("departments",
        departmentServiceImpl.readDepartments());
        return "dept_result";
    }

        }
```

After a successful authentication, the `AppSecurityConfig` will redirect to
`/deptform.html` as the default success page.

12. Create a `LoginController` that will provide all the handler methods of the `AppSecurityConfig`:

```
@Controller
public class LoginController {

@RequestMapping(value="/login.html",
  method=RequestMethod.GET)
public String login(@RequestParam(name="error",
  required=false) String error, Model model) {

    try {
      if (error.equalsIgnoreCase("true")) {
        String errorMsg = "Login Error";
        model.addAttribute("errorMsg", errorMsg);
      }else{
        model.addAttribute("errorMsg", error);
      }
    } catch (NullPointerException e) {
      return "login_form";
    }
    return "login_form";
  }

@RequestMapping("/logout.html")
public String logout() {
  return "logout_form";
}
@RequestMapping("/after_logout.html")
public String afterLogout() {
  return "after_logout_form";
}

@RequestMapping("logerr.html")
public String logerr() {
  return "logerr_form";
}
}
}
```

The custom login page /login.html must be configured and recognized by the org.springframework.security.config.annotation.web.builders.HttpSecurity API. Likewise, the /logout.html must be the AppSecurityConfig's custom logout entry which will redirect to /after_logout.html after a successful logout.

13. Create the views for the `/logout.html`, `/after_logout.html` and `/login.html`. The login transaction must be using the POST HTTP method:

```
<%@ page language="java" contentType="text/html;
charset=ISO-8859-1" pageEncoding="ISO-8859-1"%>
<%@ taglib prefix="c" uri="http://java.sun.com/jsp/jstl/core"%>
<%@ taglib prefix="spring"
uri="http://www.springframework.org/tags" %>
<%@ taglib prefix="form"
uri="http://www.springframework.org/tags/form"%>
<!DOCTYPE html>
<html>
<head>
<meta http-equiv="Content-Type" content="text/html;
charset=ISO-8859-1">
<title><spring:message code="login_title" /></title>
</head>
<body>
  <c:if test="${ not empty errorMsg }">
      <em><c:out value='${ errorMsg }'/></em><br/>
  </c:if>
  <form action="<c:url value='/login.html' />"
    method="POST">
      <spring:message code="user"   />
<input type="text" name="username" /><br/>
      <spring:message code="password"   />
<input type="text" name="password" /><br/>
      <input type="submit" value="Login" />
  </form>
</body>
</html>
```

14. Next, create the physical views for the `DepartmentController`'s `/deptform.html` form and the `/dept_result.html` result view pages. The form view must be implemented this way:

```
<%@ page language="java" contentType="text/html;
charset=ISO-8859-1" pageEncoding="ISO-8859-1"%>
<%@ taglib prefix="c" uri="http://java.sun.com/jsp/jstl/core"%>
<%@ taglib prefix="spring"
uri="http://www.springframework.org/tags" %>
<%@ taglib prefix="form"
uri="http://www.springframework.org/tags/form"%>
<!DOCTYPE html>
<html>
<head>
<meta http-equiv="Content-Type" content="text/html;
```

```
        charset=ISO-8859-1">
        <title><spring:message code="dept_title"  /></title>
        </head>
        <body>
          <c:if test="${ not empty username }">
              Username is <em><c:out value='${ username}'/>
              </em><br/>
              Password is <em><c:out value='${ password }'/>
              </em><br/>
              Role(s) is/are: <em><c:out value='userRole'/>
              </em><br/>
          </c:if>
          <form:form modelAttribute="departmentForm"
            method="POST">
            <spring:message code="dept_id"  />
            <form:input path="deptId"  /><br/>
            <spring:message code="dept_name"  />
            <form:input path="name"  /><br/>
            <input type="submit" value="Add Department" />
          </form:form>
        </body>
        </html>
```

While the result view looks like this snippet:

```
        <%@ page language="java" contentType="text/html;
        charset=ISO-8859-1" pageEncoding="ISO-8859-1"%>
        <%@ taglib prefix="c" uri="http://java.sun.com/jsp/jstl/core"%>
        <%@ taglib prefix="spring"
        uri="http://www.springframework.org/tags" %>
        <%@ taglib prefix="form"
        uri="http://www.springframework.org/tags/form"%>
        <!DOCTYPE html>
        <html>
        <head>
        <meta http-equiv="Content-Type" content="text/html;
        charset=ISO-8859-1">
        <title><spring:message code="dept_title"  /></title>
        </head>
        <body>
           <h1><spring:message code="dept_list"  /></h1>
           <table border="1">
              <c:forEach var="dept" items="${ departments }">
                  <tr>
                      <td>${ dept.deptId }</td>
                      <td>${ dept.name }</td>
                      <c:url var="delUrl"
                        value="/deldept.html/${dept.deptId}" />
```

```
                    <td>
                    <a href="<c:out
                     value='${ delUrl }'/>">DELETE</a></td>
                    <c:url var="updateUrl"
                     value="/updatedept.html/${dept.id}" />
                    <td><a href="<c:out
                       value='${ updateUrl }'/>">UPDATE</a>
                       </td>
                </tr>
             </c:forEach>
          </table>
        <br>
      <a href="<c:url value='/deptform.html'/>">
         Add More Department</a> <br/>
         <em>This is for CSRF Logout</em>
      <c:url var="logoutUrl" value="/logout.html"/>
         <form action="${logoutUrl}" method="post">
         <input type="submit" value="Log out" />
         </form>
       </body>
      </html>
```

15. Reuse and update the `view.properties`, `messages_en_US.properties` configuration for the view mappings and view label bundles, respectively. Also, reuse `jdbc.properties` for the MySQL connection details. Place all these files in the `src\main\resources\config` folder.

16. `clean`, `build`, and `deploy`. Start the application through `https://localhost:8443/ch04/login.html`. Using the user and password registered in the `org.springframework.security.config.annotation.authentication.builders.AuthenticationManagerBuilder` of `AppSecurityConfig` context, proceed adding a new department record and try viewing all the records stored. After clicking logout, you will be redirected to the logout success page:

17. After the logout success page, any controller-defined URL will always redirect users to /login.html view; otherwise, a HTTP Status 404 will be issued.

18. Try running the application using HTTP at port 8080 and the security model will always redirect it to /login.html, causing HTTP Status 404, because HTTP and port 8080 is not yet mapped to HTTPS and port 8483.

How it works...

The authentication and authorization starts with extending the class WebSecurityConfigurerAdapter. This class provides AppSecurityConfig the inherited methods that are important in establishing the users, channels, and request endpoints for the authentication and authorization rules.

First, it has HttpSecurity that applies web-based security rules for specific HTTP or HTTPS requests. It has a built-in antMatchers() that will scrutinize which URL requests will be covered by the authentication rules and which will not. This method can also determine which HTTP methods are allowed to be authenticated or not. In the meantime, HttpSecurity only allows /login.html, /login.html?error=true and /after_logout.html to be executed without user authentication.

Moreover, the API has http.formLogin().loginPage(), which determines what view page will be the entry point for authentication. Likewise, it also has the methods http.formLogin().logoutUrl() and http.formLogin().logoutSuccessUrl() to register views related to logout processing. In XML-based context definitions, this API class is equivalent to the <http> element in Spring Security's namespace configuration.

Second, the configuration has the WebSecurity class that has the ignoring() method that will identify which URL request will not be subject to security rules at the general level. Restrictions through this class are often applied to static resources such as JavaScript, CSS, and image paths.

Lastly, it provides AuthenticationManagerBuilder, which has methods such as inMemoryAuthentication(), used in creating usernames, passwords, and roles. The inMemoryAuthentication() is the most basic and internal way of setting up user details. When it comes creating roles, it has the method roles() which asks for the role name without the prefix "ROLE_". It is authorities() that has the expression format "ROLE_XXX".

After completing the security model `AppSecurityConfig`, we apply this to our `SpringContextConfig`, not only to execute all the rules, but to create eventually the `springSecurityFilterChain`, which is considered the core API repository of the Spring Security architecture. In order for `springSecurityFilterChain` to be functional at runtime, the `delegatingFilterProxy` filter class must be registered in `ServletContext` by implementing `AbstractSecurityWebApplicationInitializer`. The filter rolls out all the security rules imposed by `AppSecurityConfig`. In this recipe, using `Filter.Registration` to add the filter to `ServletContext` gives us an exception:

```
SEVERE [localhost-startStop-1]
org.apache.catalina.core.StandardContext.filterStart Exception starting
filter delegatingFilterProxy
  org.springframework.beans.factory.NoSuchBeanDefinitionException: No bean
named 'delegatingFilterProxy' available
```

Once `AppSecurityConfig` is loaded, it imposes one entry point to the application through the URL `/login.html`. This security model will just redirect the user from an authentication error to the URL request `/login.html?error=true`. It requires the user to log out properly to protect the application through `/logout.html`.

This recipe hasn't covered CSRF yet, use `http.csrf().disable()` for now. CSRF will be discussed in a later recipe. At this point, Spring Security 4.2.2 has been set up over Spring 5.0 MVC.

Mapping sessions to channels and ports

In preparation for reactive and concurrent web programming in the later chapters, Tomcat 9.0 was installed in Chapter 1, *Getting Started with Spring* to use **TLS** to enable **HTTPS**. This recipe will showcase how Spring Security 4.2.2 manages all URL requests to run on secured HTTP protocols only.

Getting started

Open web project `ch04` and create another security model restricting all URL requests to execute on top of the secured HTTP at port `8443`.

How to do it...

After the initial setup and configuration, it is time to experiment with the Spring Security 4.2.2 module:

1. Let us now disable the previous AppSecurityConfig model by applying comment symbols to its @Configuration and @EnableWebSecurity annotations:

```
//@Configuration
//@EnableWebSecurity
public class AppSecurityConfig extends
  WebSecurityConfigurerAdapter {
    // refer to sources

}
```

 The use of the @Order annotation can be another option instead of manually commenting the annotations in AppSecurityConfig. This also generates a precedence rule whenever we have a series of security models, although there are slight inconsistencies when @Order is used after their roll-out.

2. Create another security model named AppSecurityModelA with the same in-memory user details and WebSecurity URL exemptions, but with some highlights on the HttpSecurity configuration for HTTPS security rules:

```
@Configuration
@EnableWebSecurity
public class AppSecurityModelA extends
    WebSecurityConfigurerAdapter{
    @Override
    protected void configure(AuthenticationManagerBuilder auth)
throws Exception {
        // refer to sources
    }
    @Override
    protected void configure(HttpSecurity http) throws
        Exception {
            http
              .requiresChannel()
              .anyRequest().requiresSecure()
              .and().authorizeRequests()
              .antMatchers("/login**", "/after**").permitAll()
              .anyRequest().authenticated()
              .and().formLogin()
              .loginPage("/login.html")
```

```
                .defaultSuccessUrl("/deptform.html", false)
                .failureUrl("/login.html?error=true")
                .and()
                .logout().logoutUrl("/logout.html")
                .logoutSuccessUrl("/after_logout.html");
            http
            .portMapper()
                .http(8080).mapsTo(8443);
            http.csrf().disable();
        }
        @Override
        public void configure(WebSecurity web) throws
          Exception {
            // refer to sources
          }
      }
```

3. Update `SpringContextConfig` by importing `AppSecurityModelA`, replacing the previous security context definition:

```
@Import(value = { AppSecurityModelA.class })
@Configuration
@EnableWebMvc
@ComponentScan(basePackages = "org.packt.secured.mvc")
public class SpringContextConfig {   }
```

4. Save all files. Then `clean`, `install`, and `deploy` the project.

 Shut down Tomcat 9 and remove the previously deployed ch04 project and its WAR file for this recipe to work. Clear also all the browser sessions.

How it works...

This recipe highlights how Spring MVC transactions will behave even when a wrong HTTP and port channel is accidentally used in executing the request. In the previous recipe, the login request was executed through `http://localhost:8080/ch04/login.html` and the security model did not allow this execution even with the correct user credentials. Since our Tomcat 9.0 is using HTTPS, we need to include a solution in our security model that will force redirection of all URL request transactions from HTTP at port 8080 to HTTPS using port 8443. The easiest solution is to configure the `http.requiresChannel()` method, which can restrict any requests from running on HTTP but with HTTPS instead.

The `requiresChannel()` method outputs a `ChannelRequestMatchRegistry` class that lists all the URL requests that can be executed in HTTPS. Some applications consider `/login.html` as a non-HTTP request, thus the line `http.requiresChannel().antMatcher ("/login.html").requiresInsecure()` is indicated in the model. But in this recipe, we will include all URLs as part of the HTTP transactions, thus the line `http.requiresChannel().anyRequest().requiresSecure()` in our `AppSecurityModelA` context. In an XML-based context definition, this process is equivalent to the metadata:

```
<intercept-url pattern="/**" access="isAuthenticated()"
requires-channel="http"/>
```

What follows after the HTTPS registration is the typical `authorizeRequests()` invocation asking for the usual authentication and authorization rules.

With regard to port matching, `HttpSecurity` also has a `portMapper()` method, which forces a port to be redirected to another port, just like in our case wherein running requests on port `8080` will just be executed forcedly to port `8443`. When using XML-based Spring Security configuration, port mapping is done through:

```
<security:port-mappings>
      <security:port-mapping http="8080" https="8443"/>
  </security:port-mappings>
```

To wrap up, using this security model on a non-TLS Tomcat installation will give you:

Customizing the authentication process

Using Spring Security's `/login` by default will just provide us with the built-in user authentication and authorization processes. This whole operation is being controlled by `springSecurityFilterChain`'s built-in `AuthenticationManager` class that matches the user credentials declared as in-memory users and roles to the incoming login credentials.

But there are instances where login processing must be customized to cater for some special validation procedures, such as explicitly banning some users or roles and sanitation of login credentials. This recipe will show you how to override the internal `/login` processing.

Getting started

Use the same project, `ch04`, and create a new security model that will implement a chain of authentication processing using providers and a custom authentication manager.

How to do it...

Let us now implement another security model that uses a custom authentication process instead of the default:

1. First, create a new security context definition, `AppSecurityModelB`, which presents the overriding of the `http.formLogin().loginProcessingUrl()` and the customization of the authentication manager and its providers:

```
@Configuration
@EnableWebSecurity
public class AppSecurityModelB extends
    WebSecurityConfigurerAdapter{
  @Autowired
  private AuthenticationProvider appAdminProvider;
  @Autowired
  private AuthenticationProvider appHRProvider;
  @Autowired
  private AuthenticationManager appAuthenticationMgr;
  @Override
  protected void configure(AuthenticationManagerBuilder auth)
throws Exception {   }

  @Override
  protected void configure(HttpSecurity http) throws Exception
{
```

```
        http
          .authorizeRequests()
          .antMatchers("/login_form**","/after**")
          .permitAll()
          .anyRequest().fullyAuthenticated()
          .and()
          .formLogin()
          .loginPage("/login_form.html")
          .loginProcessingUrl("/login_process")
          .defaultSuccessUrl("/deptform.html")
          .failureUrl("/login_form.html?error=true")
          .and()
          .logout().logoutUrl("/logout.html")
          .logoutSuccessUrl("/after_logout_url.html");
        http.csrf().disable();
    }
    @Override
    public void configure(WebSecurity web) throws Exception {
        // refer to sources
    }
    @Override
    protected AuthenticationManager authenticationManager()
        throws Exception {
        return new ProviderManager(Arrays.asList(
            appAdminProvider, appHRProvider ),
          appAuthenticationMgr);
    }
}
```

In the `authenticationManager()` method, observe the order of the injected custom providers inside the `org.springframework.security.authentication.ProviderManager`'s constructor. The order of execution starts from the leftmost provider up to the parent authentication manager `appAuthenticationMgr`. Notice also that all the user credentials and roles are not configured using `AuthenticationManagerBuilder` anymore.

 Be sure to save this class inside `org.packt.secured.mvc.core`.

2. Implement the preceding two providers indicated, namely `AppAdminProvider` and `AppHRProvider`, and save them in `org.packt.secured.mvc.core.manager`. The first provider, `AppAdminProvider`, just checks if the user is `admin` with a password of "admin". If the credential is correct, it sets its `ROLE_ADMIN` and passes the authentication chain its `Authentication` details; otherwise, it throws `BadCredentialsException`:

```
@Component
public class AppAdminProvider implements AuthenticationProvider
{

  @Override
  public Authentication authenticate(Authentication
      authentication) throws AuthenticationException {
    String name = authentication.getName();
    String password =
      authentication.getCredentials().toString();
    if (name.equalsIgnoreCase("admin") &&
        password.equalsIgnoreCase("admin")) {
      Set<SimpleGrantedAuthority> authorities =
new HashSet<>();
        authorities.add(new
          SimpleGrantedAuthority("ROLE_ADMIN"));
        return new
          UsernamePasswordAuthenticationToken(name,
        password, authorities);
    } else {
      throw new BadCredentialsException("Invalid Admin
        User");
    }
  }

  @Override
  public boolean supports(Class<?> authentication) {
      return authentication.equals(
        UsernamePasswordAuthenticationToken.class);
  }
}
```

3. The second, `AppHRProvider`, checks if the user is using the `hradmin` account, builds its user roles, and returns its `Authentication` details. The same `BadCredentialsException` is thrown if it is not the valid user:

```
@Component
public class AppHRProvider implements AuthenticationProvider {

  @Override
  public Authentication authenticate(Authentication
    authentication) throws AuthenticationException {

    // refer to sources
    if (name.equalsIgnoreCase("hradmin") &&
      password.equalsIgnoreCase("hradmin")) {
      Set<SimpleGrantedAuthority> authorities =
            new HashSet<>();
      authorities.add(
          new SimpleGrantedAuthority("ROLE_HR"));
      return new UsernamePasswordAuthenticationToken(name,
          password,authorities);
    } else {
      throw new BadCredentialsException("Invalid HR User");
    }
  }

  @Override
  public boolean supports(Class<?> authentication) {
    // refer to sources
  }
}
```

If a diamond operator (<>) that is used to simplify the instantiation of generic classes does not work, configure Maven Compiler Plugin in `pom.xml` to contain:

```
<configuration>
    <source>1.8</source>
    <target>1.8</target>
</configuration>
```

Or, add the following POM properties:

```
<properties>
    <maven.compiler.source>1.8</maven.compiler.source>
    <maven.compiler.target>1.8</maven.compiler.target>
</properties>
```

4. The security model will not be complete without the custom implementation of the parent provider, the AppAuthenticationManager. This authentication manager builds the whole user and their corresponding user account just as AuthenticationManagerBuilder did previously, with the in-memory user credentials:

```
@Component
public class AppAuthenticationMgr
    implements AuthenticationManager {
    @Override
    public Authentication authenticate(Authentication
        authentication) throws AuthenticationException {

        System.out.println(AppAuthenticationMgr.class);
        String name = authentication.getName();
        String password =
            authentication.getCredentials().toString();
        if (name.equalsIgnoreCase("sjctrags") &&
            password.equalsIgnoreCase("sjctrags")) {
            Set<SimpleGrantedAuthority> authorities =
                    new HashSet<>();
            authorities.add(new
                SimpleGrantedAuthority("ROLE_USER"));
            return new UsernamePasswordAuthenticationToken(name,
                password, authorities);
        } else if (name.equalsIgnoreCase("admin") &&
            password.equalsIgnoreCase("admin")) {
            Set<SimpleGrantedAuthority> authorities =
                new HashSet<>();
            authorities.add(new
                SimpleGrantedAuthority("ROLE_ADMIN"));
            return new UsernamePasswordAuthenticationToken(name,
                password, authorities);
        } else if (name.equalsIgnoreCase("hradmin") &&
            password.equalsIgnoreCase("hradmin")) {
            Set<SimpleGrantedAuthority> authorities =
                new HashSet<>();
            authorities.add(new
                SimpleGrantedAuthority("ROLE_HR"));
            return new UsernamePasswordAuthenticationToken(name,
```

```
            password, authorities);
      } else if(name.equalsIgnoreCase("guest")){
        Set<SimpleGrantedAuthority> authorities =
          new HashSet<>();
        authorities.add(new
            SimpleGrantedAuthority("ROLE_ANONYMOUS"));
        return new AnonymousAuthenticationToken(name,
            "ANONYMOUS", authorities);
      } else{
        throw new BadCredentialsException("Not Valid User");
      }
    }
  }
```

The custom `AuthenticationManager` includes `guest` as its anonymous user to be used, in the later recipes.

5. Update the `SpringConfigContext` to accommodate this security model. Also add the package of the provider in its `@ComponentScan` annotation:

```
@Import(value = { AppSecurityModelB.class })
@Configuration
@EnableWebMvc
@ComponentScan(basePackages = {"org.packt.secured.mvc",
    "org.packt.secured.mvc.core.manager" }
public class SpringContextConfig {    }
```

Comment on all the class-level annotations of the previous security model classes to avoid conflict or use `@Order` to establish a series of security model hierarchies.

6. Create a separate login view (`/login_form.html`) that will highlight the overridden `/login` URL for login processing:

```
<%@ page language="java" contentType="text/html;
charset=ISO-8859-1" pageEncoding="ISO-8859-1"%>
<%@ taglib prefix="c" uri="http://java.sun.com/jsp/jstl/core"%>
<%@ taglib prefix="spring"
uri="http://www.springframework.org/tags" %>
<%@ taglib prefix="form"
uri="http://www.springframework.org/tags/form"%>
<!DOCTYPE html>
<html>
```

```
<head>
<meta http-equiv="Content-Type" content="text/html;
charset=ISO-8859-1">
<title>Just Another Login Form</title>
</head>
<body>
  <c:if test="${ not empty errorMsg }">
    <em><c:out value='${ errorMsg }'/></em><br/>
  </c:if>
  <form action="/ch04/login_process" method='POST'>
    <table>
      <tr>
        <td>User:</td>
        <td><input type='text' name='username' value=''>
        </td>
      </tr>
      <tr>
        <td>Password:</td>
        <td><input type='password' name='password' />
        </td>
      </tr>
      <tr>
        <td colspan='2'><input name="submit" type="submit"
          value="submit" />
        </td>
      </tr>
      <tr>
        <td colspan='2'><input name="reset" type="reset" />
        </td>
      </tr>
    </table>
  </form>
</body>
</html>
```

7. Save this file inside `src/main/webapp/login_process`.

8. Update the `LoginController` by implementing a `GET` request method for the `/login_form.html` view page:

```
@RequestMapping(value = {"/login_form.html"},
  method = RequestMethod.GET)
public String login_form(@RequestParam(name="error",
  required=false) String error, Model model) {
    try {
      if (error.equalsIgnoreCase("true")) {
        String errorMsg = "Login Error";
        model.addAttribute("errorMsg", errorMsg);
```

```
              }else{
                model.addAttribute("errorMsg", error);
              }
            } catch (NullPointerException e) {
              return "login_form_url";
            }
            return "login_form_url";
        }
```

9. Create a separate after-logout view page
    (`src\main\webapp\login_process\after_logout_form.html`) to redirect
    the user to `/login_form.html`. Also, implement a typical `@Controller` of this
    new view page. Make the previous controllers as reference.

10. Update `views.properties` and `messages_en_US.properties` for the new
    view.

11. Save all files. `clean`, `build`, and `deploy`. Run
    `https://localhost:8443/ch04/login_form.html` to test the custom
    `AuthenticationProvider` and the overridden `login-processing-url`. Try
    logging in using all the user credentials indicated in the
    `AuthenticationManagerBuilder` and observe what happens.

How it works...

First, the recipe encourages developers to override the default URL `/login`, the default
login processing for Spring Security 4.x. To avoid conflicts with the previous configuration,
we must declare a new URL through the `http.formLogin().loginProcessingUrl()`
method, given that this URL is non-existent and non-controller-based. This new processing
URL must be executed using a `POST` request; otherwise, a `HTTP status 405` will be
thrown.

Second, the recipe highlights the customization of the whole authentication and authorization process. The Spring Security architecture lies mainly with who will use the MVC application and what access levels each user will have. To depend on the default framework mechanism is not acceptable, especially in cases where the security requirement becomes complex and unconditional. In order for the module to comply with the security requirement, it is recommended to implement a customized version of the AuthenticationManager. This class only requires one method to be overridden, and that is authenticate(), which returns an Authentication object once the access is allowed, throws AuthenticationException if the access is not allowed, or returns a null object for certain conditions.

AuthenticationManager delegates the authentication process to a chain of providers, which needs to be implemented to avoid a fat custom AuthenticationManager. To inject the custom manager and its providers, WebSecurityConfigurerAdapter's authenticationManager() must be overridden to establish the new authentication chain comprised of the list of providers and the custom parent authentication manager.

This recipe is designed so that the first provider to be executed during /login_process is the AppAdminProvider. This provider will redirect the user to /deptform.html once the user credentials are considered valid; otherwise, the next provider, AppHRProvider, will be next to run its authenticate() method. An exception must be thrown from AppHRProvider to trigger the execution of AppAuthenticationManager, which gives us the conclusion that the last to authenticate() is the parent authentication manager. Returning null values will also trigger the authentication chain. The whole chaining process is indicated in the following diagram:

The only problem with designing authentication chaining is when all the providers and managers do not cooperate to achieve one security goal. The tasks of each node in the chain *must be mutually-exclusive and must not create inconsistencies and conflicts* that can make the login/logout mechanism out of control.

In this recipe, every AuthenticationException thrown by each provider or the parent manager leads to the execution of the failureUrl(). This exception is not a normal runtime exception and can only be caught inside the chain. Some implementations of AuthenticationException that can be used to classify login credential-related exceptions are AuthenticationServiceException, BadCredentialsException, SessionAuthenticationException, and UsernameNotFoundException.

Customizing the Spring Security authentication does not only involve the implementation of the authentication chain but also the building of user credentials and their roles. This recipe eliminated the creation of an in-memory user databank but instead created an internal and programmatical way of building user credentials through the use of providers and authentication managers.

Implementing authentication filters, login success, and failure handlers

The previous recipe taught us how to create a custom authentication manager and a chain of providers that can help control the different gateways of authentication and authorization processes. Now, we will expand on customization, covering the setup of a filter stack and its handlers.

Getting started

This recipe will create a security model out of Spring Security 4.2.2, where there is a filter chain of security transactions which includes all the managers and providers of the previous recipe, with the addition of security objects called handlers. This recipe is the most important part of this chapter when it comes to stretching the flexibility of the security architecture of the Spring Security framework.

How to do it...

Let us now add important supporting components to the authentication process established by the previous recipe:

1. Create and apply two filters needed to establish a security filter chain in this new security model. Implement our first filter interface, `org.springframework.security.web.authentication.UsernamePasswordAuthenticationFilter`, which will intercept the authentication and authorization process every time `/login` is called. Save this `AppAuthenticationFilter` class in `org.packt.secured.mvc.handler` package:

```
public class AppAuthenticationFilter extends
    UsernamePasswordAuthenticationFilter {
```

```
@Override
protected void
    successfulAuthentication(HttpServletRequest
  request, HttpServletResponse response, FilterChain
  chain, Authentication authResult) throws IOException,
    ServletException {
  Collection<? extends GrantedAuthority> authorities =
    authResult.getAuthorities();
  List<String> roles = new ArrayList<String>();
  for (GrantedAuthority a : authorities) {
    roles.add(a.getAuthority());
  }
  String name = obtainPassword(request);
    String password = obtainUsername(request);
  UsernamePasswordAuthenticationToken userDetails =
  new UsernamePasswordAuthenticationToken(name, password,
      authorities);
  setDetails(request, userDetails);
  chain.doFilter(request, response);
}

@Override
protected void
  unsuccessfulAuthentication(HttpServletRequest
  request, HttpServletResponse response,
    AuthenticationException failed) throws IOException,
      ServletException {

  response.sendRedirect("/ch04/login.html?error=true");
}
@Override
public Authentication
   attemptAuthentication(HttpServletRequest
    request, HttpServletResponse response)
      throws AuthenticationException {
  String name = obtainPassword(request);
    String password = obtainUsername(request);
  SecurityContext context =
      SecurityContextHolder.getContext();
  Authentication auth = null;
  if(context.getAuthentication() == null){
    auth = new UsernamePasswordAuthenticationToken(
        name, password);
    setDetails(request,
        (UsernamePasswordAuthenticationToken) auth);
  }else{
    auth = (AnonymousAuthenticationToken)
        context.getAuthentication();
```

```
            return auth;
      }
      return auth;
   }
}
```

This class has three overridden methods responsible for filtering incoming authentication requests, namely `attemptAuthentication()`, which is executed once an anonymous user attempts to access the `/login`, `successfulAuthentication()`, which runs after an authentication has been created either from an authenticated or valid anonymous user, and lastly, `unsuccessfulAuthentication()`, which is responsible for global error page redirection, equivalent to executing `http.formLogin.failureUrl()`. Authentication is classified into two types, `org.springframework.security.authentication.UsernamePasswordAuthenticationToken` and `org.springframework.security.authentication.AnonymousAuthenticationToken`.

 Do not apply `@Component` on any filter implementation because it will give you `java.lang.IllegalArgumentException`: `authenticationManager` must be specified.

2. The next custom filter implementation in our filter stack is the `org.springframework.security.web.authentication.AnonymousAuthenticationFilter`, which is responsible for managing anonymous user access. Save this class `AppAnonAuthFilter` together with the previous filter:

```
public class AppAnonAuthFilter
      extends AnonymousAuthenticationFilter {
   private String principal;
   private String key;
   private List<GrantedAuthority> authorities;
     public AppAnonAuthFilter(String key) {
         super(key);
         this.key = key;
   }
   public AppAnonAuthFilter(String key, Object principal,
       List<GrantedAuthority> authorities) {
      super(key, principal, authorities);
      this.key = key;
      this.principal = principal.toString();
      this.authorities = authorities;
   }
```

```
@Override
protected Authentication
    createAuthentication(HttpServletRequest request) {
  if(principal.equalsIgnoreCase(
     request.getParameter("username")) ){
     AnonymousAuthenticationToken authTok =
     new AnonymousAuthenticationToken(key, principal,
      authorities);
     SecurityContext context =
       SecurityContextHolder.getContext();
     context.setAuthentication(authTok);
     return authTok;
  }
  return null;
  }
}
```

This class creates an `Authentication` object once an anonymous account `guest` has been detected; otherwise, it just throws `null` to the Spring Security container. This filter must be programmed not to create conflict with the processes of the `UsernamePasswordAuthenticationFilter` class.

 Do not apply `@Component` on any filter implementation because it will give you a `HTTP status 500`.

3. As helper objects, handlers are triggered by security models every time an `Authentication` object is thrown. A custom success authentication handler assists filter chains in defining the different default success URLs after a successful user authentication process. This class also overrides the `formLogin.defaultSuccessUrl()` and gives the application several options of default view pages depending on the roles of the users:

```
@Component
public class CustomSuccessHandler extends
    SimpleUrlAuthenticationSuccessHandler {
    private RedirectStrategy redirectStrategy =
new DefaultRedirectStrategy();
    @Override
    protected void handle(HttpServletRequest request,
      HttpServletResponse response, Authentication
        authentication) throws IOException {
        String targetUrl = targetUrl(authentication);
        if (response.isCommitted()) {
            System.out.println("Can't redirect");
```

```
            return;
        }
        redirectStrategy.sendRedirect(request, response,
            targetUrl);
    }
    protected String targetUrl(Authentication
            authentication) {
        String url = "";
        Collection<? extends GrantedAuthority> authorities =
        authentication.getAuthorities();
        List<String> roles = new ArrayList<String>();
        for (GrantedAuthority a : authorities) {
            roles.add(a.getAuthority());
        }
        if (isUserRole(roles)) {
            // add user-related transactions here
url = "/deptform.html";
        } else if (isAdminRole(roles)){
            // add admin-related transactions here
            url = "/deptform.html";
        } else if (isHrAdminRole(roles)){
            // add admin-related transactions here
url = "/deptform.html";
        } else{
            url = "/deptform.html";
        }
        return url;
    }
        // refer to sources
}
```

4. Save this file in `org.secured.mvc.core.handler`.

5. Another handler called the logout handler must be custom implemented to provide routes once `/logout` is triggered, depending on the roles of the users. This class overrides `formLogin.logoutSuccessUrl()`:

```
@Component
public class CustomLogoutHandler extends
    SimpleUrlLogoutSuccessHandler {
    private RedirectStrategy redirectStrategy =
new DefaultRedirectStrategy();
    @Override
    public void onLogoutSuccess(HttpServletRequest request,
        HttpServletResponse response, Authentication
        authentication) throws IOException, ServletException {
        String targetUrl = targetUrl(authentication);
        if (response.isCommitted()) {
```

```
            System.out.println("Can't redirect");
            return;
        }
        redirectStrategy.sendRedirect(request, response,
            targetUrl);
    }
    protected String targetUrl(Authentication authentication) {
        String url = "";
        Collection<? extends GrantedAuthority> authorities =
         authentication.getAuthorities();
        List<String> roles = new ArrayList<String>();
        for (GrantedAuthority a : authorities) {
            roles.add(a.getAuthority());
        }

        if (isUser(roles)) {
            url = "/after_logout.html?message="
+ "Thank your, User!";
        } else if (isAdmin(roles)){
            url = "/after_logout.html?message="
+ "Thank you, Admin!";
        } else if (isHrAdmin(roles)){
            url = "/after_logout.html?message="
+ "Thank you, HR!";
        }
        return url;
    }
    // refer to sources
}
```

6. The last handler essential to this recipe is the handler that will be executed when the user /login fails. Though this class has a limited scope of work, this can be useful in scrutinizing error messages depending on the nature of the validation error or the type of AuthenticationException:

```
@Component
public class CustomFailureHandler extends
   SimpleUrlAuthenticationFailureHandler {
  private RedirectStrategy redirectStrategy = new
    DefaultRedirectStrategy();
  @Override
  public void onAuthenticationFailure(HttpServletRequest
     request, HttpServletResponse response,
     AuthenticationException exception) throws IOException,
          ServletException {

    String targetUrl = "";
```

```
            if(exception instanceof BadCredentialsException){
              targetUrl = "/login.html?error="
                    + exception.getMessage();
            }
            else {
              targetUrl = "/login.html?error=true";
            }

            // refer to sources
            redirectStrategy.sendRedirect(request, response,
                targetUrl);
        }
    }
```

7. Together with the previous custom authentication manager and providers, construct the proper model that will highlight the whole custom security architecture:

```
@Configuration
@EnableWebSecurity
public class AppSecurityModelC extends
    WebSecurityConfigurerAdapter {
  // refer to sources
  @Override
  protected void configure(AuthenticationManagerBuilder auth)
throws Exception {   }
  @Override
  protected void configure(HttpSecurity http) throws Exception
{
        http
            .anonymous().authorities("ROLE_ANONYMOUS")
            .and()
            .authorizeRequests()
            .antMatchers("/login**", "/after**").permitAll()
            .antMatchers("/deptanon.html").anonymous()
            .anyRequest().authenticated()
            .and()
            .formLogin()
            .loginPage("/login.html")
            .defaultSuccessUrl("/deptform.html")
            .failureHandler(customFailureHandler)
            .successHandler(customSuccessHandler)
            .and()
            .addFilterBefore(appAnonAuthFilter(),
                UsernamePasswordAuthenticationFilter.class)
            .addFilter(appAuthenticationFilter(
authenticationManager()))
            .logout().logoutUrl("/logout.html")
```

```
            .logoutSuccessHandler(customLogoutHandler)
            .and()
      .exceptionHandling().authenticationEntryPoint(
            setAuthPoint());
      http.csrf().disable();
      }
   }
```

8. Implement the authentication filter that will assess all incoming valid users. Include this inside the `AppSecurityModelC` context definition:

```
@Bean
public UsernamePasswordAuthenticationFilter
   appAuthenticationFilter(AuthenticationManager authMgr) {
      AppAuthenticationFilter filter =
         new AppAuthenticationFilter();
      filter.setRequiresAuthenticationRequestMatcher(
      new AntPathRequestMatcher("/login.html", "POST") );
      filter.setAuthenticationManager(authMgr);
      return filter;
   }
```

9. Create another filter that will assess users that are not considered valid users and will allow `guest` or `anonymous` access to the application:

```
@Bean
public AnonymousAuthenticationFilter
         appAnonAuthFilter(){
      List<GrantedAuthority> anonAuth = new ArrayList<>();
      anonAuth.add(new
      SimpleGrantedAuthority("ROLE_ANONYMOUS"));
      AppAnonAuthFilter anonFilter =
         new AppAnonAuthFilter("ANONYMOUS","guest",anonAuth);
      return  anonFilter;
   }
```

10. To register into Spring Security container the preceding filters, create an authentication manager by overriding the `authenticationManager()` of the `WebSecurityConfigurerAdapter`:

```
@Override
protected AuthenticationManager authenticationManager()
      throws Exception {
      // refer to sources
   }
```

11. Since we have bypassed the default filter configuration of the Spring Security framework, it is mandatory to tell the security platform when to trigger either of the filters implemented by injecting a new `AuthenticationTrustResolver`:

```
@Bean
public AuthenticationTrustResolver trustResolver() {
  return new AuthenticationTrustResolver() {

    @Override
    public boolean isRememberMe(final Authentication
authentication) {
      return true;
    }

    @Override
    public boolean isAnonymous(final Authentication
authentication) {
      Collection<? extends GrantedAuthority> auths =
      authentication.getAuthorities();
      List<String> roles = new ArrayList<String>();
      for (GrantedAuthority a : auths) {
        roles.add(a.getAuthority());
      }
      if(roles.contains("ROLE_ANONYMOUS") || roles.size() ==
0){
        return true;
      }
      else{
        return false;
      }
    }
  };
}
```

12. Together with `AuthenticationTrustResolver`, implementation is a new `AuthenticationEntryPoint` to tell the platforms what URL to trigger with the custom filters created in preceding steps.

```
@Bean
public AuthenticationEntryPoint setAuthPoint(){
  return new AppAuthPoint("/login.html");
}
```

13. Create an additional @Controller for the request transactions of our anonymous account guest:

```
@Controller
public class AnonymousController {
    @RequestMapping(value="/deptanon.html")
    public String anonPage(){
        return "dept_anon";
    }
}
```

14. Create the additional view page /deptanon.html for the default view page of our anonymous account inside the src/main/webapp/anonymous_sites directory:

```
<html><head>
<meta http-equiv="Content-Type" content="text/html;
charset=ISO-8859-1">
<title>Anonymous</title>
</head>
<body>
    <h1>Anonymous Account</h1>
    <p>This content is for our beloved guest wants to check
our DEPARTMENT database. Enjoy!
    <em><a href="<c:url value='/login.html'/>">You want some more
about us? Login!.</a></em>
</body>
</html>
```

15. Update the views.properties for the added view details.

16. Be sure to update the SpringContextConfig by importing the new AppSecurityModelC and including org.packt.secured.mvc.core.handler in its @ComponentScan.

17. Save all files. Just like in the recent recipes, always clear the browser sessions and remove the previously deployed ch04 project in the Tomcat 9 server. clean, build, and deploy the Maven project.

How it works...

The main idea is to create a customized filter chain that will manage the whole access to the application. In this recipe, the authentication procedure for valid users and the anonymous account has been overridden to accommodate some details not inherent to the framework. For instance, the framework recognizes anonymous access, but it does not provide a set of rules for it. The recipe creates an anonymous `guest` account whose access to the application will be redirected by
`org.springframework.security.web.AuthenticationEntryPoint` to its own content page, which is `/deptanon.html`. This conveys that the anonymous access is `restricted` from accessing the `/deptform.html`, which is only for the authenticated users. The assessment of any anonymous access is the major responsibility of
`AnonymousAuthenticationFilter`, with the intervention also of the
`UsernamePasswordAuthenticationFilter`. The former checks first if the authentication request is a `guest` or is bearing an anonymous access `key` before the authentication process creates the `AnonymousAuthenticationToken`. Otherwise, it throws `null` for the latter to create a `UsernamePasswordAuthenticationToken`, indicating that the access is not anonymous and must undergo the authentication process by the manager and its providers. Thus, its configuration will not work without the injection of the custom
`AuthenticationManager` and `AuthenticationProvider` provided in the previous recipe:

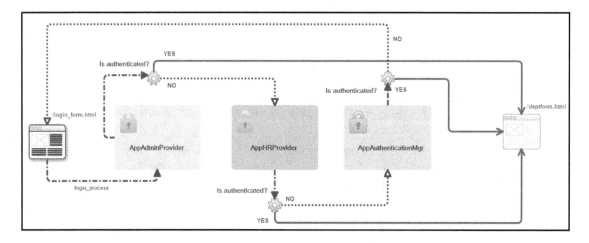

The validation of whether the Authentication is anonymous or not is the ultimate job of org.springframework.security.authentication.AuthenticationTrustResolver , which completes the puzzle of why the filters and the authentication providers communicate each other. The AuthenticationTrustResolver evaluates all the Authentication objects thrown by filters and providers into the container at runtime. It is also the exact object that helps the AuthenticationEntryPoint determine when to redirect a user to an anonymous page.

Security filters must be implemented properly so as not to contradict each other or to interfere with the results of some filter methods. To avoid unexpected results, HttpSecurity has methods (custom filters) that can set the order of filter execution, and these are:

- addFilter: This adds a custom Spring Security filter anywhere in the filter chain
- addFilterBefore: This adds a custom filter before an existing specified filter class in the chain
- addFilterAfter: This adds a custom filter after an existing specified filter class in the chain
- addFilterAt: This adds a custom filter at the location of an existing specified filter class in the chain

On the other hand, the security chain will not be complete without the existence of the custom handlers, such as CustomSuccessHandler, CustomFailureHandler, and CustomLogoutHandler. Both CustomSucessHandler and CustomFailureHandler are triggered to manage the different page redirections during the login processing while CustomLogoutHandler provides different logout redirections once the /logout process is executed. The framework's DefaultRedirectStrategy is used to manage the redirection of each handler without specifying the context paths.

Because of Spring Security's flexibility, its filter chain may contain several custom chains as needed by the application, and some of the widely used ones are LogoutFilter, ConcurrentSessionFilter, X509AuthenticationFilter, CasAuthenticationFilter, and JaasApiIntegrationFilter.

These security filters can store specific user details and information to `SecurityContext` and can be accessed by any of the components of the application. This object can only be accessed through
`org.springframework.security.core.context.SecurityContextHolder`.

Creating user details

The previous recipes introduced us to how to store user details using in-memory and providers and filters. This time the correct manner of storing user credentials and roles will be showcased without bothering with the providers and filters.

Getting started

Use the Maven project ch04 again and create another security model imposing the use of `org.springframework.security.core.userdetails.UserDetails` and
`org.springframework.security.core.userdetails.UserDetailsService`.

How to do it...

Instead of hardcoding the user details inside the security model, we will implement a service layer that will programmatically generate a username and password for the application:

1. Let us create the `UserService` interface, as follows that will generate hardcoded data for the `UserDetails`:

```
public interface UserService {
    public String getUserCredentials(String username);
    public Set<String> getuserRoles(String username);
}
```

2. Save this file in our `org.secured.mvc.service` since this is just an application-based native service.

3. Then, implement the interface through `UserServiceImpl` as follows:

```
@Service("userService")
public class UserServiceImpl implements UserService{

    @Override
```

```
public String getUserCredentials(String username) {
  Map<String, String> credentials = new HashMap<>();
  credentials.put("sjctrags", "sjctrags");
  credentials.put("admin", "admin");
  credentials.put("hradmin", "hradmin");
  return credentials.get(username);
}

@Override
public Set<String> getuserRoles(String username) {
  Map<String, Set<String>> roles = new HashMap<>();
  Set<String> userA = new HashSet<>();
  Set<String> userB = new HashSet<>();
  Set<String> userC = new HashSet<>();
  userA.add("ROLE_USER");
  userB.add("ROLE_ADMIN");
  userB.add("ROLE_USER");
  userC.add("ROLE_HR");
  userC.add("ROLE_ADMIN");
  roles.put("sjctrags", userA);
  roles.put("admin", userB);
  roles.put("hradmin", userC);
  return roles.get(username);
}
}
```

4. Now, create an implementation of `UserDetailsService`, which retrieves the user information through its username and provides this corresponding information to `SecurityContext`:

```
@Service("authUserService")
public class AuthUserService implements UserDetailsService {
  @Autowired
  private UserService userService;

  @Override
  public UserDetails loadUserByUsername(String username)
    throws UsernameNotFoundException {
    String password =
      userService.getUserCredentials(username);
    UserDetails user = new User(username, password, true,
      true,
    true, true, getAuthorities(username));
    return user;
  }
  private Set<GrantedAuthority> getAuthorities(String
username){
    Set<GrantedAuthority> authorities =
```

```
              new HashSet<GrantedAuthority>();
          for(String role : userService.getuserRoles(username)) {
              GrantedAuthority grantedAuthority =
                new SimpleGrantedAuthority(role);
              authorities.add(grantedAuthority);
          }
          return authorities;
      }
  }
```

5. Place this class inside the `org.packt.secured.mvc.core.service` package. We will be injecting this class inside our Spring Security container.

6. Design now the `AppSecurityModelD` that will utilize `UserDetails` and `UserDetailsService` for storing and retrieving user identification:

```
@Configuration
@EnableWebSecurity
public class AppSecurityModelD extends
    WebSecurityConfigurerAdapter {
  // refer to sources
@Autowired
@Qualifier("authUserService")
private UserDetailsService userDetailsService;
    @Override
    protected void configure(AuthenticationManagerBuilder auth)
throws Exception {
        auth.userDetailsService(userDetailsService);
        auth.eraseCredentials(false);
        }
    @Override
    protected void configure(HttpSecurity http) throws Exception
{
        http
          .authorizeRequests()
          .antMatchers("/login**", "/after**").permitAll()
          .anyRequest().authenticated()
          .and()
          .formLogin()
          .loginPage("/login.html")
          .defaultSuccessUrl("/deptform.html")
          .failureUrl("/login.html?error=true")
          .successHandler(customSuccessHandler)
          .and()
          .logout().logoutUrl("/logout.html")
          .logoutSuccessHandler(customLogoutHandler);
        http.csrf().disable();
    }
```

```
        @Override
        public void configure(WebSecurity web) throws Exception {
            // refer to sources
        }
    }
```

7. For evidence that `UserDetails` have been injected into `SecurityContext`,
utilize the `CustomSuccessHandler` and `CustomLogoutHandler` of the previous
recipe. Modify a little bit the `CustomLogoutHandler` to extract the user
credentials and roles using the `java.security.Principal` object:

```
@Component
public class CustomLogoutHandler extends
    SimpleUrlLogoutSuccessHandler {
  private RedirectStrategy redirectStrategy =
    new DefaultRedirectStrategy();
  @Override
  public void onLogoutSuccess(HttpServletRequest request,
    HttpServletResponse response, Authentication
     authentication) throws IOException, ServletException {
     String targetUrl = targetUrl(authentication);
         // refer to sources
     redirectStrategy.sendRedirect(request, response,
        targetUrl);
  }
  protected String targetUrl(Authentication authentication) {
    UserDetails p =
       (UserDetails )authentication.getPrincipal();
    String username = p.getUsername();
    String password = p.getPassword();
    String url = "";
    Collection<? extends GrantedAuthority> authorities =
         p.getAuthorities();
    List<String> roles = new ArrayList<String>();
    for (GrantedAuthority a : authorities) {
          roles.add(a.getAuthority());
    }
        if (isUser(roles)) {
          url = "/after_logout.html?message=" + " Thank
          your, " + username + " with password " + password
            +" and role(s):" + roles;
        }
      // refer to sources
        return url;
    }
    // refer to sources
}
```

8. Be sure to update `SpringContextConfig` by importing the new `AppSecurityModelD` and including the `org.packt.secured.mvc.core.service` in its `@ComponentScan`.

9. Save all files. `clean`, `build`, and `deploy` the Maven project.

How it works...

This recipe opens other options of storing and managing user information and credentials aside from the in-memory or hardcoding way. This is the most appropriate way to manage user details and authorities through the use of the `UserDetailsService` interface, which injects `UserDetails` into the `SecurityContext`. The `UserDetailsService` is an interface used in building the user account through the user's username, password, and `GrantedAuthorities`. It has a required `loadUserByUsername()` method which asks for the username of the user to build and inject into the container an object called `UserDetails`. This `UserDetails` is another interface that holds the user information, which is later encapsulated into authentication objects found in filters, providers, and handlers. A default implementation of this interface is `org.springframework.security.core.userdetails.User`, which is capable of saving the username, password, and granted authorities together with some toggle values as to whether the object is lockable and/or within expiration.

Generating encrypted passwords

This recipe explains how to protect the plain text password using different hashing algorithms with or without using salt.

Getting started

Use the same `ch04` project, applying a different security model which focuses on how to inject an encryption algorithm into the security container to enable password encoding and matching during the authentication process.

How to do it...

The following recipe shows how to create an encrypted password:

1. To implement an encrypted authentication, let us start with a custom class,
   `AppPasswordEncoder`, that serves as a compendium of some popular
   `PasswordEncoder` APIs:

```
public class AppPasswordEncoder {

    public String md5Encoder(String password, String salt) {
        Md5PasswordEncoder md5PasswordEncoder =
            new Md5PasswordEncoder();
        md5PasswordEncoder.setEncodeHashAsBase64(true);
        md5PasswordEncoder.setIterations(32);
        String encoded =
            md5PasswordEncoder.encodePassword(password, salt);
        return encoded;
    }
    public String bcryptEncoder(String password) {
        BCryptPasswordEncoder bCryptPasswordEncoder =
            new BCryptPasswordEncoder();
        String encoded =
            bCryptPasswordEncoder.encode(password);
        return encoded;
    }
    public String standardEncoder(String password) {
        StandardPasswordEncoder standardPasswordEncoder =
            new StandardPasswordEncoder();
        String encoded =
            standardPasswordEncoder.encode(password);
        return encoded;
    }
}
```

Among these three built-in common `PasswordEncoder`, it is only
`Md5PasswordEncoder` that has support for custom
`org.springframework.security.authentication.dao.SaltSource`. The
rest have a default internal salt generation. Save this file inside the
`org.packt.secured.mvc.core.password` package.

2. Slightly modify the `getUserCredentials()` method of `UserServiceImpl` to include the encoded password for each user. `Md5PasswordEncoder` is used for this recipe:

```
@Service("userService")
public class UserServiceImpl implements UserService{

    @Override
    public String getUserCredentials(String username) {
        Map<String, String> credentials = new HashMap<>();
        AppPasswordEncoder encoder = new AppPasswordEncoder();
        // Without salt
        /*
        credentials.put("sjctrags",
encoder.md5Encoder("sjctrags", null));
        credentials.put("admin",
encoder.md5Encoder("admin", null));
        credentials.put("hradmin",
encoder.md5Encoder("hradmin", null));
        */
        // With Salt (username as salt)
        credentials.put("sjctrags",
encoder.md5Encoder("sjctrags", "sjctrags"));
        credentials.put("admin",
encoder.md5Encoder("admin", "admin"));
        credentials.put("hradmin",
encoder.md5Encoder("hradmin", "hradmin"));
        return credentials.get(username);
    }

    @Override
    public Set<String> getuserRoles(String username) {
        // refer to sources
    }
}
```

This recipe will be applying salt for every hashing procedure of `Md5PasswordEncoder` to strengthen the randomness of the hash generation. To disable salting, just set the second parameter of `md5Encoder()` to `null`.

3. Now, create the security model `AppSecurityModelE` that will allow injection of the `Md5PasswordEncoder` bean into the container in order to encode the password of our `UserDetails`:

```
@Configuration
@EnableWebSecurity
public class AppSecurityModelE extends
        WebSecurityConfigurerAdapter{

  // refer to sources
  @Override
  protected void configure(AuthenticationManagerBuilder auth)
throws Exception {
    // Hashing without salt
    //   auth.userDetailsService(userDetailsService)
    //        .passwordEncoder(md5PasswordEncoder());

    // Hashing with salt
     auth.authenticationProvider(authProvider());
     auth.eraseCredentials(false);
  }
  @Override
  protected void configure(HttpSecurity http) throws Exception
{
          // refer to sources
  }
  @Override
  public void configure(WebSecurity web) throws Exception {
        // refer to sources
  }
  @Bean
  public Md5PasswordEncoder md5PasswordEncoder(){
     Md5PasswordEncoder md5 = new Md5PasswordEncoder();
     md5.setEncodeHashAsBase64(true);
     md5.setIterations(32);
     return md5;
  }
  @Bean
  public DaoAuthenticationProvider authProvider() {
     DaoAuthenticationProvider daoProvider =
       new DaoAuthenticationProvider();
     daoProvider.setPasswordEncoder(md5PasswordEncoder());
     daoProvider.setUserDetailsService(userDetailsService);
     ReflectionSaltSource saltHash =
       new ReflectionSaltSource();
     saltHash.setUserPropertyToUse("username");
     daoProvider.setSaltSource(saltHash);
```

```
                          return daoProvider;
              }
        }
```

Since this recipe adds salt to hashing, the class
`org.springframework.security.authentication.dao.DaoAuthenticati`
`onProvider` will be used to configure the encoding of `userDetailsService`
using `md5PasswordEncoder()` with `SaltSource`.

4. Update `SpringContextConfig` to consider the new security model.
5. Save all files. `build`, `install`, and `deploy` the project.

How it works...

In any Spring MVC application, passwords must always be encoded using secured hashing
algorithms. Spring Security 4.2.2 still supports hashing algorithms combined with a proper
salt to generate strong hash values. Once a `PasswordEncoder` is injected into the container,
Spring Security executes password encoding and matches the result to the `UserDetails`
and `password` property. When encoding is configured, Spring Security will now recognize
the encrypted values instead of the default text value. Implementing this recipe is a two-
way process because the `PasswordEncoder` in the container will not give appropriate
matches if the passwords stored in `UserDetails` are not encoded by the same algorithm
using the same number of iterations, and the same salt property, if there is one. The hash
generated by the security model must match the same hash in `UserDetails` in order to
proceed with the authentication process.

Applying Security to MVC methods

From architectural-level authorization, we go down to the access levels of our service and
controller methods. This recipe will design a role-based authorization imposed on some
essential transactions of the MVC application.

Getting started

We will utilize the same `ch04` project, but this time we will focus on role-based
authorization of the service and request methods.

How to do it...

1. Before we apply Spring Security on some service methods, let us open the
   `UserServiceImpl` class and add the following authorization: a super-user role
   to `hradmin` by adding `ROLE_USER` to its existing set of authorities; `ROLE_ADMIN`
   and `ROLE_USER` authorities to the "`admin`" account; and `ROLE_USER`
   authorization to the "`sjctrags`" account:

   ```
   @Service("userService")
   public class UserServiceImpl implements UserService{

       // refer to sources
     @Override
     public Set<String> getuserRoles(String username) {
       Map<String, Set<String>> roles = new HashMap<>();
       Set<String> userA = new HashSet<>();
       Set<String> userB = new HashSet<>();
       Set<String> userC = new HashSet<>();
       userA.add("ROLE_USER");
       userB.add("ROLE_ADMIN");
       userB.add("ROLE_USER");
       userC.add("ROLE_HR");
       userC.add("ROLE_ADMIN");
       userC.add("ROLE_USER");
       roles.put("sjctrags", userA);
       roles.put("admin", userB);
       roles.put("hradmin", userC);
       return roles.get(username);
     }
   }
   ```

2. Impose access restrictions to our `DepartmentService` interface by applying
   role-based authorization using the Spring Security annotations `@Secured`,
   `@PreAuthorize`, and `@PostAuthorize`:

   ```
   public interface DepartmentService {
     @Secured("ROLE_USER")
     public List<Department> readDepartments();
     @Secured("ROLE_USER")
     public void addDepartment(DepartmentForm dept);
     @Secured("ROLE_ADMIN")
     public void removeDepartment(Integer deptId);
     @PreAuthorize("hasRole('USER') AND hasRole('HR')")
     public void updateDepartment(DepartmentForm dept, Integer
   id);
     @PreAuthorize("hasRole('USER') AND hasRole('HR')")
   ```

```
    public Department getDeptId(Integer id);
  }
```

 Do not apply these changes to the implementation class.

3. Create another `@Controller` that will contain restricted request methods. This class, `RestrictedController`, has a `GET` method that exposes banned departments once a `ROLE_HR` or `ROLE_ADMIN` accesses `/deptbanned.html`:

```
@Controller
public class RestrictedController {
  @PreAuthorize("hasRole('HR') OR hasRole('ADMIN')")
  @RequestMapping("/deptbanned.html")
  public String bannedDepts(){
    return "banned";
  }
}
```

4. Create a view page for `/deptbanned.html`, which lists all banned departments. Update the `views.properties` and `messages_en_US.properties` for this additional view.

5. Create a new security context, `AppSecurityModelF`, which contains the complete configuration for this recipe:

```
@Configuration
@EnableWebSecurity
@EnableGlobalMethodSecurity(prePostEnabled = true,
    securedEnabled=true)
public class AppSecurityModelF extends
    WebSecurityConfigurerAdapter {
  // refer to sources

  @Override
  protected void configure(AuthenticationManagerBuilder auth)
throws Exception {
    auth.authenticationProvider(authProvider());
    auth.eraseCredentials(false);
    }
  @Override
  protected void configure(HttpSecurity http) throws Exception
{
    http
      .authorizeRequests()
```

```
        .antMatchers("/login**","/after**")
        .permitAll()
        .anyRequest().authenticated()
        .and()
        .formLogin()
        .loginPage("/login.html")
        .defaultSuccessUrl("/deptform.html")
        .failureUrl("/login.html?error=true")
        .successHandler(customSuccessHandler)
        .and()
        .logout().logoutUrl("/logout.html")
        .logoutSuccessHandler(customLogoutHandler)
        .and()
        .exceptionHandling()
        .accessDeniedPage("/access_denied.html");
  http.csrf().disable();
}
@Override
public void configure(WebSecurity web) throws Exception {
        // refer to sources
}
  @Bean
  public Md5PasswordEncoder md5PasswordEncoder(){
    // refer to sources
}
  @Bean
  public DaoAuthenticationProvider authProvider() {
      // refer to sources
}
}
```

6. In order for the @Secured, @PreAuthorize, and @PostAuthorize annotations to be functional, the class-level annotation @EnableGlobalMethodSecurity must be configured, setting prePostEnable and securedEnabled to true.

7. Lastly, create a view page /acces_denied.html, which is triggered if access to a restricted transaction is detected.

8. Update SpringContextConfig to consider the new security model.

9. Save all files. clean, build, and deploy the project.

How it works...

Spring Security has three annotations that can be applied to methods with restricted, confidential, or exclusive access. The `@Secured` annotation is used when there is only one authorized role allowed to execute a specific method based on the security policies. But if there is more than one role allowed in the access, with some special and complicated conditions, `@PreAuthorize` and `@PostAuthorize` must be used.

`@PreAuthorize` verifies the roles before executing the method, while `@PostAuthorize` checks the roles after executing the restricted method. The latter works most often with functions because its verification always includes `returnObject` together with the attached roles. Both of the annotations use Spring Expression Language in establishing the access control. It can restrict the access only to `hasRole("ADMIN") AND hasRole("HR")`, or to users who are `both hasRole("ADMIN") AND hasRole("USER")`. `@Secured` does not support expression-based access control.

These annotations will not serve their purpose if the `@EnableGlobalMethodSecurity` is not configured at the class-level of the security context definition. This main annotation has three properties to set:

- `prePostEnabled`: This is a Boolean property that enables or disables the use of `@PreAuthorize` and `@PostAuthorize`
- `secureEnabled`: This is a Boolean property that enables or disables the use of `@Secured`
- `jsr250Enabled`: This is a Boolean property that enables or disables the use of some JSR-250 annotations for restrictions

Lastly, method restrictions can be applied not only to service methods, but also to `@Controller` request handlers, as shown by the `RestrictedController`.

Creating roles and permissions from the database

We have utilized `UserDetailsService` and `UserDetails` interfaces in handling user credentials and information but the information, still came from `HashMap` with `static` data. This recipe will show us how to archive all the user credentials and information to a database to be fetched by a custom `UserDetails` class.

Getting started

Open the MySQL server to alter our `hrs` schema. Also, utilize the same project `ch04` for this recipe.

How to do it...

1. Before we start the main recipe, let us add the following tables in our `hrs` schema:

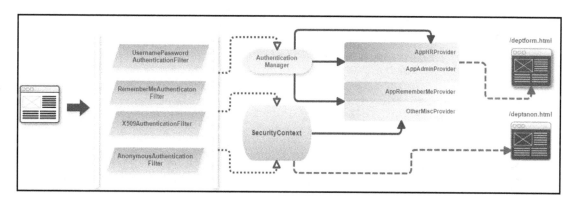

2. The `userdetails` class will contain the usual general user information, while `logindetails` contains the `username`, `password`, and `encrypted password` of each user. On the other hand, `role_permission` contains all the roles and access permissions of each user in `logindetails`. A *Permission* is defined as the allowable CRUD transaction to be performed by a user, such as READ, WRITE, VIEW, DELETE, and REPORT, which is different from the usual *Role*. A role ADMIN, for instance, can have ADMIN_UPDATE and ADMIN_DELETE permissions.

3. With the newly added tables, generate the model for each table and create a typical DAO interface that will add, retrieve, update, and delete the records:

```
public interface LoginDao {
  public List<Role> getUserRoles();
  public Role getUserRole(int id);
  public List<Permission> getPermissions();
  public Permission getPermission(int id);
  public List<RolePermission>
    getUserGrantedAuthority(int userId);
  public List<AccountLogin> getUsers();
  public AccountLogin getUser(String username);
}
```

4. Implement a @Repository implementation of this interface using SimpleJdbcInsert and JdbcTemplate.

5. Inside the package org.packt.secured.mvc.core.user, create custom UserDetails that will store all logindetails with some additional transactions, such as sorting the GrantedAuthority and username/password validation:

```
public class AppUserDetails implements UserDetails {
    private String password;
    private final String username;
    private final Set<GrantedAuthority> authorities;
    private final boolean accountNonExpired;
    private final boolean accountNonLocked;
    private final boolean credentialsNonExpired;
    private final boolean enabled;
    @Override
    public Collection<? extends GrantedAuthority>
getAuthorities() {
        return authorities;
    }

    // refer to sources

    public AppUserDetails (String username, String
      password, boolean enabled, boolean accountNonExpired,
        boolean credentialsNonExpired,
        boolean accountNonLocked,
        Collection<? extends GrantedAuthority>
            authorities) {

      if (((username == null) || "".equals(username)) ||
        (password == null)) {
```

```
        throw new IllegalArgumentException(
                "Empty values are not allowed");
    }

    this.username = username;
    this.password = password;
    // refer to sources
}

private static SortedSet<GrantedAuthority>
    sortAuthorities(Collection<? extends
      GrantedAuthority> authorities) {
    SortedSet<GrantedAuthority> sortedAuthorities =
      new TreeSet<GrantedAuthority>(
            new AuthorityComparator());
    for (GrantedAuthority grantedAuthority :
      authorities) {
        sortedAuthorities.add(grantedAuthority);
    }
    return sortedAuthorities;
}

private static class AuthorityComparator implements
        Comparator<GrantedAuthority>, Serializable {

    public int compare(GrantedAuthority g1,
GrantedAuthority g2) {
        // refer to sources
        return g1.getAuthority()
        .compareTo(g2.getAuthority());
    }
  }
}
```

6. Afterwards, create another `UserDetailsService` inject and use `LoginDao` to retrieve the user details for the custom `AppUserDetails`:

```
@Service("authJdbcUserService")
public class AuthJdbcUserService implements
    UserDetailsService{
  @Autowired
  private LoginDao loginDaoImpl;

  @Override
  public UserDetails loadUserByUsername(String username)
throws UsernameNotFoundException {
    AccountLogin login = loginDaoImpl.getUser(username);
```

```
        // refer to sources
      UserDetails user = new
           AppUserDetails(login.getUsername(),
            login.getEncPassword(),true, true, true, true,
            getAuthorities(username, login));
      return user;
    }
    private Set<GrantedAuthority> getAuthorities(String
       username, AccountLogin login){
      List<RolePermission> roleperms =
        loginDaoImpl.getUserGrantedAuthority(login.getId());
      // refer to sources
      return authorities;
    }
}
```

7. Populate `logindetails` with the encoded password using the same injected `PasswordEncoder`:

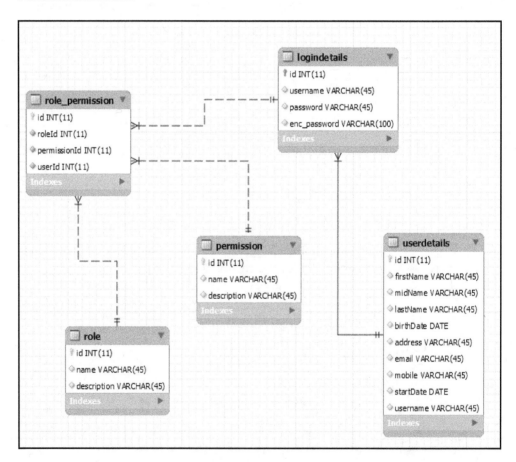

8. Create `AppSecurityModelE2,` having `authJdbcUserService` injected as the new `UserDetailsService`:

```
@Configuration
@EnableWebSecurity
public class AppSecurityModelE2 extends
    WebSecurityConfigurerAdapter{
  // refer to sources
  @Autowired
  @Qualifier("authJdbcUserService")
  private UserDetailsService userDetailsService;
  @Override
  protected void configure(AuthenticationManagerBuilder auth)
throws Exception {

    auth.authenticationProvider(authProvider());
    auth.eraseCredentials(false);
  }
// refer to sources
@Bean
public DaoAuthenticationProvider authProvider() {
    DaoAuthenticationProvider daoProvider =
        new DaoAuthenticationProvider();
    daoProvider.setPasswordEncoder(md5PasswordEncoder());
    daoProvider.setUserDetailsService(userDetailsService);
    ReflectionSaltSource saltHash =
        new ReflectionSaltSource();
    saltHash.setUserPropertyToUse("username");
    daoProvider.setSaltSource(saltHash);
    return daoProvider;
}
}
```

9. Update `SpringContextConfig` to consider the new security model.
10. Save all files. `clean`, `build`, and `deploy` the project.

How it works...

For some specific scenarios, UserDetails can be customized in order to add some validations and constraints needed to build complete user credentials. In this recipe, we added a simple Comparator to arrange all the authorities alphabetically. There is also a username and password validation to check whether the account is not null. Moreover, all credentials must come from a custom UserDetailsService that injects LoginDao to retrieve all logindetails that match the username. Instead of hardcoding the data in a HashMap, the service will use a query transaction to supply all the needed credential to AppUserDetails. It is recommended to use a separate @Service that will generate the encoded password prior to the logindetails execution.

Managing and storing sessions

Spring Security does not only manage the user authentication and access authorization, but also controls the sessions the application uses in its entire lifespan. This recipe will design a security model that focuses on session management and controls.

Getting started

Open again the same ch04 project with another security model emphasizing session management and control.

How to do it...

1. Simple session handling implementation starts with creating a session as Cookie, which manages a maximum of one session per user access, deletes the session after /logout, and redirects view pages once the session expires or is compromised:

```
@Configuration
@EnableWebSecurity
@EnableGlobalMethodSecurity(prePostEnabled = true,
            securedEnabled=true)
public class AppSecurityModelG extends
   WebSecurityConfigurerAdapter {
  // refer to sources
  @Override
```

```
    protected void configure(AuthenticationManagerBuilder auth)
throws Exception {
        auth.authenticationProvider(authProvider());
        auth.eraseCredentials(false);
    }


    @Override
    protected void configure(HttpSecurity http) throws Exception
{
        http
            .authorizeRequests()
            .antMatchers("/login**", "/after**").permitAll()
            .antMatchers("/session*").permitAll()
            .anyRequest().authenticated()
            .and()
            .formLogin()
            .loginPage("/login.html")
            .defaultSuccessUrl("/deptform.html")
            .failureUrl("/login.html?error=true")
            .successHandler(customSuccessHandler)
            .and()
            .logout().logoutUrl("/logout.html")
            .logoutSuccessHandler(customLogoutHandler)
            .invalidateHttpSession(true)
            .deleteCookies("JSESSIONID")
            .and()
            .exceptionHandling()
      .accessDeniedPage("/access_denied.html");
        http.sessionManagement()
            .sessionCreationPolicy(
SessionCreationPolicy.IF_REQUIRED)
            .maximumSessions(1)
            .expiredUrl("/session_expired.html")
            .and()
            .enableSessionUrlRewriting(true)
            .invalidSessionUrl("/session_invalid.html");
            http.csrf().disable();
        }
    @Override
    public void configure(WebSecurity web) throws Exception {
            // refer to sources
    }
      @Bean
      public Md5PasswordEncoder md5PasswordEncoder(){
          // refer to sources
    }
      @Bean
      public DaoAuthenticationProvider authProvider() {
```

```
                // refer to sources
        }
    }
```

2. For the concurrent session control, inject
   `org.springframework.security.web.session.HttpSessionEventPublis`
   `her` into the `SpringContextConfig` definition. Update also `@Import` to load
   `AppSecurityModelG`:

```
@Import(value = { AppSecurityModelG.class })
@Configuration
@EnableWebMvc
@ComponentScan(basePackages = {"org.packt.secured.mvc",
  "org.packt.secured.mvc.core.manager",
        "org.packt.secured.mvc.core.handler",
            "org.packt.secured.mvc.core.service"})
public class SpringContextConfig {
    @Bean
    public HttpSessionEventPublisher
      httpSessionEventPublisher() {
        return new HttpSessionEventPublisher();
    }
}
```

3. Set the session expiry age by implementing `HttpSessionListener`. Save this
   class together with the `SpringWebInitializer`:

```
public class AppSessionListener implements
        HttpSessionListener{

    @Override
    public void sessionCreated(HttpSessionEvent event) {
      System.out.println("app session created");
      event.getSession().setMaxInactiveInterval(10*60);
    }

    @Override
    public void sessionDestroyed(HttpSessionEvent event) {
      System.out.println("app session destroyed");
    }
}
```

4. Register this listener at the `ServletContext` level of the application. Also configure in `SpringWebInitializer` the mode of storing the session, which is done through `Cookie`:

```
@EnableWebMvc
@ComponentScan(basePackages = "org.packt.secured.mvc")
@Configuration
public class SpringWebInitializer implements
    WebApplicationInitializer {
  @Override
  public void onStartup(ServletContext container)
     throws ServletException {
       // refer to sources
   }

    private void addRootContext(ServletContext container) {
        // Create the application context
        AnnotationConfigWebApplicationContext rootContext =
          new AnnotationConfigWebApplicationContext();
        rootContext.register(SpringContextConfig.class);
        // Register application context with
        //ContextLoaderListener
        container.addListener(
          new ContextLoaderListener(rootContext));
        container.addListener(new AppSessionListener());
        container.setInitParameter("contextConfigLocation",
          "org.packt.secured.mvc.core");
        container.setSessionTrackingModes(
          EnumSet.of(SessionTrackingMode.COOKIE));
       // if URL, enable sessionManagement URL rewriting
      }
    private void addDispatcherContext(ServletContext
container) {
         // refer to sources
    }
  }
```

 Sessions can be stored in the browser as `SessionTrackingMode.COOKIE`, `SessionTrackingMode.URL`, or `SessionTrackingMode.SSL`.

5. Save all files. `clean`, `build`, and `deploy` the new project.

6. Open the Chrome browser and run our application. Log in using the `sjctrags` account.

7. Then, open the Firefox browser and run the same URL, and log in using the same `sjctrags` account. Since the security model limits the maximum session to 1, the `/session_expired.html` is executed.

How it works...

The first configuration detail that needs to be decided is *when the session will be created*. Spring Security 4.2.2 supports multiple ways of creating sessions:

- Always during transactions without any constraints (`SessionCreationPolicy.ALWAYS`)
- Only when required by the application (`SessionCreationPolicy.IF_REQUIRED`)
- Stop creating any but use existing sessions (`SessionCreationPolicy.NEVER`)
- Stop creating nor use sessions during the entire lifespan of the application (`SessionCreationPolicy.STATELESS`)

Among these four types, the `SessionCreationPolicy.IF_REQUIRED` fits with login-based applications.

The next decision is how to control the concurrent access to the application. With the help of `HttpSessionEventPublisher`, the architecture offers developers control through `http.sessionManagement().maximumSession()`. Once a user reaches this limit, `HttpSecurity` has the option to offer `http.sessionManagement().maxSessionsPreventsLogin(true)` to the user or not but, either of the options can lead to `/session_expired.html`.

On the other hand, it is always recommended to enable URL rewriting in any MVC application for cases in which the browser is restricted to run *cookies*. Whether `ServletContext` stores the session as `Cookie` in the browser, or as a request parameter in a URL, it is always advisable to use `http.sessionManagement().enableSessionUrlRewriting(true)` to avoid possible runtime exceptions when the browser's cookies support is disabled.

Lastly, it is important that after `/logout`, all sessions must be invalidated or killed for security reasons. `http.logout().invalidateHttpSession(true)` is applicable to deleting all types of sessions, while `http.logout().deleteCookies("JSESSIONID")` only applies once the application is in `SessionTrackingMode.COOKIE` mode.

Solving Cross-Site Request Forgery (CSRF) and session fixation attacks

CSRF occurs when a user who is currently logged in has accidentally processed an unknown link or event which tries to execute a valid transaction using suspicious request parameters, which may lead to some disastrous and catastrophic effects to the database, network, or even to the system infrastructure. On the other hand, **session fixation** happens when a user accidentally leaves his session open after logging out, and through this idle session an exploit happens because someone maliciously uses the existing session ID and variables to execute unwanted transactions. Invalidating sessions does not guarantee a solution to session fixation attacks; thus, this recipe will explain how Spring Security can protect Spring MVC applications from these two vulnerabilities.

Getting started

The same `ch04` project will be used to execute a security model which gives us the best and immediate solutions for preventing CSRF and session fixation attacks from happening.

How to do it...

To avoid confusion and conflict with the rules established in the other security context models:

1. Let us create a separate security model, `AppSecurityModelH`, that enables CSRF support and invalidates previous sessions and session attributes after creating a new one:

```
@Configuration
@EnableWebSecurity
public class AppSecurityModelH extends
  WebSecurityConfigurerAdapter{
  @Override
  protected void configure(AuthenticationManagerBuilder auth)
throws Exception {
        auth.inMemoryAuthentication()
           .withUser("sjctrags")
              .password("sjctrags").roles("USER");
    }
  @Override
  protected void configure(HttpSecurity http) throws Exception
{
        http
          .authorizeRequests()
          .antMatchers("/login*").permitAll()
          .anyRequest().authenticated()
          .and()
          .formLogin()
          .antMatchers("/login*", "/after**").permitAll()
          .defaultSuccessUrl("/deptform.html")
          .failureUrl("/login.html?error=true")
          .and().logout().logoutUrl("/logout.html")
          .logoutSuccessUrl("/after_logout.html");
        http.csrf().csrfTokenRepository(
          CookieCsrfTokenRepository.withHttpOnlyFalse());
        http.sessionManagement().sessionFixation()
          .newSession();
    }
  @Override
  public void configure(WebSecurity web) throws Exception {
        // refer to sources
    }
}
```

2. For CSRF support to work properly inside a session, all navigations must be driven by a `POST` method. Also, use the Spring Form tag library `<form:form>` to generate form components, because CSRF tokens are automatically generated inside the `<form:form>` tag.

3. Save all files. `clean`, `build`, and `deploy` the `ch04` project.

How it works...

This recipe tackles two issues, namely the prevention of CSRF and session fixation, in Spring MVC applications. When it comes to session fixation, Spring Security provides default protection which invalidates the previous sessions but copies all session attributes to the newly created one. This mechanism is called the `http.sessionManagement().sessionFixation().migrateSession()` type of preventing session fixation attacks. But there are two more options developers can use, and these are `newSession()` and `none()`. `newSession()` is preferred for this recipe because it deletes the entire past sessions, including session data, which gives confidence that no exploits can penetrate through older sessions or use the session data. The method `none()` is the scariest because it does not delete any previous sessions.

On the other hand, deleting `http.csrf().disable()` means the security model enables CSRF support for the application. Enabling CRSF support means injecting or customizing the `CsrfTokenRepository` interface that will generate tokens to be stored in every specific session created by Spring Security. The default repository is session-based and is derived from the `HttpSessionCsrfTokenRepository` class, but another solution is to implement `OncePerRequestFilter` to generate and store tokens without using any sessions. Customizing filters such as `OncePerRequestFilter` opens solutions for AJAX or plain JavaScript to interact with the tokenization processes through the retrieval of the two generated tokens, **XSRF-TOKEN** and `X-XSRF-TOKEN`.

This recipe uses `org.springframework.security.web.csrf.CookieCsrfTokenRepository`, which generates and stores the **XSRF-TOKEN** as cookie data:

In order for CSRF support to work with sessions, all form transactions and navigations must be in `POST` request transactions, with the use of the Spring Form tag library `<form:form>` to spare us from creating AJAX to manually generate and attach the token per view page. Any access to authenticated pages without the specified token will give users the `HTTP status 404`, which indicates that the application is sensitive to CSRF.

Anonymous pages are not included in the CSRF tokenization process, so hyperlinks and typical HTML forms can be used on these pages.

Solving Cross-Site Scripting (XSS) and clickjacking attacks

The difference between cross-site scripting attacks and CRSF or session fixation is the presence of an injected third-party JavaScript or malicious script in **XSS**, whose objective is to sniff form transactions and perform exploits. **Clickjacking** is another attack which uses X-Frame-Options to inject exploits on a specific part of a page through frames.

Aside from properly escaping or encoding HTML properties, outgoing header variables must be sanitized to avoid XSS and clickjacking attacks. This recipe will highlight how Spring Security 4.2.2 can help shield all the outgoing headers from malicious attacks.

Getting started

Using the same ch04, this recipe will highlight how to control response headers to avoid XSS attacks during form transactions.

How to do it...

To prevent **XSS** attacks in our form transactions:

1. Let's create a new security model that enables *header filtering or sanitation,* which is inherent to the Spring Security 4.2.2 framework:

```
@Configuration
@EnableWebSecurity
public class AppSecurityModelI extends
    WebSecurityConfigurerAdapter{
  @Override
  protected void configure(AuthenticationManagerBuilder auth)
throws Exception {
        // refer to sources
  }
  @Override
  protected void configure(HttpSecurity http) throws Exception
{
      // refer to sources
        http.csrf().disable();

        http.headers().defaultsDisabled().cacheControl()
         .and().headers().httpStrictTransportSecurity()
```

```
                          .and().contentTypeOptions().disable()
                          .frameOptions().deny()
                          .and().addHeaderWriter(
                            new StaticHeadersWriter(
                             "X-Content-Security-Policy",
                             "default-src 'auth'"));
                    }
                    @Override
                    public void configure(WebSecurity web) throws Exception {
                          // refer to sources
                    }
              }
```

2. Save all files. `clean`, `compile`, and `deploy` the ch04 project.

How it works...

Response headers must also be protected from exploitation by adding security headers or by filtering the default outgoing header information of the application. Preferably, applications must attain the following headers related to the caching browser history:

```
Cache-Control: no-cache, no-store, max-age=0, must-revalidate
Pragma: no-cache
Expires: 0
```

`HttpSecurity` has `headers().defaultsDisabled().cacheControl()`, which disables caching information in the browser history.

To avoid content sniffing and illegal injection of scripts, `HttpSecurity` has the ability to disable content type options through the method `headers().contentTypeOptions().disable()`. The execution of this method results in a security header:

```
X-Content-Type-Options: nosniff
```

Since the recipe uses HTTPS, it is advisable to use **HTTP Strict Transport Security** (**HSTS**) in order to avoid illegal interception during redirection. Interception happens when there is an erroneous shift from HTTPS to HTTP transactions, wherein the response headers and credentials are accidentally exposed outside of the security. HTTPS can avoid the leak by managing any request to proceed always with HTTPS mode consistently during any accidental `sideshifting` of protocols. Executing the `http.headers().httpStrictTransportSecurity()` method enables HTTPS, but use this only in secured HTTP mode.

On the other hand, clickjacking can be avoided by setting `X-FRAME-OPTIONS` to:

```
X-Frame-Options: DENY
```

This is done through the `http.headers().frameOptions().deny()` method. Moreover, to protect the application from all direct XSS attacks, we need to add the security header

```
X-XSS-Protection: 1; mode=block
```

by executing `http.headers().xssProtection().block(true)`.

Lastly, for the browser to know from what static location these CSS, JS, and images will be loaded, the `Content-Security-Policy` header must be configured to indicate the location of these resources for the browser to recognize. The method `http.headers().addHeaderWriter(new StaticHeadersWriter("X-Content-Security-Policy","default-src 'self'"))` tells the browser that all resources should be coming from the context root of the page.

Creating interceptors for login data validation

Interceptors of Spring 5.0 can still be used to implement audit trails, transaction monitoring, session tracking, and additional request functionalities. These components filter and evaluate all incoming requests before they reach the `@Controller`. This recipe will show how interceptors can be a great help for the authentication process and session management.

Getting started

This last recipe is an add-on to the Spring Security framework. Although interceptors are Spring MVC components, these support classes can help manage some parts of the security chain. This recipe will utilize `ch04` and will update some of our context definition classes.

How to do it...

To apply an interceptor that will monitor and evaluate the /login.html request:

1. Let us create a class of HandlerInterceptor type that keeps track of the access time of each user:

```
public class LoginInterceptor implements
    HandlerInterceptor{

@Override
public void afterCompletion(HttpServletRequest request,
  HttpServletResponse response, Object handler,
Exception ex) throws Exception {
        System.out.println("INFO LOG ......
        Fully Done login transaction.....");
}

@Override
public boolean preHandle(HttpServletRequest request,
  HttpServletResponse response, Object handler)
    throws Exception {
System.out.println("INFO LOG ......
Beginning login transaction.....");
Long startLog = System.currentTimeMillis();
Cookie startTime = new Cookie("startLog",
    startLog.toString());
response.addCookie(startTime);
System.out.println("INFO LOG ......
Done Computing Start Time.....");
return true;
}

@Override
public void postHandle(HttpServletRequest request,
  HttpServletResponse response, Object handler,
ModelAndView modelAndView) throws Exception {
System.out.println("INFO LOG ......
        User Successfuly logged in.....");
 }
}
```

The interface org.springframework.web.servlet.HandlerInterceptor has been used to implement the three helper methods, namely preHandle(), postHandle(), and afterCompletion().

2. Implement another interceptor using the class
   `org.springframework.web.servlet.handler.HandlerInterceptorAdapt`
   `er`, whose task is to audit the time duration the user has spent with the
   application. This component also logs the end of the whole MVC transactions:

```
public class AfterLogoutInterceptor extends
   HandlerInterceptorAdapter{
   @Override
   public boolean preHandle(HttpServletRequest request,
      HttpServletResponse response, Object handler)
      throws Exception {
System.out.println("INFO LOG ......
Entering After Logout transaction.....");
   Long startLog = null;
   Cookie[] allCookies = request.getCookies();
   for(Cookie c : allCookies){
      if(c.getName().equalsIgnoreCase("startLog")){
         startLog = Long.parseLong(c.getValue());
         System.out.println(c.getValue());
         break;
      }
    }
   long elapsed = System.currentTimeMillis() -
         startLog.longValue();
   System.out.println("----------Time Elapsed: " +
      (elapsed/1000) + " sec ---------------");
   return true;
}
@Override
public void afterCompletion(HttpServletRequest request,
   HttpServletResponse response, Object handler,
      Exception ex) throws Exception {
      System.out.println("INFO LOG ......
      Fully Done Logout transaction.....");
   }
}
```

3. To make the interceptors work, open the root context
   `SpringDispatcherConfig` and override the `addInterceptors()` to register
   the two custom interceptors, `LoginInterceptor` and
   `AfterLogoutInterceptor`:

```
@Override
public void addInterceptors(InterceptorRegistry registry) {
   registry.addInterceptor(
new LoginInterceptor()).addPathPatterns("/login.html");
   registry.addInterceptor(
```

```
        new AfterLogoutInterceptor())
        .addPathPatterns("/after_logout.html*");
    }
```

4. Save all files. `Clean`, `build`, and `deploy` the `ch04` project.

How it works...

This recipe simply adds an additional Spring MVC component that can listen to and handle
support for any request transactions involved in the authentication and authorization
process. `HandlerInterceptor` and `HandlerInterceptorAdapter` work like filters, but
the filter is more powerful and general when it comes to the scope of work. Filters are
configured in `ServletContext`, while interceptors are injected in the Spring context
definition through the `addInterceptors()` method of `InterceptorRegistry`. When it
comes to scope, interceptors are convenient to use when the Spring platform is used, rather
than implementing Filter. Creating interceptors is appropriate for applying DRY coding
principles wherein code blocks are written repeatedly across the platform. Additionally,
they can help the framework with logging, profiling, authorization-related validation, and
minimal filtering tasks.

All interceptors contain three methods, and these are:

- `preHandle()`: This is executed before the actual request is executed
- `postHandle()`: This is executed after a request is executed
- `afterCompletion()`: This is executed after the whole request transaction is
  completed

Using interceptors is optional and mapping them to the correct request paths using the
`InterceptorRegistry.addInterceptor().addPathPatterns` needs extra caution,
because the patterns used to specify the URL here are path expressions and not the usual
normal URL. Generating these patterns may cause some paths not to be included or
excluded. It is always advisable to include `excludePathPatterns()` and
`includePathPatterns()` to ensure that request URL paths are valid.

5
Cross-Cutting the MVC

Interceptors are not only confined to managing requests but also to establishing a set of behaviors of the applications, such as transaction logging, data transaction management, custom authorization and authentication, managing services, caching, and workflow simulation.

Spring 5.0 still supports AOP, which is a programming paradigm that implements a functionality or *concern* which may not be part of the business process but is essential to some areas of the application. These *concerns* or sets of behaviors are linked to some objects in order to work, like the `HandlerInterceptor` (which can intercept anywhere in the application).

There are two main classifications of *concerns* and these are the *major concerns*, which cater to only a single component of the Spring MVC, and the *global concerns*, which are applied throughout the application and also may affect the whole transaction flow.

The following recipes will cover how to implement *major concerns* such as managing the request handlers, services, and DAO transactions. Moreover, some of the recipes will also discuss exception handling, logging, custom security, managing session and request attributes, and restricting user access, which are all part of the *global concerns*.

In this chapter, you will learn the following:

- Logging and auditing service methods
- Managing DAO transactions
- Monitoring services and request handlers
- Validating parameters and arguments
- Managing exceptions
- Implementing the caching mechanism
- Intercepting request transactions

- Implementing user authentication
- Accessing with restrictions
- Controlling concurrent user access
- Implementing a mini-workflow using AOP

Logging and auditing service methods

Aspect-Object Programming (AOP) is known in many applications as an immediate solution for logging or auditing. This first recipe will introduce the concept and components of AOP in Spring 5.0 as it implements the service logging and auditing features of an MVC application through the use of the Log4J framework.

Getting started

Create a new Eclipse Maven project, ch05, with the web.xml-lessServletContext declaration. Add all the previous libraries of *Spring 5.0, Servlet 3.1, JSP 2.3, JUnit 4*, and other related plugins to the Maven configuration. Follow Chapter 1, *Getting Started with Spring*, for building the context definitions.

How to do it...

Before implementing AOP components, let us first implement logging by following these steps:

1. The previous has already created some POJOs, so just copy the Employee model, the supporting DAO and service interfaces, and their corresponding implementation classes. Place all model classes in a new package, org.packt.aop.transaction.model.data, all DAO components in org.packt.aop.transaction.dao, and all services in org.packt.aop.transaction.service.

2. Add the updated Log4J libraries to the pom.xml:

```
<dependency>
  <groupId>log4j</groupId>
  <artifactId>log4j</artifactId>
  <version>1.2.17</version>
</dependency>
```

3. Create the `log4j.properties` containing the needed configuration details such as the *type of appenders to be used, message formats to be applied,* and the *location of the log file*:

```
# LOG4J configuration
log4j.rootLogger=INFO, Appender1, Appender2
log4j.appender.Appender1=org.apache.log4j.ConsoleAppender
log4j.appender.Appender1.layout=org.apache.log4j.PatternLayout
log4j.appender.Appender1.layout.ConversionPattern=%-7p %d [%t]
%c %x - %m%n
log4j.appender.Appender2=org.apache.log4j.FileAppender
log4j.appender.Appender2.File=C\:\\logs\\ch05.log
log4j.appender.Appender2.layout=org.apache.log4j.PatternLayout
log4j.appender.Appender2.layout.ConversionPattern=%-7p %d [%t]
%c %x - %m%n
```

4. Save this file in `src/main/resources/` of your Maven project.

5. To start with AOP, include in the repository the `AspectJ` plugin which is an AOP extension for implementing aspects:

```
<dependency>
    <groupId>org.aspectj</groupId>
    <artifactId>aspectjrt</artifactId>
    <version>1.8.10</version>
    <scope>runtime</scope>
</dependency>
<dependency>
    <groupId>org.aspectj</groupId>
    <artifactId>aspectjtools</artifactId>
    <version>1.8.10</version>
</dependency>
```

6. Create an `@Aspect` class inside the package `org.packt.aop.transaction.core` that will manage the logging *concerns* of `EmployeeService`. This class will cut across any `EmployeeService` method execution just to monitor the status of the service calls. This class must be injected as an `@Component` bean of the container:

```
import org.apache.log4j.Logger;

@Component
@Aspect
public class EmployeeAspect {
  private Logger logger =
      Logger.getLogger(EmployeeAspect.class);
  @Before("execution(* org.packt.aop.transaction.service
```

```
 .impl.EmployeeServiceImpl.*(..))")
 public void logBeforeEmployeeTransactions(
    JoinPoint joinPoint){

 logger.info("EmployeeAspect.logBeforeEmployeeTransactions()
 detected : " + joinPoint.getSignature().getName());
  }
 @After("execution(* org.packt.aop.transaction.service
 .impl.EmployeeServiceImpl.*(..))")
 public void logAfterEmployeeTransactions(
    JoinPoint joinPoint) {
 logger.info("EmployeeAspect.logAfterEmployeeTransactions()
  detected : " + joinPoint.getSignature().getName());
   }
 }
```

7. The two methods inside the aspect class are called *advices*.

   The `logBeforeEmployeeTransactions()` is a type of `@Before` advice which means its execution is triggered after any `EmployeeServiceImpl` method execution is encountered.

   On the other hand, the `logAfterEmployeeTransactions()` is an `@After` advice which is called after any execution of the `EmployeeServiceImpl` advisced methods.

   Both methods implement the needed logging *concerns*. The expressions inside `@After` and `@Before` advices are called **Pointcuts**, which tells the advices when to execute.

8. Create more `@Aspect` classes that will cover specific service transactions such as `EmployeeDeleteAspect`, `EmployeeInsertAspect`, `EmployeeReadAspect`, and `EmployeeUpdateAspect`. The following is an implementation of `EmployeeUpdateAspect`, which highlights the `args()` expression used to capture the arguments of the adviced `updateEmployee()` method. The `args()` is also part of the Pointcut expression:

```
@Component
@Aspect
public class EmployeeUpdateAspect {
private Logger logger =
    Logger.getLogger(EmployeeUpdateAspect.class);
@Before("execution(* org.packt.aop.transaction.service
.impl.EmployeeServiceImpl.updateEmployee(..))
&& args(empForm, id)")
```

```
public void logBeforeUpdateEmp(JoinPoint joinPoint,
    EmployeeForm empForm, int id) {
      // refer to sources
}
@After("execution(* org.packt.aop.transaction.service
.impl.EmployeeServiceImpl.updateEmployee(..))
&& args(empForm, id)")
public void logAfterUpdateEmp(JoinPoint joinPoint,
EmployeeForm empForm, int id) {
      // refer to sources
}


}
```

 If the adviced method has no arguments, avoid using `args()` because it will lead to compiler errors or non-execution of the `Aspect` class. Keyword `args()` includes all the local parameters of the adviced method.

9. For a Spring container to recognize aspects, apply the `@EnableAspectJAutoProxy` annotation to the application context definition `SpringContextConfig`, which will enable the support for handling aspect classes and other related annotations.

10. Create a test class, `TestEmployeeService`, to evaluate if logging and AOP are successfully integrated into the MVC application:

```
@RunWith(SpringJUnit4ClassRunner.class)
@WebAppConfiguration
@ContextConfiguration(classes = { SpringDbConfig.class,
    SpringDispatcherConfig.class })
public class TestEmployeeService {

  @Autowired
  private EmployeeService employeeServiceImpl;
  @Test
  public void testPersistEmployee(){
    EmployeeForm form = new EmployeeForm();
    form.setFirstName("Sherwin");
    form.setLastName("Tragura");
    form.setAge(38);
    // refer to sources
  }
  @Test
  public void testReadEmployees(){
    List<Employee> emps =
      employeeServiceImpl.readEmployees();
```

```
            assertNotNull(emps);
        }
        @Test
        public void testReadOneEmp(){
          Employee emp = employeeServiceImpl.readEmployee(10);
        }
        @Test
        public void testDelEmp(){
          employeeServiceImpl.delEmployee(11111);
        }
    }
```

How it works...

Aspect classes contain implementations that can be executed on some or any areas of the MVC platform to modularize the performance of the application. These aspects execute features that are not really part of the MVC components but can be triggered to become part of the system at runtime, fulfilling the software *concerns* they are assigned to. Aspect classes are denoted by the annotation @Aspect.

Technically, methods written inside aspects are called *advices* and can be classified into five, namely @Before, @After, @Around, @AfterReturning, and @AfterThrowing. This recipe only highlighted @Before methods, which are called before the execution of adviced methods, and @After, which is triggered after any execution of its methods. Adviced methods are the transactions intercepted by these advices and can be determined by their assigned Pointcut expressions.

Both @After and @Before advices have an optional parameter, JoinPoint, which represents all the adviced methods being executed. It contains properties such as getThis(), which returns the class name carrying the adviced method (such as EmployeeServiceImpl), and getSignature(), which returns an object containing the method signature of the adviced method.

The correctness of writing the advices depends on the Pointcut and the method signature of the concerned method(s). If the adviced methods do not return any value, the advices must not return one otherwise it will not be executed by the application. In the case of request handlers and other services that return a particular object, advices have the option to return the same object type or just void.

With regard to return values, advices may return a specific Java type or a generic object. Aside from `JoinPoint`, advices can include the parameters of the adviced methods using the `args()` expression. All variables found in `args()` must be declared as local parameters using specific types or Object.

On the other hand, Pointcuts can also be a source of errors if not formulated properly:

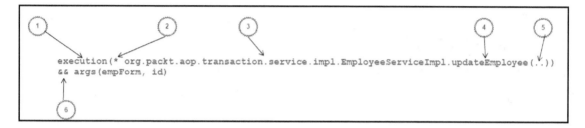

The preceding diagram showing the Pointcut expression is made up of the following components:

- Expression (1) is the command that will trigger the execution; sometimes the `within` command is used
- Expression (2) is the return statement of the adviced methods; (*) means all possible return types including `void`
- Expression (3) is the location path where the adviced methods are to be found; it includes the package and the name of the class
- Expression (4) is the name of the adviced method
- Expression (5) is the possible parameters of the adviced method; the notation (..) means all possible numbers and types of parameters
- Expression (6) is the logical operator used to augment more than one expression; `&&` is interpreted as AND, while `||` denotes the typical OR

Aside from observing the correct format, the effectiveness of Pointcut is also measured through how loose or tight it covers the concerned areas of the application. Thus, developers must determine first what aspects are for global and specific *concern* implementation before designing and generating the advices and their Pointcuts.

Managing DAO transactions

Aspects do not only intercept the service layer but also the data transaction layer. This recipe will give us a concrete scenario when AOP is needed in most DAO transactions. Aspects implemented for the DAO layer are just limited to logging, tracing, and validating tasks due to undesirable effects when transactions become complex.

Getting started

Open `ch05` and add an `@Aspect` that will filter `null` record(s) from `JdbcSimpleInsert` and `JdbcTemplate`.

How to do it...

Our first AOP implementation will be applied for managing DAO transactions. Follow the following procedure to log all the DAO transactions using *aspects*, *advices* and *Pointcuts*:

1. Before this recipe starts, be sure to have the `EmployeeDao` and `EmployeeDaoImpl` inside the packages `org.packt.aop.transaction.dao` and `org.packt.aop.transaction.dao.impl`, respectively.

2. To apply aspects to our DAO transactions, let us create an `@Aspect` inside the package `org.packt.aop.transaction.core` that will monitor `getEmployees()` and `getEmployee()` methods from `EmployeeDaoImpl`, and will verify if the returned values are `null` or not. If `null`, this aspect will create an object of the same type just to avoid `NullPointerException`:

```
@Component
@Aspect
public class ManageNullsDao {

    private Logger logger =
        Logger.getLogger(ManageNullsDao.class);

    @Around("execution(* org.packt.aop.transaction.dao
    .impl.EmployeeDaoImpl.getEmployees(..))")
    public Object safeDaoEmps(ProceedingJoinPoint joinPoint)
        throws Throwable {

        logger.info("ManageNullsDao.safeDaoEmps() detected : "
                    + joinPoint.getSignature().getName());
        Object emps = joinPoint.proceed();
```

```
      if (emps == null) {
        return new ArrayList();
      } else {
        return emps;
      }
    }

    @Around("execution(* org.packt.aop.transaction.dao
    .impl.EmployeeDaoImpl.getEmployee(..))")
    public Object safeDaoOneEmp(ProceedingJoinPoint
      joinPoint) throws Throwable {

      logger.info("ManageNullsDao.safeDaoOneEmp()
        detected : " + joinPoint.getSignature().getName());
      Object emp = joinPoint.proceed();
      if (emp == null) {
        return new Employee();
      } else {
        return emp;
      }
    }
  }
```

3. Execute again the `TestEmployeeService` with an empty `employee` table. Use `assertNotNull()` to check if the result of `getEmployees()` is still `null`.

How it works...

The aspect class `ManageNullsDao` consists of two `@Around` advices which intercept the execution of `getEmployees()` and `getEmployee()` of `EmployeeDaoImpl`. It is not because of its before and after execution why this recipe chose `@Around` as the appropriate advice, but its capability to extract the return value of the adviced method. The `@Around` advice has an optional parameter, `ProceedingJoinPoint`, that controls the execution of the adviced method through its `proceed()` method. Calling `proceed()` is equivalent to executing `getEmployees()`, which will return a generic type Object. After the object has been retrieved, validation of whether it is `null` happens. Whatever the result of the validation is, the advice method aims to replace all `null` values so that any component executing `getEmployes()` or `getEmployee()` can avoid runtime exceptions.

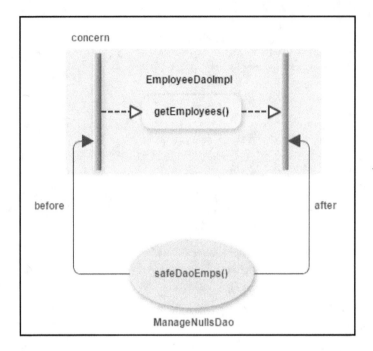

The preceding diagram shows how @Around wraps the adviced method and provides some implementation before and after the adviced method is executed.

Monitoring services and request handlers

Aspects has some trade-offs when used to intercept DAO transactions. Most often we use aspects to monitor services and @Controller transactions. This recipe will show us the easiest way to monitor service and request transactions using transaction management.

Getting started

Open ch05 and add an @Aspect that will monitor EmployeeController's deleteRecord() request handler and EmployeeServiceImpl's readEmployee() using a custom annotation.

How to do it...

After the DAO layer, let us monitor all service and `@Controller` request transactions by following these steps:

1. This is the first recipe that will showcase the use of custom transaction management annotations in formulating Pointcuts for advices. Using Reflection APIs, create the following method-level annotation inside the `org.packt.aop.transaction.annotation` package:

```
@Retention(RetentionPolicy.RUNTIME)
@Target(ElementType.METHOD)
public @interface MonitorService {   }
```

2. To make `@MonitorTransaction` transaction-aware, implement `org.springframework.transaction.PlatformTransactionManager` and place it inside `org.packt.aop.transaction.core`:

```
@Component
public class TransactionManager implements
    PlatformTransactionManager {

    @Override
     public void commit(TransactionStatus status)
       throws TransactionException { }
    @Override
    public TransactionStatus
       getTransaction(TransactionDefinition definition)
                   throws TransactionException {
           return new SimpleTransactionStatus();
     }
    @Override
    public void rollback(TransactionStatus status)
        throws TransactionException { }
}
```

3. Inject the custom `TransactionManager` bean into the `SpringContextConfig` container and extract `org.springframework.transaction.support.TransactionTemplate`, which will be used by the advices:

```
@Configuration
@EnableWebMvc
@EnableAspectJAutoProxy
@ComponentScan(basePackages = {"org.packt.aop.transaction",
"org.packt.aop.transaction.core",
```

```
    "org.packt.aop.transaction.annotation"})
public class SpringContextConfig {
    @Autowired
    private PlatformTransactionManager transactionManager;
    // refer to sources
    @Bean("template")
    TransactionTemplate transactionTemplate(){
        TransactionTemplate template =
            new TransactionTemplate();
        template.setTransactionManager(transactionManager);
        return template;

    }

}
```

4. Implement an aspect class that includes a Pointcut that filters all methods, that has @MonitorTransaction, and contains an advice that recognizes the custom annotation as the main trigger to execute some events with the help of TransactionManager:

```
@Component
@Aspect
public class MonitorServiceAspect {
    @Autowired
    private TransactionTemplate template;

    private Logger logger =
        Logger.getLogger(MonitorTransactionAspect.class);

    @Around("execution(* *(..)) && @annotation(monitor)")
    public void logIt(ProceedingJoinPoint pjp,
            MonitorService monitor) {
      template.execute(s->{
            try{
                Employee employee = (Employee)
                    pjp.proceed();
                logger.info(employee.getFirstName());
            } catch (Throwable ex) {
                throw new RuntimeException();
            }
            return null;
        });
    }

}
```

5. Apply now the preceding annotation to the `readEmployee()` method of
`EmployeeServiceImpl`:

```
@Service
public class EmployeeServiceImpl implements EmployeeService {
    @Autowired
    private EmployeeDao employeeDaoImpl;

    @MonitorService
    @Override
    public Employee readEmployee(@NegativeArgs
        Integer empId) {
            return employeeDaoImpl.getEmployee(empId);
    }

    // refer to sources
}
```

6. Create another custom annotation, `@MonitorRequest`, using *step 1* to *step 5*.
   Implement also a `MonitorRequestAspect` that will use the annotation to trigger
   a logging event for the `deleteRecord()` handler of `EmployeeController`:

```
@Component
@Aspect
public class MonitorRequestAspect {
    @Autowired
      private TransactionTemplate template;

    private Logger logger =
        Logger.getLogger(MonitorRequestAspect.class);

    @Around("execution(* *(..)) && @annotation(monitor)")
    public void logIt(ProceedingJoinPoint pjp,
        MonitorRequest monitor) {
      String methodName = pjp.getSignature().getName();
      template.execute(s->{
            try{
                logger.info("executing request handler: " +
                    methodName);
            } catch (Throwable ex) {
                    throw new RuntimeException();
            }
            return null;
        });
    }
}
```

7. Save all files. Then `clean`, `install`, and `deploy` the project. Check `ch05.log` to verify the result.

How it works...

Aspects can monitor and control `@Transactional` methods by including `org.springframework.transaction.annotation.Transactional` in its Pointcuts. But `@Transactional` can only be applied to methods that require Spring transaction management such as JPA and Hibernate transactions. For general-purpose methods, a custom transaction-aware annotation must be applied in order for aspects to monitor them.

The class `org.springframework.transaction.PlatformTransactionManager` is used to implement a general transaction management solution to general bean classes or methods. Together with `@Aspect` classes, customizing transactions becomes easy by extracting `TransactionTemplate` from `PlatformTransactionManager`.

The transactional behavior is executed by the `execute ()` method of `TransactionTemplate`, which is realized by the advices of the `@Aspect` that monitors the methods with the help of custom annotation. The inclusion of the custom annotation in its Pointcut triggers the execution of the advice whenever the transaction is executed.

This programmatic style of implementing transaction management is always applied to the service layer. Monitoring secured services can also be done by applying this recipe.

Validating parameters and arguments

Custom annotations can also be aspects to validate if arguments passed to `@Service` methods are appropriate or not. The following recipe will use AOP paradigms to intercept parameter passing.

Getting started

Open `ch05` and add an `@Aspect` that will utilize custom annotation to validate the employee ID parameter of the `readEmployee()` service method of `TransactionTemplate`.

How to do it...

Let us now perform validation on method arguments by doing the following steps:

1. This recipe will start with the creation of a class-level annotation which is not a transactional type, just like in the previous recipe. Using again the Reflection API, implement an annotation that will be used by an @Aspect to intercept parameter passing.

```
@Retention(RetentionPolicy.RUNTIME)
@Target(ElementType.PARAMETER)
public @interface NegativeArgs { }
```

2. Since a valid employee ID is a positive number, create an aspect that will validate if the empId argument passed onto readEmployee() of EmployeeServiceImpl is a non-negative number, using the custom annotation @NegativeArgs:

```
@Component
@Aspect
public class NegativeArgsAspect {
    private Logger logger =
        Logger.getLogger(NegativeArgsAspect.class);
    @Pointcut("execution(*
    *(@org.packt.aop.transaction.annotation.NegativeArgs
    (*), ..))")
    protected void myPointcut() {
    }
    @AfterThrowing(pointcut = "myPointcut() && args(empId)",
        throwing = "e")
    public void afterThrowingException(JoinPoint joinPoint,
            Exception e, Integer empId) {
        if(empId < 0){
            logger.info("cannot be negative number");
        }
    }

    @AfterReturning(pointcut = "myPointcut() &&
        args(empId)")
    public void afterSuccessfulReturn(JoinPoint joinPoint,
            Integer empId) {
        if(empId < 0){
            logger.info("cannot be negative number");
        }
    }
}
```

3. Apply the annotation to the `readEmployee()` of `EmployeeServiceImpl`:

```
@MonitorService
@Override
public Employee readEmployee(@NegativeArgs Integer
    empId) {
        return employeeDaoImpl.getEmployee(empId);
}
```

4. Inside the test class `TestEmployeeService`, create a test method that will trigger the validation:

```
@Test
public void testReadEmpMonitor(){
  Employee emp = employeeServiceImpl.readEmployee(-11);
}
```

How it works...

This recipe offers a defensive way of validating any method's arguments during its execution. Using a typical custom annotation, aspects can validate any arguments in any methods, throw an `Exception`, or replace the value with some defaults at runtime.

Aggressive use of aspects in validating arguments can cause unexpected runtime errors or the degradation of software performance.

Managing exceptions

Spring 5.0 has built-in API classes such as `HandlerExceptionResolver` and `@AdviceController` to handle `@Controller` exceptions, but this recipe will create another way to manage exceptions through an improvised handler implemented using the AOP paradigm.

Getting started

Open `ch05` and add another aspect component that will monitor all methods of `EmployeeServiceImpl` and will catch all types of exceptions once encountered.

How to do it...

Let us improvise exception handling using AOP concepts by doing these steps:

1. Just like in the previous recipe, verify if `Employee` models classes and its service implementations are in their respective packages. We will still be using the `Jdbctemplate`-based CRUD transactions.

2. Other than transactions, `@Aspect` can also be used to trace and log some exceptions. Let us now add an aspect named `ExceptionUpdateAspect` in the package `org.packt.aop.transaction.core` that will contain two `@AfterThrowing` advices, namely `logExceptionUpdateEmp()`, which will be triggered once the `updateEmployee()` method encounters an `Exception`, and `logExceptionEmployee()`, which is applied to all of the methods in `EmployeeServiceImpl`:

```
@Component
@Aspect
public class ExceptionUpdateAspect {
  private Logger logger =
      Logger.getLogger(ExceptionUpdateAspect.class);
  @AfterThrowing(pointcut="execution(*
  org.packt.aop.transaction
  .service.impl.EmployeeServiceImpl.updateEmployee(..))
  && args(empForm,id)", throwing = "e")
  public void logExceptionUpdateEmp(JoinPoint joinPoint,
    EmployeeForm empForm, int id, Throwable e)
      throws Throwable {
      // refer to sources
  }
  @AfterThrowing(pointcut="within(org.packt.aop.transaction
  .service.impl.EmployeeServiceImpl)", throwing = "e")
  public void logExceptionEmployee(JoinPoint joinPoint,
    Throwable e) throws Throwable {
      // refer to sources
  }
}
```

3. Execute the `TestEmployeeService` and test the `updateEmployee()` method.

How it works...

The @AfterThrowing advice methods are only executed when an **exception** is thrown by the adviced methods in the EmployeeServiceImpl. adviced methods are not required to implement try-catch or throw exceptions for @AfterThrowing to be valid. Once any concerned method encounters an exception, @AfterThrowing will be triggered following the capture of the Exception object through its throwing attribute. There are possibilities that some of the advices will not be performed due to the execution of @AfterThrowing.

Implementing the caching mechanism

Applying custom AOP to @Repository transactions must be used with caution because it might ruin the performance of the database CRUD transactions instead of improving them. All @Repository and @Transactional Spring components can be managed by built-in Spring aspects through generating a *Pointcut* such as execution(@org.springframework.transaction.annotation.Transactional * *(..)). Adding more custom aspects will, however, bring degradation to the DAO layer's performance. Aside from managing null values, @Repository only needs a custom @Aspect when caching large amounts of data records that are frequently accessed.

Object caching is one of the solutions that helps an application enhance its performance through storing into the memory all frequently accessed data from the database. Instead of incurring database READ overhead, caching will allow only the execution of a query transaction when its data is not yet saved in the memory. This recipe will create a custom aspect that will manage object caching.

Getting started

This recipe will be using Ehcache as the caching mechanism. The same project, ch05, will be used for this recipe.

How to do it...

Let us implement another way of object caching through these steps:

1. Aside from logging and auditing, aspects can also be used to trigger caching. To enable `Ehcache` in Spring 5.0, include the following Maven dependency in the `pom.xml`:

```
<dependency>
    <groupId>net.sf.ehcache</groupId>
    <artifactId>ehcache</artifactId>
    <version>3.3.1</version>
</dependency>
```

2. Define all the caches to be used by the application in an XML file named `ehcache.xml`. Place this configuration file in `src/main/resources`:

```
<?xml version="1.0" encoding="UTF-8"?>
<ehcache xmlns:xsi="http://www.w3.org/2001/XMLSchema-instance"
  xsi:noNamespaceSchemaLocation="ehcache.xsd"
  updateCheck="true"
  monitoring="autodetect"
  dynamicConfig="true">

  <diskStore path="C://ch05cached" />

  <cache name="employeesCache"
    maxEntriesLocalHeap="500"
    maxEntriesLocalDisk="500"
    eternal="false"
    diskSpoolBufferSizeMB="20"
    timeToIdleSeconds="300" timeToLiveSeconds="600"
    memoryStoreEvictionPolicy="LFU"
    transactionalMode="off">
    <persistence strategy="localTempSwap" />
  </cache>
</ehcache>
```

 If the operating system used is macOS or Linux, point `diskStore` to the desired folder location using the correct file system path.

3. Open the `SpringDispatcherConfig` in `org.packt.aop.transaction.dispatcher` and initialize the following `org.springframework.cache.ehcache.EhCacheManagerFactoryBean` and `org.springframework.cache.CacheManager` beans to the container:

```
import org.springframework.cache.CacheManager;
import org.springframework.cache.ehcache.EhCacheCacheManager;
import
org.springframework.cache.ehcache.EhCacheManagerFactoryBean;
// refer to sources
@EnableWebMvc
@ComponentScan(basePackages="org.packt.aop.transaction")
@PropertySource("classpath:config/jdbc.properties")
@Configuration
public class SpringDispatcherConfig extends
        WebMvcConfigurerAdapter{
@Inject
private ResourceLoader resourceLoader;

// refer to sources
  @Bean
  public CacheManager cacheManager(){
    CacheManager cm = new EhCacheCacheManager(
      ehCacheCacheManager().getObject());
    return cm;
  }

  @Bean
  public EhCacheManagerFactoryBean ehCacheCacheManager() {
    EhCacheManagerFactoryBean cmfb =
        new EhCacheManagerFactoryBean();
    cmfb.setConfigLocation(resourceLoader
      .getResource("classpath:ehcache.xml"));
    cmfb.setShared(true);
    return cmfb;
  }
}
```

4. Create an `@Aspect` that will intercept the `getEmployees()` method in `EmployeeDaoImpl` and will manage the caching of its return value, which is a `List<Employee>`:

```
import net.sf.ehcache.Cache;
import net.sf.ehcache.CacheManager;
import net.sf.ehcache.Element;
  // refer to sources
@Component
@Aspect
public class CacheListenerAspect {
  @Autowired
  private CacheManager cacheManager;
  private Logger logger =
    Logger.getLogger(CacheListenerAspect.class);
  @Around("execution(* org.packt.aop.transaction.dao
  .impl.EmployeeDaoImpl.getEmployees(..))")
  public Object cacheMonitor(ProceedingJoinPoint joinPoint)
    throws Throwable  {

    logger.info("executing " +
     joinPoint.getSignature().getName());
    Cache cache = cacheManager.getCache("employeesCache");
    logger.info("cache detected is  " + cache.getName());
    logger.info("begin caching.....");
    String key = joinPoint.getSignature().getName();
    logger.info(key);
    if(cache.get(key) == null){
      logger.info("caching new Object.....");
      Object result = joinPoint.proceed();
      cache.put(new Element(key, result));
      return result;
    }else{
      logger.info("getting cached Object.....");
      return cache.get(key).getObjectValue();
    }
  }
}
```

5. Save all files. Stop the Tomcat server first and then start it again due to cache installation. Then `clean`, `build`, and `deploy` the project.

How it works...

Spring 5.0 supports several cache implementations such as Gemfire, Guava Cache, and Ehcache. Since `Ehcache` is the most widely used type, this recipe injected `org.springframework.cache.ehcache.EhCacheCacheManager` to implement the `CacheManager` abstraction and instantiated `org.springframework.cache.ehcache.EhCacheManagerFactoryBean` to generate `net.sf.ehcache.Cache` into the `diskStore`. One of the caches named `employeesCache` is being utilized by the `CacheListenerAspect`, which intercepts the `getEmployees()` of the `EmployeeDaoImpl` class. This aspect class has an `@Around` advice named `cacheMonitor()` that caches always the first batch of `List<Employees>` data returned by `getEmployees()` in order to prevent the method from accessing the database again the next time it is executed by the application.

Although this solution is quite helpful and flexible, some developers still use `@EnableCaching`, the built-in Spring cache, to use Spring's popular annotations such as `@Cacheable` and `@CacheEvict`.

Intercepting request transactions

The previous chapter ended up with a recipe that used `HandlerInterceptor` and `HandlerInterceptorAdapter` as the mediums for handling incoming and outgoing request attributes and session data of any request handler in a `@Controller`, for security and transaction management purposes. This recipe will provide another option for how to mimic the functionality of these two Spring MVC API classes.

Getting started

Open the same project, ch05, and add a `@Controller` that will implement requests and responses for our employee login and menu transactions.

How to do it...

Aside from JEE **Filter** implementation, let us use aspect to intercept some request-response transactions:

1. Aside from implementing `Filter`, one obvious solution to monitor sessions during pre and post login transactions is to create interceptors. In the package `org.packt.aop.transaction.controller`, create a `LoginController` that will provide a login form and an employee list results page:

```
@Controller
public class LoginController {
  @Autowired
  private EmployeeService employeeServiceImpl;
  @RequestMapping(value="/login_emps.html",
      method=RequestMethod.GET)
  public String login(Model model, HttpServletRequest req){
    int browserNo = (Integer)
        req.getAttribute("browserNo");
    if(browserNo == 3){
      model.addAttribute("error", "Browser Not Supported");
      return "browser_error";
    }
    return "login";
  }
  @RequestMapping(value="/login_emps.html",
      method=RequestMethod.POST)
  public ModelAndView loginSubmit(ModelMap model,
    @RequestParam("username") String username,
    @RequestParam("password") String password){

    // refer to sources
    return new
        ModelAndView("redirect:/menu_emps.html",model);
  }
  @RequestMapping(value="/menu_emps.html",
      method=RequestMethod.GET)
  public String menu(Model model, HttpServletRequest req){
    List<Employee> emps =
        employeeServiceImpl.readEmployees();
    model.addAttribute("emps", emps);
    return "menu";
  }
  @RequestMapping(value="/empty_login.html",
      method=RequestMethod.GET)
  public String emptylogin(){
      // refer to sources
```

```
    }
    @RequestMapping(value="/browser_error.html",
        method=RequestMethod.GET)
    public String browserError(){
        // refer to sources
    }
}
```

2. Create an `@Aspect` class that will intercept `/login_emps.html` in processing the incoming `HttpServletRequest`. The class will filter and check the browser type of the user and will trigger the `/browser_error.html` page if the application is accessed through Internet Explorer:

```
@Component
@Aspect
public class LoginProxyAspect {
    private Logger logger =
        Logger.getLogger(LoginProxyAspect.class);
    @Pointcut("within(@org.springframework
    .stereotype.Controller *))")
    public void classPointcut() {  }
    @Pointcut("execution(*
    org.packt.aop.transaction.controller
    .LoginController.login(..))")
    public void loginPointcut() {  }
    @Before("classPointcut() && loginPointcut()
    && args(model,req) && @annotation(mapping)")
    public String browserCheck(JoinPoint joinPoint,
        Model model, HttpServletRequest req,
      RequestMapping mapping) throws ServletException,
        IOException{
        logger.info("executing " +
            joinPoint.getSignature().getName());
        logger.warn("MVC application trying to
check browser type...");
        String loginRequestMethod =
            mapping.method()[0].name();
        String username = req.getParameter("username");
        String password = req.getParameter("password");
        req.setAttribute("username", username);
        req.setAttribute("password", password);
        logger.info("executing " +
            joinPoint.getSignature().getName() + " which is a "
            + loginRequestMethod + " request");
        if(loginRequestMethod.equalsIgnoreCase("GET")){
            Enumeration<String> headers =
                req.getHeaderNames();
```

```
while(headers.hasMoreElements()){
String headerName = headers.nextElement();
if(headerName.equalsIgnoreCase("user-agent")){
    String browserType =
        req.getHeader(headerName);
    if(browserType.contains("Chrome")){
        req.setAttribute("browserNo", 1);
        logger.info("MVC application uses
            Chrome...");
    }else if (browserType.contains("Firefox")){
        req.setAttribute("browserNo", 2);
        logger.info("MVC application uses
            Firefox...");
    }else{
        req.setAttribute("browserNo", 3);
        logger.info("MVC appstops...");
    }
    break;
}
}
}
return "login";
}
}
```

3. Save all files. Then `clean`, `build`, and `deploy` the ch05 project.

How it works...

In this scenario, the appropriate advice that will retrieve all the request headers of the incoming request for /login_emps.html is the @Before advice. The aspect class LoginProxyAspect intercepts the incoming request to retrieve the user-agent header in order to prohibit all transactions from running on Internet Explorer. After detecting the type of browser, the browserCheck() advice creates a request attribute, browserNo, for the /login_emps.html to know what browser typed was used.

Another highlight of this recipe is the use of the @Pointcut annotation. @Pointcut is used when creating an independent rule for join points to be applied anywhere within the aspect class. Usually, when the Pointcut expression gets complicated, we use the @Pointcut annotation to simplify and break down the expression to simple terms. For the annotation to run correctly, it must be defined by a void method without any implementation at all, such as the loginPointcut() and classPointcut() of LoginProxyAspect.

The interception process is configured by the join point rules of `loginPointcut()` and `classPointcut()`. The former includes all the `login()` methods in `LoginController` with any local parameter values and return values, while the latter monitors all the `@Controller` class transactions. `@Pointcut` can limit the *concerns* to controllers just by invoking the `@` symbol together with the package of the `@Controller` annotation interface. In usual cases, the `within` command tells advices to include all methods inside a package (for example, `within(org.packt.aop.transaction.controller)`) or sub-packages (for example, `within(org.packt.aop.transaction..*)`). The interception will not be complete without the `@annotation`, which limits our *concerns* to only the request hander defined by `@RequestMapping`.

This recipe has `browserCheck()` advice that intercepts the `@Controller` request handler method, named login, without any restriction on the local parameters and return value.

Implementing user authentication

Although Spring Security is the most straightforward and easy solution for securing any Spring MVC applications, software designers always need the option of customizing the authentication procedure for non-complex and small-scale security requirements. This recipe will provide the solution for how to use `@Aspect` and advices in implementing security modules.

Getting started

Open `ch05` and add the following `@Aspect` to the `loginSubmit()` request handler of `EmployeeController`.

How to do it...

Let us create a custom login interceptor that validates the user's credentials using database authentication:

1. This recipe uses aspects to pre- and post-validate user credentials using the authentication services provided by the previous recipes. Create an aspect class, `LoginAuthAspect`, which contains the following `@Pointcut` definitions and a `Log4J` logger:

```
@Component
@Aspect
public class LoginAuthAspect {
  private Logger logger =
      Logger.getLogger(LoginAuthAspect.class);
  @Autowired
  private LoginService loginServiceImpl;
  @Pointcut("within(@org.springframework.stereotype
  .Controller *)")
  public void classPointcut() { }
  @Pointcut("execution(*
  org.packt.aop.transaction.controller
  .LoginController.loginSubmit(..))")
   public void loginSubmitPointcut() { }

}
```

2. Inside the @Aspect class, implement a @Before advice that will intercept loginSubmit(), verify if the transaction is POST, and audit the username and password that tried to log in to the application:

```
@Before("classPointcut() && loginSubmitPointcut() &&
@annotation(mapping)")
public void registerParams(JoinPoint joinPoint,
    RequestMapping mapping) throws ServletException,
        IOException{

    HttpServletRequest req = ((ServletRequestAttributes)
    RequestContextHolder.getRequestAttributes())
        .getRequest();
    logger.info("executing " +
    joinPoint.getSignature().getName());
    String loginRequestMethod = mapping.method()[0].name();
    logger.info("executing " +
      joinPoint.getSignature().getName() + " which is a "
        + loginRequestMethod + " request");
    if(loginRequestMethod.equalsIgnoreCase("POST")){
    String username =  req.getParameter("username");
    String password =  req.getParameter("password");
    logger.warn("MVC application detected access from
      user: " + username + " with password: " + password );
  }
}
```

3. The next advice is `authCredentials()`, which is an `@After` advice that will evaluate further the user credentials based on what is recorded in the `employee` table. The advice will just generate a `Boolean` session attribute, `authenticated`, which will be set to `true` if the user is a valid one based on `SimpleJdbcInsert` and `JdbcTemplate`:

```
@After("classPointcut() && loginSubmitPointcut() &&
@annotation(mapping)")
public void authCredentials(JoinPoint joinPoint,
    RequestMapping mapping) throws ServletException,
        IOException{

    HttpServletRequest req = ((ServletRequestAttributes)
    RequestContextHolder.getRequestAttributes())
        .getRequest();
    logger.info("executing " +
    joinPoint.getSignature().getName());
    String loginRequestMethod = mapping.method()[0].name();
    logger.info("executing " +
    joinPoint.getSignature().getName() + " which is a "
        + loginRequestMethod + " request");
    if(loginRequestMethod.equalsIgnoreCase("POST")){
        String username =
            (String)req.getParameter("username");
        String password =
(String) req.getParameter("password");
        AccountLogin access =
         loginServiceImpl.getUserAccount(username.trim());
        req.getSession().setAttribute("authenticated",
         false);
        if(access != null){
            if(access.getPassword()
.equalsIgnoreCase(password.trim())){
            logger.info("user " + username +" with
                password " + password + " valid");
            req.getSession().setAttribute("authenticated",
true);
            req.getSession().setAttribute("userId",
                access.getId());
            }else{
    req.getSession().setAttribute("authenticated",
                false);
            }
        }
    }
}
```

4. Save all files. Then `clean`, `build`, and `deploy` the project.

How it works...

Obviously, this recipe is a flexible type of implementation and everyone can modify this recipe given their own set of login scenarios. But one thing is for sure, AOP can establish database connections using Spring JDBC. Moreover, advices can also verify the HTTP request type of an adviced method. In the case of `loginSubmit()`, both advice methods check first if the incoming transactions are `POST` ones.

If there is a need to extract the `HttpServletRequest`, it is not necessary to alter the local parameters of the advices and the *concerns*. The best way is to use `org.springframework.web.context.request.RequestContextHolder` to retrieve the `HttpServletRequest` object and `org.springframework.web.context.request.ServletWebRequest` for the `HttpServleResponse` object:

```
HttpServletRequest req = ((ServletRequestAttributes)
RequestContextHolder.getRequestAttributes()).getRequest();
ServletWebRequest servletWebRequest=new ServletWebRequest(req);
HttpServletResponse response=servletWebRequest.getResponse();
```

Accessing with restrictions

If we can use AOP to customize the user authentication process, we can also use it to establish the access control list and authorization rules.

Getting started

Given the roles, permissions, and permission sets of Chapter 4, *Securing Spring MVC Applications*, this recipe will implement the record deletion of employee records to `ROLE_HR` only. Open the Maven Eclipse `ch05` project, and add the following features.

How to do it...

Let us simulate Spring Security's authorization process by using AOP concepts:

1. Although authorization can be implemented using the Spring Security framework, this recipe will provide us with another solution using AOP concepts. Inside the package `org.packt.aop.transaction.controller`, create an `EmployeeController` which will delete a record given an `empId` detail:

```
@Controller
public class EmployeeController {
  @Autowired
  private EmployeeService employeeServiceImpl;
  @RequestMapping("/deldept.html/{deptId}")
  public String deleteRecord(Model model,
    @PathVariable("deptId") Integer deptId){
    employeeServiceImpl.delEmployee(deptId);
    model.addAttribute("emps",
        employeeServiceImpl.readEmployees());
    return "menu";
  }
}
```

2. Modify the view page `/menu_emps.html` to include the DELETE transaction for every record, as shown in the following screenshot:

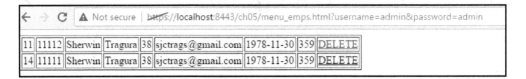

3. Now, create an `@Aspect` class that will intercept the `deleteRecord()` request handler of `EmployeeController` to filter the user permissions of the currently logged in user. Once the user clicks DELETE, the advice method will be triggered to allow the deletion only if the user has ROLE_HR; otherwise, a redirection to `/banned.html` will occur:

```
@Component
@Aspect
public class DeleteAuthorizeAspect {
    private Logger logger =
        Logger.getLogger(DeleteAuthorizeAspect.class);
```

```
@Autowired
private LoginService loginServiceImpl;
@Pointcut("within(@org.springframework.stereotype
.Controller *))")
public void classPointcut() {  }
@Pointcut("execution(*
org.packt.aop.transaction.controller
.EmployeeController.deleteRecord(..))")
public void delPointcut() {  }
@Around("classPointcut() && delPointcut()
&& @annotation(mapping)")
public String delEmployee(ProceedingJoinPoint joinPoint,
   RequestMapping mapping) throws Throwable{

  HttpServletRequest req = ((ServletRequestAttributes)
  RequestContextHolder.getRequestAttributes())
    .getRequest();
  logger.info("executing " +
    joinPoint.getSignature().getName());
  int userId = (Integer)req.getSession()
    .getAttribute("userId");
  System.out.println("userId" + userId);
  List<RolePermission> permission =
    loginServiceImpl.getPermissionSets(userId);
  if(isAuthroize(permission)){
  logger.info("user " + userId
    + " is authorized to delete");
  joinPoint.proceed();
    return "menu";
  }else{
   logger.info("user " + userId + " is NOT authorized to
      delete");
   return "banned";
  }
}

private boolean isAuthroize(List<RolePermission>
   permission){
  Set<String> userRoles = new HashSet<>();
  Set<String> userPerms = new HashSet<>();
  // refer to sources

  if(userRoles.contains("ROLE_HR")){
     return true;
  }
  return false;
}
}
```

4. Save all files. Then `clean`, `build`, and `deploy` the project.

How it works...

If in `Chapter 4`, *Securing Spring MVC Applications*, we used `UserService` to create the `User` object containing the `GrantedAuthority`. This chapter provided us with another mechanism to implement and utilize the access control rules of the application through an `@Around` advice. The first thing `DeleteAuthorizeAspect` does is extract the session attribute `userId` generated by the `LoginAuthAspect` of the previous recipe. At this point, aspects can interact with each other using session and request attributes. Now, after retrieving the `empId` of the currently logged in user, the `delEmployee()` advice will query the permission sets assigned to the user through `LoginServiceImpl`. The advice will only permit the deletion if one of the roles confirmed is `ROLE_HR`, otherwise this page will be shown on the screen:

Controlling concurrent user access

Concurrent access control can also be feasible in AOP since we can improvise the authentication process through the `@Aspect` interception. If aspects can communicate with each other through session attributes, we can utilize the existing session of the application to count the number of user accesses per account.

Getting started

Update `LoginAuthAspect` in order to manage the number of allowable user access privileges an account can utilize.

How to do it...

Without using Spring Security, let us simulate concurrent user control by using AOP and following these steps:

1. Create a @Bean of Map type that will hold all usernames that are currently logged in to the application. Inject this Map in SpringContextConfig:

```
Configuration
@EnableWebMvc
@EnableAspectJAutoProxy
@ComponentScan(basePackages="org.packt.aop.transaction")
public class SpringContextConfig {
  @Bean
  public Map<String,Integer> authStore(){
    return new HashMap<>();
  }
}
```

2. Update the authCredentials() advice method of LoginAuthAspect to include the validation of the total number of open accesses a current user has:

```
@After("classPointcut() && loginSubmitPointcut()
&& @annotation(mapping)")
public void authCredentials(JoinPoint joinPoint,
    RequestMapping mapping) throws ServletException,
      IOException{

  HttpServletRequest req =
    ((ServletRequestAttributes)RequestContextHolder
     .getRequestAttributes()).getRequest();
  logger.info("executing " +
    joinPoint.getSignature().getName());
  String loginRequestMethod = mapping.method()[0].name();
  logger.info("executing " +
    joinPoint.getSignature().getName()
    + " which is a " + loginRequestMethod + " request");
  if(loginRequestMethod.equalsIgnoreCase("POST")){
  String username =  (String)req.getParameter("username");
  String password = (String) req.getParameter("password");
  AccountLogin access =
    loginServiceImpl.getUserAccount(username.trim());
  req.getSession().setAttribute("authenticated", false);
  if(access != null){
   if(access.getPassword().equalsIgnoreCase(
     password.trim())){
      logger.info("user " + username +" with password "
```

```
                              + password + " valid");
                    if(authStore.containsKey(username)){
                        if(authStore.get(username) == 2){
                            logger.info("user " + username +" with password "
                                + password + " is already logged in");
                            req.getSession().setAttribute("authenticated",
                                false);
                        }else{
                            int numSess = authStore.get(username);
                            authStore.put(username, ++numSess);
                            req.getSession().setAttribute("authenticated",
                                true);
                            req.getSession().setAttribute("userId",
                            access.getId());
                        }
                    }else{
                        authStore.put(username, 1);
                        req.getSession().setAttribute("authenticated", true);
                        req.getSession().setAttribute("userId",
                        access.getId());
                    }
                }
            }
        }
    }
}
```

In this recipe, a user is only allowed to open up to two accounts of the same username, otherwise, the user will be redirected to the /login_emps.html.

3. Save all files. Then clean, build, and deploy the updated ch05 project.

How it works...

Although there are so many ways, this recipe used a java.util.Map as a global authStore for usernames which is accessed always by LoginAuthAspect to check whether a certain account is currently using the application. If the valid user has not accessed the session at all, it will be registered into the store with one as the number of currently open accounts. Once the same user successfully logs in to the application using another browser, the advice will check first if the number of open accesses is less than two, otherwise, the user will be redirected to /login_emps.html. Now, aside from checking the existence of the user in the database, the @Around advice authCredentials() will limit the privilege of the user given a maximum number of allowable accesses per account.

Implementing a mini-workflow using AOP

Unlike HandlerInterceptor, this chapter has proven that the AOP paradigm is the best mechanism for creating modules that can intercept requests, services, data transactions, security modules, and cache providers. Given the correct *concerns* and delineation of tasks, a set of @Aspect classes can optimize the modularity of the MVC application, which enhances the core features of the application. This last recipe will create a simple web application that will simulate a document rendition workflow based on popular enterprise records and document management systems, such as *Alfresco*.

Getting started

Let us create a new Maven project, ch05-wf, to replicate the setup and configuration done in the previous project. Given all the different types of advices and @Pointcut definitions, we need to implement the following high-level activity diagram from scratch using AOP principle and Spring MVC concepts:

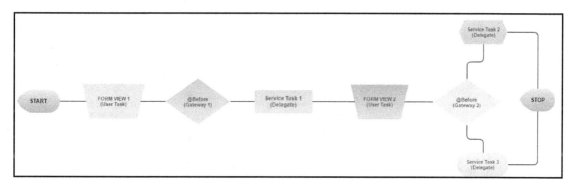

How to do it...

To summarize the whole concept of AOP, let us simulate a mini-workflow design which uses Spring AOP concepts:

1. Although Spring 5 can still support BPMN 2.0, it has another way to simulate a workflow of transactions using aspects. Let us define all user task executors as Spring form @Controller requests. userTask1 will ask what type of *rendition type* the actor wants all the information to be saved as, and userTask2 will ask for the *email type* the user wants the generated document to be sent as:

```
@Controller
public class UserTaskController {
    @RequestMapping("/wf/start.html")
    public RedirectView renderUserTask(Model model){
        String renditionType = "pdf";
        model.addAttribute("renditionType", renditionType);
        return new RedirectView("/wf/approval.html",true);
    }
    @RequestMapping("/wf/approval.html")
    public RedirectView emailUserTask(Model model){
        String notificationType = "yahoo";
        model.addAttribute("notificationType",
          notificationType);
        return new RedirectView("/wf/end.html",true);
    }
    @ResponseBody
    @RequestMapping("/wf/end.html")
    public String stopActivity(){
        return "done";
    }
}
```

2. Workflow events will be implemented using AOP and must be placed inside a org.packt.aop.workflow.core package. The startEvent will be implemented by the StartEventAspect that simply provides the initial notification that the workflow has started:

```
@Component
@Aspect
public class StartEventAspect {
    private Logger logger =
      Logger.getLogger(StartEventAspect.class);
    @Pointcut("within(@org.springframework.stereotype
    .Controller *)")
    public void classPointcut() {}
```

```
@Pointcut ("execution (*
org.packt.aop.workflow.controller.UserTaskController
.renderUserTask (..)) ")
public void taskPointcut () {}
@Before ("classPointcut () && taskPointcut ()   &&
@annotation (mapping)")
public void sequence (JoinPoint joinPoint,
    RequestMapping mapping) throws Throwable{
       logger.info ("starting rendition workflow....");
    }
}
```

3. After providing the rendition type to the `renderUserTask ()` request, the first
    transaction event will be triggered, the `RenderEventAspect`. This will execute
    the process to convert all unstructured data to either PDF, XLS, or RTF format:

```
@Component
@Aspect
public class RenderEventAspect {
    @Autowired
    private RenderDelegate renderDelegate;

    @Pointcut ("within (@org.springframework.stereotype
    .Controller *)")
    public void classPointcut () {}
    @Pointcut ("execution (*
org.packt.aop.workflow.controller.UserTaskController.emailUserT
ask (..)) ")
    public void taskPointcut () {}
    @Before ("classPointcut () && taskPointcut ()   &&
    @annotation (mapping)")
    public void sequence (JoinPoint joinPoint, RequestMapping
        mapping) throws Throwable{
           HttpServletRequest req =
((ServletRequestAttributes) RequestContextHolder.getRequestAttri
butes ()).getRequest ();
           String rendetionTyupe =
(String) req.getParameter ("renditionType");
           if (rendetionTyupe.equalsIgnoreCase ("pdf")) {
              renderDelegate.callRenderPDFservice ();
           } else if (rendetionTyupe.equalsIgnoreCase ("xls")) {
              renderDelegate.callRenderXLSservice ();
           } else if (rendetionTyupe.equalsIgnoreCase ("rtf")) {
              renderDelegate.callRenderRTFservice ();
           }
       }
    }
}
```

4. Then, workflow will execute the `emailUserTask()` request which will ask for the email type where the document will be forwarded. After providing either **GMAIL** or **YAHOO**, the `NotificationEventAspect` will be triggered to execute the email transaction:

```
@Component
@Aspect
public class NotificationEventAspect {
    @Autowired
    private NotificationDelegate notificationDelegate;
    @Pointcut("within(@org.springframework.stereotype
    .Controller *)")
    public void classPointcut() {}
    @Pointcut("execution(*
    org.packt.aop.workflow.controller.UserTaskController
    .stopActivity(..))")
    public void taskPointcut() {}
    @Before("classPointcut() && taskPointcut()  &&
    @annotation(mapping)")
    public void sequence(JoinPoint joinPoint, RequestMapping
        mapping) throws Throwable{
            HttpServletRequest req =
              ((ServletRequestAttributes)RequestContextHolder
                .getRequestAttributes()).getRequest();
          String notificationType =
              req.getParameter("notificationType");
          if(notificationType.equalsIgnoreCase("yahoo")){
            notificationDelegate.sendYahooDocs();
          }else if(notificationType
              .equalsIgnoreCase("gmail")){
            notificationDelegate.sendGmailDocs();
          }
    }
}
```

5. The workflow will culminate by triggering the `EndEventAspect`:

```
@Component
@Aspect
public class EndEventAspect {
    private Logger logger =
    Logger.getLogger(EndEventAspect.class);
    @Pointcut("within(@org.springframework.stereotype
    .Controller *)")
    public void classPointcut() {}
    @Pointcut("execution(*
    org.packt.aop.workflow.controller.UserTaskController
```

```
        .stopActivity(..))")
        public void taskPointcut() {}
        @After("classPointcut() && taskPointcut()    &&
        @annotation(mapping)")
        public void sequence(JoinPoint joinPoint, RequestMapping
            mapping) throws Throwable{
            logger.info("end of rendition workflow....");
        }
    }
```

6. The delegates or services will be executed by the events to perform the necessary rendition algorithms and email notification. All delegates will be placed inside the org.packt.aop.workflow.delegate package:

```
@Component
public class RenderDelegate {
    private Logger logger =
Logger.getLogger(RenderDelegate.class);
    public void callRenderPDFservice(){
        logger.info("converting data to PDF format...");
    }
     public void callRenderRTFservice(){
        logger.info("converting data to RTF format...");
    }
     public void callRenderXLSservice(){
        logger.info("converting data to XLS format...");
    }
}

@Component
public class NotificationDelegate {
    private Logger logger =
Logger.getLogger(NotificationDelegate.class);
    public void sendGmailDocs(){
        logger.info("sending docs to GMAIL...");
    }
    public void sendYahooDocs(){
        logger.info("sending docs to YAHOO...");
    }
}
```

7. Controllers will determine the *gateway paths* of the workflow.
8. Create some additional @Aspect for logging, small-scale security rules, and custom caching for frequently retrieved objects.
9. Save all files. Then clean, deploy, and install ch05-wf and run the first activity task.

How it works...

In a BPMN 2.0 workflow design, a gateway is used to manage the flow of execution and is also capable of executing services needed to generate output. In a customized workflow, AOP can be used as a gateway protocol, wherein it can determine the request flow after every user task. Some @Aspect classes can have heavy implementation and some may have lighter tasks depending on the workflow specifications. By knowing the repercussions of using AOP in creating software, designers can avoid overlaps and gaps between *concerns* and advices. Also, @Aspect implementation must not cause degradation to the performance of the application; thus, it must focus on the lighter concerns of the specification.

6
Functional Programming

One of the main reasons why Spring 5.0's framework was created is to fully integrate functional programming when implementing the asynchronous web framework. The so-called functional web framework has a reactive core that has its own annotation, interfaces, and classes for handling requests. Thus, to fully understand reactive programming in Spring is to know the core platform of Java functional programming.

The main idea of functional programming is to build a set of definitions to evaluate computer instructions. Each definition is a concise, single, and atomic expression that calls another occurrence of expressions which, collectively, can give a simplified result. Although functional programming is an old programming methodology based on mathematical principles, it is now being integrated in Java for the purposes of creating a transition from an imperative way of programming to a more reduced, clear, agile and robust style of coding. But aside from the tangible improvements it can give to Spring, functional programming can help developers focus on the problems instead of spending so much time on implementing complex and cluttered low-level implementations.

This chapter will introduce a new face of Java that can be used to solve synchronous and asynchronous Spring web projects.

In this chapter, you will learn the following:

- Implementing lambda expressions using anonymous inner classes
- Creating lambda expressions using @FunctionalInterface
- Building the built-in functional interfaces
- Applying method and constructor references
- Using the Stream API
- Applying streams to collections
- Applying streams to NIO 2.0
- Using parallel streams

Implementing lambda expressions using anonymous inner classes

The implementation of functional programming principles in Java has started with the use of anonymous inner classes. Starting with Java 1.7, an abstract method of a certain interface now can be implemented using anonymous inner classes, and even without using the **implements** keyword, given that it has only one abstract method.

Getting started

Create an Eclipse Maven project, ch06, and pattern the Maven configurations from the previous chapter's pom.xml. Copy the previous SpringContextConfig, SpringDbConfig, SpringDispatcherConfig, and SpringWebinitializer and place them inside their new respective packages under the org.packt.functional.codes core package. Update the DispatcherServlet configuration details and all the copied context definition classes to set up the new project. Reuse also the Employee model and DAO classes used previously.

How to do it...

Functional programming in Java can be illustrated by an interface with one abstract method. Let us now showcase functional programming in Java by doing these steps:

1. Let us create a typical EmployeeRecord interface in org.packt.function.codes.service. The interface has only one method, as follows:

    ```
    public interface EmployeeRecord {
        public Employee getServiceRecord(Integer empid);
    }
    ```

2. Afterwards, implement EmployeeRecord using an *anonymous inner class*:

    ```
    @Service("employeeService")
    public class EmployeeServiceImpl {
      @Autowired
      private EmployeeDao employeeDaoImpl;
      public Employee getEmployee(Integer empid){
        EmployeeRecord emp = new EmployeeRecord(){
    ```

```
@Override
public Employee getServiceRecord(Integer empid) {
  Iterator<Employee> iterate =
    employeeDaoImpl.getEmployees().iterator();
  while(iterate.hasNext()){
    Employee e = iterate.next();
    if(e.getEmpId().equals(empid)){
      return e;
    }
  }
  return new Employee();
}
};
  return emp.getServiceRecord(empid);
  }
}
```

3. In `src\test\java`, create a test class, `TestEmployeeService`, to test the `getEmployee()` service method:

```
@RunWith(SpringJUnit4ClassRunner.class)
@WebAppConfiguration
@ContextConfiguration(classes = { SpringDbConfig.class,
    SpringDispatcherConfig.class })
public class TestEmployeeService {
  @Autowired
  private EmployeeServiceImpl employeeService;

  @Test
  public void testEmployeeRec(){
    Employee emp = employeeService.getEmployee(11111);
    System.out.format("%s \n", emp.getFirstName());
  }
}
```

How it works...

Lambda expression is the sole reason why functional programming is now natively supported in Java. Some languages name lambda expression as a closure or anonymous method, but all these terms refer to only one concept and that is *animosity in implementation*. Lambda is independent of any class surrounding it and can be returned as an object that may vary from one instance to another. It is defined by the parameters and returned values of the abstract method assigned to a particular interface.

A custom implementation of lambda becomes possible with the use of anonymous inner classes. Anonymous inner classes use *overriding* techniques in order to implement the interface method. Java 1.7 allows for a `Runnable` interface to be implemented using lambda:

```
Runnable job = new Runnable(){
  @Override
  public void run() {
    // Transactions
  }
};
```

Likewise, the `Comparator` interface used to compare a `String`, `array`, or `List` can also be instantiated in this manner:

```
Comparator<String> compareTool = new Comparator<String>(){
    @Override
    public int compare(String o1, String o2) {
      return 0;
    }
};
```

Implementing lambda expression using @FunctionInterface

Java 1.8 has formalized the lambda expression implementation through the use of the `@FunctionalInterface` annotation and the inclusion of the new specification on anonymous functions. This recipe will open a new technique in creating lambda expression.

Getting started

Using the same Eclipse project and `EmployeeServiceImpl`, add the needed service methods using `@FunctionInterface` components.

How to do it...

Many of the API classes in Java 1.8 use functional interfaces to simplify service implementation by applying the principles of functional programming. To illustrate what functional programming is, let us implement the following steps:

1. Create another version of the `EmployeeRecord` interface of the previous recipe that uses the `@FunctionalInterface` annotation:

```
@FunctionalInterface
public interface EmployeeRecordService {
  public List<Employee> getEmployees();
}
```

2. Also in `org.packt.function.codes.service`, create a functional interface that highlights a method with parameters:

```
@FunctionalInterface
public interface ComputeSalaryIncrease {
  public double increase(double current, double increase);

  default public double demote(double current, double
      decrease){
    return current - (0.2*decrease);
  }
  static public double rateAppraisal(double current){
    return current * 0.2;
  }
}
```

3. Open `EmployeeServiceImpl` and create `getEmployees()` that implements `EmployeeRecordService`:

```
public List<Employee> getEmployees(){
    EmployeeRecordService employees =
       ()->{ return employeeDaoImpl.getEmployees();  };
    return employees.getEmployees();
}
```

4. Adding the method `updateSalary()` under that will implement `ComputeSalaryIncrease`:

```
public double updateSalary(double current, double
    increase){

    ComputeSalaryIncrease salaryInc = (currSal, inc)->{
```

```
double proRate = currSal + (inc *0.2);
return proRate;
    };
return salaryInc.increase(current, increase);
}
```

5. Open `TestEmployeeService` and add the following test methods:

```
@Test
public void testComputeSalary(){
  System.out.println(employeeService.updateSalary(2000,
      500));
}

@Test
public void testShowEmployees(){
   Iterator<Employee> iterate =
        employeeService.getEmployees().iterator();
   while(iterate.hasNext()){
      Employee temp = iterate.next();
      System.out.format("%s \n", temp.getFirstName());
   }
}
```

How it works...

The formalization of lambda expressions in Java 1.8 is all documented in JSR 335, which covers the `@FunctionalInterface` annotation to create custom functional interfaces, built-in functional interfaces, and Stream APIs with lots of useful `mapping`, `sorting`, `filtering`, `reduction`, and `aggregate` methods. But what is most important is the recognition of anonymous functions which have the following form:

```
() -> { System.out.println("lambda expression"); }
```

The left-hand side of the arrow symbol is the area of inferred parameters and the right-hand side is the body of the anonymous function which *can be a simple expression or a block of statements.* An anonymous function is technically a reduced lambda expression.

In this form, the lambda expression is said to be implementing the correct interface method when its parameters and return types match the abstract method. If the abstract method has zero parameters, just like in `getEmployees()`, the left-hand side of the expression remains empty. But in the case of `updateSalary()`, where there are two double parameters, the lambda expression must contain two local variables at the left-hand side, which are inferred to be double types. Since these two methods output a value, a `return` statement must be found in their respective implementation body bearing the value of the function. And if the implementation requires a more complex and lengthy logic, the body part of this form can still be treated as a typical anonymous inner class where variables and constants are declared and initialized, just like what is emphasized in `updateSalary()`.

This new syntax of lambda expression has nothing to do with the existence of the `@FunctionalInterface` annotation. The use of this annotation is only to restrict one interface to have only one abstract method, otherwise, a compilation error will be issued by the compiler. Moreover, the use of the annotation `@FunctionaInterface` allows us to add more methods to our interfaces, namely the *default and static methods*, which are allowed by Java 1.7 and above.

The *default methods* are instance-scoped methods that become available once the lambda expression of the said `@FunctionalInterface` has been successfully implemented. They are defined by the keyword `default`.

Unlike in a normal interface, static methods can now be created in `@FunctionalInterface` and can be accessed at interface level. Functional interfaces can have more than one default or static method. The `ComputeSalaryIncrease` interface contains one default and one static method.

Applying the built-in functional interfaces

Java 1.8 also introduced some built-in functional interfaces that can be used directly in different lambda expressions. `Predicate`, `Consumer`, `Supplier`, and `Function` are some of the functional interfaces of the newly created package `java.util.function`, which will be highlighted in this recipe.

Getting started

Using the same Eclipse project and `EmployeeServiceImpl`, add the needed service methods using the pre-defined function interfaces of Java 1.8.

How to do it...

There are some built-in functional interfaces that Java 1.8 can provide in order to create services depending on the type of transactions needed to be implemented. To illustrate how to use these functional interfaces, follow these steps:

1. Add another method to `EmployeeServiceImpl` that will retrieve and filter employees with an age greater than 25:

```java
public List<Employee> getEmployeesFunc(){
    Predicate<Employee> qualifiedEmps =
        (e) -> e.getAge() > 25;
    List<Employee> newListEmps = new ArrayList<>();
    Iterator<Employee> iterate =
        employeeDaoImpl.getEmployees().iterator();
    while(iterate.hasNext()){
        Employee e = iterate.next();
        if(qualifiedEmps.test(e)){
            newListEmps.add(e);
        }
    }
    return newListEmps;
}
```

Using the `Predicate` functional interface is one way of establishing a logical expression to be used for object validation. Its abstract method `test()` is implemented using lambda expression.

2. Add this method that evaluates employee records given two series of Predicates, AND-ed, to comprise a filtering rule. This service method will fetch all qualified employees with `age > 25` belonging to a certain `deptId`:

```java
public List<Employee> getEmployeePerDept(int deptId){
    Predicate<Employee> qualifiedEmps =
        (e) -> e.getAge() > 25;
    Predicate<Employee> groupEmp =
        (e) -> e.getDeptId() == deptId;
    Predicate<Employee> rule =
        qualifiedEmps.and(groupEmp);
    List<Employee> newListEmps = new ArrayList<>();
    Iterator<Employee> iterate =
        employeeDaoImpl.getEmployees().iterator();
    while(iterate.hasNext()){
        Employee e = iterate.next();
        if(rule.test(e)){
            newListEmps.add(e);
```

```
        }
    }
    return newListEmps;
}
```

3. Create another method that generates random tickets for employee complaints. This method uses the `Supplier` functional interface for constructing a lambda expression that only gives a value without any input:

```
public int employeeTicket(){
    Supplier<Integer> generateTicket =
       () -> (int)(Math.random()*200000);
    return generateTicket.get();
}
```

The `Supplier` functional interface has an implemented abstract method, `get()`, which can give the expected result generated by its lambda expression.

4. Add the method `printEmployeeNotQuaified()`, which prints all employee records with the classification of whether an employee is QUALIFIED or NOT based on age:

```
public void printEmployeeNotQuaified(){
    Consumer<Employee> showNotQualified =
    (e) ->{
        if(e.getAge().intValue() > 25){
          System.out.format("%s %s %s\n",
            e.getFirstName(),
            e.getLastName(), "QUALIFIED");
        }else {
          System.out.format("%s %s %s\n",
            e.getFirstName(),
            e.getLastName(), "NOT QUALIFIED");
      }
    };
    Iterator<Employee> iterate =
        employeeDaoImpl.getEmployees().iterator();
    while(iterate.hasNext()){
      Employee e = iterate.next();
      showNotQualified.accept(e);
    }
}
```

This method highlights the use of `Consumer` that uses the lambda expression to accept an input of any object, but will only process transactions and not return any output. It has an implemented abstract method, `accept()`, that executes the lambda expression.

5. Lastly, add the following method that uses `Function` to convert an object to another form. In this case, the method wants to extract only the age values in order to compute the average age of all the employees:

```java
public double getAverageAge(){
    double avg = 0.0;
    Function<Employee, Integer> getAge = (e) -> e.getAge();
    Iterator<Employee> iterate =
        employeeDaoImpl.getEmployees().iterator();
    while(iterate.hasNext()){
        Employee e = iterate.next();
        avg += getAge.apply(e);
    }
    return avg;
}
```

The functional interface has an abstract method, `apply()`, which extracts the `age` element from the whole record.

How it works...

Built-in functional interfaces are also available in current Java and can be used as a new programming paradigm for the DAO and services of any Spring MVC applications. Aside from the importance of lambda expression, these built-in functional interfaces help convert imperative programming the functional programming style, where all transactions are in the form of functions which can be called repeatedly by other functions one after the other. The presence of these interfaces provides a clear picture that DAO, services, or any generic transactions can be implemented in a composed and uncluttered set of commands, which can be maintained and managed well when compared to low-level and complex iterations and method calls.

Instead of having complicated logical expressions, we can create and join two `Predicates`, each with simple and clear logical statements written in lambda expression in order to form a larger `Predicate` that will evaluate if an object satisfies the combined rule or not. Here, we have a series of `Predicate` function interfaces joined together to implement one method, `test()`, without having confusing and messy parentheses and a lengthy logical statement. `Predicate` functional interfaces have three default methods, `and()`, `or()`, and `negate()`, used to call other `Predicates` to perform AND, OR, and NOT operations, respectively.

Aside from `Predicate`, there is `Consumer`, which is another built-in functional interface purposely used to accept an object in order to generate results without returning any functional value. It has a default method, `andThen()`, which takes another `Consumer` to create a series of `Consumer` implementations.

`Supplier` is quite the opposite of `Consumer` because its lambda expression has no parameter but has a return value. On the other hand, `Function` is a functional interface used in mapping transactions where an original object type is mapped to another type. It has default methods such as `compose()`, `andThen()`, and `identity()`. The `andThen()` method is used to call another `Function` given that the first `Function` is executed before the second one, while `compose()` is used to call another `Function` wherein the execution starts with the second `Function` and is then followed by the first one. Both of the methods are used to generate a series of conversions. The `identity()` method is just used to return the same original type.

Each of these functional interfaces mentioned has their own primitive, binary, and unary versions.

Applying method and constructor references

Some of the lambda expressions can be simplified using some valid short-hand forms, given that a certain method or keyword can satisfy the implementation of the concerned functional interfaces. Instead of writing the full-blown expressions with the parameters and curly braces, we intend to reduce lambda expression as much as possible to apply the principles of functional programming. This recipe will highlight how to optimize a lambda expression used in object instantiation and method calls.

Getting started

Open the same project, ch06, and let us implement service classes that utilize built-in functional interfaces using method and constructor references.

How to do it...

To illustrate the use of method and constructor references, follow these steps:

1. Create a service implementation named EmployeeDataService, which will provide instances of empty Employee instances and a zero-sized ArrayList object for a list of employees. Also, it has a method that converts an employee's birthday from a long value to a java.util.Date object:

```java
@Service("employeeDataService")
public class EmployeeDataService {
  public Employee createEmployee(){
    Supplier<Employee> newEmp = Employee::new;
    return newEmp.get();
  }
  public List<Employee> startList(){
    Supplier<List<Employee>> newList = ArrayList::new;
    return newList.get();
  }

  public Date convertBday(long bdayLong){
    Function<Long, Date> bday = Date::new;
    return bday.apply(bdayLong);
  }
}
```

2. Then, create another service class, `GenericReferences`, which shows lambda expressions successfully implemented by just calling on some custom or API instances and static methods. The following first method showcases how to implement, straightforwardly, the functional interfaces through using some built-in static methods of any Java or Spring API:

```
@Service("genericRef")
public class GenericReferences {
  public int convertInt(String strVal){
    Function<String,Integer> convertToInt =
        Integer::parseInt;
    return convertToInt.apply(strVal);
  }
}
```

3. Add the second method to `GenericReferences` that gives the shorthand way of implementing lambdas through calling some methods that throw any exceptions (risky methods):

```
public Date convertBday(String bdayStr){

SimpleDateFormat sdf = new SimpleDateFormat("MM/dd/yyyy");
  Function<String,Date> birthday = t -> {
    Date bdate = null;
    try {
        bdate = sdf.parse(t);
    } catch (ParseException e) {
    bdate = null;
    }
   return bdate;
  };
 return birthday.apply(bdayStr);
}
```

The method `convertBday()` uses a risky method `parse()` of `SimpleDateFormat` to convert the input `String` to the `Date` object, given the input mask `MM/dd/yyyy`. Since `parse()` needs to be handled by a `try-catch` block, the only simple form that it can get is the original lambda expression form.

4. Lastly, add the following method that uses the static method to implement a functional interface in a shorter lambda expression form:

```
public boolean midYearStarted(Date started){
    Date midYear = new Date("117,5,30");
    Predicate<Date> midDayCheck = midYear::before;
    return midDayCheck.test(started);
}
```

How it works...

If a functional interface is written to simply return an object through instantiation, with or without the presence of constructor argument(s), we can use a constructor reference to implement its abstract method. This simplifies the implementation of a lambda expression by having the class name of the object concatenated to two colons (:) followed by the new keyword. The createEmployee() method uses a constructor reference to implement a Supplier that will provide an empty Employee object. For some classes that require constructor parameters to instantiate, convertBday() shows us that the constructor reference is feasible for creating the object. But there is only one case where we cannot push this short-hand form, and that is when the constructor of the class throws any exceptions (risky constructor).

The constructor reference is one special type of method reference that refers to a constructor of a class. A method reference replaces the common lambda expression form as long as the functional interfaces are satisfied with the result of the method that is not considered risky.

The method reference can also be applied to a typical instance and static methods, too. The convertInt() method depicts the replacement of the curly braces form with in the Integer::parseInt statement. The parseInt() method is a static method of the int wrapper class, which is one of the best candidates for this short-hand form. Likewise, any instance method can be subject to a method reference, just like in the midYearStarted() method, wherein a certain employment start date is verified. In this method, the Predicate is implemented using a method reference to the method before() of the Date object. A method reference to an instance method requires an instance object of the class needed to implement the functional interface.

The method reference is not always applicable to all technical requirement, thus the original lambda form is still suggested for implementing functional interfaces.

Using the Stream API

A stream in Java is a sequence of functional definitions or scripts that work as a pipelined operation, wherein each of these definitions outputs another stream, creating a flow of stream operations expected to provide an end result. A stream is an outcome of a certain combination of functional interfaces, code reduction, and some lambda operations. It is also the first major attempt towards parallelizing some transactions in Java using internal multithreading. This recipe will highlight how to create Java streams from `List`, `Set`, and arrays of data.

Getting started

Open the same project `ch06` and let us add service classes that will show us how to start creating `java.util.stream.Stream` from the given `EmployeeDao` transactions and test data.

How to do it...

There are few ways to create Java stream objects from a typical collection or array data store. To use the Stream API, do the following steps:

1. Let us create an experimental service class, `EmployeeStreamService`, which consists of service methods dedicated to stream methods. This first method only shows how to extract streams from `employeeDaoImpl`:

```
@Service("employeeStreamService")
public class EmployeeStreamService {
  @Autowired
  private EmployeeDao employeeDaoImpl;
  public void getCollectionStreams(){
    Stream<Employee> serial =
        employeeDaoImpl.getEmployees().stream();
    Stream<Employee> parallel =
        employeeDaoImpl.getEmployees().parallelStream();
  }
}
```

2. Next, add another method that illustrates how to extract stream data from an existing `List<String>` or `Set<String>` collection:

```
public void getListData(){
    List<String> employeeIDS =
        Arrays.asList("23234", "353453", "22222",
            "5555", "676767");
    Stream<String> streamsIds = employeeIDS.stream();
    Set<String> candidates = new HashSet<String>();
    candidates.add("Joel");
    candidates.add("Candy");
    candidates.add("Sherwin");
    Stream<String> streamCandidates =
        candidates.stream();
}
```

3. Lastly, the method below will show us how to extract a stream from an array of `long`, `int`, and `double` data:

```
public void getArrayData(){
    int[] ages = {24, 33, 21, 22, 45};
    IntStream ageStream = Arrays.stream(ages);
    double[] salaries = {33000.50, 23100.20, 45000.50};
    DoubleStream salStream = Arrays.stream(salaries);
    long[] longDates = {23434432342L, 11123343435L,
        34343342343L};
    LongStream dateStream = Arrays.stream(longDates);
}
```

4. Save all files.

 Always apply generics to stream objects to avoid explicit object conversion and some other type-related warnings.

How it works...

There are two types of `java.util.stream.Stream`, namely the sequential and parallel streams, but this recipe will focus on the sequential stream type. The sequential stream consists of sequential aggregate operations executing one after another, just like in a serial type of operation. All these operations occur in one single thread, wherein each operation outputs its own stream object:

On the other hand, the parallel stream assigns randomly these aggregate operations to several threads, allowing some of them to execute in parallel:

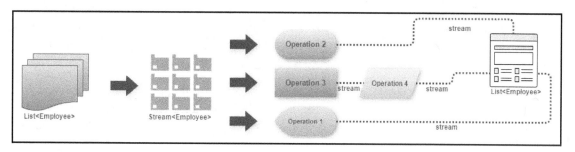

Once a stream is used and consumed, it cannot be reused for a second time; thus, it might be quite expensive when it comes to memory usage at some point when streams are badly needed all throughout a platform. Moreover, streams are taken cautiously with processing requirements with a heavy computation, because they use threading in executing all their pipelined operations.

Streams can be directly extracted from Set and List. The generated streams will contain all Collection data but cannot change them, whatever Stream operations are applied. When it comes to arrays of primitive types such as int, long, and double, Java 1.8 has a special kind of generic Stream class that can handle stream object transformation, namely the IntStream, LongStream, and DoubleStream. All these classes have common operations which can also be found in Stream API.

Applying streams to collections

Java stream is currently used to transform, manipulate, consume, reduce, and/or transfer data without changing its data structure. Since a Stream object is not a data structure, it is designed to be generated by some of the most popular data structures in Java, namely arrays and collections, to perform a faster declarative way of data processing. It also has some utility methods that can generate data structures from the baseline.

Getting started

Open project ch06 again and add some services that will manipulate EmployeeDao data using stream methods.

How to do it...

The previous recipe provided with the process for how to generate the Stream objects from a source data structure. It is time to scrutinize and study the operations involved in stream objects:

1. Open again the class EmployeeStreamService in the package org.packt.functional.codes.service.impl and add this set of methods that initializes Employee, arrays and converts List<Employee> to Employee[] using some Stream methods:

```java
public Stream<Employee> createEmptyArrayStream(){
    Stream<Employee> stream = Stream.empty();
    return stream;
}

public Stream<Employee> createUnlimitedStream(){
    Stream<Employee> stream =
Stream.generate(() -> {return new Employee();})
.limit(10);
    return stream;
}
public Stream<Employee> createArrayFromOf(Employee[]
    empArr){
    Stream<Employee> empStream = Stream.of(empArr);
    return empStream;
}

public Employee[] convertStreamToArray(
Stream<Employee> arrStream){
    Employee[] newArrayEmps =
    arrStream.toArray(Employee[]::new);
    return newArrayEmps;
 }
public void createCustomArrayStream(){
    Employee emp1 = new Employee();
    Employee emp2 = new Employee();
    Stream<Employee> emptyRecs = Stream.of(emp1, emp2);
    Consumer<Employee> showRecs = System.out::println;
    emptyRecs.forEach(showRecs);
```

```
    }
    public Stream<Employee> createArrayStream(Employee[]
        empArr){
        Stream<Employee> empStream = Arrays.stream(empArr);
        return empStream;
    }
    public Employee[] arrayStream(){
        Stream<Employee> serial =
        employeeDaoImpl.getEmployees().stream();
        IntFunction<Employee[]> sizeEmpArr =
            (size) -> new Employee[size];
        Employee[] arrEmps = serial.toArray(sizeEmpArr);
        return arrEmps;
    }
```

The preceding methods focus on ways to create streams of objects from the start. Creating an empty `Stream<Employee>` is shown by `createEmptyArrayStream()`, while `createUnlimitedStream()` generates either an unlimited or limited number of `Employee` streams. The `createCustomArrayStream()` method, on the other hand, creates `Employee` objects at runtime and stores them in a `Stream` object for rendering transactions using an internal iterator, `foreach()`. Other methods show how to extract streams from arrays or collections.

On the other hand, the `convertStreamToArray()` method accepts an existing stream of `Employee` objects and converts it to an array of `Employees` using a constructor reference. Likewise, the `arrayStream()` method executes the same conversion but uses the `IntFunction` functional interface to instantiate the `Employee[]`.

2. The Stream API has a list of *intermediate aggregate methods* that are lazily executed until the last aggregate operation is reached. Add the following method that shows how to use `filter()` in order to select `Employee` objects that meet the preceding age 25 limit:

```
    public List<Employee> getEmployeesAge(){
        AgeLimitService ageLimit = ()->{
          return employeeDaoImpl.getEmployees()
                .stream()
                .filter((Employee e)-> e.getAge() > 25)
                .collect(Collectors.toList());
        };
        return ageLimit.qualifiedEmps();
    }
```

The `AgeLimitService` is a custom functional interface implemented in the `org.packt.functional.code.service` as:

```
@FunctionalInterface
public interface AgeLimitService {
    public List<Employee> qualifiedEmps();
}
```

3. Add another method that highlights the use of the `sorted()` operation with `Comparator<Employee>` for sorting `Employee` objects. Lambda expression is used to implement the `Comparator` interface:

```
public List<Employee> getSortedEmployees(){
    Comparator<Employee> compareEmp =
    (e1, e2) -> e1.getLastName().compareTo(e2.getLastName());
    List<Employee> newListEmps =
        employeeDaoImpl.getEmployees()
            .stream()
            .sorted(compareEmp )
            .collect(Collectors.toList());
    return newListEmps;
}
```

4. The following method showcases one of the most widely-used aggregate methods, `map()`, which takes a `Function` functional interface that converts one object type to another:

```
public Set<String> getDistinctNames(){
    Function<Employee,String> allNames =
    (e) -> e.getFirstName();
    Set<String> setNames = employeeDaoImpl.getEmployees()
        .stream()
        .filter((a) -> a.getAge() > 25)
        .map(allNames)
        .collect(Collectors.toCollection(HashSet::new));
    return setNames;
}
```

5. Some variations of the `map()` method accept the `ToIntFunction`, `ToDoubleFunction`, or `ToLongFunction` function interfaces in order to generate combined end results such as the `average()`, `count()`, or `sum()` of all the objects. The following is a method that uses the `mapToInt()` method that extracts the average age of all employees:

```
public double getAverageAge(){
    ToIntFunction<Employee> sizeEmpArr =
```

```
        (e) -> e.getAge();
    return employeeDaoImpl.getEmployees()
    .stream()
    .mapToInt(sizeEmpArr).average().getAsDouble();
}
```

6. For manipulating existing data without changing the original data structure, the `replaceAll()` method through its lambda expression can return a new `List`, `Set`, or `array` of data objects, given some reflected changes. The following is a method that uses `replaceAll()` to write all `firstNames` and `lastNames` in all caps:

```
public List<Employee> updateNames(){
    List<Employee> newListEmps=
        employeeDaoImpl.getEmployees();
    newListEmps.replaceAll((e) ->{
      e.setFirstName(e.getFirstName().toUpperCase());
      e.setLastName(e.getLastName().toUpperCase());
      return e;
    });
    return newListEmps;
}
```

7. Other intermediate operations, such as `limit(n)` and `distinct()`, can be used as special types of filtering methods which will add more constraints on the retrieval of records. The `distinct()` operation returns a stream of unique elements based on the given `Predicate`, whereas `limit(n)` extracts the first n objects from the container:

```
public List<Employee> getOldestEmps(){
    Predicate<Employee> checkNotQualified =
      (e) -> e.getAge() < 25;
    Comparator<Employee> compareAge =
      (e1, e2) -> e1.getAge().compareTo(e2.getAge());
    return employeeDaoImpl.getEmployees().stream()
        .filter(checkNotQualified)
        .sorted(compareAge)
        .limit(3)
        .distinct()
        .collect(Collectors.toList());
}
```

8. Aside from the intermediate aggregate operations, there are also terminal operations in Stream that trigger the execution of the whole sequence of operations, and `reduce()` is one of them. The combination of the `map()` and `reduce()` methods is one of the most robust pairs of intermediate methods in generating basic statistical and mathematical operations on some list or arrays of data objects. The following method shows how `reduce()` can combine the list of numeric values from a `List<Employee>`, given a *summation* formula, to give the sum of all `Employee` ages. The formula may vary from one requirement to another:

```
public double sumAge(){
    BinaryOperator<Integer> addAgeEmp =
(age1, age2) -> age1 + age2;
    Function<Employee,Integer> ageList =
      (e) -> e.getAge();
    double sum = employeeDaoImpl.getEmployees()
        .stream()
        .map(ageList)
        .reduce(0, addAgeEmp);
    return sum;
}
```

The `reduce()` method needs an initial value and a formula in the form of the `BinaryOperator` functional interface. Moreover, its output is always a single-valued end result.

9. Another terminal operation is the `collect()` method that groups together all data objects in a stream and returns them as a list, set, or array. It uses some mutable reduction operations found in the class `java.util.stream.Collectors`. The following is a service method that returns all employees with an age greater than 25 in the form of a `List`:

```
public List<Employee> getEmployeesFunc(){
    Predicate<Employee> qualifiedEmps =
      (e) -> e.getAge() > 25;
    List<Employee> newListEmps =
      employeeDaoImpl.getEmployees()
          .stream()
          .filter(qualifiedEmps)
          .collect(Collectors.toList());
    return newListEmps;
}
```

10. Aside from `Collectors.toList()`, `Collectors.toSet()` and
    `Collectors.toMap()`, a stream can also be stored in other mutable containers
    such as `LinkedList` or `LinkedHashSet` through the use of the
    `Collectors.toCollection()` static method:

```
public Set<String> getDistinctNames(){
    Function<Employee,String> allNames =
        (e) -> e.getFirstName();
    Set<String> setNames = employeeDaoImpl.getEmployees()
        .stream()
        .filter((a) -> a.getAge() > 25)
        .map(allNames)
        .collect(Collectors
        .toCollection(LinkedHashSet::new));
    return setNames;
}
```

11. The last popular terminal operation is `forEach()`, which implements the
    `java.lang.Iterable` interface to iterate internally all objects passed on it. The
    following method shows the `firstName`, `lastName`, and `age` of all records:

```
public void showAllEmployees(){
    Consumer<Employee> showAll = (e) -> {
        System.out.format("%s %s %d\n", e.getFirstName(),
        e.getLastName(), e.getAge());
    };
    employeeDaoImpl.getEmployees()
        .stream()
        .forEach(showAll);
}
```

12. There are also terminal operations that return `Boolean` because their purpose is
    to validate a particular input requirement. The following service method searches
    and returns `true` whenever one `Employee` record is found to have an age of less
    than 25:

```
public boolean validateAgeNotQualified(){
    Predicate<Employee> checkNotQualified =
        (e) ->  e.getAge() < 25;
    return employeeDaoImpl.getEmployees()
.stream()
.anyMatch(checkNotQualified);
}
```

How it works...

This recipe discusses three groups of methods under the `java.util.stream.Stream` class, and these are the *stream creation methods, intermediate operations,* and *terminal stream methods.*

Streams can be generated in many ways, but the most straightforward technique is to use the static method `of()` when creating a stream from individual objects or from an existing array, and the collection's instance `stream()` method when creating a sequential stream from a `List`, `Set`, or `Map` of mutable containers. The `Stream` class has a static method, `empty()`, which can create a zero-size stream, while another static, `generate()`, produces an infinite stream of objects.

The second batch of operations is the set of methods that fills up the pipeline of streams that are executed only once the compiler executes the last stream operation. These `Stream` methods are summarized as follows:

- `filter()`: Removes some of the `stream` objects based on criteria or conditions implemented in the `Predicate` functional interface
- `sorted()`: Sorts the stream objects based on the comparator's rule for comparison, written in lambda expression
- `map()`, `flatMap()`, `mapToInt()`, `mapToDouble()`, `mapToLong()`: Maps each original `Stream` object to a new object type, based on some variations of `Function` implemented to extract a certain result
- `limit()`: Cuts the size of the stream to be retrieved based on a certain `Predicate`
- `distinct()`: Retrieves a unique list of stream objects based on `Predicate`

The preceding intermediate methods only update, manipulate, extract, define, streamline, and remove data without changing the original data structure.

The last batches of stream methods are the so-called terminal operations which are the last operations to appear in the pipeline of streams. Their returned value is either mutable containers (for example, collections or arrays) or void. There are five known methods under this group, namely `count()`, `match()`, `findFirst()`, `forEach()`, `collect()` with `Collectors`, and `reduce()`. The `forEach()` method internally iterates all `Stream` objects and can output all of them using `OutputStream`. The `reduce()` method asks a formula to perform transactions on stream objects in order to generate a single-valued result. On the other hand, the return type of `collect()` operations depends on the static method of the `Collectors` class. It can return a mutable container when `Collectors.toList()`, `Collectors.toSet()`, `Collectors.toMap()`, or `Collectors.toCollection()` is called. Or, it can return a single-value element if the method calls `Collectors.averagingInt()`, `Collectors.counting()`, or `Collectors.summingInt()`, for instance. On the other hand, the `match()` method has so many variations, such as `allMatch()`, which returns `true` if all objects satisfy the `Predicate`, `noneMatch()`, that returns `true` if none of the objects satisfy the Predicate, and `anyMatch()`, which returns `true` if one stream object fulfills the Predicate input. Pretty straightforwardly, the method `count()` returns the number of stream objects, while `findFirst()` returns the first object given a particular constraint.

Applying streams to NIO 2.0

Collections can not only provide `Stream` objects, but also NIO 2.0 classes. The following recipe will provide us with some service methods on file transactions that utilize stream operations.

Getting started

Open project `ch06` again and add some services that will manage dump files containing employee information.

How to do it...

NIO 2.0 APIs are known for their stream-based operations for reading and writing files. We use NIO 2.0 in many communication and data transformation modules. In this recipe, Stream API will be applied to perform some file operations using NIO 2.0:

1. Let us create another service class, `EmployeeFileStreamService`, in the package `org.packt.functional.codes.service.impl`. Add the following method that will retrieve the context of a dump file using NIO 2.0 and Stream APIs:

```
public void viewFileContent(String empFile) throws IOException{
    Consumer<String> readStr = System.out::println;
    Stream<String> content = null;
    Path path = Paths.get(empFile);
    content = Files.lines(path, Charset.defaultCharset());
    content.map(String::toUpperCase)
             .forEach(readStr);
    content.close();
}
```

2. Add a method that opens a dump file and counts the number of employee records:

```
public long countRecsInFile(String empFile) throws IOException{
    long numWords = 0;
    Stream<String> content = null;
    Path path = Paths.get(empFile);
    content = Files.lines(path, Charset.defaultCharset());
    numWords = content
         .map(line -> Arrays.stream(line.split(" ")))
         .count();
    content.close();
    return numWords;
}
```

3. The following method searches for a directory or file based on the specified extension and returns all of the searches to the caller:

```
public String searchFilesDir(String filePath, String
    extension) throws IOException{

    Path root = Paths.get(filePath);
    int depth = 3;
    Stream<Path> searchStream =
       Files.find(root, depth, (path, attr) ->
```

```
                String.valueOf(path).endsWith(extension));
    String found = searchStream
        .sorted()
        .map(String::valueOf)
        .collect(Collectors.joining(" / "));
    searchStream.close();
    return found;
}
```

4. The next method will search and list all documents with a preferred extension from a specific directory:

```
public void viewDirFiles(String dirPath, String extension)
throws IOException{
  Consumer<String> readStr = System.out::println;
  Stream<Path> stream =
    Files.list(Paths.get(dirPath)).sequential();
  stream.map(String::valueOf)
      .filter(path -> path.endsWith(extension))
      .forEach(readStr);
}
```

5. The following are two methods that highlight the use of `BufferedReader` and `Stream`. The `viewDirBuffered()` method retrieves all documents from a specified directory, while the other method, `countRecByAge()`, counts the number of records having a particular age:

```
public void viewDirBuffered(String dirPath) throws IOException{
  Consumer<String> readStr = System.out::println;
  BufferedReader buff =
    Files.newBufferedReader(Paths.get(dirPath));
  buff.lines()
      .map(String::toLowerCase)
      .forEach(readStr);
}
public long countRecByAge(String filePath, int age)
throws IOException{
  Path path = Paths.get(filePath);
  BufferedReader reader = Files.newBufferedReader(path);
  long numRec = reader
      .lines()
      .filter(line -> line.contains(age+""))
      .count();
return numRec;
}
```

6. Always close the stream after reading. Streams are not needed when writing on a file; rather, use NIO 2.0 classes and methods for writing.

7. Create a test dump file for testing and save it in `src/test/java`. A sample `employee_list.txt` may contain data separated by spaces:

```
sherwin john tragura 39
owen salvador estabillo  35
```

How it works...

Java New IO (NIO) 2.0 is a buffered-based set of I/O interfaces and classes that makes file reading and writing a flexible pair of operations. Its non-blocking mode enables the APIs to work with threads in reading and writing through some channels. Among all the APIs it has, the concern of this recipe is the utility class, `java.nio.file.Files`, which contains a method that supports `Stream` operations for file and directory transactions.

The `Files.lines()` method returns a stream of text so that the file-reading operation can be more optimized and refined through the use of functional interfaces and stream operations. Moreover, the `Files.find()` and `Files.walk()` methods retrieve a stream of all file and directory objects that can be further streamlined through the use of pipelined stream operations. Even the `BufferedReader` class that is used by NIO 2.0 to open a file for reading and writing has support for `Stream` operations.

Using parallel streams

The previous recipe described how to generate the two types of streams, but did not mention more about parallel streams. This final recipe will explore the pros and cons of using parallel streams.

Getting started

Open project `ch06` again to add service methods that will compare and contrast the two types of streams, *sequential* and *parallel streams*. The services will use the same `EmployeeDao` for the JDBC transactions.

How to do it...

All the preceding recipes highlighted the sequential stream which is common to many stream-based transactions. Let us now generate the parallel stream form by following these steps:

1. Create a service class, `EmployeeParallelStreamService`, inside the same package as the previous service classes. Add the following version of `showAllEmployees()` that uses `parallelStream()` to `forEach()` all employee records:

```
public void showAllEmployees(){
    Consumer<Employee> showAll = (e) -> {
      System.out.format("%s %s %d\n",
         e.getFirstName(), e.getLastName(), e.getAge());
    };
    employeeDaoImpl.getEmployees()
       .parallelStream()
       .forEach(showAll);
}
```

2. Create the test class that will prove that `parallelStream()` provides multi-processing when executing the pipelined `Stream` operations:

```
@RunWith(SpringJUnit4ClassRunner.class)
@WebAppConfiguration
@ContextConfiguration(classes = { SpringDbConfig.class,
  SpringDispatcherConfig.class })
public class TestEmployeeParallelStreamService {
  @Autowired
  private EmployeeParallelStreamService
    employeeParallelStreamService;
  @Test
  public void testParallelViewRecs(){
    System.out.println("*********ITERATION 1********");
    employeeParallelStreamService.showAllEmployees();
    System.out.println("********ITERATION 2*********");
    employeeParallelStreamService.showAllEmployees();
    System.out.println("******************************");
  }
}
```

Every snapshot of the test method execution will give us a different random order of employee records, as follows:

```
***********EXECUTION 1************
Sherwin Tragura 22
Joel Enage 45
Jerry Mayo 42
Sherwin Tragura 38
***********EXECUTION 2************
Sherwin Tragura 22
Joel Enage 45
Sherwin Tragura 38
Jerry Mayo 42
**********************************
```

3. Add the following service methods to `EmployeeParallelStreamService` that will show all the threads that `parallelStream()` utilizes when compared to the sequential version:

```
public double getSequentialAverageAge(){
    ToIntFunction<Employee> sizeEmpArr =
     (e) -> {
       System.out.println("Thread: " +
         Thread.currentThread().getName());
       return e.getAge();
     };
    return employeeDaoImpl.getEmployees()
      .stream()
      .mapToInt(sizeEmpArr)
      .average().getAsDouble();
}
public double getParallelAverageAge(){
    ToIntFunction<Employee> sizeEmpArr = (e) -> {
       System.out.println("Thread: " +
       Thread.currentThread().getName());
       return e.getAge();
     };
    return employeeDaoImpl.getEmployees()
.parallelStream()
.mapToInt(sizeEmpArr)
.average().getAsDouble();
}
```

4. Add the test method in `TestEmployeeParallelStreamService` that will test and execute the preceding service's methods:

```
@Test
public void compareComputation(){
System.out.println("**********PARALLEL************");
System.out.println("Average: " +
 employeeParallelStreamService.getParallelAverageAge());
    System.out.println("**********SEQUENTIAL**********");
    System.out.println("Average: " +
   employeeParallelStreamService
.getSequentialAverageAge());
System.out.println("*******************************");
}
```

Executing this test will give us the following console log:

```
***********PARALLEL*****************
Thread: main
Thread: ForkJoinPool.commonPool-worker-3
Thread: ForkJoinPool.commonPool-worker-1
Thread: ForkJoinPool.commonPool-worker-2
Average: 36.75
***********SEQUENTIAL**************
Thread: main
Thread: main
Thread: main
Thread: main
Average: 36.75
*********************************
```

5. Add another service method that custom generates a thread pool for `parallelStream()`, to be used in computing the average employee age:

```
public double getAverageMoreProcessors()
    throws InterruptedException, ExecutionException{
    ToIntFunction<Employee> sizeEmpArr =
    (e) -> {
       System.out.println("Thread: " +
         Thread.currentThread().getName());
       return e.getAge();
      };
    Callable<Double> task =
       () -> employeeDaoImpl.getEmployees()
                 .stream()
.mapToInt(sizeEmpArr)
.average().getAsDouble();
```

```
        ForkJoinPool forkJoinPool = new ForkJoinPool(4);
        double avgAge = forkJoinPool.submit(task).get();
        return avgAge;
    }
```

How it works...

Both types of stream use threads in `java.util.concurrent.ForkJoinPool` to execute all aggregate methods. The only difference is that the sequential stream uses only one thread, while the parallel one uses the default number of threads offered by the CPU of the machine. To enable `parallelStream()` is much easier than managing the threads that it uses. If the default number of threads degrades the parallel processing mechanism, `ForkJoinPool` can be customized by setting the number of allowable threads, which must not be more than the number of core processors present in the machine. But the stream pipeline must be wrapped in a `java.util.concurrent.Callable` object in order to be executed by the thread pool.

Since `parallelStream()` uses concurrent threads, it can help lower the processing time of some generic transactions only. But it has several drawbacks on synchronized transactions that involve *saving mutable objects, connecting to remote services, processing tightly-coupled transactions,* and *computing highly complicated mathematical and statistical formulas.* It also has some bad effects on APIs such as `LinkedHashSet`, `LinkedList`, and `TreeSet`, because some of its operations require non-thread-safe objects.

7
Reactive Programming

We continue to learn the Java functional programming paradigm in this chapter because some of the upcoming recipes will still require the APIs of `java.util.function` while building Reactive web components and Stream-based transactions.

This chapter discusses some of the new APIs needed to create Java events that are discrete, asynchronous, and non-blocking which are used in communication between a *message* sender and the recipient in many applications. This communication will eventually create a loosely-coupled and message-driven environment involving one or more Streams of Object. The model sounds similar to building message-driven transactions in **Java Message Service (JMS)** and **Advanced Message Queuing Protocol (AMQP)** but not exactly, since this communication model deals more with adaptive and scalable Streams of objects that can control data requests and even self-manage the data flow when bad data propagation occurs. When communication pitfalls happen, these APIs will just exit the data propagation without any exceptions as if nothing serious has happened. Moreover, these events are responsive in real-time given all possible requests and can somehow use the functional programming paradigm. This chapter will be all about building these kinds of events, which lead to **Reactive programming** concepts.

Reactive programming is needed mostly for transmitting or transferring a Stream of live data with no guarantee of **zero transmission error** and **predictable data capacity**. Its goal is to control the transmission of data to avoid traffic or starvation on either side of the transmitter and receiver. Since *Streams* play a great role in Reactive applications, these data transmissions are carried out using **multithreading** and **concurrency** techniques which can provide a non-blocking and asynchronous data flow even when data errors are encountered.

This chapter will highlight **Reactive Stream** APIs with the major inclusion of **Project Reactor 3.x** and **RxJava 2.x**. Spring 5 supports Reactive and asynchronous web applications that apply the mentioned Reactive tools in transforming and merging Streams of data using Java 1.8 JVM and above.

In this chapter you will learn how to perform the following tasks:

- Applying the observer design pattern using Reactive Streams
- Creating Mono<T> and Flux<T> publishers
- Implementing the Subscriber<T> interface
- Using java.util.function in Flux and Mono publishers
- Applying backpressure to Mono<T> and Flux<T>
- Managing task executions using schedulers
- Creating concurrent and parallel subscriptions
- Managing asynchronous data emissions
- Implementing Stream transformation and manipulations
- Testing Reactive data transactions
- Implementing Reactive events using RxJava 2.x

Applying the observer design pattern using Reactive Streams

Reactive programming started as a Reactive Streams model initially implemented in the .NET Framework but popularized by Pivotal and Netflix. This programming paradigm is supported by a specification used by many developers to extend and implement libraries that can solve Reactive-related problems. JavaScript, Python, and Java are some of the languages that have already shown their support by including this specification in their platforms. Based on the Reactive Stream JVM specification, Java 1.8 and above can now support Reactive programming. Java 1.9, especially, has a dedicated **Flow API** (java.util.concurrent.Flow) which consists of all the Reactive Streams API written within the context of Java language specification.

This chapter will introduce Reactive programming concepts and will provide recipes on how this paradigm started using the popular observer design pattern.

Getting started

The Reactive model was conceived by the **Reactive Streams 1.x** specification and includes four simple interfaces, namely the `Publisher`, `Subscriber`, `Subscription`, and `Processor`. Its slim platform composition makes it the most straightforward and flexible specification for Reactive programming both in Web and Android development. It aims to provide sets of rules and guidelines on how to utilize these interfaces by using any kind of programming language to get rid of asynchronous data requests. This chapter will focus more on **Reactor Project 3.x** (Reactor Core 3.x) as the core implementer of Reactive Streams.

How to do it...

This recipe highlights the main APIs involved in implementing the Reactive programming specification:

1. Create a **Spring Maven** project ch07. This project will consist of only native services to highlight **Reactive Streams 1.x** interfaces and **Reactor 3.x** implementation classes.

2. Copy `DispatcherServlet`, `SpringContextConfig`, `SpringDbConfig`, `SpringDispatcherConfig`, and `SpringWebinitializer` from the previous chapter and update the details of these application contexts. Use a new core page named `org.packt.Reactive.codes`. Also reuse the `Employee` model and DAO classes used in the previous recipes.

3. Configure the `pom.xml` file to include all the libraries used in the previous chapter such as the `Junit 4, Log4J, Spring 5.0.0.BUILD-SNAPSHOT, Servlet 3.x, JSP 2.3`, and MySQL JDBC connector.

4. For **Reactive Stream 1.0**, add the following Maven dependencies in `pom.xml`:

```xml
<dependency>
  <groupId>org.ReactiveStreams</groupId>
  <artifactId>Reactive-Streams</artifactId>
  <version>1.0.0</version>
</dependency>
<dependency>
  <groupId>org.ReactiveStreams</groupId>
  <artifactId>Reactive-Streams-tck</artifactId>
  <version>1.0.0</version>
  <scope>test</scope>
</dependency>
```

5. For the Reactive implementation classes, add the following dependencies of **Reactor Project 3.0**:

```
<dependency>
  <groupId>io.projectreactor</groupId>
  <artifactId>reactor-core</artifactId>
  <version>3.0.7.RELEASE</version>
</dependency>
```

6. Inside the package `org.packt.Reactive.core.service`, create a service interface `EmployeeStreamservice` that consists of the following abstract methods:

```
public interface EmployeeStreamservice {
    public Mono<Void> showThreads();
    public Publisher<Employee> readEmployees();
    public Publisher<Employee> readEmployee(Integer empId);
    public Publisher<String> getValidEmployees();
}
```

7. To start this chapter, implement `Publisher<Void>` that will prove that all Streams are threaded. Create an implementation class named `EmployeeStreamserviceImpl` that will implement the abstract method `showThreads ()` using `org.ReactiveStreams.Publisher` as shown in the following code snippet:

```
@Service
public class EmployeeStreamserviceImpl
implements EmployeeStreamservice {

    @Autowired
    private EmployeeDao employeeDaoImpl;

    @Override
    public Publisher<Void> showThreads() {
      Runnable task = () ->{
        System.out.println(Thread.currentThread().getName());
      };
      Mono<Void> execThread = Mono.fromRunnable(task);
      return execThread;
    }
}
```

8. To avoid synchronous ways of retrieving a list of the `Employee` model records from the database, establish a data retrieval mechanism using the observer design pattern where `Publisher` can wrap raw data, convert it into a Stream of objects that can be managed using its set of events asynchronously and transfer the Streams to its different subscribers. Add the following method to our implementation class:

```
@Override
public Publisher<Employee> readEmployees() {
  Publisher<Employee> publishedEmployees=
  Flux.fromIterable(employeeDaoImpl.getEmployees());
  return publishedEmployees;
}
```

9. Publishers cannot be executed without having any subscribers listening to them. A Subscriber is a recipient and can be a simple service, `@Controller`, or a module that needs the published Streams. At this point, create a test class `TestEmployeeStreamservice` that will implement `org.ReactiveStreams.Subscriber` to run `showThreads()` and `eadEmployees()` as follows:

```
@RunWith(SpringJUnit4ClassRunner.class)
@WebAppConfiguration
@ContextConfiguration(classes = { SpringDbConfig.class,
SpringDispatcherConfig.class })
public class TestEmployeeStreamservice {

  @Autowired
  private EmployeeStreamservice employeeStreamserviceImpl;

  @Test
  public void testStreamThread(){
    Subscriber<Void> mySubscription = newSubscriber<Void>() {

      @Override
      public void onComplete() {
        System.out.println("---End of Stream --");
      }

      @Override
      public void onError(Throwable e) {
        System.out.println("--Transmission Error --");
      }
      @Override
      public void onSubscribe(Subscription subs) {}
```

```
            @Override
            public void onNext(Void none) {   }

        };
employeeStreamserviceImpl.showThreads().subscribe(mySubscriptio
n);
    }

  @Test
    public void testReadEmployees(){
    Subscriber<Employee> mySubscription = new
Subscriber<Employee>() {

        @Override
        public void onComplete() {
           System.out.println("*-------End of Stream -------");
        }

        @Override
        public void onError(Throwable e) {
           System.out.println("*----Transmission Error ----");
        }

        @Override
        public void onNext(Employee emp) {
           System.out.format("%d %s %s %d\n",emp.getId(),
           emp.getFirstName(), emp.getLastName(), emp.getAge());
        }

        @Override
        public void onSubscribe(Subscription subs) {
           subs.request(Long.MAX_VALUE);
        }

    };
    employeeStreamserviceImpl.readEmployees().
    subscribe(mySubscription);
  }
}
```

10. Retrieving a single `Object` from a service method can also be handled by a publisher but it will require one service transaction to be state-ready for multithreading or concurrency. A `java.util.concurrent.Callable` package is required to wrap and convert these transactions into thread-ready functions that will return an individual `Stream` object. The following code snippet is an implementation that retrieves an employee record in asynchronous mode:

```
@Override
public Publisher<Employee> readEmployee(Integer empId) {
  Callable<Employee> task = () ->
employeeDaoImpl.getEmployee(empId);
  Publisher<Employee> publishedEmployee =
Mono.fromCallable(task);
  return publishedEmployee;
}
```

11. Add the following test case to our `TestEmployeeStreamservice` that will create a subscriber to `readEmployee(Integer empId)`:

```
@Test
public void testReadSingleEmployee(){
  Subscriber<Employee> mySubscription = new
Subscriber<Employee>() {

    @Override
    public void onComplete() {
      System.out.println("-----End of Stream -----");
    }

    @Override
    public void onError(Throwable e) {
      System.out.println("--Transmission Error ----");
    }

    @Override
    public void onNext(Employee emp) {
      System.out.format("%d %s %s %d \n", emp.getId(),
      emp.getFirstName(), emp.getLastName(), emp.getAge());
    }

    @Override
      public void onSubscribe(Subscription subs) {
      subs.request(Long.MAX_VALUE);
    }
  };
  employeeStreamserviceImpl.readEmployee(14).
```

```
    subscribe(mySubscription);
  }
```

12. A Stream of objects returned by publishers can consist of different events working asynchronously to process live data in order to extract the desired final output stream. If all the events did not encounter `java.lang.Error` or `java.lang.Exception` then the publisher will emit the desired value, exit, and signal a completion. Otherwise, it will emit an error value or message and will gracefully end the transmission. Following is an implementation of `getValidEmployees()` that computes a gradient from the employee's age and returns a list of employee names in `Strings`:

```
@Override
public Publisher<String> getValidEmployees(){
  Function<Employee, String> validEmps = (e) -> {
    double ageGradient = (int) ( 1 / (e.getAge() - 22));
    if (ageGradient == 0){
      return e.getFirstName() + " " + e.getLastName();
    }else{
      return null;
    }
  };
  Runnable completion = () ->{
    System.out.println("**** End of List*****");
  };

  Publisher<String> publishedEmployees= Flux
  .fromIterable(employeeDaoImpl.getEmployees()).map(validEmps)
  .onErrorReturn("Invalid Employee").doOnComplete(completion);
  return publishedEmployees;
}
```

The preceding publisher has a method `map()` which processes all elements sequentially from `fromIterable()` to generate another stream. From the snippet, its main task is to execute the functional interface `Function` that concatenates the employee's first name and last names given that the age's gradient is equal to 0, otherwise the function will return `Null`. The `Null` Stream data triggers an error in publishers.

13. Add the following test case that will show us the result once risky `getValidEmployees()` is executed. Be sure to have an employee record with age 22 to trigger an error:

```
@Test
public void testGetValidEmployees(){
```

```
    Subscriber<String> mySubscription = new Subscriber<String>()
{

    @Override
    public void onComplete() { }

    @Override
    public void onError(Throwable e) {   }

    @Override
    public void onNext(String name) {
      System.out.format("Employee: %s \n", name);
    }

    @Override
    public void onSubscribe(Subscription subs) {
      subs.request(Long.MAX_VALUE);
    }
};
    employeeStreamserviceImpl.getValidEmployees()
    .subscribe(mySubscription);
}
```

When `Publisher` triggers `onErrorReturn()` and `doOnComplete()`, `Subscriber` does not need to write any snippets in its `onError()` and `onComplete()` overrides.

14. Save all files. Execute all the test cases in `TestEmployeeStreamservice` and observe how the Publisher-Subscriber model works in the Reactive Streams specification.

How it works...

Highlighted in this recipe are two of the most important Reactive Streams interfaces, `Publisher` and `Subscriber`. These main APIs impact the interactive and Reactive model of data Stream emission from the data provider to the recipient component. The main goal of these interfaces is to implement the flow of the data objects during emission and also to provide the other to programming languages or web frameworks the opportunity to custom implement the Reactive specification depending on the purpose.

The blueprint of the `Publisher` interface is implemented using the following template:

```
public interface Publisher<T> {
  public void subscribe(Subscriber<? super T> s);
}
```

Here, `T` is the type of Stream object and `subscribe()` is the way `Subscriber<T>` connects to live data Stream emissions. There is no other way of executing all the `Publisher<T>` events but to connect to `subscriber(s)`.

Moreover, a publisher can be composed of blocking and non-blocking operators that can be executed asynchronously to process a Stream of elements. For instance, the `getValidEmployees()` method extracts a Stream of the `Employee` objects through `fromIterable()` that becomes the observable or subject for the subscribers to listen to. While generating the stream, another Stream function, `map()` is executed side-by-side with `fromIterable()` to convert each Stream object to another form creating a separate stream. Thus, if there are other additional operators in the event, there will be levels of independent, threaded Streams that will be working asynchronously to formulate the final data emission:

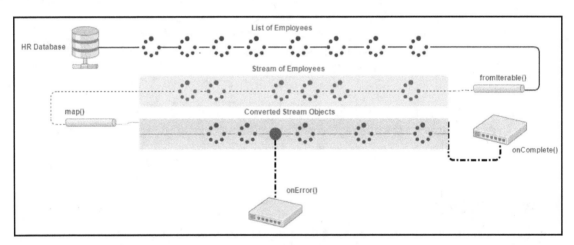

Whenever a **Throwable** is encountered by any of the Stream layers, the risky layer of `operator(s)` in the preceding diagram will just execute its `onError()` operator in order for `Publisher<T>` to exit as if nothing happens. In normal non-asynchronous cases, two or more methods can be executed sequentially, one after the other which might not be good whenever server-side exceptions or slow database connections occur (such as starvation or degradation of resources). Tightly-coupled processes will always replicate more problems in an application.

On the other hand, a `Subscriber` interface is designed to contain the following template:

```
public interface Subscriber<T> {
  public void onSubscribe(Subscription s);
  public void onNext(T t);
  public void onError(Throwable t);
  public void onComplete();
}
```

Here, `onComplete()` is the method that will be signaled to execute after a successful data emission; `onError()` is the operator triggered when `Throwable` is encountered during the `Publisher` event execution; `onNext()` is the method that retrieves each Stream object; and lastly `onSubscribe()`, which bears the very essential `Subscription` interface that has a `request()` method is used to control the number of data objects fired in each transmission. There is no guarantee that a subscriber will always get the same Stream provided by publishers in its previous emissions. Also, the final Stream can contain a single-entity (`Mono<T>`) or a list of data (`Flux<T>`).

Stream operators in publishers are quite similar to threaded operators in the Stream pipeline of `java.util.stream.Stream` presented in Chapter 6, *Functional Programming*. Some of the operators require a functional interface implemented using Lambda expressions just like in the recipes. Some require a transaction to be thread-ready through wrapping it with a `Callable` object. Thus, we can conclude that Reactor Core 3.x supports functional Reactive programming using the Java 1.8 APIs of `java.util.function`.

Creating Mono<T> and Flux<T> publishers

Reactor Core 3.x has two specific implementations of `Publisher<T>` namely `Mono<T>` and `Flux<T>`. If `Subscriber<T>` expects at most one Stream element, `Mono<T>` must be generated. And if at least one is needed to be transmitted, it must be the `Flux<T>` type. This recipe will expound on how to use these Stream types.

Getting started

This recipe will be about how to use `Mono<T>` and `Flux<T>` Stream types given raw data from unit tests and forms. Although they were used in the previous recipe in generating `Publisher<T>` Streams, nothing has been mentioned about their basic usage. The same Maven project, ch07 will be used for this particular recipe.

How to do it...

After the generic API classes, let us deal with the specific APIs of Spring Reactor 3.0 by using the following steps:

1. Create a service interface `EmployeeNativeStreamservice` that contains some non-DAO related services which will exhibit how to use Stream types. The following are the abstract methods to be implemented:

```
public interface EmployeeNativeStreamservice {
    public Mono<String> processFormUser(String name);
    public Flux<String> getFormUsers(String... names);
    public Flux<Integer> getAllAge(Integer[] age);
}
```

2. The first method to implement is `processFormUser()` that will accept a username and executes asynchronous operators in order to format the original `String` value. Trivial as it may be, this method will tell us how to process a single object through `Mono<T>` using several operations running synchronously on the main thread. This method will start showcasing some of the core `Publisher<T>` operations such as `doOnNext()`, `doOnSuccess()`, and `doOnError()`. The `doOnext()` operation is a very essential method since it is triggered when this publisher emits data. If a `Throwable` object is emitted in any of the operators, an additional threaded operator `onErrorReturn()` is ready to be invoked to perform a safe exit. Create an implementation `EmployeeNativeStreamserviceImpl` class and drop the following lines of code as follows:

```
@Service
public class EmployeeNativeStreamserviceImpl
implements EmployeeNativeStreamservice {
    @Override
    public Mono<String> processFormUser(String name) {
        Function<String,String> upper = (str) -> str.toUpperCase();
        Predicate<String> longName = (str) -> str.length() > 5;
        Consumer<String> success = (str) ->
        System.out.println("successfully processed: " + str);
        Consumer<Throwable> error = (e) ->
        System.out.println("encountered an error: : " +
e.getMessage());
        Consumer<String> onNext =
        (s) -> System.out.println("approved: " + s);
        Mono<String> makeoverName = Mono.just(name)
        .filter(longName)
        .map(upper)
```

```
        .doOnSuccess(success)
        .doOnError(error)
        .doOnNext(onNext)
        .onErrorReturn("invalid Name");
        return makeoverName;
    }
}
```

3. Secondly, add the method `getFormUsers()` in the following code snippet that accepts an array of user names through a variable argument list, concatenates a verification tag `---VALID USER` and then converts all usernames to uppercase. For error handling, another option is to invoke `defaultIfEmpty()` to emit a default value if the resulting Stream is empty. Also at this point, `Flux<T>` has its own distinct methods `doOnComplete()` and `doOnTerminate()`.These asynchronous operators are executed by this `Flux<T>` Stream type to convert arrays or lists of elements into Streams:

```
@Override
public Flux<String> getFormUsers(String... names) {
        Function<String,String> upper =
(str) -> str.concat("---VALID USER");
        Comparator<String> ascSort =
(str1, str2) -> str1.compareTo(str2);
        Runnable complete = () -> {
            System.out.println("completed processing");
        };
        Runnable terminate = () -> {
            System.out.println("terminated with problems");
        };
        Consumer<String> onNext =
(s) -> System.out.println("validated: " + s);
        Flux<String> userNames = Flux.just(names)
            .map(upper)
            .sort(ascSort)
            .defaultIfEmpty("empty list")
            .doOnNext(onNext)
            .doOnComplete(complete)
            .doOnTerminate(terminate)
            .doOnError(Exception.class,
(e) -> System.out.println("exits gracefully"));
        return userNames;
}
```

4. Lastly, implement getAllAge() which accepts an array of Integers, adds 10 to each age, and traces all Publisher-Subscriber internal operations happening at the main thread. Also present in this snippet is retryWhen() which uses time delay to implement error recovery:

```
@Override
public Flux<Integer> getAllAge(Integer age[]) {
    Function<Integer, Integer> addBufferAge =
        (a) -> a + 10;
    Flux<Integer> allAges = Flux
            .just(age)
            .map(addBufferAge)
            .retryWhen(opionFlux -> Flux.range(10, 100)
                    .flatMap(i ->
                        Flux.just(i).map(addBufferAge)))
    .log("Adding 10",
            java.util.logging.Level.INFO);
        return allAges;
}
```

5. Add the following logback dependencies for the log() operator:

```
<dependency>
    <groupId>ch.qos.logback</groupId>
    <artifactId>logback-classic</artifactId>
    <version>1.2.3</version>
</dependency>
```

6. Save EmployeeNativeStreamserviceImpl. Create a test class to execute all three service methods.

How it works...

Both Mono<T> and Flux<T> types are not the same technically as compared to typical data structures like arrays and List because the latter are fixed memory chunks representing the types of data to be stored while the former is a series of elements generated periodically, which cannot be referenced by an initial and last index. The Stream can be unpredictable since it can be full for a certain period and empty during busy transmissions. Every data emission may contain a different set of actual data depending on the backpressure applied to the Stream object .

A `Mono<T>` publisher generates a Stream of 0 or 1 `data` objects and consists of threaded operations that execute asynchronously creating layers of internal Streams. It has core operations such as `doOnSuccess()` which is triggered to execute once all the operations exited without any errors. Its data emission triggers the method `doOnNext()` which can be appropriate to execute logging or external tasks. In the service method `processFormUser()`, a Stream of `String` objects is being manipulated by the `map()` and `filter()` operators which are both asynchronous in nature. The threaded `filter()` requires `java.util.function.Predicate` to process only those strings with greater than five alphanumeric characters whereas `map()` executes `java.util.function.Function` to convert the filtered Stream object to uppercase. If the object does not qualify with `filter()`, the resulting Stream will return `Null`. To accept `null` data, `Mono` has a method, `justOrEmpty()` that will pre-empt any instances of `NullPointerException` triggered by processing `Null` Streams. Reactive Streams prohibits the use of `Null` values in any of its operations:

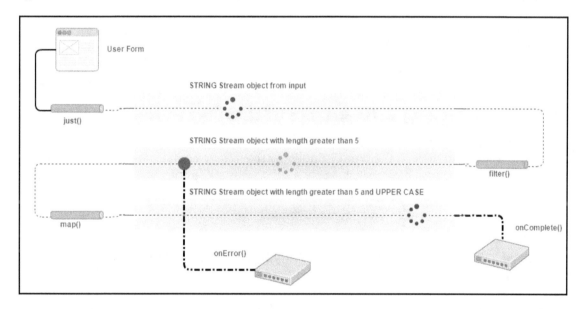

If a series of data is involved, the `Flux<T>` Stream type is used but it only requires non-null inputs. To generate `Flux<T>` from raw data, it uses the `just()` method just like `Mono<T>` but some of its operators are for multiple-data Streams. A `Flux` Stream can emit an infinite amount of data using `doOnNext()` before `doOnComplete()` or `doOnError()` is triggered.

To handle `java.lang.Error` or `java.lang.Exception`, both `Mono<T>` and `Flux<T>` can invoke `onErrorReturn()` to return a value that represents an error flag, `doOnError()` to determine the type of exception, and execute `Consumer<T>` when the transmission error happens or `retry()`/`retryWhen()` to signal a re-subscription after a `range()` of time with delays. To verify the new `Subscription` object, invoke `doOnSubscribe()`.

Sometimes `defaultIfEmpty()` is called to return any arbitrary value just to avoid a `null` value result which is not tolerated by `Publisher<T>` and `Subscriber<T>`. And to check as to where along the way the event got a null value, a `log()` method is present to show all transaction logs for the purpose of auditing and tracing. It shows all the series of `onNext()` calls to verify the situations during each Stream operation. The method uses the `logback` framework in generating the log messages.

Some publishers are created for the purpose of creating dummy tests and providing defaults to risky Streams. These Streams without data emissions are created through `Mono.empty()` and `Flux.empty()`. And in some rare cases we invoke `Mono.never()` to create a `Mono<T>` Stream that does not execute any callback functions such as `onComplete()` and `onError()`.

Implementing the Subscriber<T> interface

Publishers cannot be executed without a Subscriber. There are a few ways to implement a subscriber and it depends on the type of publisher they are to connect to. This recipe will provide some snippets on how to instantiate a subscriber and implement its callback events.

Getting ready

This recipe will be utilizing the same `ch08` to highlight the different implementation of `Subscriber<T>`.

How to do it...

To render or retrieve the emitted data, a subscription API must be created. Perform the following steps on how to implement `Subscriber<T>`:

1. Create a test class `TestEmployeeNativeStreamservice` that will verify some of the methods in the previous `EmployeeNativeStreamservice`. Add the following test method that executes `processFormUser()` using `Subscriber<T>` implemented through `java.util.function.Consumer<T>`:

```
@RunWith(SpringJUnit4ClassRunner.class)
@WebAppConfiguration
@ContextConfiguration(classes = {
SpringDbConfig.class, SpringDispatcherConfig.class })
public class TestEmployeeNativeStreamservice {

@Test
public void testMonoUserA(){

Consumer<String> convertUser = (str) ->
        System.out.println("String object: " + str);
employeeNativeStreamserviceImpl
.processFormUser("sjct").subscribe(convertUser);
}
}
```

2. Add another test method that generates a subscriber using a method reference in functional programming. This time, this test case aims to run the `getAllAge()` method:

```
@Test
public void testFluxAgeArray(){
        List<Integer> bufferedAge = new ArrayList<>();
        employeeNativeStreamserviceImpl
.getAllAge(new Integer[]{1,2,3,4})
.subscribe(bufferedAge::add);
        for(Integer age: bufferedAge){
            System.out.println(age);
        }
}
```

3. Another subscriber that can execute `processFormUser()` is instantiated using the Reactor Stream's `Subscriber<T>` API which is depicted in the method as follows:

```
@Test
public void testMonoUserC(){
  Subscriber<String> subscriber = new Subscriber<String>(){

      @Override
      public void onComplete() {
          System.out.println("Mono Streams ended
 successfully.");
      }

      @Override
      public void onError(Throwable e) {
          System.out.println("Something wrong happened.
             Exits now.");
  }

      @Override
      public void onNext(String name) {
          System.out.println("String object: " + name);
      }

      @Override
      public void onSubscribe(Subscription subs) {
          subs.request(Long.MAX_VALUE);
      }
  };

  employeeNativeStreamserviceImpl
         .processFormUser("sjctrags").subscribe(subscriber);
  }
```

The anonymous inner class is used to implement `Subscriber<T>`.

4. Save the file. Execute all test cases to view all the results.

How it works...

The subscriber is Observer<T> in the Reactive Stream model and its main objective is to listen to and observe the subject of the model which is either Mono<T> or Flux<T>. The full creation of a subscriber happens when org.reactiveStreams.Subscriber is used to override the four callback methods namely onSubscribe(), onNext(), onComplete(), and onError(). These methods can be enabled only if the publishers' counterparts of these are not invoked.

The onSubscribe() callback method manages the subscription mechanism of the subscriber by configuring the emission rate of Stream objects. This method is responsible for issuing a subscription to publishers and also managing the requests of data emission per delay per period. The Subscription<T> interface is part of this method which contains the following blueprint:

```
public interface Subscription {
  public void request(long n);
  public void cancel();
}
```

To render each Stream object either OutputStream or Collection, onNext() is executed. Different implementations can be executed within this method as long as all requirements fit within the scope of an anonymous inner class.

When the subscriber receives all the needed Stream objects from the publisher without a problem, it triggers its onComplete() method. Since this method is the last one to be called, all the necessary finishing touches such as data transformation, database persistence, or buffered writing are included in this method. But in case Throwable is encountered along the way, subscriber will trigger its onError() function which becomes the last execution instead.

The other way of generating subscribers is to implement Java 1.8's Consumer<T> functional interface. Using Lambda expression, we can construct an implementation that can expose all the data Stream objects without the limitation of an anonymous inner class.

And since Subscriber<T> supports Lambda expressions, method references can also be accepted as one way of generating subscribers that will log all Stream objects in a console or add them in a data repository.

Applying backpressure to Mono<T> and Flux<T>

Retrieving elements from `array` or `Collection` is different from data retrieval in Mono<T> or Flux<T>. In a typical data retrieval operation, the control of data emission depends on whether subscribers will pull it or not. The process can be very fast when a number of elements is practically manageable but dangerously slow when data abruptly increases. Once the subscriber or receiver becomes overwhelmed with the volume of data emission, some parts of the application may starve and will lead to memory leak. Backpressure is the process of controlling the flow of the data Stream to avoid an overflow of data emission between fast `Publisher<T>` and slow `Subscriber<T>`. It aims to maintain an optimal performance of any Reactive events even in worst-case scenarios.

Getting ready

Here, we will use Maven project `ch08` and add the code for backpressure.

How to do it...

Date emissions in Streams are affected by the backpressure operations used to extract the data. Let us define some backpressure operations by doing the following steps:

1. Create a separate service class, `EmployeeBatchStreamservice` that will showcase some abstract methods that will utilize time-related operators that are needed in setting up backpressure on Stream types:

```
public interface EmployeeBatchStreamservice {
    public Mono<Employee> selectOneEmployee();
    public Flux<Employee> selectSomeEmpRecords();
    public Flux<List<Employee>> getEmployeesByBatch();
    public Flux<String>    getTimedFirstNames();
    public Flux<Employee> selectEmpDelayed();
    public Flux<Employee> getDeferredEmployees();
}
```

2. The first event to implement is `selectOneEmployee()` that emits only one Stream object and converts it to a `Mono<Employee>` type. The `doOnCancel()` method is always invoked in time-related operators like this since these types of Stream operators trigger the `onCancel()` method periodically. Add this method to our `EmployeeBatchStreamserviceImpl` implementation class:

```
@Service
public class EmployeeBatchStreamserviceImpl
implements EmployeeBatchStreamservice {
@Autowired
private EmployeeDao employeeDaoImpl;
@Override
public Mono<Employee> selectOneEmployee() {
        Runnable cancel = () ->{
            System.out.println("Stream is cancelled");
};
Mono<Employee> oneRecord =
            Flux.fromIterable(employeeDaoImpl.getEmployees())
.doOnCancel(cancel)
            .log()
.take(1)
.singleOrEmpty();
        return oneRecord;
}
}
```

The main reason why there is a need to manage the emission of `Mono<T>` even though it only contains one piece of data is because in some circumstances, it may be empty.

3. Next, the method `selectSomeEmpRecords()` transmits only those Stream objects that are only covered within a specific emission period and skips two of them during the operation:

```
@Override
public Flux<Employee> selectSomeEmpRecords() {
Flux<Employee> takeSomeRecs =
        Flux.fromIterable(employeeDaoImpl.getEmployees())
.log()
.skip(2)
.take(Duration.ofMillis(4));
    return takeSomeRecs;
}
```

4. The third method to implement emits groups of Stream objects wherein each

group contains n elements:

```
@Override
public Flux<List<Employee>> getEmployeesByBatch() {
    Flux<List<Employee>> recordsByBatch =
        Flux.fromIterable(employeeDaoImpl.getEmployees())
.log()
.buffer(2);
    return recordsByBatch;
}
```

The operator `buffer(n)` returns a Stream of Collection where each Collection contains the group of Stream objects.

5. One of the most essential operators used in executing expensive or unstable sources of data is the `defer()` operator. It provides asynchronous execution to `Publisher<T>` that needs to be run in the background as an independent thread while proceeding with the next operators. This asynchronous method prevents other operators from interfering with the progress or status of the running `Publisher<T>`. The following method uses the `defer()` method to wrap an assumed heavy and unstable DAO transaction while `filter()` waits for its `Predicate<T>` to process the controlled data stream:

```
@Override
public Flux<Employee> getDeferredEmployees() {
    Predicate<Employee> validAge =
(e) -> e.getAge() > 25;
    Supplier<Flux<Employee>> deferredTask =
()->Flux.fromIterable(
employeeDaoImpl.getEmployees());
    Flux<Employee> deferred =
        Flux.defer(deferredTask).log().filter(validAge);
    return deferred;
}
```

6. One way to manage `defer()` operations is to use `timeout()` to explicitly provide a period of waiting for the subscriber to fulfil its subscription. Following is a method implemented for the subscriber to wait 300 milliseconds, otherwise it will trigger its `onError()` method:

```
@Override
    public Flux<String> getTimedFirstNames() {
        Function<Employee, String> firstNames =
```

```
    (e) -> e.getFirstName();
        Supplier<Flux<String>> deferredTask =
    ()->Flux.fromIterable(
    employeeDaoImpl.getEmployees())
                .map(firstNames);
        Flux<String> timedDefer = Flux.defer(deferredTask)
    .log()
    .timeout(Duration.ofMillis(300));
        return timedDefer;
    }
```

7. To execute this method properly, be sure to override the `onError()` method of the subscriber just in case `onCancel()` is triggered. Create `TestEmployeeBatchStream` and add the following test method:

```
@Test
public void testTimedFirstNames(){
        employeeBatchStreamserviceImpl.getTimedFirstNames()
    .subscribe(new Subscriber<String>(){

            @Override
            public void onComplete() {      }

            @Override
            public void onError(Throwable arg0) {
                System.out.println("time is out....");
            }

            @Override
            public void onNext(String data) {
                System.out.println(data);
        }

            @Override
            public void onSubscribe(Subscription subs) {
                subs.request(Long.MAX_VALUE); }
        });
    }
```

8. If there is a need to delay the emission of each element for m seconds given a period of 1 hour, the operators `take()` and `delayElements(m)` are used. Combinations of these threaded operations can push any number of data Streams to the subscriber. A `Null` Stream object is also a valid, expected result so error handling must be ready for these kinds of computations:

```
@Override
public Flux<Employee> selectEmpDelayed() {
        Supplier<Flux<Employee>> deferredTask =
()->Flux.fromIterable(
employeeDaoImpl.getEmployees());
        Flux<Employee> oneRecord = Flux.defer(deferredTask)
.take(Duration.ofHours(1))
.delayElements(Duration.ofSeconds(10));
        return oneRecord;
}
```

9. The other way of implementing backpressure is to override the `onSubscribe()` method of `Subscriber<T>` to request from `Publisher<T>` the emission rate of the resulting stream. This Stream request is done by the subscriber through the use of `request(t)` wherein the subscriber will be expecting t Stream objects per emission. Open the test class `TestEmployeeBatchStream` and add the following test case:

```
@Test
public void testByRequest(){
        Subscriber<Employee> subscriber =
new Subscriber<Employee>(){

        @Override
        public void onComplete() { }

        @Override
        public void onError(Throwable arg0) {   }

        @Override
        public void onNext(Employee emp) {
            System.out.println(emp);
        }

        @Override
        public void onSubscribe(Subscription subs) {
            subs.request(2);
        }
    };
    employeeBatchStreamserviceImpl.selectSomeEmpRecords()
```

```
    .subscribe(subscriber);
}
```

How it works...

Reactive applications use backpressure to manage of Stream of data flow from publishers to subscribers. It can be either a `pull` or `push` backpressure model depending on the requirements of the event. The `pull` data retrieval model is the one controlled by the subscriber which might be causing degradation or starvation whenever an empty promise Stream object is emitted by the publisher. A similar scenario is exhibited by the `testByRequest()` test case where the subscriber used the `request()` method of Subscription to tell the publisher how many Stream objects to emit per batch. On the other hand, we have a `push` model where the publisher controls the emission using some threaded operators such as `timeout()`, `delayElements()`, `buffer()`, `skip()`, and `take()`. This method promotes resiliency which means that the publisher will not be causing too much stress on its subscribers by sending an overflowing or empty stream. Given the possible chances of an empty stream, the `push` model can manage `Throwable` or execute `Mono.error()` to avoid memory leaks.

There are cases where some operations exceed the given time of execution due to I/O transactions, network problems, or huge volumes of data. Stream operators that are affected by these circumstances are wrapped by a `defer()` asynchronous method to prevent others from interfering with the ongoing status of the deferred operation. Using this method is a good start in formulating asynchronous transactions with backpressure for events that consume too many resources. Given different subscribers, the `defer()` method ensures a new Stream for each subscriber.

Some of the delay operations are deprecated so it would be wise to use the updated Reactor Core 3.0 operators. Moreover, for the time-driven operators, `onCancel()` is always triggered and `doOnCancel()` can be invoked for further `Runnable` tasks or events.

Managing task executions using Schedulers

All `Mono<T>` and `Flux<T>` Streams use the main thread for executing all its processors, which in some circumstances, can create starvation in some applications that are waiting for the main thread to be released. Eventually, exceptions from both publisher and subscriber can be thrown due to the starvation generated by the thread problems. This recipe will discuss creating thread workers that will lighten up the load of the main thread.

Getting ready

Open project ch08 again and add some services that will illustrate the different ways to create schedulers or thread executors.

How to do it...

To apply schedulers on our Stream operators, let us perform the following steps:

1. Create a service class EmployeeScheduledStreamservice that contains the following methods that will make use of the custom dispatcher and thread executor on the main thread:

```
public interface EmployeeScheduledStreamservice {
    public Flux<Employee> createPublisherThread();
    public Flux<Employee> createSubscriberThread();
    public Flux<Employee> createBothThreads();
    public Flux<Employee> createPubAndMain();
    public Flux<String> createSchedGroupPub();
    public Flux<String> createSchedGroupSub();
    public Flux<Employee> elasticFlow();
    public Flux<String> selectNamesScheduler();
}
```

2. The first method to implement is createPublisherThread() which creates a scheduler that triggers a fixed and single-threaded executor-based worker that will host the subscription to Mono<T> or Flux<T> Streams in the background, making the main thread available for other processes. Following is the EmployeeScheduledStreamserviceImpl class which generates a separate Scheduler for a publisher:

```
@Service
public class EmployeeScheduledStreamserviceImpl
implements EmployeeScheduledStreamservice {
    @Autowired
private EmployeeDao employeeDaoImpl;

@Override
    public Flux<Employee> createPublisherThread() {
        Scheduler pubWorker =
Schedulers.newSingle("pub-thread");
        Predicate<Employee> validAge =
(e) -> {
            System.out.println("filter thread: "
```

```
            + Thread.currentThread().getName());
         return e.getAge() > 25;
      };
      Supplier<Flux<Employee>> deferredTask =
()->{
            System.out.println("defer thread: "
+ Thread.currentThread().getName());
            return Flux.fromIterable(employeeDaoImpl
.getEmployees());
         };
      Flux<Employee> deferred =
         Flux.defer(deferredTask).filter(validAge)
.publishOn(pubWorker);
      return deferred;
   }
   }
```

3. Implement a method that uses a separate, single-threaded executor-based worker for the subscriber's callback execution and loads all the publisher threaded operations to the main thread. The following is another addition to the service class:

```
@Override
public Flux<Employee> createSubscriberThread() {
      Scheduler subWorker =
Schedulers.newSingle("sub-thread");
      Predicate<Employee> validAge = (e) -> {
         System.out.println("filter thread: "
+ Thread.currentThread().getName());
         return e.getAge() > 25;
      };
      Supplier<Flux<Employee>> deferredTask = ()->{
         System.out.println("defer thread: "
+ Thread.currentThread().getName());
      return Flux.fromIterable(employeeDaoImpl
.getEmployees());
         };
      Flux<Employee> deferred =
         Flux.defer(deferredTask).filter(validAge)
.subscribeOn(subWorker);
      return deferred;
   }
```

4. Next, implement `createBothThreads()` that uses separate threads for the publisher's subscription and scheduler's `Consumer` or callback executions:

```
@Override
public Flux<Employee> createBothThreads() {
        Scheduler subWorker =
Schedulers.newSingle("sub-thread");
        Scheduler pubWorker =
Schedulers.newSingle("pub-thread");
        Predicate<Employee> validAge = (e) -> {
            System.out.println("filter thread: "
+ Thread.currentThread().getName());
            return e.getAge() > 25;
        };
        Supplier<Flux<Employee>> deferredTask = ()->{
            System.out.println("defer thread: "
+ Thread.currentThread().getName());
            return Flux.fromIterable(employeeDaoImpl
.getEmployees());
        };
        Flux<Employee> deferred =
            Flux.defer(deferredTask).filter(validAge)
.subscribeOn(subWorker)
.publishOn(pubWorker);
        return deferred;
}
```

5. There are some cases when we isolate some non-critical publisher subscription operations from risky, expensive, or deferred transactions by loading these critical operations into the background thread. In this case, two threads will be utilized by the publishers, the main one and the one generated by a scheduler. Following is a method `createPubAndMain()` that shows another option for using `Schedulers`:

```
@Override
public Flux<Employee> createPubAndMain() {
        Scheduler pubWorker =
Schedulers.newSingle("pub-thread");
        Predicate<Employee> validAge = (e) -> {
            System.out.println("filter thread: "
+ Thread.currentThread().getName());
            return e.getAge() > 25;
        };
        Supplier<Flux<Employee>> deferredTask = ()->{
            System.out.println("defer thread: "
+ Thread.currentThread().getName());
            return Flux.fromIterable(employeeDaoImpl
```

```
.getEmployees());
   };
   Flux<Employee> deferred = Flux.defer(deferredTask)
.publishOn(pubWorker)
.filter(validAge);
   return deferred;
}
```

6. If a pool of schedulers is required to be assigned on each Stream operator, then this recipe fits to that requirement. In this model, each task will be assigned randomly to any available worker for `flatMap()` processing. The following is the implementation of the `createSchedGroupPub()` method that generates 8 workers wherein one worker will be chosen to execute the publisher operations. Moreover, the recipe creates a separate scheduler for the subscriber:

```
@Override
public Flux<String> createSchedGroupPub() {
   Scheduler subWorker = Schedulers.newSingle("sub-thread");
   Scheduler parallelGrp = Schedulers.newParallel("pub-grp", 8);
   Function<Employee, String> allCapsNames = (emp) ->
   emp.getFirstName().toUpperCase() + " " +
   emp.getLastName().toUpperCase();
   Flux<String> grpFlux = Flux.fromIterable(employeeDaoImpl
   .getEmployees()).publishOn(parallelGrp).flatMap((emp)->{
      System.out.println("flatMap thread: " +
      Thread.currentThread().getName());
      return
Mono.just(emp).map(allCapsNames).subscribeOn(subWorker);
   });
   return grpFlux;
}
```

There is no concurrency concept yet in this recipe. After executing this method, only one worker will be tasked to do every subscriber event. This recipe is just about creating groups of schedulers and how the platform chooses the available thread to do the publisher's tasks.

7. If we can allot a group of schedulers to subscriptions, we can also do it with the subscriber's callback. The following is a method that generates a group of schedulers that will execute the `Consumer<T>` transaction of `Subscriber<T>`:

```
@Override
public Flux<String> createSchedGroupSub() {
        Scheduler pubWorker =
Schedulers.newSingle("pub-thread");
        Scheduler parallelGrp =
Schedulers.newParallel("sub-grp", 8);
        Function<Employee, String> allCapsNames =
(emp) -> emp.getFirstName().toUpperCase() + " "
+ emp.getLastName().toUpperCase();
        Flux<String> strFlux =
            Flux.fromIterable(employeeDaoImpl
.getEmployees())
                    .publishOn(pubWorker)
                    .flatMap((str)->{
                        System.out.println("flatMap thread: "
+ Thread.currentThread().getName());
                        return Mono.just(str).map(allCapsNames)
.subscribeOn(parallelGrp);
                    });
        return strFlux;
}
```

8. When the event is unsure as to whether to utilize a single or group of n workers, `Schedulers.elastic()` is executed to dynamically create the required pool of workers that are cacheable and reusable after every Stream operation:

```
@Override
public Flux<Employee> elasticFlow() {
        Scheduler elastic =
Schedulers.newElastic("elastic-worker");
        Predicate<Employee> validAge = (e) -> {
            System.out.println("filter thread: "
+ Thread.currentThread().getName());
            return e.getAge() > 25;
        };
        Supplier<Flux<Employee>> deferredTask = ()->{
            System.out.println("defer thread: "
+ Thread.currentThread().getName());
            return Flux.fromIterable(employeeDaoImpl
.getEmployees());
        };
        Flux<Employee> deferred = Flux.defer(deferredTask)
.filter(validAge)
```

```
        .subscribeOn(elastic);
            return deferred;
    }
```

9. Lastly, some of the publisher operators require `Schedulers` as parameters just like the `window()` operation that creates an internal sub-Flux based on a delimiter that splits the whole `Flux<T>` sequence starting from the first recognized Stream element. The following method shows how `window()` works with a `Scheduler`:

```
@Override
public Flux<String> selectNamesScheduler() {
    Scheduler winWorker =
Schedulers.newSingle("window-thread");
    Function<Employee, String> allCapsNames =
(emp) -> emp.getFirstName().toUpperCase() + " "
+ emp.getLastName().toUpperCase();
    Flux<String> convertWindows =
        Flux.fromIterable(employeeDaoImpl.getEmployees())
            .windowTimeout(2,
Duration.ofMillis(20), winWorker)
                .flatMap(str -> str
                    .map(allCapsNames)
                    .collectList()
                    .map(name ->
                    StringUtils
.collectionToCommaDelimitedString(name))
                );
    return convertWindows;
}
```

How it works...

To apply more asynchronous approaches in generating `Mono<T>` and `Flux<T>`, schedulers are recommended by the Reactive Stream specification to lessen the load of the main thread. With schedulers, operators can be allowed to execute using many threads. Generally, it provides asynchronous boundaries to all threaded operators of the publisher.

There are many ways to generate and use schedulers; one is the use of timed operators like `timeout()`, `delayElements()`, and `skip()` which are showcased in the previous recipe. These types of methods have built-in schedulers that are run in the background once executed. Some are created just to become an argument of a publisher operation just like `window()` presented in `selectNamesScheduler()` where the two sub-Flux Streams are managed by separate threads. The use of `publishOn()` is one way to manage Streams using multiple threading by having different threads for the subscriptions. Subscribers observe all the publisher Streams through the scheduler specified by `publishOn()`. The `Scheduler.newSingle()` factory method is used to generate a single thread that will process the needed computations. The location where `publishOn()` is called matters because it is the point where the rest of the operations will shift to a new scheduler from the main thread.

On the other hand, assigning another thread to the Subscriber's `onComplete()`, `onError()`, and `onNext()` is another popular technique for multithreading which is done through `subscribeOn()`.

Since dispatchers and executors are almost obsolete in this latest version of Reactor Core 3.x, the `Scheduler` will stand as a dispatcher with an embedded executor that will truly solve major synchronization problems and thread management on the `Mono<T>` and `Flux<T>` Streams.

There are other commands from schedulers that can be useful in initiating thread execution such as `Schedulers.immediate()` which triggers work immediately on the current thread and `Schedulers.elastic()` which is suited for I/O related tasks which can contain a pool of threads.

Creating concurrent and parallel emissions

Besides multithreading, it is possible to achieve concurrency and parallelism with Reactor Core. This recipe is still about `Scheduler` but in parallel mode. The clear concept of parallelism is all about having these n operations distributed to m workers that are executed independently of each other. This recipe will utilize `Schedulers` to enable parallelism in Reactive Streams.

Getting ready

Open project `ch07` again and add the following service that shows different ways of how to implement concurrent and parallel Streams using `Schedulers` and some Reactive Core 3.x operators.

How to do it...

To implement concurrent and parallel Stream emissions, perform the following steps:

1. Add the following service class in our `org.packt.reactive.code.service` package. This class contains method templates that will detail parallelism and concurrency based on Reactive Streams specification:

```
public interface EmployeeParallelStreamservice {
    public Flux<String> parallelEmployeeNames();
    public Flux<GroupedFlux<Integer, Integer>>
        parallelGrpAvg();
    public Flux<String> repeatExecs();
}
```

2. Create an implementation class `EmployeeParallelStreamserviceImpl` that will contain a method `parallelEmployeeNames()` designed to utilize a pool of eight threads in order to get the full names of all employees. All these threads must work on each task in parallel mode. In short, this method implements a parallel `Flux`:

```
@Service
public class EmployeeParallelStreamserviceImpl
implements EmployeeParallelStreamservice{
    @Autowired
    private EmployeeDao employeeDaoImpl;

    @Override
    public Flux<String> parallelEmployeeNames() {
        Function<Employee, String> names = (emp) -> {
            System.out.println("flatMap thread: "
+ Thread.currentThread().getName());
            return emp.getFirstName().charAt(0) +
                emp.getLastName();
        };
        Flux<String> parallelEmpFlux =
            Flux.fromIterable
(employeeDaoImpl.getEmployees())
```

```
            .parallel(8)
            .runOn (Schedulers.parallel())
            .sequential()
            .map(names);
        return parallelEmpFlux;
    }
}
```

3. Another method `repeatExecs()` implements another design for parallelism wherein the Stream will be repeatedly run m times after each `onComplete()`:

```java
@Override
public Flux<String> repeatExecs() {
    Function<Employee, String> names =
(emp) ->{
        System.out.println("flatMap thread: "
+ Thread.currentThread().getName());
        return emp.getFirstName().charAt(0) +
            emp.getLastName();
    };
    Flux<String> parallelEmpFlux =
        Flux.fromIterable(employeeDaoImpl.getEmployees())
            .repeat(2)
            .parallel(8)
            .runOn (Schedulers.parallel())
            .sequential()
              .map(names)
            .doOnSubscribe(subscription -> {
                    System.out.println(subscription);
                });
    return parallelEmpFlux;
}
```

4. The last method in this recipe will show us a solution on how to implement grouped parallel `Flux`. This implementation is so rare that it is only opted for when there is a need to parallelize the subscriber's callback too:

```java
@Override
public Flux<GroupedFlux<Integer, Integer>> parallelGrpAvg() {
    Function<Employee, Integer> ages = (emp) -> {
        System.out.println("flatMap thread: "
+ Thread.currentThread().getName());
        return emp.getAge();
    };
    Flux<GroupedFlux<Integer, Integer>> parallelEmpFlux =
        Flux.fromIterable(employeeDaoImpl.getEmployees())
            .delaySubscription(
```

```
Duration.of(500L, ChronoUnit.MILLIS))
            .parallel(8)
            .runOn (Schedulers.parallel())
            .map(ages)
            .groups();
        return parallelEmpFlux;
}
```

How it works...

An operator that consumes more time in computations is a serious problem when creating Streams. Usually, when operations are involved in some I/O tasks, file content retrieval, or selecting records from an archive data warehouse, it is always recommended to generate threads that work in parallel mode in order to attend to these heavy operations.

Parallelism starts with a parallel() operator which creates a pool of t threads. These t threads will eventually become rails of parallel Flux after the runOn() method is invoked. After all the parallel tasks are done executing, these Streams can be merged into one resulting Stream by calling the sequential() method. It is a must to call sequential() since subscription cannot be parallelized easily. But, to really implement 100% parallelism where the subscription process is also part of the concurrency, use grouped parallel flux. Each rail is internally paired to a subscription through an internally-created key, to represent a grouped parallel flux of Stream type Flux<GroupedFlux<java.lang.Integer,T>>. Applying groups is the same concept of implementing parallelism to publisher-subscriber by grouping basis.

To add more concurrency power to the reactor stream, we can include the repeat() operator to repeat the Stream processes at least once. After the completion of all Streams, repeat() triggers re-subscription eventually executing parallel(), runOn(), and sequential() operators again and again with an unpredictable task assignment to the thread pool. Also, the subscription will also be effective and traceable if certain backpressure will be applied like the use of the delayElements() operator.

Managing continuous data emission

All the Streams generated by the previous recipes need to be subscribed in order to emit data Streams. This kind of data Stream is called the cold stream. Many of the real-time applications nowadays need services that emit a data Stream continuously once the server starts even without any subscription. Thus, data emission in this recipe is not bounded by any subscribers which gives each subscriber a different set of Streams every now and then within such a period. This recipe will discuss snippets that implement synchronous and non-blocking Stream operations.

Getting ready

This chapter will be using `ch07` again to implement services that use `ConnectableFlux<T>` and `Processor<T>`.

How to do it...

This will be the first recipe that will implement a continuous stream:

1. Let us create a service class `EmployeeHotStreamservice` that contains the following template methods:

```
public interface EmployeeHotStreamservice {
    public ConnectableFlux<String> freeFlowEmps();
    public void monoProcessorGetEmployee(Integer id);
    public void fluxProcessorGetEmployee(List<Integer> ids);
    public void validateNamesTopic(List<String> names);
    public void validateNamesWorkQueue(List<String> names);
    public void validateNamesReplay(List<String> names);
    public void validateNamesUnicast(List<String> names);
}
```

2. The first method to implement is `freeFlowEmps()` which uses `ConnectableFlux<T>` in its implementation of a continuous data Stream flow. Add the following implementation class with the implemented `freeFlowEmps()` method. This method also introduces `cache()` that stores current value for later computations, if there are any:

```
@Service
public class EmployeeHotStreamserviceImpl
implements EmployeeHotStreamservice {
```

```
    @Autowired
    private EmployeeDao employeeDaoImpl;
    @Override
    public ConnectableFlux<String> freeFlowEmps() {
        List<String> rosterNames = new ArrayList<>();
        Function<Employee, String> familyNames =
(emp) -> emp.getLastName().toUpperCase();
        ConnectableFlux<String> flowyNames =
            Flux.fromIterable(employeeDaoImpl.getEmployees())
.log().map(familyNames).cache().publish();
        flowyNames.subscribe(System.out::println);
        flowyNames.subscribe(rosterNames::add);
return flowyNames;
    }
}
```

3. To show the connection process, add the following test class that will trigger the data Stream emission to the two subscribers:

```
@RunWith(SpringJUnit4ClassRunner.class)
@WebAppConfiguration
@ContextConfiguration(classes = { SpringDbConfig
        .class, SpringDispatcherConfig.class })
public class TestEmployeeHotStreamservice {
    @Autowired
    private EmployeeHotStreamservice
        employeeHotStreamserviceImpl;

    @Test
    public void testConnectFluxProcessor(){
        employeeHotStreamserviceImpl.freeFlowEmps().connect();
    }
}
```

4. One of the best solutions in generating hot Streams is the use of `Processor<T>` which stands as a complete event broadcaster that commands the execution of all its Stream operations in at least one subscriber. Following is a method that utilizes a synchronous event broadcaster that is only used to signal all event executions in at least one subscriber synchronously:

```
@Override
public void monoProcessorGetEmployee(Integer id) {
    MonoProcessor<Integer> future =
        MonoProcessor.create();
    Consumer<Integer> checkEmp = (rowId) ->{
        if(employeeDaoImpl.getEmployee(rowId) == null){
            System.out.println("Employee with id: "
```

```
+ rowId + " does not exists.");
          }else{
              System.out.println("Employee with id: "
+ rowId + " exists.");
          }
      };
    Mono<Integer> engine = future
          .doOnNext(checkEmp)
          .doOnSuccess(emp -> {
              System.out.println("Employee's age is "
+ employeeDaoImpl.getEmployee(emp).getAge());
              System.out.println("Employee's dept is: "
+ employeeDaoImpl.getEmployee(emp).getDeptId());
          })
          .doOnTerminate((sup, ex) ->
          System.out.println("Transaction terminated
                    with error: " +ex.getMessage()))
          .doOnError(ex -> System.out.println("Error: "
+ ex.getMessage()));
    engine.subscribe(System.out::println);
    future.onNext(id);
    int valStream = future.block();
    System.out.println("Employee's ID again is: " +
          valStream);
  }
```

5. Another processor is `FluxProcessor<T>` which broadcasts the data emission to its `subscriber(s)` mainly exposing the process of emission:

```
@Override
public void fluxProcessorGetEmployee(List<Integer> ids) {
      Function<Integer,Integer> checkEmp = (id) ->{
        if(!(employeeDaoImpl.getEmployee(id) == null)){
          return employeeDaoImpl
              .getEmployee(id).getAge();
        }else{
          return -1;
        }
      };
      FluxProcessor<Integer, Integer> cpuFlow =
        EmitterProcessor.create();
      Flux<Integer> fluxp = cpuFlow.map(checkEmp);
      Flux<Integer> gradientNum = cpuFlow.map((num) ->
num + 1000);
      fluxp.subscribe(System.out::println);
      gradientNum.subscribe(System.out::println);
      for(Integer id: ids){
        cpuFlow.onNext(id);
```

```
        }
        cpuFlow.onComplete();
    }
```

6. A specialized `EmitterProcessor<T>` that caches all its Stream elements for future computations and also allows asynchronous event executions to its `subscriber(s)` is called `ReplayProcessor<T>`. Because of its built-in `cache()`, this processor remembers the previous element and emits it to the next subscriber for another event processing while maintaining an asynchronous boundary between subscribers. Following is `validateNamesReplay()` that implements the basic semantics for `ReplayProcessor<T>`:

```
@Override
public void validateNamesReplay(List<String> names) {
    ReplayProcessor<String> replayProcessor =
        ReplayProcessor.create();
    Function<String,String> appendLic =
(name) -> name.concat(".112234");
    Function<String,String> appendKey =
(name) -> name.concat("-AEK2345J");
    Function<String,String> upperCase =
(name) -> name.toUpperCase();
    Flux<String> formatter1 =
replayProcessor.filter((s) ->
        s.length() > 4).map(appendLic);
    Flux<String> formatter2 =
replayProcessor.filter((s) ->
        s.startsWith("J")).map(appendKey);
    Flux<String> formatter3 =
replayProcessor.filter((s) ->
        s.endsWith("win")).map(upperCase);

    formatter1.subscribe(System.out::println);
    formatter2.subscribe(System.out::println);
    formatter3.subscribe(System.out::println);

    for(String name : names){
       replayProcessor.onNext(name);
    }
    replayProcessor.onComplete();
}
```

7. An asynchronous version of `EmitterProcessor<T>` that signals all execution of all its events per data Stream element asynchronously is called `TopicProcessor<T>`. This processor needs more backpressure solutions to capture correctly the execution of each subscriber because of its high concurrency features:

```
@Override
    public void validateNamesTopic(List<String> names) {
        TopicProcessor<String> topicProcessor =
                TopicProcessor.create();
        Function<String,String> appendLic =
(name) -> name.concat(".112234");
        Function<String,String> appendKey =
(name) -> name.concat("-AEK2345J");
        Function<String,String> upperCase =
(name) -> name.toUpperCase();
        Flux<String> formatter1 =
topicProcessor.filter((s) ->
                s.length() > 4).map(appendLic);
        Flux<String> formatter2 =
topicProcessor.filter((s) ->
                s.startsWith("J")).map(appendKey);
        Flux<String> formatter3 =
topicProcessor.filter((s) ->
                s.endsWith("win")).map(upperCase);

        formatter1.subscribe(System.out::println);
        formatter2.subscribe(System.out::println);
        formatter3.subscribe(System.out::println);

        for(String name : names){
           topicProcessor.onNext(name);
        }
        topicProcessor.onComplete();

    }
```

8. The next processor, `WorkQueueProcessor<T>`, is also an asynchronous signal broadcaster like `TopicProcessor<T>` that evenly distributes each element to the next available subscriber. The objective is to share the load fairly to all subscribers which is the same idea with the Round Robin process distribution. Some of the elements might appear or not depending on the constraints given in each event:

```
@Override
    public void validateNamesWorkQueue(List<String> names) {
        WorkQueueProcessor<String> wqueueProcessor =
            WorkQueueProcessor.create();
```

```
        Function<String,String> appendLic =
(name) -> name.concat(".112234");
        Function<String,String> appendKey =
(name) -> name.concat("-AEK2345J");
        Function<String,String> upperCase =
(name) -> name.toUpperCase();
        Flux<String> formatter1 =
wqueueProcessor.filter((s) ->
            s.length() > 4).map(appendLic);
        Flux<String> formatter2 =
wqueueProcessor.filter((s) ->
            s.startsWith("J")).map(appendKey);
        Flux<String> formatter3 =
wqueueProcessor.filter((s) ->
            s.endsWith("win")).map(upperCase);

        formatter1.subscribe(System.out::println);
        formatter2.subscribe(System.out::println);
        formatter3.subscribe(System.out::println);

        for(String name : names){
            wqueueProcessor.onNext(name);
        }
        wqueueProcessor.onComplete();
    }
```

9. Lastly, a special kind of processor that caches data elements but can only distribute them to strictly one subscriber is `UnicastProcessor<T>` which is used in `validateNamesUnicast()`. This `UnicastProcessor<T>` is usually used for events that require asynchronous queue-based fusion of Streams:

```
@Override
public void validateNamesUnicast(List<String> names) {
        UnicastProcessor<String> unicastProcessor =
            UnicastProcessor.create();
        Function<String,String> appendLic =
(name) -> name.concat(".112234");
        Function<String,String> appendKey =
(name) -> name.concat("-AEK2345J");
        Function<String,String> upperCase =
(name) -> name.toUpperCase();
        Flux<String> formatter1 =
unicastProcessor.filter((s) ->
            s.length() > 4).map(appendLic);
        // CANNOT RUN ANYMORE THE SUBSCRIBERS BELOW
        //Flux<String> formatter2 =
        // unicastProcessor.filter((s) ->
```

```
//      s.startsWith("J")).map(appendKey);
//Flux<String> formatter3 =
//      unicastProcessor.filter((s) ->
// s.endsWith("win")).map(upperCase);

formatter1.subscribe(System.out::println);
for(String name : names){
    unicastProcessor.onNext(name);
}
unicastProcessor.onComplete();
}
```

How it works...

Hot Streams are preferred in applications in which some of its features depend on data resources that are not fixed and most of the time unknown. To avoid overflows and series of exceptions and leaks, hot Streams are used for the recipients not to pull the data but just to connect and listen to incoming Streams, if any, and observe the built-in backpressure and concurrent loosely coupled event executions.

This recipe highlighted two ways to generate hot Streams and that is through `ConnectableFlux<T>` and `Processor<T>`. The easiest way of converting a typical cold Stream to a hot Stream is through the use of `ConnectableFlux<T>`. This flux creates a continuous flow of Stream from a data repository or from a huge datasource wherein the flow of execution has started even before any recipients connect to it. Since `ConnectableFlux<T>` does not need `subscribe()` to execute it, the only way to observe its Stream is to establish a connection. The recipient must explicitly call `connect()` and the very reason why no subscription is needed is its behavior as both publisher and subscriber. This Flux supports multiple subscriptions as seen in this recipe, `freeFlowEmps()` which creates a hot Stream that implements a continuous flow of current `Employee` Stream elements from the current snapshot of the database with two subscribers doing different result `Callback` executions.

On the other hand, using `Processor<T>` is more robust, pre-packaged, and direct than the former. It has a built-in asynchronous computing capability to execute Stream operations and has back-pressure support. Some of these processors have a caching mechanism to execute proper subscriptions. Just like `ConnectableFlux<T>`, a processor is both a publisher and a subscriber and the only way to use the hot Stream they generate is to `connect()` with them too.

Implementing Stream manipulation and transformation

Now we have seen some recipes showing concepts such as basic implementation of Reactive Stream interfaces and hot Stream generation, it is time to present a recipe that will enumerate some useful Stream operators needed to combine two or more Streams, compute single-valued result using reduction, provide gateways of data emissions, group together single-threaded Streams, and transform them to non-Stream data.

Getting ready

Open project ch07 again to add the following services that showcase important operators for Stream manipulations and transformations.

How to do it...

There are other Stream operations that can be useful when it comes to data transformation, conversion, manipulation, and augmentation. To illustrate how to use these deterministic operations, perform the following steps:

1. Let us create a service class EmployeeTransformDataStream that will be applying these kind of Stream operations:

```
public interface EmployeeTransformDataStream {
    public Flux<String> mergeWithNames(List<String> others);
    public Flux<String> concatWithNames(List<String>
        others);
    public Flux<Tuple2<String,String>>
        zipWithNames(List<String> others);
    public Flux<String> flatMapWithNames(List<String>
        others);
    public Mono<Integer> countEmpRecReduce();
    public Flux<GroupedFlux<String, String>> groupNames();
    public Flux<String> chooseEmission(List<String> others);
    public String blockedStreamData();
    public Iterable<String> iterableData();
}
```

2. The first method to implement carries two `Flux<T>` that need to be combined whenever the events of the first `Flux<T>` must be applied to it while the events of the second applies to both of them. Add the following service implementation with the use of the `concatWith()` operation:

```
@Service
public class EmployeeTransformDataStreamImpl
implements EmployeeTransformDataStream {
@Autowired
private EmployeeDao employeeDaoImpl;
@Override
public Flux<String> concatWithNames(List<String> others) {
    Function<Employee, String> names =
(emp) -> emp.getFirstName() + "---validated";
    Function<Employee, Mono<String>> flatMapName =
(emp) -> Mono.just(emp).map(names);
    Flux<String> concatNames =
        Flux.fromIterable(employeeDaoImpl.getEmployees())
            .flatMap(flatMapName)
                .concatWith(Flux.fromIterable(others))
                    .map(String::toUpperCase)
                    .distinct()
                    .sort((s1, s2) -> s1.compareTo(s2));
        return concatNames;
}
}
```

3. To add transformation, the method `concatWithNames()` also includes `distinct()` that allows no duplicate entries and `sort()` which uses `Comparator<T>` interface.

4. Next, implement `mergeWithNames()` that uses `mergeWith()` to combine two `Flux<T>` given that the operations are only applied to their respective `Flux<T>` stream. The method combines the results of the last two events:

```
@Override
public Flux<String> mergeWithNames(List<String> others) {
        Function<Employee, String> names =
(emp) -> emp.getFirstName() + "---validated";
        Function<Employee, Mono<String>> flatMapName =
(emp) -> Mono.just(emp).map(names);
        Flux<String> mergedNames =
                Flux.fromIterable(employeeDaoImpl
.getEmployees())
                    .flatMap(flatMapName)
                    .mergeWith(Flux.fromIterable(others)
                    .map(String::toUpperCase)
```

```
                    .sort((s1, s2) -> s1.compareTo(s2)));
        return mergedNames;
    }
```

5. The method `zipWithNames()` combines two `Flux<T>` and creates a `reactor.util.function.Tuple2`. A **tuple** is a finite ordered list of two or more values. In this method, we create a tuple of 2 using a `zipWith()` method:

```
@Override
public Flux<Tuple2<String,String>>
zipWithNames(List<String> others) {
        Function<Employee, String> names =
(emp) -> emp.getFirstName() + "---validated";
        Function<Employee, Mono<String>> flatMapName =
(emp) -> Mono.just(emp).map(names);
        Flux<Tuple2<String,String>> zipNames =
            Flux.fromIterable(employeeDaoImpl.getEmployees())
                .flatMap(flatMapName)
                .zipWith(Flux.fromIterable(others));
        return zipNames;
    }
```

6. To retrieve the values from `Tuple2`, we have the following test `TestEmployeeTransformDataStream` class as follows:

```
@RunWith(SpringJUnit4ClassRunner.class)
@WebAppConfiguration
@ContextConfiguration(classes = { SpringDbConfig
        .class, SpringDispatcherConfig.class })
public class TestEmployeeTransformDataStream {
    @Autowired
private EmployeeTransformDataStream
        employeeTransformDataStreamImpl;

@Test
public void testZipWith(){
        List<String> names = Arrays.asList("John", "Johnwin",
            "Jolina", "Owin");
        employeeTransformDataStreamImpl
.zipWithNames(names).subscribe((tuple) -> {
System.out.println(tuple.getT1() + "-" +
        tuple.getT2());
        });
    }
}
```

7. Aside from tuples, another operation can transform the Stream of elements into groups based on an input key. The flux generated by `groupBy()` is a flux of `GroupedFlux<T, T>` which can contain a varying number of Stream elements depending on what is common among them. The following method `groupNames()` shows how to group together Streams based on their initial character as key:

```
@Override
public Flux<GroupedFlux<String, String>> groupNames() {
      Function<Employee, String> names =
(emp) -> emp.getFirstName().toLowerCase();
      Flux<GroupedFlux<String, String>> grpsNames =
          Flux.fromIterable(employeeDaoImpl.getEmployees())
             .map(names)
             .groupBy(key -> key.charAt(0)+"");
      return grpsNames;
}
```

8. To test this method, add another test case to `TestEmployeeTransformDataStream` that will show how to retrieve each `GroupedFlux<String, String>` and will show their keys:

```
@Test
public void testGroupBy(){
    List<String> names =
Arrays.asList("John", "Johnwin", "Jolina", "Owin");
    employeeTransformDataStreamImpl.groupNames()
.subscribe((grp) ->{
              grp.collectList().subscribe((list)->{
                 System.out.println("Key: " + grp.key() + " "
                    + list);
              });
       });
}
```

9. The method `countEmpRecReduce()` computes the sum of all age data using the `reduce()` method. The same method is used to compute other aggregate results such as finding the minimum, maximum, and average values. This method always converts the Stream result to the `Mono<T>` stream:

```
@Override
public Mono<Integer> countEmpRecReduce() {
      Function<Employee, Integer> ages =
(emp) -> emp.getAge();
      Function<Employee, Mono<Integer>> flatMapAge =
(emp) -> Mono.just(emp).map(ages);
```

```
Mono<Integer> count =
    Flux.fromIterable(employeeDaoImpl.getEmployees())
        .flatMap(flatMapAge)
        .reduce((total, increment) -> total +
            increment);
return count;
}
```

10. If the requirement asks for a conversion of Streams to `Object` or `Iterable<T>`, operations such as `block()`, `blockLast()`, `blockFirst()`, and `iterable()` methods are used. These are synchronous operations that are sometimes not used because of their blocking capability. Following are two methods that convert Streams to `String` and `Iterable<String>`:

```
@Override
public String blockedStreamData() {
    Function<Employee, String> names =
(emp) -> emp.getFirstName();
    String blockStringVal =
    Flux.fromIterable(employeeDaoImpl
.getEmployees())
                    .map(names).blockFirst();
    return blockStringVal;
}

@Override
public Iterable<String> iterableData() {
    Function<Employee, String> names =
(emp) -> emp.getFirstName();
    Iterable<String> namesIterate =
    Flux.fromIterable(employeeDaoImpl
.getEmployees())
                .map(names).toIterable();
    return namesIterate;
}
```

11. When implementing gateways of Streams wherein the first Stream to emit data will be the final stream, `firstEmitting()` is used. The following recipe determines which among the three `Flux<T>` will emit the first data Streams:

```
@Override
public Flux<String> chooseEmission(List<String> others) {
    Function<Employee, String> names =
(emp) -> emp.getFirstName();
    Flux<String> sideA = Flux.fromIterable(others)
            .delayElements(
Duration.ofMillis(200));
```

```
                    Flux<String> sideB =
                      Flux.fromIterable(employeeDaoImpl.getEmployees())
                          .map(names)
                          .delayElements(Duration.ofMillis(300));
                    Flux<String> sideC = Flux.fromIterable(others)
                                                .take(2);
                    Flux<String> chosen = Flux.firstEmitting(sideA,
                  sideB, sideC);
                   return chosen;
                  }
```

12. Lastly, an operator widely used, especially in this chapter is `flaptMap()` which is capable of running multiple `Publisher<T>` asynchronously processing transactions and later merging them into an interleaved sequence of Stream data results that can be subscribed in sequential or parallel mode. The following is a method that will illustrate how `flatMap()` provides data transformation during some computations with the help of `repeat()` and `delayElements()`:

```
                  @Override
                  public Flux<String> flatMapWithNames(List<String> others) {
                        Flux<String> flatMaps = Flux.fromIterable(others)
                              .flatMap((str) ->{
                  return Mono.just(str).repeat(3)
                  .map(String::toUpperCase)
                  .delayElements(Duration.ofMillis(1));
                              });
                        return flatMaps;
                  }
```

How it works...

Once the original non-Stream data is converted into Streams, all of them undergo several transformations and manipulations based on what operations are involved in the Reactive event. Previous recipes have used `map()`, `sort()`, and `filter()` to change the nature of the original stream. Now, this recipe has added some of the non-blocking and asynchronous operations that do not only involve manipulation of one Stream but a group of Streams.

The concatWith() method combines two sequences, one at a time, applying a set of operations with different levels of augmentation. The simpler version of this is concatMap() which merges all the sequences before applying any of the operations to produce the final augmented stream. On the other hand, mergeWith() augments two Streams with their respective operations already executed. Whereas, zipWith() creates tuples of 2, up to 8 depending on the needs of the event. All of these operations flatten all the Streams to arrive at only one Stream at the end. One of the popular generic flattening operations is flatMap() which combines result Streams of more than one Publisher<T> and creates one final stream.

There are some useful operations that are non-blocking, for instance blockFirst() and blockLast() which extract the final or initial Stream data, respectively. Some blocking operations like toIterable() create a collection of data ready for traversals, count() which gives the amount of Stream data per emission, and single() which creates Mono<T> from the final stream.

Just like the reduce() pipeline operator in Chapter 6, *Functional Programming*, Publisher<T> supports reduce() in the execution of java.util.function.BiFunction<T, T, T> for summation, average, standard deviation, and variance of any numerical Stream elements. This aggregator is best paired with map() in dealing with computing non-numerical data Streams.

Streams can also be emitted through chunks with the use of the groupBy() operator. This operator is a best example of a transformer which groups together Stream data based on common criteria called keys instead of passing them as individual elements.

And when it comes to choosing which Streams to emit first, the firstEmitting() operator accepts more than one Stream and lets the fastest Stream emit first to its subscribers. Depending on the backpressure applied and volume of data, firstEmitting() does not guarantee that the first to emit will always be the fastest in all circumstances.

Testing Reactive data transactions

Using the Spring Test framework, Reactive Stream events can be tested using reactor.test.StepVerifier which contains all the expectations and verifications needed to validate whether the output Stream data complies with the expected result or if the event is not properly composed of the appropriate operators.

Getting ready

Open the same `ch07` project and create a number of test cases depicting the use of
`StepVerifier`.

How to do it...

Aside from typical `@Test` execution, Reactive Stream has a dedicated API called
`StepVerifier`, which can be used to verify if its Stream emission is appropriate for a
certain requirement. Let us use the following steps to test Reactive Stream operations:

1. `StepVerifier` is part of the Reactor Core add-ons so add this dependency to
   `pom.xml`:

   ```
   <dependency>
       <groupId>io.projectreactor.addons</groupId>
       <artifactId>reactor-test</artifactId>
       <version>3.0.7.RELEASE</version>
        <scope>test</scope>
   </dependency>
   ```

2. Create a test class `TestEmployeUsingVerifier` that creates a test case that
   highlights `StepVerifier` in testing `Publisher<T>`, `Mono<T>` and `Flux<T>`
   data emissions. `StepVerifier` can check if the operators involved are risky, can
   simulate a subscription, can validate expected data values and compare them
   with actual values, and can verify if `Throwable` are thrown during emissions:

   ```
   @RunWith(SpringJUnit4ClassRunner.class)
   @WebAppConfiguration
   @ContextConfiguration(classes = { SpringDbConfig
           .class, SpringDispatcherConfig.class })
   public class TestEmployeUsingVerifier {
      @Autowired
      private EmployeeStreamservice
            employeeStreamserviceImpl;
      @Autowired
      private EmployeeTransformDataStream
            employeeTransformDataStreamImpl;

   @Autowired
      private EmployeeBatchStreamservice
            employeeBatchStreamserviceImpl;
      @Test
      public void testEmpNames(){
   ```

```
        StepVerifier
                .create(employeeStreamserviceImpl.getFirstNames())
.expectSubscription()                    .expectNext("Sherwin")
.expectNext("Owen")                      .thenCancel()
.log().verify();
}
}
```

3. If the `Publisher<T>` to be tested has unstable and non-periodic emissions due to voluminous data sources and intermittent connections, a different `StepVerifier` must be created which can wait until all considerable emissions have been generated. The following is a test case that tests a risky `Publisher<T>` and waits for 2 seconds before verifying the expected data:

```
@Test
public void testEmpNamesVirtual(){
        StepVerifier.withVirtualTime(
() -> employeeBatchStreamserviceImpl
.getTimedFirstNames())
                .expectSubscription()
                .thenAwait(Duration.ofSeconds(2))
                .expectNext("Rey")
                .expectNext("Sherwin")
                .thenCancel()
                .log().verify();
    }
```

4. Verifying the expected test data results can be written much more simply. Create the test case in the following code snippet that verifies three names using only one `expectNext()` invocation:

```
@Test
public void testOnComplete() {
    List<String> names = Arrays.asList("John", "Johnwin",
        "Jolina", "Owin");
    StepVerifier.create(employeeTransformDataStreamImpl
.concatWithNames(names))
            .expectNext("Johnwin", "Owin", "Riza")
            .expectComplete()
            .verify();
}
```

5. Lastly, we can use `StepVerifier` to test `GroupedFlux<T,T>` wherein the test case must consider a list of names that will be verified as one group. The following test case checks if a group contains `["jerry", "joel"]` as a group:

```
@Test
public void testGroup() {
    StepVerifier
        .create(employeeTransformDataStreamImpl
    .groupNames()
    .blockFirst())
        .expectSubscription()
        .expectNext("joel")
        .expectNext("jerry")
        .expectComplete()
        .verify();
}
```

A `blockFirst()` method has been invoked to randomly test one group.

How it works...

Using StepVerifier is optional and it is categorized as an add-on to the Reactor Core 3.x libraries. This class needs `Publisher<T>` to test in order to be created. There are two ways to create StepVerifier: through its `create()` and `withVirtualTime()`. When testing stable and predictable Streams with uniform and controlled backpressure, the `create()` method is used. Whereas if testing unstable Streams with highly unpredictable emissions, `withVirtualTime()` is used because it uses a scheduler and virtual time delay to wait for the publisher to emit the necessary elements before the expectations and verifications.

After creating the object, there are methods to use to set expectations like `expectComplete()`, `expectError()`, and `expectSubscription()`. To compare data values to the incoming Streams, `expectNext()` is called with the data as its arguments. To assume cancellation of subscription, at any point in the verification, `thenCancel()` can be invoked.

Lastly, to verify all expectations are in compliance with the event, we call `verify()`. Usually at the end part the `StepVerifier.AssertionError` will be thrown if one expectation fails; otherwise, all the formulae match the desired subscription result.

Implementing Reactive events using RxJava 2.x

There are other Reactive implementations that can still be used with Spring 5.x applications and one is RxJava 2.x. Under Apache license, RxJava is now a widely used Reactive programming port in many android applications. It has a huge number of APIs that can implement extensive and highly-threaded operations with Reactive approach. Behind its huge set of packages, RxJava follows the Reactive Stream specification.

Getting ready

Lastly, an additional service class will be added to ch07 through which a new approach will be shown on how to create publishers and subscribers using the RxJava approach.

How to do it...

This last recipe will show us how Spring 5 can integrate with other Reactive Stream implementation such as RxJava 2.0:

1. In order for our Spring 5 platform to work perfectly with RxJava, add the following Maven dependencies to the pom.xml configuration:

```
<dependency>
<groupId>io.Reactivex.rxjava2</groupId>
<artifactId>rxjava</artifactId>
<version>2.1.0</version>
</dependency>
```

2. Create a service class EmployeeRxJavaService that contains the following template methods summarizing all RxJava events:

```
public interface EmployeeRxJavaService {
   public Observable<Employee> getEmployeesRx();
   public Single<Employee> getEmployeeRx(int empid);
   public Flowable<String> getFirstNamesRx();
   public Flowable<String> getEmpNamesRx();
   public Flowable<String> getEmpNamesParallelRx();
   public Flowable<String> combinedStreamRx(List<String>
others);
   public ConnectableObservable<String> freeFlowEmps();
}
```

3. The `Publisher<T>` interface in Reactor Core is equivalently `Observable<T>` in RxJava. Similarly, `Observable<T>` sends data to its subscribers implementing the concept of observer design pattern. Following is a service method `getEmployeesRx()` that converts records of employees to a Stream of data using `Observable<T>`:

```
@Service
public class EmployeeRxJavaServiceImpl
implements EmployeeRxJavaService {
    @Autowired
    private EmployeeDao employeeDaoImpl;

    @Override
    public Observable<Employee> getEmployeesRx() {
        Observable<Employee> publishedEmployees =
Observable.fromIterable(employeeDaoImpl.getEmployees());
        return publishedEmployees;
}
}
```

4. To subscribe with `Observable<T>`, we need to implement its own `io.reactivex.functions.Consumer<T>` or override the callback of `Observer<T>`. RxJava has its own set of functional interfaces and it does support the Java 1.8 Stream APIs unlike Reactor Core. Following is a test class that contains two ways to subscribe with observables:

```
@RunWith(SpringJUnit4ClassRunner.class)
@WebAppConfiguration
@ContextConfiguration(classes = { SpringDbConfig
        .class, SpringDispatcherConfig.class })
public class TestEmployeeRxJavaService {
    @Autowired
    private EmployeeRxJavaService employeeRxJavaServiceImpl;
    @Test
    public void testEmployeeData(){
        Observer<Employee> mySubscription =
new Observer<Employee>() {

            @Override
            public void onComplete() {
                System.out.println("subscription completed");
            }

            @Override
            public void onError(Throwable ex) {
                System.out.println("problems encountered"
```

```
                      + ex.getMessage());
                  }

                  @Override
                  public void onNext(Employee emp) {
                      System.out.format("Employee: %s \n",
                          emp.getEmpId());
                  }

                  @Override
                  public void onSubscribe(Disposable arg0) {
                      System.out.println("subscription started");
                  }
              };
              employeeRxJavaServiceImpl.getEmployeesRx()
      .subscribe(mySubscription);
          }
          @Test
          public void testEmployeeDataConsumer(){
              Consumer<Employee> consume = (emp) ->{
                  System.out.println(emp.getFirstName());
              };
              employeeRxJavaServiceImpl.getEmployeesRx()
      .subscribe(consume);
          }
      }
```

5. To create a single-valued Stream which can contain at most one value,
   Single<T> is used. It is not a subclass of Observable<T> but it behaves like a
   Mono<T> publisher that can trigger onSuccess() or onError(). The following
   is getEmployeeRx() that can emit an Employee record or an error by executing
   a Callable task:

```
      @Override
      public Single<Employee> getEmployeeRx(int empid) {
          Callable<Employee> task =
      () -> employeeDaoImpl.getEmployee(empid);
          Single<Employee> emp = Single.fromCallable(task);
          return emp;
      }
```

6. If Reactor Core has `Flux<T>`, RxJava has `Flowable<T>` that supports backpressure, transformation, grouping, multithreading, and concurrency operations. The method `getFirstNamesRx()` converts records of `Employees`, extracts their first names and converts all `String` Stream data to uppercase:

```
@Override
public Flowable<String> getFirstNamesRx() {
    Function<Employee, Publisher<String>> firstNames =
(emp) -> Mono.just(emp.getFirstName())
.map(String::toUpperCase);
Flowable<String> emps =
    Flowable.fromIterable(employeeDaoImpl.getEmployees())
 .flatMap(firstNames);
    return emps;
}
```

7. To create schedulers, RxJava uses `io.reactivex.schedulers.Schedulers` to create different `io.reactivex.Scheduler` for the observables and observers. To assign `thread(s)` for `Observable<T>` to process its operations, the method `subscribeOn()` is invoked. These threads are where the subscriptions happen. On the other hand, `Observer<T>` callbacks or Lambda expressions can be done in threads assigned by `observeOn()`:

```
@Override
public Flowable<String> getEmpNamesRx() {
    Scheduler observerWorker = Schedulers.single();
    Scheduler subscriberWorker = Schedulers.newThread();
    Function<Employee, String> names =
(emp) -> emp.getFirstName() + emp.getLastName();
    Flowable<String> emps = Flowable
.fromIterable(employeeDaoImpl.getEmployees())
        .map(names)
.observeOn(observerWorker)
.subscribeOn(subscriberWorker);
    return emps;
}
```

8. Parallelism can be designed in most of the RxJava events by creating a thread-pool that will work in parallel mode. The generation of these threads is done by invoking `Schedulers.computation()` which is shown in the following code snippet:

```java
@Override
public Flowable<String> getEmpNamesParallelRx() {
    Function<Employee, String> names = (emp) ->{
        System.out.println("flatMap thread: "
+ Thread.currentThread().getName());
return emp.getFirstName().charAt(0) +
    emp.getLastName();
    };
    Flowable<String> parallelEmpFlux =
Flowable.fromIterable(employeeDaoImpl
.getEmployees())
            .map(names)
            .subscribeOn(Schedulers.computation());
    return parallelEmpFlux;
}
```

9. Also, the RxJava has its own operations that will provide Stream transformation and manipulations just like `sorted()` for sorting numeric and character-based Stream elements and `zipWith()` to create tuples of Stream elements. Create the folllowing method that utilizes the following two operators:

```java
@Override
public Flowable<String> combinedStreamRx(List<String> others) {
    Function<Employee, String> names =
(emp) -> emp.getFirstName() + "---validated";
    Flowable<String> zipNames = Flowable
.fromIterable(employeeDaoImpl.getEmployees())
        .map(names)
        .sorted()
        .zipWith(others,(str1, str2) ->
String.format("%s. %s", str1, str2));
    return zipNames;
}
```

10. Just like Reactor Core, RxJava can also provide operations or events that can generate hot Streams. These Streams are always flowing and the only way for its subscribers to extract the Streams is through the `connect()` method. It can allow several subscriptions which eventually connect to the hot Stream to start the emission. Create the following method that generates `ConnectableObservable<T>` from a cold Stream of Employee records:

```
@Override
public ConnectableObservable<String> freeFlowEmps() {
        List<String> rosterNames = new ArrayList<>();
        Function<Employee, String> familyNames =
(emp) -> emp.getLastName().toUpperCase();
        ConnectableObservable<String> flowyNames =
            Observable
.fromIterable(employeeDaoImpl.getEmployees())
.map(familyNames).cache()
.publish();
        flowyNames.subscribe(System.out::println);
        flowyNames.subscribe(rosterNames::add);
        return flowyNames;
}
```

11. Lastly, create a test method that will execute the preceding method:

```
@Test
public void testConnectFluxProcessor(){
employeeRxJavaServiceImpl.freeFlowEmps().connect();
}
```

How it works...

Unlike any other implementation, the RxJava 2.0 is one of the earliest favorites when it comes to Reactive programming. Many supporting features and enhancements have been added to its libraries and now it has several API classes and interfaces that can be used to generate Reactive events.

The publishers are called `Observable<T>` which are Streams of elements listened to by `Observer<T>` which are the subscribers in Reactor. There are four types of `Observable<T>` and two are highlighted in the recipe namely `Single<T>` which is the same as `Mono<T>` in concept and `Flowable<T>` which is similar to `Flux<T>`. The other two are `Maybe<T>` and `Completable<T>` wherein the former emits an element, and error or void while the latter only `onComplete()` or error without returning any element.

When it comes to asynchronous and threaded operations, it has its own version of `sort()`, `zipWith()` and many others discussed in the previous recipes. Aside from similarities with Reactor 3.x, there are also some differences when it comes to APIs such as creating schedulers. In RxJava 2.x, there are five types that can be generated by `io.Reactivex.Scheduler` and these are `immediate()`, `newThread()`, `trampoline()`, `computation()`, and `io()`. To create a single-threaded executor, `newThread()` is invoked while thread-pool for parallel processing is generated by calling `computation()`. Calling `trampoline()` has a somewhat similar result to `elastic()` in Reactor 3.x wherein threads are revived from the cache to be used for the next operation.

Another thing that makes RxJava different from Reactor 3.x is the absence of support for Java-based functional interfaces and Streams. All `Function<T>`, `Consumer<T>`, and `Supplier<T>` used in this recipe are APIs of its `io.reactivex.functions` and do not belong to `java.util.function` of Java 1.8 and above. Whether it may or may not affect Spring 5 applications, what is essential is that RxJava can be a strong option for Reactive programming solutions in the Spring 5 framework.

8
Reactive Web Applications

Since Spring Framework 3.1, the `ApplicationContext` has been supporting scalable, dynamic, real-time, and huge transactions through its non-blocking and asynchronous request handlers. The previous concepts of functional and reactive programming will be very helpful in realizing every recipe of this chapter, through which the progression of Spring Framework's support on non-blocking and asynchronous MVC will be illustrated piece-by piece, starting from the very start of asynchronous `@Controller` and services up to this day on functional and reactive web support.

Certain areas of this chapter will provide proof that Spring 5 still supports the previous foundation of asynchronous MVC configuration, including some of its new enhancements on concurrency specified by Java 1.8 and above. Also, the chapter will cover some supported view technology that can recognize the Reactor's `Publisher<T>` data stream. Another inclusion is the integration of Spring Security to the platform and how it is applied to threads created by `TaskExecutor` through the command of the `DispatcherServlet`. Most importantly, the core part will cover the experimentation on how complete the support of Apache Tomcat 9 and Spring 5 on Reactive Stream 1.x specification is, which is the starting point of Spring `WebFlux` framework. This part of the discussion will need some flashbacks to recipes with regard to the functional programming of Chapter 6, *Functional Programming* and reactive programming using Reactor Core 3.0 and RxJava 2.x of Chapter 7, *Reactive Programming*.

In this chapter, you will learn the following:

- Configuring the TaskExecutor
- Implementing @Async services
- Creating asynchronous controllers
- Creating @Scheduled services
- Using Future<T> and CallableFuture<T>

- Using Mono<T> and Flux<T> publishers for services
- Creating Mono<T> and Flux<T> HTTP response
- Integrating RxJava 2.0
- Using FreeMarker to render Publisher<T> stream
- Using Thymeleaf to render Publisher<T> stream
- Applying security on TaskExecutors

Configuring the TaskExecutor

It is appropriate to start this chapter with a recipe that will deal with the processing of huge request transactions, slicing them into pieces to be assigned for thread pool synchronously executions and managing their callbacks to arrive at a final response. In short, the recipe below will enumerate on how to enable asynchronous Spring 5 MVC platform.

Getting started

Using the Eclipse STS from Chapter 1, *Getting started with Spring*, create a Maven Project ch08 with a core package org.packt.web.reactive to start with.

How to do it...

Let us start this chapter with a new set up and configuration for the new ch08 project and with the following steps:

1. Add in its pom.xml and all the needed Maven core libraries and dependencies such as the *Spring 5, Servlet 3.1, JSP 2.3.1, JSTL 1.2, MySQL Connector 5.1.x, HikariCP 2.5.x*, and *Log4J 1.2*.
2. Just like in the previous chapters, create similar empty classes, namely SpringWebinitializer, SpringWebinitializer, SpringContextConfig, and SpringDbConfig. Store them in their respective packages and configure them according to what's been done previously.

3. To enable asynchronous request transactions with callbacks, the Spring 5
    platform must utilize *at least Servlet 3.1* container since this version supports
    multithreading in web applications. Open `SpringWebinitializer` and enable
    `<async-supported/>` in a `JavaConfig` manner:

```
@EnableWebMvc
@ComponentScan(basePackages = "org.packt.reactive.codes")
@Configuration
public class SpringWebinitializer
implements WebApplicationInitializer {
    @Override
    public void onStartup(ServletContext container)
throws ServletException {
        addRootContext(container);
        addDispatcherContext(container);
    }

   // refer to sources
    private void addDispatcherContext(ServletContext
        container) {

        AnnotationConfigWebApplicationContext
         dispatcherContext =
            new AnnotationConfigWebApplicationContext();
   dispatcherContext.register(
SpringDispatcherConfig.class);
        ServletRegistration.Dynamic dispatcher =
         container.addServlet("ch08-servlet",
            new DispatcherServlet(dispatcherContext));
        dispatcher.addMapping("/");
        dispatcher.setLoadOnStartup(1);
        dispatcher.setAsyncSupported(true);
    }
}
```

The entire book officially uses **Apache Tomcat 9**, which generates its
threads from the thread pool.

4. Since we will be generating executor services that will generate threads later, we need to configure `server.xml` to set the maximum and minimum number of threads in the Tomcat container. Most importantly, there is a need to change our Tomcat's Java connector to `org.apache.coyote.http11.Http11NioProtocol` for optimal server performance and management of multiple threads during context root execution:

```
<Connector port="8443"
    protocol="org.apache.coyote.http11.Http11NioProtocol"
            minProcessors="3"
            maxProcessors="10"
            maxThreads="1000" SSLEnabled="true">
    <UpgradeProtocol
    className="org.apache.coyote.http2.Http2Protocol" />
        <SSLHostConfig honorCipherOrder="false">
            <Certificate
                certificateKeyFile="conf/spring5packt.key"
                    certificateFile="conf/spring5packt.crt"
                    keyAlias="spring5server"
                    type="RSA" />
        </SSLHostConfig>
</Connector>
```

5. Afterwards, configure the thread generation process for the application. Create the context configuration below that implements `org.springframework.scheduling.annotation.AsyncConfigurer` responsible for injecting `org.springframework.core.task.TaskExecutor` into the Spring container. The context definition must have a class level annotation `@EnableAsync` to trigger asynchronous processing anywhere in the platform:

```
import java.util.concurrent.Executor;
import java.util.concurrent.Executors;

@EnableAsync
@Configuration
@ComponentScan(basePackages = {"org.packt.web.reactor"})
public class SpringAsynchConfig implements AsyncConfigurer {
    /*
        @Override
        public Executor getAsyncExecutor() {
            ThreadPoolTaskExecutor executor = new
                ThreadPoolTaskExecutor();
            executor.setCorePoolSize(5);
            executor.setMaxPoolSize(9);
            executor.setQueueCapacity(50);
```

```
            executor.setThreadNamePrefix("Ch08Executor-");
        executor.setWaitForTasksToCompleteOnShutdown(true);
            executor.setKeepAliveSeconds(5000);
            executor.setAwaitTerminationSeconds(1000);
            executor.initialize();
            return executor;
        }
    */
/*

        @Override
        public Executor getAsyncExecutor () {
            SimpleAsyncTaskExecutor executor =
new SimpleAsyncTaskExecutor();
            executor.setConcurrencyLimit(100);
            return executor;
        }
    */
    @Override
    public Executor getAsyncExecutor () {
        ConcurrentTaskExecutor executor =
            new ConcurrentTaskExecutor(
        Executors.newFixedThreadPool(100));
        executor.setTaskDecorator(new TaskDecorator() {
            @Override
            public Runnable decorate (Runnable runnable) {
                return () -> {
                    long t = System.currentTimeMillis();
                    runnable.run();
                    System.out.printf("Thread %s has a
                        processing time:
%s%n", Thread.currentThread().getName(),
(System.currentTimeMillis() - t));
                };
            }
        });
        return executor;
    }
}
```

 Preceding there are three executor types, but this recipe uses
`ConcurrentTaskExecutor`.

How it works...

Before reactive programming, asynchronous web features were already part of the previous Spring core used in huge multiple transactions and batch processing. Up to this day, the interface `TaskExecutor` is needed to generate threads for the MVC platform. It has several implementation types, but the ones widely used are the `SimpleAsyncTaskExecutor`, `ThreadPoolTaskExecutor`, and `ConcurrentTaskExecutor`.

SimpleAsyncTaskExecutor

The `SimpleAsyncTaskExecutor` has the least configuration properties since it *does not reuse* any threads, but creates a new one once an execution happens. If the concurrency limit has been reached, this executor blocks all requests and puts them in a queue until a slot is available.

ThreadPoolTaskExecutor

The next executor, `ThreadPoolTaskExecutor` is quite the opposite, since it has several properties to configure for thread management. This type has a scheduling management support which depends on the properties exposed such as `setKeepAliveSeconds(n)`, `setQueueCapacity(n)`, and `setAwaitTerminationSeconds(n)`.

ConcurrentTaskExecutor

On the other hand, the `ConcurrentTaskExecutor` runs the same as the `ThreadPoolTaskExecutor` but in a more flexible manner. It has a decorator which is executed as a runnable task that can be utilized to add some monitoring and statistics for its task execution.

There is only one `TaskExecutor` that can be injected into the container implemented by `AsyncConfigurer`. This happens because we have only one method, `getAsyncExecutor()`, to override in order to inject that sole `TaskExecutor` appropriate for the applications.

This entire configuration will not be triggered without invoking the class-level `@EnableAsync` in the custom `SpringAsyncConfig` context definition. In the case that `getAsyncExecutor()` has not been overridden, it will inject `SimpleAsyncTaskExecutor` by default.

Implementing @Async services

It's not only controllers that can be non-blocking in Spring 5; the service layer can too. Just like its lower versions, Spring 5 also supports asynchronous services to implement concurrent service transactions in the background. This recipe will highlight `Callable<T>` and `@Async` Spring native services.

Getting started

Open the current Maven project `ch08` and implement some methods that run asynchronously.

How to do it...

Spring 5 offers asynchronous service layer that can be called by any asynchronous controllers. Let us build these service layer using the following steps:

1. Before we start this recipe, the use of `@Async` requires a thorough and appropriate configuration of any `TaskExecutor` type in `SpringAsynchConfig` including some proxy-related configurations on `@EnableAsync` annotation.

2. Create a package `org.packt.web.reactor.service` and add `EmployeeService` with some template methods:

```
public interface EmployeeService {
    public CompletableFuture<List<Employee>>
        readEmployees();
    public Callable<List<Employee>> readEmployeesCall();
    public Future<Employee>  readEmployee(Integer empId);
    public void addEmployee(EmployeeForm emp);
    public void updateEmployee(EmployeeForm emp, int id) ;
public void delEmployee(Integer empId);
}
```

3. Any Spring 5 service can be converted to the asynchronous type just by having it return a `Callable<T>` task. Usually, it is mandatory for synchronous services to return `Callable<T>`, even when if it is created to be `void` by default. Create `EmployeeServiceImpl` by implementing `readEmployeesCall()` which retrieves a list of employees and wraps it with a `Callable` task:

```
@Service
public class EmployeeServiceImpl implements EmployeeService {
    @Autowired
    private EmployeeDao employeeDaoImpl;

@Override
    public Callable<List<Employee>> readEmployeesCall() {
        Callable< List<Employee> > task =
new Callable< List<Employee> >() {
                @Override
                public  List<Employee>  call () throws
                    Exception {
System.out.println("controller:readEmployeesCall
task executor: " +
    Thread.currentThread().getName());
                    Thread.sleep(6000);
                    List<Employee> empList =
                        employeeDaoImpl.getEmployees();
                    return empList;
                }
        };
        return task;
    }
}
```

4. Another option for creating non-blocking services is to apply the `@EnableAsync` feature in the Spring platform. With this annotation, the `@Async` can now be attached to service methods with or without a return value, in order to run its transaction asynchronously:

```
@Async
@Override
public CompletableFuture<List<Employee>> readEmployees() {
    Supplier<List<Employee>> supplyListEmp = ()->{
        System.out.println("service:readEmployees task
        executor: " + Thread.currentThread().getName());
        System.out.println("processing for 5000 ms");
        try {
            Thread.sleep(6000);
        } catch (InterruptedException e) {
```

```
        e.printStackTrace();
      }
      return employeeDaoImpl.getEmployees();
    };
    return CompletableFuture.supplyAsync(supplyListEmp);
}


@Async
@Override
public void addEmployee(EmployeeForm empForm) {
  Employee emp = new Employee();
  emp.setDeptId(empForm.getEmpId());
  emp.setFirstName(empForm.getFirstName());

  // refer to sources
  try {
    System.out.println("service:addEmployee task executor: " +
    Thread.currentThread().getName());
    System.out.println("processing for 1000 ms");
    Thread.sleep(1000);
  } catch (InterruptedException e) {   }
  employeeDaoImpl.addEmployeeBySJI(emp);
}


@Async
public Future<Employee> readEmployee(Integer empId) {
  try {
    System.out.println("service:readEmployee(empid) task
executor: " +
    Thread.currentThread().getName());
    System.out.println("processing for 2000 ms");
    Thread.sleep(2000);
  } catch (InterruptedException e) { }
  return new AsyncResult<>(employeeDaoImpl.getEmployee(empId));
}


@Async
@Override
public void updateEmployee(EmployeeForm empForm, int id) {
  Employee emp = new Employee();
  emp.setDeptId(empForm.getEmpId());
  emp.setFirstName(empForm.getFirstName());

  // refer to sources
  try {
    System.out.println("service:updateEmployee task
    executor: " + thread.currentThread().getName());
    System.out.println("processing for 1000 ms");
```

```
    Thread.sleep(1000);
  } catch (InterruptedException e) { }
  employeeDaoImpl.updateEmployee(emp);
}

@Async
@Override
public void delEmployee(Integer empId) {
  try {
    System.out.println("service:delEmployee task
    executor: "   + Thread.currentThread().getName());
    System.out.println("processing for 1000 ms");
    Thread.sleep(1000);
  } catch (InterruptedException e) { }
  employeeDaoImpl.delEmployee(empId);
}
```

 Combining @Async with Callable<T> will not work for Spring 5 service implementation due to some proxy-related issues.

5. Now, create a full-blown form controller that will perform the *adding of new employees* and *retrieving the list of employees* from the data source using the recently implemented non-blocking methods:

```
@Controller
@RequestMapping(value="/react/empform.html")
public class EmployeeController {
   @Autowired
   private EmployeeService employeeServiceImpl;
   @Autowired
   private DepartmentService departmentServiceImpl;
   @InitBinder("employeeForm")
   public void initBinder(WebDataBinder binder){
      binder.registerCustomEditor(Integer.class, "age",
new AgeEditor());
      binder.registerCustomEditor(Date.class,
new DateEditor());
   }
   @RequestMapping(method=RequestMethod.GET)
   public String employeeForm(Model model){
      EmployeeForm employeeForm = new EmployeeForm();
      model.addAttribute("employeeForm", employeeForm);
      references(model);
      return "emp-form";
   }
```

```
@RequestMapping(method=RequestMethod.POST)
public String employeeList(Model model, @Validated
    @ModelAttribute("employeeForm") EmployeeForm
        employeeForm, BindingResult result){
    try {
employeeServiceImpl.addEmployee(employeeForm);
        List<Employee> empList = employeeServiceImpl
.readEmployees().get(5000, TimeUnit.SECONDS);
        model.addAttribute("empList", empList);
    } catch (InterruptedException e) { }
catch (ExecutionException e) { }
catch (TimeoutException e) { }
    return "emp-list";
}
    private void references(Model model){
        List<Integer> deptIds = new ArrayList<>();
        List<Department> depts =
            departmentServiceImpl.readDepartments();
        Iterator<Department> iterate = depts.iterator();
        while(iterate.hasNext()){
            deptIds.add(iterate.next().getId());
        }
        model.addAttribute("deptIds", deptIds);
    }
}
```

6. For creating reports and updating and deleting records of employees, we have this `ReportController` below that will showcase how to invoke `@Async` methods with `Thread.sleep(n)`. The following request handler accesses the `CompletableFuture<T>` result from an asynchronous `readDepartments()` of `DepartmentService` through a risky `get()` method:

```
@Controller
public class ReportController {
    @Autowired
    private DepartmentService departmentServiceImpl;
    @Autowired
    private EmployeeService employeeServiceImpl;
    @RequestMapping(value="/react/viewdepts.html",
        method=RequestMethod.GET)
    public String viewDepts(Model model){
        try {
            model.addAttribute("departments",
                departmentServiceImpl
.readDepartments().get(5000,
        TimeUnit.MILLISECONDS));
        } catch (InterruptedException e) { }
```

```
catch (ExecutionException e) { }
catch (TimeoutException e) { }
      return "dept-list";
    }
```

7. Another way of retrieving result from `CompletableFuture<T>` task is through its non-risky `join()` method, which does not throw `InterruptedException` when something wrong happens during the asynchronous process:

```
@RequestMapping(value="/react/viewemps.html",
method=RequestMethod.GET)
public String viewEmps(Model model){
   List<Employee> empList =
employeeServiceImpl.readEmployees().join();
    model.addAttribute("empList", empList);
    return "emp-list";
}
```

8. There are `@Async` methods that perform asynchronous with the help of `Thread.sleep()` just to delay the process and to avoid thread-related Exception like the following `delEmployee()` of `EmployeeService`:

```
@RequestMapping(value={"/react/delemp.html/{empId}"})
public String deleteRecord(Model model, @PathVariable("empId")
Integer empId){
    try {
      employeeServiceImpl.delEmployee(empId);
      Thread.sleep(1000);
      List<Employee> empList = employeeServiceImpl
      .readEmployees().get(5000, TimeUnit.SECONDS);
      model.addAttribute("empList", empList);
    } catch (InterruptedException e) { }
    catch (ExecutionException e) { }
    catch (TimeoutException e) { }
    return "emp-list";
}
```

9. One way of executing asynchronous services is to use the `supplyAsync()` *static* method of `CompletableFuture<T>` that requires a `Supplier<T>` functional interface, as shown by the following request handler:

```
@RequestMapping(value={"/react/updateemp.html/{id}"},
method=RequestMethod.POST)
public String updateRecordSubmit(Model
model, @PathVariable("id") Integer id, @Validated
@ModelAttribute("employeeForm")
```

```
EmployeeForm employeeForm, BindingResult result){

   Consumer<List<Employee>> processResult = (empList) ->{
     model.addAttribute("empList", empList);
   };
   Supplier<List<Employee>> asyncSupplier = () ->{
     try {
       employeeServiceImpl.updateEmployee(employeeForm, id);
       Thread.sleep(1000);
       return employeeServiceImpl.readEmployees().get(5000,
       TimeUnit.SECONDS);
     } catch (InterruptedException e) {
       e.printStackTrace();
     } catch (ExecutionException e) {
       e.printStackTrace();
     } catch (TimeoutException e) {
       e.printStackTrace();
     }
     return null;
   };
   CompletableFuture.supplyAsync(asyncSupplier)
   .thenAccept(processResult);
   return "emp-list";
}
private void references(Model model){
   List<Integer> deptIds = new ArrayList<>();
   List<Department> depts = departmentServiceImpl
   .readDepartments().getNow(new ArrayList<>());
   // refer to sources
   model.addAttribute("deptIds", deptIds);
}
```

10. Use the `EmployeeDao` implementation from `Chapter 3`, *Implementing MVC Design Pattern*, on JDBC concepts.

11. Import the `AgeEditor` and `DateEditor` of the previous chapters.

12. Utilize the message bundles, view mappings and view pages from `Chapter 3`, *Implementing MVC Design Pattern*.

13. Save all files. Then `clean`, `build`, and `run` transactions. Run each request handler several times and observe `/logs/tomcat9-stdout.xxxx-xx-xx.log`:

```
service:readEmployees task executor: pool-3-thread-4
processing for 5000 ms
service:addEmployee task executor: pool-3-thread-3
processing for 1000 ms
Thread pool-3-thread-3 has a processing time:  1012
Thread pool-3-thread-4 has a processing time:  5003
```

```
service:delEmployee task executor: pool-3-thread-5
processing for 1000 ms
service:readEmployees task executor: pool-3-thread-6
processing for 5000 ms
Thread pool-3-thread-5 has a processing time:   1072
Thread pool-3-thread-6 has a processing time:   5002
```

How it works...

Building *asynchronous services* is recommended only for long transaction queues, voluminous transactions, and remote processing that experiences intermittent server communication. In the previous Spring versions, @Service methods that return Callable<T> are automatically considered non-blocking. It can be invoked by the anyRequest() handler - either synchronous or asynchronous - to execute its task. Another option is to use the method-level annotation @Async which can be applied to services that returns a value or void. Once DispatcherServlet encounters the @Async annotation, it tells TaskExecutor to allot a separate thread for its own asynchronous execution. Any controller or service that invokes the @Async method will not wait for its completion unless managed by Thread.sleep() method. This annotation is strictly valid to public methods, which should not be invoked within the class implementation *per se*. Exceptions will be thrown if these restrictions are violated.

Aside from Callable<T>, this recipe includes some services that return Future<T> and CompletableFuture<T> which are object containers required to be returned by asynchronous services. These APIs will be expounded in the next recipe.

Creating asynchronous controllers

For enhanced performance and faster request handling, asynchronous controllers have been present in any Spring instalments, to be used in cases where the service execution takes a practically large amount of time or the DAO layer retrieves an unpredictable, uncertain, erratic, and intermittent transmission of data from a certain data repository. Although rare, complex, and complicated to manage, asynchronous controllers can indeed help cut the time spent for bulk transactions compared to normal controller processing. With the use of callbacks, these types of controllers can manage unsuccessful data retrieval, which is one way of handling exceptions. Overall, given high-powered hardware resources and software applications servers, asynchronous @Controller transactions can help alleviate the unwanted acquisition of high-powered hardware specification.

Getting started

Open again `ch08` and create and add the following `@Controller` that utilizes thread pool generated by `TaskExecutor`.

How to do it...

Asynchronous results need APIs that will parse an entity or list of entities in order to generate an XML or JSON data format. Let us implement `@Controller` that parses and returns asynchronous response by following these steps:

1. To start with this recipe, add the following **Jackson Streaming APIs** for converting HTTP response to JSON format. This is because some of the request handlers will be publishing their data through `@ResponseBody`:

```xml
<dependency>
  <groupId>com.fasterxml.jackson.core</groupId>
  <artifactId>jackson-core</artifactId>
  <version>2.9.0.pr2</version>
</dependency>
<dependency>
  <groupId>com.fasterxml.jackson.core</groupId>
  <artifactId>jackson-databind</artifactId>
  <version>2.9.0.pr2</version>
</dependency>
```

2. Inside the package `org.packt.web.reactor.controller`, add the following `ServiceController` with a request handler that returns a `java.util.concurrent.Callable` data:

```java
@Controller
public class ServiceController {
   @Autowired
   private EmployeeService employeeServiceImpl;
@RequestMapping(value="/web/{id}/employeeCall.json",
produces ="application/json",
method = RequestMethod.GET,
headers = {"Accept=text/xml, application/json"})
   @ResponseBody
public Callable<Employee>
      jsonSoloEmployeeCall(@PathVariable("id") Integer id){
       Callable<Employee> task = new Callable<Employee>() {
@Override
          public Employee call () throws Exception {
```

```
        System.out.println("controller:jsonSoloEmployee
        Call task executor: " +
            Thread.currentThread().getName());
                    Thread.sleep(1000);
                    Employee emp =
        employeeServiceImpl.readEmployee(15).get();
                    System.out.println(emp.getLastName());
                    return emp;
                }
            };
            return task;
        }
    }
```

3. Using the same @Controller, add another request handler that returns
   org.springframework.web.context.request.async.WebAsyncTask
   response data:

```
    @RequestMapping(value="/web/employeeList.json",
    produces ="application/json", method = RequestMethod.GET,
    headers = {"Accept=text/xml, application/json"})
    @ResponseBody
    public WebAsyncTask<List<Employee>> jsonEmpList(){
            Callable<List<Employee>> callable =
    new Callable<List<Employee>>() {

                public List<Employee> call() throws Exception {
                    Thread.sleep(3000);
                    System.out.println("jsonEmpList task
                        executor: " +
                        Thread.currentThread().getName());
                    return employeeServiceImpl.readEmployees()
    .get();
                }
            };
        return new WebAsyncTask<List<Employee>>(1000, callable);
    }
```

4. Lastly, add another request handler, which returns a
   org.springframework.web.context.request.async.DeferredResult
   asynchronous response:

```
    @RequestMapping(value="/web/{id}/employeDR.json",
    produces ="application/json", method = RequestMethod.GET,
    headers = {"Accept=text/xml, application/json"})
    @ResponseBody
    public DeferredResult<Employee>
```

```
jsonSoloEmployeeDR(@PathVariable("id") Integer id) {
    DeferredResult<Employee> deferredResult =
new DeferredResult<>();
    deferredResult.onCompletion(() ->{
        try {
System.out.println("controller:jsonSoloEmployeeDR
task executor: " +
    Thread.currentThread().getName());
            Thread.sleep(1000);
            deferredResult.setResult(
employeeServiceImpl.readEmployee(id).get());
        } catch (InterruptedException e) { }
catch (ExecutionException e) { }
    });
    return deferredResult;
}
```

5. All these service handlers must run on a thread pool generated by the `ConcurrentTaskExecutor` configured in the previous recipe.

6. Save all files. Then `clean`, `build`, `deploy`, and `run` the transactions. Run each request handler several times and observe `C:\logs\tomcat9-stdout.xxxx-xx-xx.log`. The following is the result of the log when `jsonEmpNames()` was executed four times:

```
controller:jsonEmpNames task executor: MvcAsync1
controller:jsonEmpNames task executor: MvcAsync2
controller:jsonEmpNames task executor: MvcAsync3
controller:jsonEmpNames task executor: MvcAsync4
```

How it works...

The normal `@Controller` runs its request handler one thread at a time and uses only the default main thread of the application server. If a handler processes an HTTP request for a long period, the next transaction in the queue will be waiting for the main thread to be released from its current load. To avoid this starvation, Spring 5 still supports handlers that return `WebAsyncTask<T>`, `Callable<T>`, and `DeferredResult<T>`, which wrap a task and its result altogether to be executed by any of the threads generated by `TaskExecutor`, as authorized by `DispatcherServlet`.

If a request transaction returns a `Callable<T>`, Spring MVC coordinates with `TaskExecutor` and instructs it to create a thread for processing the `Callable` transaction. Then, the `DispatcherServlet` and all its Spring MVC components will exit to cater another request from the client but will wait for the response from that spawned thread. As more `Callable` tasks are processed by the `@Controller`, a number of threads will be running concurrently in the background that will eventually exit after its completion. The only problem with `Callable<T>` is the absence of callback methods that will synchronize its own thread executions.

Although it exhibits similar behavior and purposes to `Callable`, `DeferredResult<T>` contains callback methods that synchronize all running threads inside the task and propagate all the results before its task ends. Likewise, it has methods that save its state in a memory to be accessed by some threads during custom callbacks. If the requirement asks for an asynchronous `@Controller` to wait for all its subordinate thread executions to finish or to design a `join()` synchronization, it is recommended to wrap all its tasks in a `DeferredResult<T>` object.

To wrap `Callable` transactions with time constraints, we create a request handler that returns `WebAsyncTask<T>`. Once a controller returns a `WebAsyncTask`, the `DispatcherServlet` communicates with `WebAsyncManager` to process the wrapped `Callable<T>` given a timeout in milliseconds. Once the `Callable` task has been performed with or without errors, `WebAsyncManager` will dispatch the response to the `Dispatcherservlet` before it exits.

Relying on a synchronous `@Controller` when it comes to huge and slow request processes will cause performance degradation because it will produce a long queue waiting for the current request handler to complete its task, which means context switching from one request to another becomes expensive to client and server components.

Creating @Scheduled services

Spring 5 still supports batch processes or service transactions whose executions are triggered by time, just like any timer-based applications. The following recipe highlights the creation of batched transactions that run inside the Spring MVC container.

Getting started

Open a project, ch08, and add the following time-driven @Service methods.

How to do it...

Scheduled services are usually used to implement batch processing that can run simultaneously with the request handlers. To create these types of services, follow these steps:

1. To enable schedule-based transactions, create a context definition
   SpringScheduledConfig which implements
   org.springframework.scheduling.annotation.SchedulingConfigurer.
   Apply the class-level annotation @EnableScheduling and override the method
   configureTasks() with the preferred configurations of
   org.springframework.scheduling.concurrent.ThreadPoolTaskSchedul
   er injected in it:

   ```
   @Configuration
   @EnableScheduling
   public class SpringScheduledConfig
   implements SchedulingConfigurer {
       @Bean()
       public ThreadPoolTaskScheduler taskScheduler() {
         ThreadPoolTaskScheduler scheduler =
   new ThreadPoolTaskScheduler();
         scheduler.setPoolSize(100);
         scheduler.setThreadNamePrefix("Scheduler-");
         scheduler.setWaitForTasksToCompleteOnShutdown(true);
         scheduler.setRemoveOnCancelPolicy(true);
         return scheduler;
       }

       @Override
       public void configureTasks(ScheduledTaskRegistrar
           taskRegistrar) {
         taskRegistrar.setTaskScheduler(taskScheduler());
       }
   }
   ```

2. Now, create a service class `TimeService` which contains the following template methods:

```
public interface TimedService {
    public void batchFixedPeriod();
    public void batchCronPeriod();
    public void batchFixedDelay();
    public void batchInitialDelay();
}
```

3. Then, create an implementation class that will implement a time-triggered process that *runs every 2000 milliseconds everyday* on a separate thread generated by `ThreadPoolTaskScheduler` from its pool of threads:

```
@Service
public class TimedServiceImpl implements TimedService{
    @Scheduled(fixedRate=2000)
    @Override
    public void batchFixedPeriod() {
        System.out.println("scheduled#batchFixedPeriod: " +
            Thread.currentThread().getName());
    }
}
```

4. Add another scheduled process that uses a `cron` expression which defines its execution *every five seconds daily*:

```
@Scheduled(cron="*/5 * * * * ?")
@Override
public void batchCronPeriod() {
    System.out.println("scheduled#batchCronPeriod: " +
        Thread.currentThread().getName());
}
```

5. Create a `@Scheduled` process that runs for a *fixed period of 5000 milliseconds,* given that at the start of the execution, it incurs an *initial delay of 2000 milliseconds*:

```
@Scheduled(fixedRate=5000, initialDelay=2000)
@Override
public void batchInitialDelay() {
    System.out.println("scheduled#batchFixedDelay: " +
        Thread.currentThread().getName());
}
```

6. Lastly, implement a batch process that executes *every 5000 milliseconds with a delay of 1000 millisecond every after completion* per execution:

```
@Scheduled(fixedDelay=1000)
@Override
public void batchFixedDelay() {
        System.out.println("scheduled#batchFixedDelay: " +
            Thread.currentThread().getName());
}
```

How it works...

Time-triggered or `@Scheduled` service transactions in Spring 5 are required to return void with no parameters. This recipe highlighted some transactions that run periodically using asynchronous threads configured through the annotation property `fixedRate`. On the other hand, the service `batchFixedDelay()` runs asynchronously with a fixed delay of 1000 milliseconds defined by the property `fixedDelay`.

With regard to delay features, some batch processes can be configured to execute after a fixed period of time with some initial delays determined by the `initialDelay` property, as depicted in `batchInitialDelay()` implementation.

But the most detailed, flexible, and manageable way of implementing `@Scheduled` native services is through the `cron` configuration wherein a `cron` expression is used to schedule the transaction. Depending on the requirement, the `cron` can be easily be adjusted whenever changes happen.

The asynchronous behavior of these scheduled events is attributed to the `TaskScheduler` which manages and delegates threads to every `@Scheduled` service. It is also responsible for causing all the triggers defined in the `@Scheduled` to materialize. This `TaskScheduler` must be injected into the `SchedulingConfigurer` through the overridden method `configureTasks()`.

Using Future<T> and CallableFuture<T>

When it comes to propagating the result of an asynchronous service transaction, there are two popular APIs that are responsible for wrapping both the task and its result, namely `Future<T>` and `CallableFuture<T>`. These APIs can manage any asynchronous executions with or without a successful completion. This recipe will demonstrate the usage of these two containers and will also compare and contrast the two APIs.

Getting started

Open ch08 again and add the following `@Service` methods that return `Future<T>` and `CallableFuture<T>` task containers.

How to do it...

Another way of creating asynchronous services is using `Future<T>` and `CallableFuture<T>` as return values. Let us create these asynchronous APIs in our services by following these steps:

1. Open the `EmployeeServiceImpl` implementation class. Study the service methods `readEmployees()` and `readEmployee(id)`. The `readEmployees()` passes the whole employee record retrieval transaction to the `@Controller` in a `CompletableFuture<Employee>` form. On the other side, the `readEmployee(id)` passes the whole result as a `Future<Employee>` object.

2. Add another service class, namely `DepartmentService`, with the following templates:

```
public interface DepartmentService {

    public CompletableFuture<List<Department>>
        readDepartments();
    public void addDepartment(DepartmentForm dept);
    public void removeDepartment(Integer deptId);
    public void updateDepartment(DepartmentForm dept,
        Integer id);
    public Callable<Department> getDeptId(Integer id);


}
```

3. Implement the non-blocking and asynchronous methods of `DepartmentService` above, prioritizing on the use of `CompletableFuture<T>` and `Future<T>` as returned objects:

```
@Service
public class DepartmentServiceImpl implements DepartmentService
{
    @Autowired
    private DepartmentDao departmentDaoImpl;

    @Override
    public CompletableFuture<List<Department>>
```

```
        readDepartments() {
    try {
        Thread.sleep(5000);
    } catch (InterruptedException e) {
        e.printStackTrace();
    }
    return CompletableFuture.completedFuture(
departmentDaoImpl.getDepartments());
    }

@Async
@Override
public void addDepartment(DepartmentForm dept) {
    Department deptData = new Department();
    deptData.setDeptId(dept.getDeptId());
    deptData.setName(dept.getName());
    departmentDaoImpl.addDepartmentByJT(deptData);
}
@Async
@Override
public void removeDepartment(Integer deptId) {
    departmentDaoImpl.delDepartment(deptId);
}

@Async
@Override
public void updateDepartment(DepartmentForm dept,
        Integer id) {
    Department deptData = new Department();
    deptData.setDeptId(dept.getDeptId());
    deptData.setName(dept.getName());
    deptData.setId(id);
    departmentDaoImpl.updateDepartment(deptData);
}

@Override
public Callable<Department> getDeptId(Integer id) {
    Callable<Department> task = new
            Callable<Department>() {

      @Override
      public Department call () throws Exception {
            System.out.println("controller:readEmployeesCall
task executor: " +
      Thread.currentThread().getName());
          Thread.sleep(5000);
          Department dept =
                departmentDaoImpl.getDepartmentData(id);
```

```
            return dept;
          }
      };
      return task;
    }
  }
```

4. For the `EmployeeService` method invocation, study `EmployeeController` request handlers on how to retrieve the *list of Employees* from the `CompletableFuture<Employee>`.

5. For the `DepartmentService` method invocation, create the following `DepartmentController` that will illustrate how to retrieve asynchronous results from the `DepartmentService` services. The following `POST` request transaction saves a `Department` record within *5000* milliseconds

```
@Controller
public class DepartmentController {
    @Autowired
    private DepartmentService departmentServiceImpl;

    // refer to sources
    @RequestMapping(value="/react/deptform.html",
       method=RequestMethod.POST)
    public String submitForm(Model model,
       @ModelAttribute("departmentForm")
DepartmentForm departmentForm){
        try {
            Thread.sleep(5000);
            departmentServiceImpl.addDepartment(
departmentForm);
            model.addAttribute("departments",
                departmentServiceImpl.readDepartments()
.get(5000,  TimeUnit.MILLISECONDS));
        } catch (InterruptedException e) { }
catch (ExecutionException e) { }
catch (TimeoutException e) { }
        return "dept-list";
    }
```

6. The `GET` request below performs record data retrieval but returns an empty `Department` record once a `Throwable` happens during the process:

```
@RequestMapping(value={"/react/deldept.html/{deptId}"})
public String deleteRecord(Model model, @PathVariable("deptId")
Integer deptId){
  try {
```

```
    Thread.sleep(5000);
  } catch (InterruptedException e) { }
  departmentServiceImpl.removeDepartment(deptId);
  model.addAttribute("departments",
  departmentServiceImpl.readDepartments().getNow(new
ArrayList<>()));
  return "dept-list";
}
```

7. The following method is another way of processing Future<T> value using a separate thread pool. It allots a thread to an asynchronous method getDeptId() and requires a while loop to wait for the process to finish. When the transaction finishes without any Throwable, the record is retrieved through the get() method of Future<T>. Otherwise, custom recovery can be done.

```
@RequestMapping(value={"/react/updatedept.html/{id}"})
public String updateRecord(Model model, @PathVariable("id")
Integer id){
  ExecutorService threads = Executors.newFixedThreadPool(5);
  Future<Department> deptfuture =
  threads.submit(departmentServiceImpl.getDeptId(id));
  Department dept = null;
  while (!deptfuture.isDone()) {
    System.out.println("Thread is still busy
    processing....");
    try {
      Thread.sleep(1);
    } catch (InterruptedException e) { }
  }

  try {
    dept = deptfuture.get();
  } catch (InterruptedException e) { }
  catch (ExecutionException e) { }
  DepartmentForm departmentForm = new DepartmentForm();
  departmentForm.setDeptId(dept.getDeptId());
  departmentForm.setName(dept.getName());
  model.addAttribute("departmentForm", departmentForm);
  return "dept-form";
}
```

8. Save all files. Then clean, build, and run the application. Check the Tomcat log file for the thread execution trails.

How it works...

This recipe focuses on asynchronous tasks that output a certain object such as an `Employee`, `Department`, `ArrayList<Employee>`, or `ArrayList<Department>`. Between the two, the `Future<T>` has been exposing methods to their invokers since **Java 1.5** introduced concepts of concurrency. It has been used in wrapping tasks and its results whenever asynchronous methods returns any objects to their caller. Its implementation handler object called `AsyncResult<T>` is the one involved in wrapping beans, collections, or arrays of objects.

Since these objects are for non-blocking transactions, the `AsyncResult<T>` can be monitored and managed using the `utility` methods of `Future<T>`, namely the `isCancelled()`, `isDone()`, and `get()`. Since there are chances that the result will be void, we need to create a `while` loop to check if the task running inside `AsyncResult<T>` is still on process. Once `isDone()` returns true, we can retrieve the result through the `get()` method. Also, the `isCancelled()` can be called to monitor if the task has been cancelled by an internal background process. Study `updateRecord()` for the snippet on how to use these methods.

Whenever we have asynchronous services that return `Callable<T>`, the `java.util.concurrent.Executors` can help manage and execute the `Callable<T>` to extract `Future<T>`. In `updateRecord()` of `DepartmentController`, the non-blocking `departmentServiceImpl.getDeptId(id)` returns a `Callable<Employee>` for processing. To capture the result, the `@Controller` has to generate a new thread pool through `Executor`. In order to execute the `Callable<Employee>` task, the thread pool will execute the task at the background using its `submit()`, method which will eventually extract the `Future<Employee>`. Using all the `Future<Employee>` methods, the `Employee` object can be extracted successfully.

The real problem with using `Future<T>` as container object for tasks is the lack of callback implementation. Aside from `Thread.sleep()`, it lacks the synchronization technique to establish a well-managed sequence of cooperating or competing threads.

Thus, Java 1.8 and above has created an implementation of Future, the `CompletableFuture<T>`, that provides callbacks and extended features on asynchronous executions of tasks using its `then` methods with exception handling. Its utility methods support both blocking and non-blocking task executions. And most of all, `CompletatableFuture<T>` recognizes `@FunctionalInterface` and *lambda expressions*. In `readEmployees()` of `EmployeeService`, a `Supplier<List<Employee>>` has been generated to be executed by `CompletableFuture< List<Employee>>` in a common `ForkJoinPool` through its `supplyAsync()` method. This method also returns `CompletableFuture<T>` to the invoker. Another way of passing this container to the invoker is through its utility static method, `CompletableFuture.completedFuture()`.

Although this recipe focused much on its blocking `get()` overloads, `CompletableFuture<T>` offers other asynchronous ways of retrieving its result such as `thenAccept()` which accepts a `Consumer<T>` to process the result. An example is `updateRecordSubmit()` request handler of `ReportController`.

Using Mono<T> and Flux<T> publishers for services

Although **Spring Functional and Reactive Framework** will be discussed thoroughly in the next chapter, this recipe will provide evidence that Spring 5 MVC has a full support on **Reactor Core 3.x**'s `Mono<T>` and `Flux<T>` stream operations. This recipe will ex how to start and build Spring WebFlux applications from the ground up using the **Spring 5** platform.

Getting started

Open project `ch08` again and add some `@Service` non-blocking methods that retrieve employee data from a data source using `Flux<T>` and `Mono<T>`, manipulate them, apply backpressure to stream operations, and utilize multithreading through Reactor's **Scheduler**.

How to do it...

In the previous chapters, we have provided details about `Mono<T>` and `Flux<T>` streams and how they behave when executed using test methods. This time, let us apply the following streams in our asynchronous and reactive services by following these steps:

1. Before we start, add the Maven dependencies of **Reactor Stream 1.0** and **Reactor Core 3.x** in `pom.xml`. These libraries are also added in the previous chapter.

2. Add the following template methods on our existing `EmployeeService` of the previous recipe:

```
public interface EmployeeService {
    // refer to sources
    public Flux<Employee> readEmployeesFlux(int age);
    public Flux<Employee> readEmployeesByDescAge();
    public Flux<Employee> readEmployeesByAscLastName();
    public Flux<String> readEmpFirstNames();
    public Mono<Double> getAveAge();
}
```

3. Then, add the following implementation of asynchronous methods in its existing `EmployeeServiceImpl` using `Flux<T>` and `Mono<T>` stream operations that utilize only one thread for both publisher and subscriber operations. Add the following `readEmpFirstNames()` implementation that uses `flatMap()` to extract the first names of all employees and `sort()` them ascendingly using `Comparator`:

```
@Service
public class EmployeeServiceImpl implements EmployeeService {
// refer to sources

    @Override
    public Flux<String> readEmpFirstNames() {
        Function<Employee, Mono<String>> mapProcess =
(emp) -> Mono.just(emp).map((e)->{
            System.out.println("flux:map task executor: " +
                Thread.currentThread().getName());
            return e.getFirstName().toUpperCase();
        });
        Comparator<String> strComp = (s1, s2) ->{
           System.out.println("flux:sort task executor: " +
              Thread.currentThread().getName());
           return s1.compareTo(s2);
        };
        Flux<String> names =
```

```
      Flux.fromIterable(employeeDaoImpl
.getEmployees()).flatMap(mapProcess)
  .sort(strComp);
      return names;
    }
  }
```

4. Add the following service implementation that uses two separate threads for publisher and subscriber operations:

```
@Override
public Flux<Employee> readEmployeesFlux(int age) {
  Scheduler subWorker = Schedulers.newSingle("sub-thread");
  Scheduler pubWorker = Schedulers.newSingle("pub-thread");
  Predicate<Employee> validAge = (e) -> {
    System.out.println("flux:filter task executor: " +
    Thread.currentThread().getName());
    return e.getAge() > age;
  };
  Supplier<Flux<Employee>> deferredTask = ()->{
    System.out.println("flux:defer task executor: " +
    Thread.currentThread().getName());
    return Flux.fromIterable(employeeDaoImpl.getEmployees());
  };
  Flux<Employee> deferred = Flux.defer(deferredTask)
  .filter(validAge)
  .subscribeOn(subWorker)
  .publishOn(pubWorker);
  return deferred;
}

@Override
public Flux<Employee> readEmployeesByDescAge() {
  Scheduler subWorker = Schedulers.newSingle("sub-thread");
  Scheduler pubWorker = Schedulers.newSingle("pub-thread");
  Supplier<Flux<Employee>> deferredTask = ()->{
    System.out.println("flux:defer task executor: "+
    Thread.currentThread().getName());
    return Flux.fromIterable(employeeDaoImpl.getEmployees());
  };
  Comparator<Employee> descAge = (e1, e2) -> {
    System.out.println("flux:sort task executor: " +
    Thread.currentThread().getName());
    if(e1.getAge().compareTo(e2.getAge()) == 0){
      return 0;
    } else if(e1.getAge().compareTo(e2.getAge()) > 0){
      return -1;
    } else return 1;
```

```
};
Flux<Employee> deferred = Flux.defer(deferredTask)
.sort(descAge)
.subscribeOn(subWorker)
.publishOn(pubWorker);
return deferred;
}
```

5. Lastly, add the following service methods that returns Mono<T> streams and uses some of the generic functional interfaces such as ToIntFunction<T> in implementing stream operations:

```
@Override
public Mono<Double> getAveAge() {
  ToIntFunction<Employee> sizeEmpArr = (e) -> {
    System.out.println("flux:toIntFunction task
    executor: " + Thread.currentThread().getName());
    return e.getAge();
  };
  Callable<Double> task = () ->{
    System.out.println("flux:callable task  executor: " +
    Thread.currentThread().getName());
    return employeeDaoImpl.getEmployees().stream()
    .mapToInt(sizeEmpArr).average().getAsDouble();
  };

  Mono<Double> aveAge= Mono.fromCallable(task);
  return aveAge;
}
```

 The use of @Async, Callable<T> and other related APIs are not recommended on these types of services due to some proxy-related issues.

6. Save all files. Create a test class to test each service above.

How it works...

The **Spring WebFlux** is a new paradigm offered by Spring 5 to implement reactive and asynchronous web applications. It has a wide support on service, controllers, and web services using **Reactor Core 3.0**. This recipe provides means on how to apply `Publisher<T>` and `Subscriber<T>` core operations in building the service layers of Spring framework. Reactive service methods will throw an `Exception` when applied `@Async` because they are already composed of asynchronous and deterministic operators. The full-blown **Spring Reactive and Functional Web Framework** will be discussed in the next chapter.

Creating Mono<T> and Flux<T> HTTP response

The **Spring WebFlux** paradigm will not be complete without the `@Controller` returning `Mono<T>` and `Flux<T>` stream data.

Getting started

Add in project `ch08` a set of request handlers that returns on the client `Mono<T>` and `Flux<T>` through `@ResponseBody` annotation.

How to do it...

After using **Reactor Core** specification to build the service layer, let us apply `Mono<T>` and `Flux<T>` streams to `@Controllers` by doing these steps:

1. Open the `ServiceController` of the previous recipe again and add the following request handler showcasing the use of **Reactor Stream** operations:

```
@RequestMapping(value="/web/employeeNames.json",
produces ="application/json",
method = RequestMethod.GET,
headers = {"Accept=text/xml, application/json"})
@ResponseBody
public Callable<List<String>> jsonEmpNames(){
        Callable<List<String>> task =
new Callable<List<String>>() {
```

```
            @Override
            public List<String> call () throws Exception {
                List<String> names = new ArrayList<>();
                System.out.println("controller:jsonEmpNames
                    task executor: " +
Thread.currentThread().getName());
                Thread.sleep(5000);
                employeeServiceImpl.readEmpFirstNames()
  .subscribe((str)->{
                              names.add(str);
                    });
                return names;
            }
        };
    return task;
    }
    @RequestMapping(value="/web/employeeFlux.json",
produces ="application/json",
method = RequestMethod.GET,
headers = {"Accept=text/xml, application/json"})
    @ResponseBody
    public Flux<Employee> jsonSoloEmployeeFlux(){
        return employeeServiceImpl.readEmployeesFlux(15);
    }
    @RequestMapping(value="/web/empLastnameFlux.json",
produces ="application/json",
method = RequestMethod.GET,
headers = {"Accept=text/xml, application/json"})
    @ResponseBody
    public Flux<Employee> jsonEmpLastNameFlux(){
        return
            employeeServiceImpl.readEmployeesByAscLastName();
    }
    @RequestMapping(value="/web/empAgeFlux.json",
produces ="application/json",
method = RequestMethod.GET,
headers = {"Accept=text/xml, application/json"})
    @ResponseBody
    public Flux<Employee> jsonEmpAgeFlux(){
        return employeeServiceImpl.readEmployeesByDescAge();
    }
}
```

2. Save all files. The `clean`, `build`, and `deploy`. Run and test the request URLs in a browser.

How it works...

Since both Tomcat 9 and Spring 5 support asynchronous thread execution, request handlers can now return `Mono<T>` and `Flux<T>` data streams and receive automatic subscription with the client through the `DispatcherServlet` of Spring 5 platform. Conventionally, the `@Controller` can still programmatically execute the `Flux<T>` or `Mono<T>` cold stream through supplying the appropriate `Supplier<T>` to the stream's `subscribe()` method and wrapping the task and result in a `Callable<T>` for publishing. However, since Spring 5 understands full-blown reactive programming using **Reactor Core**, cold stream as well as hot stream can be published directly to the client. Thus, it can be concluded that the Spring 5 context fully understands reactive and functional programming.

Integrating RxJava 2.0

From our conclusion that Spring 5 understands the full language of reactive programming, this recipe will show us that this Spring version does not only supports its built-in **Reactor Core** extension but can also extend its translation to **RxJava 2.x**.

Getting started

Add the following service methods and `@Controller` request handlers to ch08 which will also highlight **RxJava 2.x** stream transactions.

How to do it...

Aside from Reactor Core, Spring 5 can work with other reactive libraries, just like the popular RxJava 2.0. Follow these steps to guide on how to integrate RxJava 2.0 with Spring 5:

1. Before we start, add the Maven dependencies of **RxJava 2.x** to pom.xml. This set of libraries has been used in the previous chapter.

2. Open the `DepartmentService` class and add the following template methods that will soon be implemented as non-blocking transactions:

```
public interface DepartmentService {
    // refer to sources
    public Observable<Department> getDeptsRx();
    public Single<Department> getDeptRx(int id);
    public Flowable<String> getDepttNamesRx();
}
```

3. Implement these template methods in `DepartmentServiceImpl` using RxJava 2.x stream APIs:

```
@Override
    public Observable<Department> getDeptsRx() {
        Observable<Department> depts=
            Observable.fromIterable(
departmentDaoImpl.getDepartments());
        return depts;
    }

    @Override
    public Single<Department> getDeptRx(int id) {
        Callable<Department> task =
() -> departmentDaoImpl.getDepartmentData(id);
        Single<Department> dept = Single.fromCallable(task);
        return dept;
    }

    @Override
    public Flowable<String> getDepttNamesRx() {
        Function<Department, Publisher<String>> firstNames =
(emp) -> Mono.just(emp.getName())
.map(String::toUpperCase);
        Flowable<String> emps =
            Flowable.fromIterable(departmentDaoImpl
.getDepartments()).flatMap(firstNames);
        return emps;
    }
```

 The use of `@Async`, `Callable<T>` and other related APIs are not recommended on these types of services due to some proxy-related issues.

4. To expose these non-blocking transactions, open again `ServiceControllers` and add the following request handlers that will invoke the newly implemented RxJava 2.x streams:

```
@RequestMapping(value="/web/{id}/deptSingle.json",
produces ="application/json",
method = RequestMethod.GET,
headers = {"Accept=text/xml, application/json"})
@ResponseBody
public Single<Department> jsonSoloDeptSingle(
@PathVariable("id") Integer id){
    return departmentServiceImpl.getDeptRx(id) ;
}
@RequestMapping(value="/web/deptList.json",
produces ="application/json",
method = RequestMethod.GET,
headers = {"Accept=text/xml, application/json"})
@ResponseBody
public Observable<Department> jsonSoloDeptList(){
    return departmentServiceImpl.getDeptsRx() ;
}
@RequestMapping(value="/web/deptNames.json",
produces ="application/json",
method = RequestMethod.GET,
headers = {"Accept=text/xml, application/json"})
@ResponseBody
public Flowable<String> jsonDeptNames(){
    return departmentServiceImpl.getDepttNamesRx() ;
}
```

5. Save all files. Then `clean`, `build`, and `deploy` this project. Run all the URLs in a browser.

How it works...

This recipe has just proven that, as long as the reactive paradigm follows the **Reactive Stream 1.x** specification, Spring 5 is capable of executing the reactive syntax of any reactive plugin or libraries other than **Reactor Core 3.x**. Using `Observable<T>`, `Single<T>`, and `Flowable<T>`, the services, as well as the `@Controller` request handler has successfully published all the results using an automatic subscription done by `DispatcherServlet`.

Using FreeMarker to render Publisher<T> stream

FreeMarker is one of the view technologies that have extended support for Spring 5. The following recipe will illustrate how **FreeMarker** templates can publish Mono<T> and Flux<T> stream data using the **Spring Reactive** module.

Getting started

Add the following viewResolver and view configuration in ch08 to compile and run FreeMarker templates.

How to do it...

Spring 5's reactive module supports FreeMarker components to provide templates to reactive contents. Let us implement FreeMarker templating using the Spring Reactive module:

1. Add the newest Maven dependencies of **FreeMarker** in pom.xml:

    ```
    <dependency>
        <groupId>org.freemarker</groupId>
        <artifactId>freemarker</artifactId>
        <version>2.3.26-incubating</version>
    </dependency>
    ```

2. To add the reactive components to the application, include the following Maven dependency that implements the Reactor Core implementation of the Reactive Streams specification:

    ```
    <dependency>
        <groupId>org.springframework</groupId>
        <artifactId>spring-web-reactive</artifactId>
        <version>${spring.version}</version>
    </dependency>
    ```

3. To avoid conflicts with other non-reactive web configurations, create a root context definition `SpringWebReactiveConfig` that implements `org.springframework.web.reactive.config.WebReactiveConfigurer`. This definition will inject all reactive view engines and resolvers needed to render `Publisher<T>` streams:

```
@EnableWebMvc
@ComponentScan(basePackages="org.packt.web.reactor")
@PropertySource("classpath:config/jdbc.properties")
@Configuration
public class SpringWebReactiveConfig
implements WebReactiveConfigurer { }
```

4. Inject the following FreeMarker bean configuration in the `SpringWebReactiveConfig` context definition. Set the FreeMarker template location in `\WEB-INF\templates`:

```
@Bean(name = "viewResolverFTL")
    public FreeMarkerViewResolver getViewResolverFtl() {
        FreeMarkerViewResolver viewResolver =
new FreeMarkerViewResolver();
        viewResolver.setPrefix("");
        viewResolver.setSuffix(".ftl");
        viewResolver.setOrder(1);
        return viewResolver;
    }
    @Bean(name = "freemarkerConfig")
    public FreeMarkerConfigurer getFreemarkerConfig() {
        FreeMarkerConfigurer config =
new FreeMarkerConfigurer();
        config.setTemplateLoaderPath("/WEB-INF/templates/");
        return config;
    }
```

5. Create a `RenderController` that will publish a list of employees in an FTL template.

```
@Controller
public class RenderController {
    @Autowired
    private EmployeeService employeeServiceImpl;
    @RequestMapping(value="/ftl/empList.html",
        method=RequestMethod.GET)
    public String usersFtl(Model model){
        model.addAttribute("employees",
employeeServiceImpl.readEmployeesByDescAge()
```

```
        .collectList().block());
                return "ftl_list_emps";
        }
    }
```

6. Inside the path `\WEB-INF\templates`, create an FTL template `ftl_list_emps.ftl` that will serve as the physical view:

```html
<!DOCTYPE html>
<html>
<head>
    <title>Ch08 FreeMarker Reactive View</title>
</head>
<body>
 <table>
   <thead>
     <tr>
       <th>Employee ID</th>
       <th>First Name</th>
       <th>Last Name</th>
       <th>Age</th>
     </tr>
   </thead>
   <tbody>
     <#list employees as e>
     <tr>
       <td>${e.empId?html}</td>
       <td>${e.firstName?html}</td>
       <td>${e.lastName?html}</td>
       <td>${e.age?html}</td>
     </tr>
     </#list>
   </tbody>
 </table>
</body>
</html>
```

7. Save all files. Then, `clean`, `build`, and `deploy`. Run the URL on the browser and expect the following result:

Employee ID	First Name	Last Name	Age
67.876	Jeremy	Irons	65
23.456	Joel	Enage	45
15	John	Tragura	38
222.222	Johnny	Refamonte	38
11.112	Sherwin	Tragura	22
44.444	Richard	Gore	0

How it works...

This is the first time that the **Spring Reactive** module has been introduced in a recipe. Although `Flux<T>` and `Mono<T>` stream data can be recognized implicitly using the Reactor Core 3.0 APIs, there are several reactive components that Spring 5 can offer which are found in this module. From Spring 5 technical documentation, this module provide supports for FreeMarker templating through its two APIs needed for reactive content parsing:
`org.springframework.web.reactive.result.view.freemarker.FreeMarkerConfigurer` and
`org.springframework.web.reactive.result.view.freemarker.FreeMarkerViewResolver`. Although these reactive APIs can only be used in **Functional and Reactive Web Framework** in `Chapter 9`, *Spring Boot 2.0*, this recipe still experimented with using the non-reactive version of these two APIs to render Reactive stream data. The recipe was successful, but FreeMarker has no parsing API or wrapper that will convert `Publisher<T>` stream to raw data for publishing. `Mono<T>` streams must execute the blocking operation `block()` in order to extract the raw data while `Flux<T>` needs to call `collectList().block()` in order to expose the `Collection<T>` data for page rendering.

Using Thymeleaf to render a Publisher<T> stream

Other than FreeMarker, Spring 5 has a strong built-in support for Thymeleaf template compilation, with the objective of rendering **Reactive Stream** data directly.

Getting started

Open the Maven project ch08 and add the following view configuration for Thymeleaf integration.

How to do it...

To use Thymeleaf as the templating procedure for rendering reactive contents, follow these steps:

1. Before this recipe starts, be sure to have the **Spring Reactive** dependency included in pom.xml since we are building now a reactive web application.

2. If the rendition requires the use of non-blocking Mono<T> and Flux<T> operations, then **Thymeleaf** is the appropriate templating library to use, because **FreeMarker** cannot directly recognize non-blocking operations. To integrate Thymeleaf for Spring 5, add the following Maven dependencies:

```
<dependency>
    <groupId>org.thymeleaf</groupId>
    <artifactId>thymeleaf-spring5</artifactId>
    <version>3.0.6.M4</version>
</dependency>
```

3. Open the SpringWebReactiveConfig context definition and inject the following Thymeleaf configuration details. Also, inject the application's ApplicationContext which is needed by SpringResourceTemplateResolver:

```
@Autowired
private ApplicationContext applicationContext;

@Bean(name ="templateResolver")
public SpringResourceTemplateResolver getTemplateResolver() {
    SpringResourceTemplateResolver templateResolver =
new SpringResourceTemplateResolver();
    templateResolver.setApplicationContext(
applicationContext);
    templateResolver.setPrefix("/WEB-INF/templates/");
    templateResolver.setSuffix(".html");
    templateResolver.setTemplateMode("XHTML");
    return templateResolver;
}
@Bean(name ="templateEngine")
```

```
public SpringTemplateEngine getTemplateEngine() {
    SpringTemplateEngine templateEngine =
new SpringTemplateEngine();
    templateEngine.setTemplateResolver(
getTemplateResolver());
    return templateEngine;
}
@Bean(name="viewResolverThymeLeaf")
public ThymeleafViewResolver getViewResolverThyme(){
    ThymeleafViewResolver viewResolver =
new ThymeleafViewResolver();
    viewResolver.setTemplateEngine(getTemplateEngine());
    viewResolver.setOrder(2);
    return viewResolver;
}
```

4. Open the `RenderController` and add the following request handler that will render a `Flux<Employee>` to a `Thymeleaf` template:

```
@RequestMapping(value="/thymeleaf/empList.html",
    method=RequestMethod.GET)
public String users(Model model){
    model.addAttribute("employees",
        new ReactiveLazyContextVariable(
employeeServiceImpl.readEmployeesByDescAge()));
    return "thyme_list_emps";
}
```

 Extension of **Thymeleaf** templates is preferred to be `.html`.

5. Create a Thymeleaf template in `\WEB-INF\templates\xxxx.html` that will serve as the physical view of the request handler above:

```
<!DOCTYPE html>
<html xmlns:th="http://www.thymeleaf.org">
 <head>
    <title>Ch08 Thymeleaf Reactive View</title>
 </head>
 <body>
    <table>
      <thead>
        <tr>
          <th>Employee ID</th>
          <th>First Name</th>
```

```
          <th>Last Name</th>
          <th>Age</th>
        </tr>
      </thead>
      <tbody>
        <tr th:each="e : ${employees}">
          <td th:text="${e.empId}"></td>
          <td th:text="${e.firstName}"></td>
          <td th:text="${e.lastName}"></td>
          <td th:text="${e.age}"></td>
        </tr>
      </tbody>
    </table>
  </body>
</html>
```

6. Save all files. Then `clean`, `build`, and `deploy` the project. Run the URL in any browser and expect the same output as the previous recipe.

How it works...

When it comes to full-blown support, Thymeleaf can translate the reactive streams to be rendered by its templates through a wrapper class called `org.thymeleaf.spring5.context.webflux.ReactiveLazyContextVariable`. This object behaves as a blocking mechanism to resolve asynchronous objects like `Mono<T>` or `Flux<T>` in order for the Thymeleaf templates to render the raw data. The translation process happens during the transition of the stream from the request handler to view.

All its templating APIs must be injected into the Spring Reactive container since Thymeleaf is one of the supported components in building reactive applications using Spring 5 platform. Similar to FreeMarker, Spring 5 has a reactive version of Thymeleaf APIs but can only be used in the next chapter.

Applying security on TaskExecutors

The last recipe for this chapter is essential in building secured reactive and asynchronous Spring MVC applications. This is all about imposing authentication and authorization rules on asynchronous services and controllers using Spring Security 4.2.x.

Getting started

Open `ch08` for the last time and apply the security rules based on Spring Security 4.2 security contexts.

How to do it...

This last recipe is an extension of the Spring Security module that is applied to asynchronous services and controllers. Follow these steps on how threads in asynchronous and reactive executions can access the user details at runtime:

1. Before this recipe starts, include inside the `pom.xml` all the needed Maven dependencies of Spring Security 4.2.2. Refer to Chapter 4, *Securing Spring MVC Applications*, recipe ;*Applying Aspect-Oriented Programming*, for this item.

2. Create a new package `org.packt.web.reactor.security.config` to contain the Security context definition derived from Chapter 4, *Securing Spring MVC Applications*, recipe *Applying Aspect-Oriented Programming*. The `inMemoryAuthentication()` security configuration will be taken as the security protocol for this recipe. Also, there will be a slight modification on the `http.sessionManagement()` operation to consider asynchronous request executions:

```
@Configuration
@EnableWebSecurity
public class AppSecurityConfig extends
    WebSecurityConfigurerAdapter {
    @Override
    protected void configure(AuthenticationManagerBuilder auth)
        throws Exception {
      auth.inMemoryAuthentication()
        .withUser("sjctrags")
.password("sjctrags").roles("USER");
    }
    @Override
    protected void configure(HttpSecurity http) throws
Exception {
        http
          .authorizeRequests()
          .antMatchers("/react/login**",
                  "/react/after**").permitAll()
          .anyRequest().authenticated()
          .and()
          .formLogin()
```

```
            .loginPage("/react/login.html")
            .defaultSuccessUrl("/react/menu.html")
            .failureUrl("/react/login.html?error=true")
            .and().logout().logoutUrl("/react/logout.html")
            .logoutSuccessUrl("/react/after_logout.html")
            .and().sessionManagement()
            .sessionCreationPolicy(
    SessionCreationPolicy.IF_REQUIRED);
            http.csrf().disable();
        }
        @Override
        public void configure(WebSecurity web) throws Exception {
          web
            .ignoring()
                .antMatchers("/resources/**")
                .antMatchers("/css/**")
                .antMatchers("/js/**")
                .antMatchers("/image/**");
        }
    }
```

3. Also include in the new package the configuration of Spring Security's `DelegatingFilterProxy` with some added support on asynchronous and non-blocking transactions:

```
    public class SpringSecurityInitializer extends
            AbstractSecurityWebApplicationInitializer {
        @Override
        protected boolean isAsyncSecuritySupported() {
            return true;
        }
        @Override
        protected EnumSet<DispatcherType>
    getSecurityDispatcherTypes() {
            return EnumSet.of(DispatcherType.ASYNC,
                DispatcherType.REQUEST, DispatcherType.FORWARD,
                DispatcherType.INCLUDE);
        }
    }
```

4. Create a service class `EmployeeParallelStreamService` inside the same package as the previous service classes. Add the following version of `showAllEmployees()` that uses `parallelStream()` to `forEach()` all employee records:

```
    public void showAllEmployees(){
    Consumer<Employee> showAll =
```

```
(e) -> {
System.out.format("%s %s %d\n",
e.getFirstName(), e.getLastName(), e.getAge());
};
employeeDaoImpl.getEmployees()
.parallelStream()
.forEach(showAll);
}
```

5. Now, apply the security protocol by integrating the `AppSecurityConfig` context definition to `SpringContextConfig` through the `@Import` annotation:

```
@Import(value = { AppSecurityConfig.class })
@Configuration
@EnableWebMvc
@ComponentScan(basePackages = {"org.packt.web.reactor",
        "org.packt.web.reactor.model"})
public class SpringContextConfig  { }
```

6. For the thread pool to access `SecurityContext` for further authentication and authorization rules, inject the following `org.springframework.beans.factory.config.MethodInvokingFactoryBean` with the necessary details to `SpringContextConfig` definition. The `SecurityContext` is only accessible by the *main thread* and not with the thread pool generated by `TaskExecutors`:

```
@Bean
    public MethodInvokingFactoryBean
            methodInvokingFactoryBean() {
      MethodInvokingFactoryBean methodInvokingFactoryBean =
new MethodInvokingFactoryBean();
      methodInvokingFactoryBean
.setTargetClass(SecurityContextHolder.class);
      methodInvokingFactoryBean
.setTargetMethod("setStrategyName");
      methodInvokingFactoryBean
.setArguments(new String[]{
SecurityContextHolder.MODE_INHERITABLETHREADLOCAL});
      return methodInvokingFactoryBean;
}
```

Omission of these lines will cause the following `NullPointerException` on the threads accessing `SecurityContext`.

```
java.util.concurrent.ExecutionException: java.lang.NullPointerException
        java.util.concurrent.CompletableFuture.reportGet(Unknown Source)
        java.util.concurrent.CompletableFuture.get(Unknown Source)
        org.packt.web.reactor.controller.ServiceController$1.call(ServiceController.java:48)
        org.packt.web.reactor.controller.ServiceController$1.call(ServiceController.java:43)
        org.springframework.web.context.request.async.WebAsyncManager.lambda$startCallableProcessing$4(WebAsyncManager.java:321)
        java.util.concurrent.Executors$RunnableAdapter.call(Unknown Source)
        java.util.concurrent.FutureTask.run(Unknown Source)
        java.lang.Thread.run(Unknown Source)
```

7. Open `EmployeeServiceImpl` and `DepartmentServiceImpl` and apply some audit logs to check if the `java.security.Principal` is propagated by all asynchronous threads. First, implement `readEmployees()` method that processes employee record retrieval for *6000* milliseconds and returns `CompletableFuture<T>`:

```
@Service
public class EmployeeServiceImpl implements EmployeeService {
    @Async
    @Override
    public CompletableFuture<List<Employee>> readEmployees() {
        Supplier<List<Employee>> supplyListEmp = ()->{
        // refer to sources
        try {
            System.out.println("readEmployees Callable
            login: " + SecurityContextHolder.getContext()
.getAuthentication().getPrincipal());
            Thread.sleep(6000);
        } catch (InterruptedException e) { }
        return employeeDaoImpl.getEmployees();
    };
        return CompletableFuture.supplyAsync(supplyListEmp);
    }
}
```

8. Implement the `readEmployeesCall()` that acceses the user credentials and returns the `Callable<t>` task:

```
@Override
public Callable<List<Employee>> readEmployeesCall() {
    Callable< List<Employee> > task = new Callable<
List<Employee> >() {
```

```
  @Override
  public  List<Employee>  call () throws
  Exception {
    // refer to sources
    System.out.println("readEmployeesCall Callable
    login: " + SecurityContextHolder.getContext()
    .getAuthentication().getPrincipal());
    Thread.sleep(6000);
    List<Employee> empList = employeeDaoImpl.getEmployees();
    return empList;
  }
};
return task;
}
```

9. Add an `@Async` method that accesses the user credentials and processes the insertion of Employee record within *1000* milliseconds:

```
@Async
@Override
public void addEmployee(EmployeeForm empForm) {
  // refer to sources
  try {
    // refer to sources
    System.out.println("addEmployee @Async login: " +
    SecurityContextHolder.getContext()
    .getAuthentication().getPrincipal());
    Thread.sleep(1000);
  } catch (InterruptedException e) { }
  employeeDaoImpl.addEmployeeBySJI(emp);
}
```

10. Methods that return `Future<T>` can also access the security user details:

```
@Async
public Future<Employee> readEmployee(Integer empId) {
  try {
  System.out.println("service:readEmployee(empid)
  task executor: " + Thread.currentThread().getName());
  System.out.println("processing for 2000 ms");
  System.out.println("readEmployee @Async login: " +
  SecurityContextHolder.getContext()
  .getAuthentication().getPrincipal());
  Thread.sleep(2000);
  } catch (InterruptedException e) { }
  return new AsyncResult<>(employeeDaoImpl.getEmployee(empId));
}
```

11. Lastly, methods that return the non-blocking and reactive `Flux<T>` and `Mono<T>` streams can also access user credentials:

```
@Override
public Flux<Employee> readEmployeesFlux(int age) {
    Scheduler subWorker = Schedulers.newSingle("sub-thread");
    Scheduler pubWorker = Schedulers.newSingle("pub-thread");
    Predicate<Employee> validAge = (e) -> {
        // refer to sources
        System.out.println("flux:filter task executor
        login: " + SecurityContextHolder.getContext()
        .getAuthentication().getPrincipal());
        return e.getAge() > age;
    };
    Supplier<Flux<Employee>> deferredTask = ()->{
        // refer to sources
        System.out.println("flux:defer task executor
        login: " + SecurityContextHolder.getContext()
        .getAuthentication().getPrincipal());
        return Flux.fromIterable(employeeDaoImpl.getEmployees());
    };
    Flux<Employee> deferred = Flux.defer(deferredTask)
    .filter(validAge).subscribeOn(subWorker)
    .publishOn(pubWorker);
    return deferred;
}
```

12. Save all files. Delete the existing `ch08` context folder in Tomcat's `/webapps` before the new deployment. Then `clean`, `install`, and `deploy` the new project with Spring Security 4.2.x. Run `https://localhost:8443/react/login.html` and log in using the given credentials.

13. After executing the services, open Tomcat's log and observe a similar output:

```
readDepartments CompletableFuture login:
org.springframework.security.core.userdetails.User@41036863:
Username: sjctrags; Password: [PROTECTED]; Enabled: true;
AccountNonExpired: true; credentialsNonExpired: true;
AccountNonLocked: true; Granted Authorities: ROLE_USER
addDepartment @Async login:
org.springframework.security.core.userdetails.User@41036863:
Username: sjctrags; Password: [PROTECTED]; Enabled: true;
AccountNonExpired: true; credentialsNonExpired: true;
AccountNonLocked: true; Granted Authorities: ROLE_USER
readEmployees Callable login:
org.springframework.security.core.userdetails.User@41036863:
```

```
Username: sjctrags; Password: [PROTECTED]; Enabled: true;
AccountNonExpired: true; credentialsNonExpired: true;
AccountNonLocked: true; Granted Authorities: ROLE_USER
```

How it works...

Spring Security 4.2.x supports both synchronous and asynchronous MVC applications. It must be noted that both DispatcherServlet and DelegatingFilterProxy must be configured to support asynchronous processes and secure all the @Controller and services of the application. Moreover, SecurityContext must be accessible to all threads by setting the Spring Security variable spring.security.strategy to MODE_INHERITABLETHREADLOCAL by injecting the bean MethodInvokingFactoryBean into the context definition.

Once this recipe works perfectly, all security concepts elaborated in Chapter 4, *Securing Spring MVC Applications*, can be applied to all of the asynchronous services in this chapter.

9
Spring Boot 2.0

All the ideas and concepts established in the previous recipes converge into this chapter which aims to showcase Spring 5 as the tool in building a reactive and functional web application. Part of this chapter will discuss recipes on how to build a complete Spring MVC application with JDBC connectivity, logging, and view technology like JSP, Thymeleaf, and FreeMarker based on the methodology provided by **Spring Boot 2.0**, the main highlight. Features like implementing JPA and REST web services will also be included to show that some popular core POM starters that have been used in the previous Spring releases, are still present in this new version. Also, there will be some recipes that will be designed to compare and contrast built-in *starter* Maven libraries of Spring Boot 2.0 against its previous stable releases.

This chapter will also provide a concrete and practical set of procedures for building an application using the new web model, the *Functional and Reactive Web Framework* of Spring 5. Some recipes will require concepts on Reactor Core 3.0, RxJava 2.x and functional interfaces to justify the full-support of reactive programming in Spring 5. This is the only chapter that will lead us on how to implement a reactive `WebApplicationContext` which is one way of crafting a reactive web application. This will also teach us how to create a reactive application that can be run as a standalone *service box* with an embedded Tomcat server that supports NIO, and a Reactor Netty server at the side for listening to Spring5's reactive request-response transactions.

In this chapter, you will learn the following:

- Building a non-reactive Spring MVC application
- Configuring Logging
- Adding JDBC Connectivity
- Building a reactive Spring MVC application
- Configuring Spring Security 5.x
- Using reactive view resolvers

- Using RouterFunction and HandlerFunction
- Implementing Spring Data with JPA
- Implementing REST services using @RestController and Spring REST
- Apply Spring Cache

Building a non-reactive Spring MVC application

Spring Boot is a development strategy or methodology in building Spring 5 applications without using too many XML configurations and annotations. Since it does not require so many setups and configurations, software development methodology becomes time-efficient and requirement-centric. Likewise, it has the default core configuration needed to run the application immediately after build and also has an easy-integration with plugins such as JDBC, Spring Security, logging, and Hibernate ORM framework. This first recipe will provide us with a clear procedure for building an enterprise application using the latest Spring Boot 2.0.

Getting started

There are many ways to create a **Spring Boot 2.0** application, but this book will try to be consistent with the use of Maven. Using the Eclipse STS in `Chapter 1`, *Getting Started with Spring*, create a Maven Project ch09 with a core package `org.packt.spring.boot` to be the root package.

How to do it...

When creating a Spring MVC application using **Spring Boot 2.0**, the first thing to consider is the Spring Boot **starter parent POM configuration**. This inherits all the Spring Boot Maven dependencies supported by the chosen Spring Boot version. In this book, version **2.0.0M2** is the updated milestone for Spring Boot 2.0 at the moment:

1. Open the newly created `pom.xml` of `ch09` and add the following starter parent configuration:

```
<project xmlns="http://maven.apache.org/POM/4.0.0"
    xmlns:xsi="http://www.w3.org/2001/XMLSchema-instance"
```

```
xsi:schemaLocation="http://maven.apache.org/POM/4.0.0
    http://maven.apache.org/xsd/maven-4.0.0.xsd">
    <modelVersion>4.0.0</modelVersion>
<groupId>org.packt.cookbook</groupId>
<artifactId>ch09</artifactId>
<version>0.0.1-SNAPSHOT</version>
<packaging>war</packaging>
    <parent>
    <groupId>org.springframework.boot</groupId>
    <artifactId>spring-boot-starter-parent</artifactId>
    <version>2.0.0.M2</version>
    <relativePath/>
    </parent>
// refer to sources
</project>
```

2. For this parent starter configuration to work, be sure to use the preceding **Maven 3.x** to compile and run the pom.xml.

3. The Spring Boot starter parent requires setting the appropriate Java version for the Spring Boot since the default compiler level is always **Java 1.6**. Since we are into Spring Boot 2.0 that supports **Spring 5**, it is necessary to set the JVM version to at least 1.8 in the <properties> configuration of pom.xml. Also included in the settings are projects UTF encodings, runnable JAR's startClass, and Maven details:

```
<project xmlns="http://maven.apache.org/POM/4.0.0"
    xmlns:xsi="http://www.w3.org/2001/XMLSchema-instance"
    xsi:schemaLocation="http://maven.apache.org/POM/4.0.0
        http://maven.apache.org/xsd/maven-4.0.0.xsd">
    <modelVersion>4.0.0</modelVersion>
<groupId>org.packt.cookbook</groupId>
<artifactId>ch09</artifactId>
<version>0.0.1-SNAPSHOT</version>
<packaging>war</packaging>
<parent>
    <groupId>org.springframework.boot</groupId>
    <artifactId>spring-boot-starter-parent</artifactId>
    <version>2.0.0.M2</version>
    <relativePath/>
</parent>
    <properties>
        <project.build.sourceEncoding>UTF-8
</project.build.sourceEncoding>
        <project.reporting.outputEncoding>UTF-8
</project.reporting.outputEncoding>
            <java.version>1.8</java.version>
```

```
            <startClass>org.packt.spring.boot.HRBootApplication
        </startClass>
            </properties>
        // refer to sources
        </project>
```

4. After configuring all the details about the starter parent, now add the **Spring Boot starters** that are needed to comprise the default configuration of the Spring Boot application. These **starter POMs** are one of the listed inherited dependencies of the starter parent. Their **version numbers** are not specified, since it is the job of the Spring Boot starter parent to figure out what versions are appropriate for the setup. Since the ultimate goal is to build a Spring MVC application, include the required starters in the <dependencies>, which is to be later configured by the **application configuration file**:

```
<dependencies>
        <dependency>
            <groupId>org.springframework.boot</groupId>
            <artifactId>spring-boot-starter-web</artifactId>
        </dependency>
    // refer to sources
    </dependencies>
```

5. Although Spring Boot 2.0 supports at least Tomcat 8.0 by default, the following starter for Tomcat embedded server can be included for some servlet container details, but be sure to set the scope to provided since we will be deploying this application to our Tomcat 9 in WAR format:

```
<dependency>
        <groupId>org.springframework.boot</groupId>
        <artifactId>spring-boot-starter-tomcat</artifactId>
        <scope>provided</scope>
    </dependency>
```

6. The next starters are needed to configure the JSTL, FreeMarker, and Thymeleaf views:

```
<dependency>
        <groupId>javax.servlet</groupId>
        <artifactId>jstl</artifactId>
    </dependency>
    <dependency>
        <groupId>taglibs</groupId>
        <artifactId>standard</artifactId>
        <version>1.1.2</version>
    </dependency>
```

```xml
<dependency>
    <groupId>org.springframework.boot</groupId>
    <artifactId>spring-boot-starter-freemarker</artifactId>
</dependency>
<dependency>
    <groupId>org.springframework.boot</groupId>
    <artifactId>spring-boot-starter-thymeleaf</artifactId>
</dependency>
```

 If there are dependencies that are not part of the starters, the version numbers of these artifacts must be specified.

7. To load all the necessary Spring Boot 2.0.0.M2 starters, add the following Maven repositories:

```xml
<repositories>
        <repository>
            <id>spring-snapshots</id>
            <url>http://repo.spring.io/snapshot</url>
            <snapshots><enabled>false</enabled></snapshots>
        </repository>
        <repository>
            <id>spring-milestones</id>
            <url>http://repo.spring.io/milestone</url>
            <snapshots>
                <enabled>true</enabled>
            </snapshots>
        </repository>
    </repositories>
    <pluginRepositories>
        <pluginRepository>
            <id>spring-snapshots</id>
            <url>http://repo.spring.io/snapshot</url>
            <snapshots>
                <enabled>false</enabled>
            </snapshots>
        </pluginRepository>
        <pluginRepository>
            <id>spring-milestones</id>
            <url>http://repo.spring.io/milestone</url>
            <snapshots>
                <enabled>true</enabled>
            </snapshots>
        </pluginRepository>
    </pluginRepositories>
```

8. To close this POM configuration, add the following Maven deployment details. The `<finalName>` determines the name of the deployed JAR or WAR file:

```
<build>
   <plugins>
       <plugin>
           <groupId>org.springframework.boot</groupId>
           <artifactId>spring-boot-maven-plugin</artifactId>
       </plugin>
   </plugins>
   <finalName>ch09</finalName>
</build>
```

If this project is ought to be deployed as a WAR application, omit the spring-boot-maven-plugin. Otherwise, the Maven plugin stays if the project will be deployed as a standalone JAR application with its embedded Tomcat server. Some of the Maven plugins are already part of the starters such as `maven-jar-plugin` and `maven-surefire-plugin`.

9. Save the `pom.xml`. Update the `ch08` Maven project given the new POM configuration.

10. Any Spring Boot application must have an execution point where all starter beans will be loaded into the container, project components will be recognized by Spring Boot default component scan, and auto-configuration will be enabled.

11. This is the *application's entry point* that helps bootstrap the application either *as standalone or servlet-based application*:

```
@SpringBootApplication
public class HRBootApplication
extends SpringBootServletInitializer   {
   @Override
    protected SpringApplicationBuilder
      configure(SpringApplicationBuilder application) {
         return application.sources(HRBootApplication.class);
    }

    public static void main(String[] args) throws Exception {
         SpringApplication.run(HRBootApplication.class, args);
    }
}
```

This component must be located in the core package
`org.packt.spring.boot` to recognize all project components through
its auto-configured component-scan capability. Also, if this project is
designed for standalone **JAR** application, register this class in the
`<startClass>` of POM's `<properties>` to be recognized as JAR's `main-class` by the parent starter.

12. To add more *non-reactive web configurations* to the `Application`, the
`@Configuration` classes must be generated to contain all the `@Bean` mappings
needed to complete the MVC platform. In the previous Spring Boot releases,
configuration classes are required to be registered in the **META-INF**, but with
this version, it is no longer required. Add the following
`WebMvcConfigurerAdapter` class in the new package
`org.packt.spring.boot.config` that enables MVC, and adds required view
resolvers, massage bundles, and static resources:

```
@Configuration
@EnableWebMvc
public class SpringMvcConfig extends WebMvcConfigurerAdapter {
    @Bean
    public InternalResourceViewResolver getViewResolver() {
        InternalResourceViewResolver resolver =
        new InternalResourceViewResolver();
        resolver.setPrefix("/WEB-INF/");
        resolver.setSuffix(".html");
        resolver.setOrder(3);
        return resolver;
    }

    @Override
    public void configureDefaultServletHandling(
        DefaultServletHandlerConfigurer configurer) {
        configurer.enable();
    }
    @Bean
    public ResourceBundleViewResolver bundleViewResolver(){
        ResourceBundleViewResolver viewResolverB =
        new ResourceBundleViewResolver();
        viewResolverB.setBasename("config.views");
        viewResolverB.setOrder(0);
        return viewResolverB;
    }
    @Bean
    public MessageSource messageSource() {
        ReloadableResourceBundleMessageSource messageSource =
```

```
        new ReloadableResourceBundleMessageSource();
    messageSource.setBasenames(
    "classpath:config/messages_en_US",
    "classpath:config/errors");
    messageSource.setUseCodeAsDefaultMessage(true);
    messageSource.setDefaultEncoding("UTF-8");
    messageSource.setCacheSeconds(1);
    return messageSource;
}
@Bean
public static PropertySourcesPlaceholderConfigurer
    propertyConfig() {
    return new PropertySourcesPlaceholderConfigurer();
}

@Override
public void addResourceHandlers(ResourceHandlerRegistry
registry) {
    registry
    .addResourceHandler("/css/**")
    .addResourceLocations("/js/")
    .setCachePeriod(31556926);
}
}
```

 The use of JSP as view is *not really recommended* because it will add more servlet-based configurations to the application, which will create so many issues on the auto-configuration processes of Spring Boot. Besides, Spring Boot supports many templating engines such as FreeMarker , Thymeleaf , Velocity, and Mustache that are directly supported by the application.

13. To use **FreeMarker** and **Thymeleaf** templates, add the following starters:

```
<dependency>
    <groupId>org.springframework.boot</groupId>
    <artifactId>spring-boot-starter-freemarker</artifactId>
</dependency>
<dependency>
    <groupId>org.springframework.boot</groupId>
    <artifactId>spring-boot-starter-thymeleaf</artifactId>
</dependency>
```

14. The next step is to set up the Thymeleaf and FreeMarker properties through the
    application configuration file. However, since we have injected into the
    application `InternalResourceViewResolver` and
    `ResourceBundleViewResolver`, conflicts arise when it comes to the ordering of
    view hierarchy. There will be no choice but to inject all the configuration `@Bean`
    for these templating engines using another non-reactive `@Configuration` class
    to be dropped inside the package `org.packt.spring.boot.config`:

```
@Configuration
@EnableWebMvc
public class SpringContextConfig  {
    @Autowired
    private ApplicationContext applicationContext;
    @Bean(name = "viewResolverFTL")
    public FreeMarkerViewResolver getViewResolverFtl() {
        FreeMarkerViewResolver viewResolver =
new FreeMarkerViewResolver();
        viewResolver.setPrefix("");
        viewResolver.setSuffix(".ftl");
        viewResolver.setOrder(1);
        return viewResolver;
    }
    @Bean(name = "freemarkerConfig")
    public FreeMarkerConfigurer getFreemarkerConfig() {
        FreeMarkerConfigurer config = new FreeMarkerConfigurer();
        config.setTemplateLoaderPath("/WEB-INF/templates/");
        return config;
    }
    @Bean(name ="templateResolver")
    public SpringResourceTemplateResolver getTemplateResolver()
{
        SpringResourceTemplateResolver templateResolver =
new SpringResourceTemplateResolver();
        templateResolver.setApplicationContext(
applicationContext);
        templateResolver.setPrefix("/WEB-INF/templates/");
        templateResolver.setSuffix(".html");
        templateResolver.setTemplateMode("XHTML");
        return templateResolver;
    }
    @Bean(name ="templateEngine")
    public SpringTemplateEngine getTemplateEngine() {
        SpringTemplateEngine templateEngine =
new SpringTemplateEngine();
templateEngine.setTemplateResolver(getTemplateResolver());
        return templateEngine;
    }
```

```
@Bean(name="viewResolverThymeLeaf")
public ThymeleafViewResolver getViewResolverThyme(){
        ThymeleafViewResolver viewResolver =
new ThymeleafViewResolver();
        viewResolver.setTemplateEngine(getTemplateEngine());
        viewResolver.setOrder(2);
        return viewResolver;
}
}
```

15. One of the most important components of this application is the application configuration file that contains all the predefined properties of the supported dependencies needed by all the auto-configuration classes found in **Spring Boot 2.0**. This file is fetched and read during bootstrap of `HRBootApplication` to supply all the properties to the auto-configuration classes enabled by the starter dependencies. This file is popular as `application.xml`, `application.properties`, or `application.yml`, and is always located in the `src/main/resources` folder:

```
server.port=8443
server.servlet.context-path=/ch09
server.ssl.key-store=spring5server.keystore
server.ssl.key-store-password=packt@@
server.ssl.keyStoreType=PKCS12
server.ssl.keyAlias=spring5server

spring.thymeleaf.cache=false
#spring.thymeleaf.template-resolver-order=2
#spring.thymeleaf.suffix=.html
spring.freemarker.cache=false
#spring.freemarker.suffix=.ftl
```

Some of the core properties of `org.springframework.boot.autoconfigure.freemarker.FreeMarkerAutoConfiguration` and `org.springframework.boot.autoconfigure.thymeleaf.ThymeleafAutoConfiguration` classes are commented because these will be bypassed by FreeMarker and Thymeleaf configuration done in the context definition previously. All `server.*` property values are to be supplied to `org.springframework.boot.autoconfigure.web.ServerProperties`, which handles the embedded server auto-configuration.

16. Create the `src/main/resources/config` folder and drop here the `views.properties`, `errors.properties`, and `messages_en_US.properties` from `ch08`, here. Modify them to fit into this recipe.

17. Create `src/main/webapp/WEB-INF/templates` and drop all test view pages in JSTL, FreeMarker, and Thymeleaf rendition formats here.

18. There are two ways how to deploy Spring Boot applications: JAR or WAR. In this recipe, this project will be deployed as a WAR as indicated in POM:

```
<project xmlns="http://maven.apache.org/POM/4.0.0"
   xmlns:xsi="http://www.w3.org/2001/XMLSchema-instance"
   xsi:schemaLocation="http://maven.apache.org/POM/4.0.0
      http://maven.apache.org/xsd/maven-4.0.0.xsd">
      <modelVersion>4.0.0</modelVersion>
   <groupId>org.packt.cookbook</groupId>
   <artifactId>ch09</artifactId>
   <version>0.0.1-SNAPSHOT</version>
      <packaging>war</packaging>
   // refer to sources
</project>
```

19. Run Maven command `clean install -U`. Deploy the WAR file *manually* in our installed Tomcat 9. The Spring Boot 2.0 project will have a directory structure like this:

How it works...

The real essence of why developers choose Spring Boot 2.0 in building applications is the principle of auto-configuration. Unlike in ground-up Spring MVC 5 development, choosing the compatible Maven artifacts to the existing Spring API version is not a problem anymore because of the presence of the parent starter POM. The only challenge is just the choosing of the external support dependencies not included in the parent starter, since the version numbers are of critical importance. For clarification, Spring Boot 2.0 is not a framework and will not replace Spring 5 since its mandate is to generate Spring 5 applications.

There is a list of starters that can be inherited from the Maven repository of Spring Boot 2.0.0.M2 and each has auto-configuration classes found in `org.springframework.boot.autoconfigure.*`. To manage these classes, the bootstrap class, which is also called the `Application` class, will enable and execute some of them with the required properties to be filled in the `application.properties` file. This class, like our `HRBootApplication`, must have a class-level `@SpringBootApplication` to register it as the entry-point of the application. Another option is to apply `@Configuration`, `@EnableAutoConfiguration`, and `@ComponentScan` collectively in order to declare an `Application` class. These three annotations are needed if we need to further customize further the bootstrapping details, just like the version of our `HRBootApplication` in the following snippet that completely bypasses FreeMarker and Thymeleaf auto-configuration processes:

```
@Configuration
@ComponentScan("org.packt.spring.boot")
@EnableAutoConfiguration(exclude={ FreeMarkerAutoConfiguration.class,
    ThymeleafAutoConfiguration.class})
public class HRBootApplication extends  SpringBootServletInitializer  {
    // refer to sources
}
```

The `HRBootApplication` is composed of two methods, namely the `main()` and the `configure()` method overridden from `org.springframework.boot.web.servlet.support.SpringBootServletInitializ er`. If the project is needed to be deployed as a standalone JAR application, the `main()` is required to be present to bootstrap the application. If the project needs to be deployed in an application server, the class must extend `SpringBootServletInitializer` to bootstrap in a servlet container using the overridden method, `configure()`.

During bootstrap, all bean components are instantiated and injected and one of them is the `org.springframework.boot.web.servlet.context.AnnotationConfigServletWeb ServerApplicationContext`, which is the context root of the non-reactive Spring MVC application. All the required properties are categorized according to auto-configuration class and are found in `https://docs.spring.io/spring-boot/docs/current/reference/html/common-applicati on-properties.html`. Depending on what starter POMs are loaded into the container, necessary properties are to be registered and configured in the `application.properties` in order to load all the configuration beans into the `ApplicationContext` container.

Configuring Logging

After a long configuration recipe on building a Spring 5 MVC application, let us discuss how to enable logging using Spring Boot 2.0

Getting started

Open `ch09` again and create and add the following `@Controller` that utilizes thread pools generated by `TaskExecutor`.

How to do it...

If logging and auditing can be enabled in a ground-up Spring 5 application, it is easier to integrate a logging mechanism in Spring Boot. Follow these steps:

1. Create the following packages that will be utilized in the succeeding recipes:

   - `org.packt.spring.boot.controller`
   - `org.packt.spring.boot.dao`
   - `org.packt.spring.boot.service`

2. Since Spring Boot 2.0 directly supports `Logback` and `SL4J` with fewer configurations, create the following `logback.xml` inside `src/main/resources`. Assign a separate logger to each package above wherein each has its own `Level` value. Also, utilize two appenders, namely `ch.qos.logback.core.ConsoleAppender` to log all the messages in Tomcat's `stdout.log` and `ch.qos.logback.core.FileAppender` to log all messages in a custom log file `/logs/ch09.log`:

```xml
<?xml version="1.0" encoding="UTF-8"?>
<configuration>
  <appender name="STDOUT"
      class="ch.qos.logback.core.ConsoleAppender">
    <encoder>
      <pattern>%d{HH:mm:ss.SSS} [%thread] %-5level %logger{36}
-
         %msg%n</pattern>
    </encoder>
  </appender>
  <appender name="FILE"
class="ch.qos.logback.core.FileAppender">
        <file>/logs/ch09.log</file>
        <encoder>
            <pattern>%d{HH:mm:ss.SSS} [%thread] %-5level
%logger{36} - %msg%n</pattern>
        </encoder>
  </appender>
  <logger name="org.packt.spring.boot" level="info">
    <appender-ref ref="FILE" />
  </logger>
   <logger name="org.packt.spring.boot.controller"
level="trace">
    <appender-ref ref="FILE" />
  </logger>
   <logger name="org.packt.spring.boot.service" level="warn">
    <appender-ref ref="FILE" />
  </logger>
    <logger name="org.packt.spring.boot.dao" level="warn">
    <appender-ref ref="FILE" />
  </logger>
  <root level="info">
    <appender-ref ref="FILE" />
  </root>
</configuration>
```

The order of the details of `logback.xml` is technically crucial. The first part of the configuration must be the settings of the appenders chosen, followed by the custom loggers, and the last will be the root logger detail. Any violations to this ordering will lead to `HTTP status 404`.

3. Open `HRBootApplication` class and update it to start using the logging feature:

```
@Configuration
@ComponentScan("org.packt.spring.boot")
@EnableAutoConfiguration(exclude={
FreeMarkerAutoConfiguration.class,
    ThymeleafAutoConfiguration.class})
public class HRBootApplication extends
SpringBootServletInitializer {

    private static Logger logger =
    LoggerFactory.getLogger(HRBootApplication.class);

    @Override
    protected SpringApplicationBuilder configure(
    SpringApplicationBuilder application) {
        logger.info("bootstrap in servlet container");
        return application.sources(HRBootApplication.class);
    }

    public static void main(String[] args) throws Exception {
        logger.info("bootstrap as a standadlone with embedded
        server");
        SpringApplication.run(HRBootApplication.class, args);
    }
}
```

4. Save all files. The `clean` and `install` and manually deploy WAR to Tomcat 9.

How it works...

Spring Boot 2.0 uses *commons-logging* as its abstraction when it comes to implementing a logging mechanism, which is the reason why it has direct support to Log4J2, Logback, and java.util.logging APIs. Since we relied on the auto-configuration of the starters, the default framework used is Logback, and Spring Boot only requires one task, and that is to create the Logback configuration file with the appropriate loggers, appenders, and the level values that can be among the following: ERROR, WARN, INFO, DEBUG, and TRACE. To open logging with tracing, register in application.properties the property trace=true. Likewise, to enable debug mode, register the property debug=true.

Adding JDBC Connectivity

At this point we are ready to create a full-blown Spring MVC project from Spring Boot 2.0 with a database backend. This recipe will showcase how to add a starter POM that will auto-configure all APIs for the implementation of java.sql.DataSource needed by all the JDBC transactions of EmployeeDao and DepartmentDao.

Getting started

Open again current Maven project ch09 and add a new POM starter to implement the JDBC transactions using MySQL.

How to do it...

Using the previous DAO and service layer, let us implement a Spring Boot 2.0 application by doing the following steps:

1. Open pom.xml and add the following starter for the Spring Boot application:

```
<dependency>
        <groupId>org.springframework.boot</groupId>
        <artifactId>spring-boot-starter-jdbc</artifactId>
</dependency>
```

 Since this starter uses HikariCP as a default connection pooling plugin, including Maven dependencies on HikariCP is now not recommended.

2. Add the MySQL connector for the JDBC connectivity:

```
<dependency>
    <groupId>mysql</groupId>
    <artifactId>mysql-connector-java</artifactId>
    <version>5.1.40</version>
</dependency>
```

3. Open the `application.properties` and add the following properties for the `org.springframework.boot.autoconfigure.jdbc.DataSourceAutoConfiguration` class:

```
spring.datasource.driverClassName=com.mysql.jdbc.Driver
spring.datasource.url=jdbc:mysql://localhost:3306/hrs?autoRecon
nect=true&useSSL=true&serverSslCert=classpath:config/spring5pac
kt.crt
spring.datasource.username=root
spring.datasource.password=spring5mysql
spring.datasource.hikari.connection-timeout=60000
spring.datasource.hikari.maximum-pool-size=5
```

4. Create a new package `org.packt.spring.boot.model.data` and copy into it all data models from Chapter 8, *Reactive Web Applications*.

5. Copy to `org.packt.spring.boot.dao` all the DAO interfaces from the previous chapter.

6. Copy the DAO implementation classes from Chapter 8, *Reactive Web Applications*, to a new package `org.packt.spring.boot.dao.impl`.

7. Since Spring Boot does no longer uses lots of annotations, there will be some modifications in the DAO implementation classes. Instead of auto-wiring objects, Spring Boot is capable of injecting `@Bean` to the constructor of any component. Thus the auto-configured `java.sql.DataSource` will be automatically injected to a constructor of any DAO implementation with a parameter as such. Follow the modifications of `EmplayeeDaoImpl` and `DepartmentDaoImpl` as follows:

```
@Repository
public class DepartmentDaoImpl implements DepartmentDao{
    private JdbcTemplate jdbcTemplate;
    private SimpleJdbcInsert jdbcInsert;
    public DepartmentDaoImpl(DataSource dataSource) {
        jdbcTemplate = new JdbcTemplate(dataSource);
        jdbcInsert = new SimpleJdbcInsert(jdbcTemplate);
    }
// refer to sources
}
```

```
@Repository
public class EmployeeDaoImpl implements EmployeeDao {
    private JdbcTemplate jdbcTemplate;
    private SimpleJdbcInsert jdbcInsert;
    public EmployeeDaoImpl(DataSource dataSource) {
        jdbcTemplate = new JdbcTemplate(dataSource);
        jdbcInsert = new SimpleJdbcInsert(jdbcTemplate);
}
// refer to sources
}
```

8. Save all files. Then `clean` and `install`. Generate the WAR file.

How it works...

Since the earlier chapters, `HikariCP` data source pooling has been used because of its fast performance when it comes to complex JDBC transactions. Spring Boot 2.0 has decided to use `HikariCP` as the default data source pooling to replace the Tomcat JDBC connection pooling. Also, auto-wiring a `java.sql.DataSource` bean object is no lonhger allowed in Spring Boot development, since it can already perform *automatic constructor injection* of `@Bean` to any component class.

Building a reactive Spring MVC application

Spring Boot 2.0 supports building reactive Spring MVC applications and also has a starter POM to provide components with **Reactor Core 3.x libraries**. Likewise, it has the capability to easily integrate with **RxJava 2.x** APIs to provide us with another option for building reactive transactions. This recipe will be about creating a web application with a 100% reactive web framework of Spring 5.

Getting started

Reopen `ch09` and prepare to build a reactive application using Spring Boot 2.0 with all non-blocking and functional components derived from the previous chapter.

How to do it...

`Chapter 8`, *Reactive Web Application*, introduced us to the reactive APIs of FreeMarker and Thymeleaf from Spring Reactive module of Spring 5. Let us now explore the reactive components of Spring Boot by doing the following steps:

1. There is only one starter POM dependency that is responsible for creating a 100% reactive application that can only be inherited from the Spring Boot 2.0 repository, and that is `spring-boot-starter-webflux`. Aside from its Spring Reactor APIs, it contains all the necessary beans needed to instantiate a reactive `AnnotationConfigServletWebServerApplicationContext` that can only be supported by Spring 5:

```
<dependency>
    <groupId>org.springframework.boot</groupId>
    <artifactId>spring-boot-starter-webflux</artifactId>
        <exclusions>
            <exclusion>
                <groupId>org.springframework.boot</groupId>
                <artifactId>spring-boot-starter-reactor-netty
</artifactId>
            </exclusion>
        </exclusions>
</dependency>
```

 Since this chapter will be using Tomcat as both the embedded and external server for deployment, exclude **Netty plugins** from the `webflux` starter. Moreover, avoid using `org.springframework.boot.experimental:spring-boot-starter-web-reactive` since it's already deprecated and now successfully replaced by the `webflux` starter.

2. Spring Boot 2.0 supports asynchronous components by default because of the `webflux` starter. Thus, copy `SpringAsynchConfig` from the previous chapter and drop this in `org.packt.spring.boot.config` without further configurations. To recall, this class triggered the use of `@Async`, `Callable`, and `DeferredResult` transactions and also generated the needed thread pool from `TaskExecutor`.

3. Add the Reactor Core 3.x dependencies to execute `Publisher<T>`, `Mono<T>`, and `Flux<T>` stream operations.

4. In order to execute `Observable<T>`, `Flowable<T>`, and `Single<T>` operations of **RxJava 2.x**, add the following Maven dependency:

```
<dependency>
    <groupId>io.reactivex.rxjava2</groupId>
    <artifactId>rxjava</artifactId>
    <version>2.1.0</version>
</dependency>
```

5. Copy all service interfaces of `ch08` to `org.packt.spring.boot.service`.

6. Copy the implementation classes of all the services of `ch08` to `org.packt.spring.boot.service.impl`.

> Comment first the lines that execute `SecurityContextHolder`.

7. Copy all the controllers except `LoginController` in `ch08` to the package `org.packt.spring.boot.controller`.

> Comment first the lines that execute `SecurityContextHolder`.

8. Copy all the form models from the previous chapter to a new package `org.packt.spring.boot.model.form`.

9. Also copy the custom property editors `AgeEditor` and `DateEditor` to `org.packt.spring.boot.editor`.

10. Use the existing DAO implementations as modified by the previous recipe.

11. Update your views, errors, and message bundle in `src/main/resources/config` to contain all the properties derived from `ch08`.

12. Apply logging to controllers, services, and DAO components.

13. Lastly, copy all the view pages from the previous `ch08` Maven project as follows:

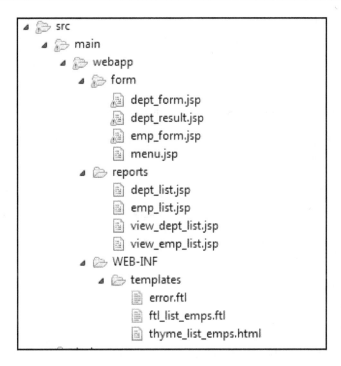

14. Save all files. Then `clean` and `install` to generate WAR files. Manually copy the WAR file from `/ch09/target to /webapps` of Tomcat 9. Access `https://localhost:8443/ch09/menu.html` and perform some form handling transactions.

How it works...

This recipe is the only way of building a 100% reactive Spring 5 web application wherein the `org.springframework.web.reactive.config.DelegatingWebFluxConfiguration` is injected into the container by Spring Boot and `@Autowire` it to the constructor of `AnnotationConfigServletWebServerApplicationContext` to generate a reactive web MVC configuration. The following bootstrap log from `/logs/ch09.log` will give us proof that the process really occurs with Spring Boot 2.0:

```
07:35:22.558 [localhost-startStop-1] INFO
o.s.b.f.s.DefaultListableBeanFactory — Overriding bean
definition for bean 'requestMappingHandlerMapping' with a
different definition: replacing [Root bean: class [null];
scope=; abstract=false; lazyInit=false; autowireMode=3;
```

```
dependencyCheck=0; autowireCandidate=true; primary=false;
factoryBeanName=org.springframework.web.servlet.config.annotati
on.DelegatingWebMvcConfiguration;
factoryMethodName=requestMappingHandlerMapping;
initMethodName=null; destroyMethodName=(inferred); defined in
class path resource
[org/springframework/web/servlet/config/annotation/DelegatingWe
bMvcConfiguration.class]] with [Root bean: class [null];
scope=; abstract=false; lazyInit=false; autowireMode=3;
dependencyCheck=0; autowireCandidate=true; primary=false;
factoryBeanName=org.springframework.web.reactive.config.Delegat
ingWebFluxConfiguration;
factoryMethodName=requestMappingHandlerMapping;
initMethodName=null; destroyMethodName=(inferred); defined in
class path resource
[org/springframework/web/reactive/config/DelegatingWebFluxConfi
guration.class]]
```

Because of this process, Spring Boot allows automatic recognition of thread pools generated by `TaskExecutor` and also allows assignment of each thread to different `@Async`, `Callable`, `DeferredResult`, `Flux<T>`, and `Mono<T>` operations. Likewise, the integration of **RxJava 2.x** does not require further property configuration details because the new web platform is now totally reactive. At this point, we have a working Spring WebFlux with a reactive platform built by Spring Boot 2.0 from the ground up.

Configuring Spring Security 5.x

With regard to easy feature or module integration, **Spring Boot 2.0** provides an easier way to integrate Spring Security to the application. This recipe will showcase how to apply the new **Spring Security 5** to a reactive web application.

Getting started

Open the Spring Boot `ch09` project and add the Spring Security 5 module into the existing application.

How to do it...

Let us now start applying security context to the previous reactive application through these steps:

1. Open `pom.xml` and add the following starter POM for **Spring Security 5**:

```
<dependency>
        <groupId>org.springframework.boot</groupId>
        <artifactId>spring-boot-starter-security</artifactId>
</dependency>
```

2. Create a new package `org.packt.spring.boot.security` and drop into it the same security context definition `AppSecurityConfig` from ch08.

3. Avoid registering `DelegatingFilterProxy` into the container since Spring Boot does it automatically by injecting `org.springframework.boot.web.servlet.DelegatingFilterProxyRegistrationBean` and mapping it to a filter name `springSecurityFilterChain`. If you include `SpringSecurityInitializer` from ch08 into this project, conflicts will arise and an exception like this will be thrown:

```
28-Jun-2017 13:01:07.219 SEVERE [https-openssl-nio-8443-exec-6]
org.apache.catalina.core.StandardContext.filterStart Exception
starting filter springSecurityFilterChain
org.springframework.beans.factory.NoSuchBeanDefinitionException
: No bean named 'springSecurityFilterChain' available
```

 There is no need to include `SpringSecurityInitializer` just to enable asynchronous support for s `pringSecurityFilterChain`, because Spring Boot enables it by default.

4. The next step is to `@Import` the `AppSecurityConfig` to apply the security protocols indicated in the security class definition to the Spring MVC project:

```
@Import(value = { AppSecurityConfig.class })
@Configuration
@EnableWebMvc
public class SpringContextConfig  {  // refer to sources }
```

5. Finally, you are now ready to use **Spring Security 5.x**. Uncomment all lines that execute `SecurityContextHolder`.

6. Copy the `LoginController` from ch08 to
   `org.packt.spring,boot.controller`.

7. Also copy the views, `login.jsp`, `logout.jsp` and `after_logout.jsp` to
   `src/main/webapp` of this project. Also update the views and message bundle
   pertaining to these view pages.

8. Save all files. Then `clean` and `install` project ch09. Manually deploy it to the
   server. Open a browser and access
   `https://localhost:8443/ch09/login.html` and supply the needed
   credentials indicated by in-memory configuration of `AppSecurityConfig`.

How it works...

As compared to the previous chapters, Spring Security is easy to configure with Spring Boot
2.0 and it gives the application the updated web security module which, in our case, is
version 5.x. To load all the needed classes and interfaces, the `spring-boot-starter-security` starter must be included in the set of Maven dependencies. Afterwards, the steps
are exactly the same as those enumerated in Chapter 4, *Securing Spring MVC Applications*,
and Chapter 8, *Reactive Web Applications*, with the exclusion of the
`DelegatingFilterProxy` initialization where we enabled the asynchronous support and
registered the **ASYNC** filter dispatcher. Thus, we can conclude that Spring Security 5.x can
be applied to a reactive web framework of Spring 5.

Using reactive view resolvers

The previous recipes showed us the procedures required to create a full reactive web
application, but there are still parts of it that need not be present, such as the use of
`InternalResourceViewResolver`, `MessageBundleViewResolver`, and the rest of the
non-reactive view resolvers of Spring 5. This recipe will recommend to us the appropriate
view engines for a reactive application.

Getting started

Let us tag ch09 as a closed project and create a separate one for this recipe that will be
named ch09-flux.

How to do it...

Let us now use the reactive view implementation that can render reactive stream data using Spring Boot:

1. Just as in the previous recipe, the only requirement for creating a full-blown reactive Spring 5 application is Spring Boot's `webflux` starter POM dependency. Also include the embedded Tomcat server as our official reactive server:

```
<dependency>
    <groupId>org.springframework.boot</groupId>
    <artifactId>spring-boot-starter-webflux</artifactId>
    <exclusions>
        <exclusion>
            <groupId>org.springframework.boot</groupId>
            <artifactId>spring-boot-starter-reactor-netty
</artifactId>
        </exclusion>
    </exclusions>
</dependency>
<dependency>
        <groupId>org.springframework.boot</groupId>
        <artifactId>spring-boot-starter-tomcat</artifactId>
</dependency>
```

 Avoid adding `spring -boot-starter -web` since the use of non-reactive components of Spring 5 will strictly not recommend the use of the `@EnableWebMvc` annotation in our context definitions.

2. Implement logging mechanism for this project similar to `ch09`.
3. Spring 5 has a reactive support for templating engines such as FreeMarker, Groovy, Thymeleaf, Velocity, and Mustache, which means these can be the appropriate options to render results from a reactive platform. Since the use of JSP is strictly prohibited, reactive FreeMarker and Thymeleaf will be configured to render data:

```
<dependency>
    <groupId>org.freemarker</groupId>
    <artifactId>freemarker</artifactId>
</dependency>
<dependency>
    <groupId>org.springframework</groupId>
    <artifactId>spring-context-support</artifactId>
</dependency>
```

```
<dependency>
  <groupId>org.springframework.boot</groupId>
  <artifactId>spring-boot-starter-thymeleaf</artifactId>
</dependency>
```

4. Create the bootstrap class similar to `ch09` inside a similar package
   `org.packt.spring.boot`:

```
@SpringBootApplication
public class HRBootApplication extends
 SpringBootServletInitializer  {

  @Override
   protected SpringApplicationBuilder
     configure(SpringApplicationBuilder application) {
        return application.sources(HRBootApplication.class);
   }
   public static void main(String[] args) throws Exception {
        SpringApplication.run(HRBootApplication.class, args);
   }

 }
```

5. Create an `application.properties` file in `src/main/resources` and add the
   following properties for the embedded Tomcat server and MySQL database
   connectivity:

```
server.port=8093
server.servlet.context-path=/ch09-flux

spring.datasource.driverClassName=com.mysql.jdbc.Driver
spring.datasource.url=jdbc:mysql://localhost:3306/hrs?autoRecon
nect=true&useSSL=true&serverSslCert=classpath:config/spring5pac
kt.crt
spring.datasource.username=root
spring.datasource.password=spring5mysql
spring.datasource.hikari.connection-timeout=60000
```

 This project will be deployed and executed as a standalone reactive web
application using a reactive embedded Tomcat server which will execute
its entire request transactions through HTTP using port 8093 .

6. Next, create reactive context definition classes that will inject all the reactive beans of **Fre**eMarker and Thymeleaf. These `@Configuration` classes have an annotation, `@EnableWebFlux` to import all the Spring WebFlux configurations including the reactive web `ApplicationContext`:

```
@Configuration
@EnableWebFlux
public class WebFluxConfig  {  // refer to sources  }
```

 There is no need to inherit or implement configuration APIs.

7. Spring 5 has a built-in support for reactive FreeMarker engine that uses the `org.springframework.web.reactive.result.view.freemarker.FreeMarkerViewResolver` and `org.springframework.web.reactive.result.view.freemarker.FreeMarkerConfigurer`. There is no need to inject all these bean objects to `WebFluxConfig` container.

8. Likewise, Spring 5 provides injected beans of reactive APIs of Thymeleaf engine such as the `org.thymeleaf.spring5.ISpringWebFluxTemplateEngine` and `org.thymeleaf.spring5.view.reactive.ThymeleafReactiveViewResolver` beans. Because of `@EnableWebFlux` all these beans are already loaded into the container so custom injection is not needed anymore.

9. Create a controller inside a package `org.packt.spring.boot.controller` that will just execute our configuration:

```
@Controller
public class FluxController {
    private Logger logger =
        LoggerFactory.getLogger(FluxController.class);
    @RequestMapping("/sampleFtl")
       public String home(ModelMap model) {
         model.addAttribute("title", "Reactive FreeMarker
Result");
         model.addAttribute("message", "Built-in
Configuration");
         logger.info("exceuting HelloController");
         return "sampleFtl";
    }
    @RequestMapping("/thymeleaf/sampleThyme")
    public String welcome(ModelMap model) {
       model.addAttribute("title", "Reactive Thymeleaf Result");
```

```
                        model.addAttribute("message", "Built-in Configuration");
                        return "sampleThyme";
            }


        }
```

10. Built-in support is different from an auto-configuration mechanism; thus, all default properties of Thymeleaf and FreeMarker reactive view resolvers and template engines are not open to change with this version of Spring Boot. `ThymeleafAutoConfiguration` and `FreeMarkerAutoConfiguration` properties are only applied only to their non-reactive APIs.

11. Store all templates in `src/main/resources/templates` because there is no other means that we can configure its template location.

12. Save all files. Run the `clean spring-boot:run` command to execute `ch09-flux` as a standalone application. Open a browser and execute `http://localhost:8093/ch09-flux/sampleFtl` and `http://localhost:8093/ch09-flux/thymeleaf/sampleThyme`.

How it works...

A full-blown reactive application does not need `spring-boot-starter-web` because the model of a reactive web framework does not only include the use of **Spring Reactor** and **RxJava 2.x** in many of its non-blocking transactions, but covers all the components of MVC and its embedded server. Spring 5 is a framework created not only to support reactive programming, but to build a totally reactive platform than can even execute as an independent reactor engine. We have come to the point where we have a clear picture of why Spring 5 was created and how powerful its reactive web framework and is which can only be utilized through Spring Boot 2.0.

Using RouterFunction and HandlerFunction

The previous recipes have shown us how to establish a **reactive** `ApplicationContext` and how Spring Boot 2.0 manages to run this reactive platform using a reactive embedded Tomcat server. This recipe will add another main feature of Spring 5 that is about building non-blocking, asynchronous, and context-independent Request-Response transactions using the functional web framework, a technique of writing a reactive version of `@Controller` and its mappings, using a domain-specific language way.

Getting started

Open the standalone Spring Boot `ch09-flux` project and add the following:
`RouterFunction<?>` and `HandlerFunction<?>`.

How to do it...

Let us implement reactive services using `HandlerFunction<T>` and `RouterFunction<T>`.
Follow these steps:

1. Before anything else, implementing a functional web framework means there will be a need to set up and configure another reactive embedded server that will execute and run these *independent services*. Since the embedded Tomcat is the one running for the whole Spring Boot 2.0 application, it will be advisable if Netty, Jetty, or Undertow were used to listen and run these independent services. This recipe chose the **Reactor Netty server** as the dedicated server for these functional-based events. Thus, now include the Netty APIs from the `webflux` starter POM:

```
<dependency>
    <groupId>org.springframework.boot</groupId>
    <artifactId>spring-boot-starter-webflux</artifactId>
</dependency>
```

2. Then, add another `webflux@Configuration` class to inject
`reactor.ipc.netty.http.server.HttpServer`:

```
@Configuration
@EnableWebFlux
public class HttpServerConfig {
    @Bean
    public  NettyContext nettyContext(ApplicationContext
context) {
```

```
        HttpHandler handler =
            DispatcherHandler.toHttpHandler(context);
        ReactorHttpHandlerAdapter adapter =
    new ReactorHttpHandlerAdapter(handler);
        HttpServer httpServer =
    HttpServer.create("localhost", Integer.valueOf("8095"));
        return httpServer.newHandler(adapter).block();
    }
}
```

 Do not use the existing port of the embedded Tomcat server to avoid conflicts. Moreover, the reactive `AplicationContext` is needed by Netty in order to listen to all registered functional web components such as `HandlerFunction<?>` and `RouterFunction<?>`.

3. Unlike in the usual `@Controller`, this functional web framework model of Spring 5 requires all `ServletRequest` and `ServletResponse` to be internally managed by the reactive `org.springframework.web.reactive.function.server.HandlerFunction`. This API is implemented using lambda expressions, `@FunctionalInterface`, Spring Reactor, RxJava, or any combinations of them. Usually, a `HandlerFunction` is created inside a `webflux` configuration class:

```
@Configuration
@EnableWebFlux
public class ReactiveControllers {
    public HandlerFunction<ServerResponse> routeMonoHandle(){
        HandlerFunction<ServerResponse> handlerMono =
            request -> ok().body(Mono.just("Mono Stream"),
                        String.class);
        return handlerMono;
    }
    public HandlerFunction<ServerResponse> handlerFluxData(){
        HandlerFunction<ServerResponse> handlerFlux =
            req -> ServerResponse.ok()
.body(fromObject("Flux Stream from String"));
        return handlerFlux;
    }
}
```

Do not apply the `@Controller` annotation since this is a `@Configuration` class.

4. Another way of writing `HandlerFunction<?>` is to create a `@Component` class that will contain all its bare implementations such as `DataHandler` that is stored inside `org.packt.spring.boot.handler`:

```
@Component
public class DataHandler {

    public Mono<ServerResponse> fluxHello(ServerRequest req) {
        return ok().body(Flux.just("Hello", "World!"),
                String.class);
    }

    public Mono<ServerResponse> stream(ServerRequest req) {
        Stream<String> streamData =
                Stream.of("i", "love", "reactive", "programming")
.sorted()
                .map((str) -> str.toUpperCase() + " ");
        Flux<String> flux = Flux.fromStream(streamData);
            return
ok().contentType(MediaType.APPLICATION_STREAM_JSON)
.body(flux, String.class);
    }
}
```

5. All these `HandlerFunction<?>` or reactive services will not be returned as a `ServetResponse` without the request URL mapping. In the traditional MVC, the `@RequestMapping` annotation maps the request handler to a **URL** that is called by the client to execute the handler. In the functional web model, `@RequestMapping` will not be used, but a router called `org.springframework.web.reactive.function.server.RouterFunction`, which will route the request to the `HandlerFunction<?>` whenever it finds a match with its registered URL. The following are injected `RouterFunction<?>` to the handlers in the `ReactiveControllers` configuration class:

```
@EnableWebFlux
public class ReactiveControllers {
    // refer to sources
    @Bean
    public RouterFunction<?> routeMono() {
            return route(GET("/mono" + "/stream"),
```

```
                    routeMonoHandle());
    }
    @Bean
    public RouterFunction<ServerResponse> handledRoute(){
        RouterFunction<ServerResponse> router =
            route(GET("/routeFluxHandle"), handlerFluxData());
        return router;
    }
}
```

6. To utilize the `DataHandler` functions, inject this bean component to the `ReactiveControllers` configuration class and use method references or lambda expression to call these `HandlerFunction` implementations:

```
@Configuration
@EnableWebFlux
public class ReactiveControllers {
    @Autowired
    private DataHandler dataHandler;

    // refer to sources
    @Bean
    public RouterFunction<ServerResponse> compundRoutes() {
            return route(GET("/routeFlux"),
dataHandler::fluxHello)
                    .andRoute(GET("/stream"),
dataHandler::stream);
        }
}
```

 The implementation of `RouterFunction<?>` here is quite complex, since it establishes two URL gateways to execute two separate `HandlerFunction<?>`.

7. Save all files. Execute the `clean spring-boot:run` command to deploy the reactive application. Open a browser and run all the *independent services* like `http://localhost:8095/stream`.

Avoid using the context root of the Tomcat embedded server for the reason that Reactor Netty here is configured to stand as a separate and container-independent reactive server.

How it works...

In the previous recipe, the `spring-boot-starter-reactor-netty` has been excluded from the POM dependencies just to avoid confusion on what embedded server to use for the standalone execution. At this point, Reactor Netty server must be included in order to listen and run these threaded and functional web components of Spring 5, namely the `HandlerFunction<?>` and `RouterFunction<?>`.

It requires having a `webflux@configuration` class in order to implement these components. Syntax errors will arise if we apply `@Controller` to the class, since `RouterFunction<?>` and `HandlerFunction<?>` together take the role of the `@Controller` and `@RequestMapping` in a typical MVC scenario. In a functional web model, `RouterFunction` is implemented to `route()` all matched requests to `HandlerFunction`. These mappings can be a simple one or chaining of `route().and.route()` stream operations. Once all these components are injected into the container, the Reactor Netty server will auto-detect and listen to all these injected `RouterFunction` because this server required the reactive `ApplicationContext` to be passed as a parameter to `ReactorHttpHandlerAdapter` in order to build and execute all these routers.

This recipe has also proven that these functional web components can execute side-by-side with all the non-reactive `@Controller` since the former uses Netty while the latter executes on top of the embedded Tomcat server. Reactor Netty is a full-blown implementation of NIO specification, which is an appropriate server for executing non-blocking, asynchronous, and reactive events and services.

This recipe will be the gateway to the next chapter, which is all about microservices development.

Implementing Spring Data with JPA

Spring Boot 2.0 still supports persistence using JPA, which avoids too many SQL scripts and Hibernate configurations. It provides auto-configuration when it comes to creating a persistence layer and, thus, it is an option to auto-configure the `hibernate.properties` and some JPA details. This recipe will illustrate how reactive applications can integrate with a non-reactive Spring Data JPA for MySQL CRUD transactions.

Getting started

Open `ch09-flux` and add a Spring Data JPA module for persistence and transaction management.

How to do it...

Spring 5 still supports Spring Data modules including Spring Data JPA. This recipe will showcase how to integrate Spring Data JPA using Spring Boot 2.0:

1. First, add the following starter POM dependency for Spring Data JPA auto-configuration:

   ```xml
   <dependency>
       <groupId>org.springframework.boot</groupId>
       <artifactId>spring-boot-starter-data-jpa</artifactId>
   </dependency>
   ```

2. Inside the package `org.packt.spring.boot.config`, create a non-`webflux` `@Configuration` to enable JPA transaction management. Spring Data JPA is not a reactive dependency, so avoid applying an `@EnableWebFlux` annotation:

   ```java
   @Configuration
   @EnableJpaRepositories(basePackages="org.packt.spring.boot.dao"
   )
   @EnableTransactionManagement
   public class SpringDataConfig {   }
   ```

 Indicating the DAO repository package is optional. Also, there is no need to inject Hibernate-related beans and JPA-related configuration into the class definition.

3. Open and validate if `application.properties` contain the correct data source details:

```
spring.datasource.driverClassName=com.mysql.jdbc.Driver
spring.datasource.url=jdbc:mysql://localhost:3306/hrs?autoRecon
nect=true&useSSL=true&serverSslCert=classpath:config/spring5pac
kt.crt
spring.datasource.username=root
spring.datasource.password=spring5mysql
spring.datasource.hikari.connection-timeout=60000
```

4. Copy the `Employee` model class from `ch08` and drop it in the `org.packt.spring.boot.model.data` package. The class must have an `@Entity` annotation to convert into a JPA entity model and a `@Table` annotation that will map it to the actual table `employee` in the `hr` database. If naming conflicts arise with the property mapping, the `@Column` can be used to map each property to the actual name of the column names. Lastly, the JPA domain model must extend `java.io.Serializable` to make it a persistent data object:

```
import javax.persistence.Entity;
import javax.persistence.GeneratedValue;
import javax.persistence.GenerationType;
import javax.persistence.Id;
import javax.persistence.Table;

@Entity
@Table(name = "employee")
public class Employee implements Serializable  {
    private Integer id;
    private Integer empid;
    private String firstname;
    private String lastname;
    private Integer age;
    private String email;
    private Date birthday;
    private Integer deptid;
    @Id
    @GeneratedValue(strategy = GenerationType.AUTO)
    public Integer getId() {
        return id;
}

// refer to sources
}
```

5. Create a package `org.packt.spring.boot.dao` and create an interface `EmployeeRepository` that extends `org.springframework.data.jpa.repository.JpaRepository`. If the requirement asks for simple CRUD operations with `Iterable<T>` return values, use `org.springframework.data.repository.CrudRepository`. If the service needs `List<T>` returned values and other additional features, use `JpaRepository`:

```
@Repository
public interface EmployeeRepository extends
            JpaRepository<Employee, Integer> {
    List<Employee> findByDeptid(Integer deptid);
    List<Employee> findByFirstname(String firstname);
    List<Employee> findByLastname(String lastname);
    List<Employee> findByAge(Integer age);
}
```

6. Then, create a service class `EmployeeService` in `org.packt.spring.boot.service` that contains the following template methods:

```
public interface EmployeeService {
    public List<Employee> findEmployeeByDeptid(Integer deptid);
    public List<Employee>
findEmployeeByFirstname(String firstname);
    public List<Employee> findEmployeeByLastname(String
lastname);
    public List<Employee> findEmployeeByAge(Integer age);
    public List<Employee> findAllEmps();
}
```

7. Afterwards, implement `EmployeeServiceImpl` using the `EmployeeRepository`:

```
@Service
@Transactional
public class EmployeeServiceImpl implements EmployeeService{
    @Autowired
    private EmployeeRepository employeeRepository;

    @Override
    public List<Employee> findEmployeeByDeptid(Integer deptid) {
        return employeeRepository.findByDeptid(deptid);
    }

    @Override
```

```
    public List<Employee>
findEmployeeByFirstname(String firstname) {
        return employeeRepository.findByFirstname(firstname);
    }

    @Override
    public List<Employee> findEmployeeByLastname(String
lastname) {
        return employeeRepository.findByLastname(lastname);
    }

    @Override
    public List<Employee> findEmployeeByAge(Integer age) {
        return employeeRepository.findByAge(age);
    }

    @Override
    public List<Employee> findAllEmps() {
        return employeeRepository.findAll();
    }
}
```

The use of @Transactional is optional since HRBootApplication enables the transaction management at the beginning.

8. Open DataHandler and add the following HandlerFunction<?> that will retrieve a stream of employees from the EmployeeRepository:

```
@Autowired
    private EmployeeService employeeServiceImpl;

public Mono<ServerResponse> empList(ServerRequest req) {
        Flux<Employee> flux =
            Flux.fromIterable(employeeServiceImpl.findAllEmps());
return
    ok().contentType(MediaType.APPLICATION_STREAM_JSON)
    .body(flux, Employee.class);
}
```

9. Then open a `ReactiveControllers` configuration class and add the following `RouterFunction<?>` that will execute the preceding `HandlerFunction<?>`:

```
@Bean
    public RouterFunction<ServerResponse> listAllEmps() {
            return route(GET("/routeEmps"),
dataHandler::empList);
    }
```

10. Save all files. Execute `clean spring-boot:run` commands. Open a browser and execute `http://localhost:8095/routeEmps`.

← → C ⌂ ⓘ localhost:8095/routeEmps

▦ Apps ▢ Design ▢ Social Tools ▢ Spring ▢ Something ▢ PHP ▢ Databases ▢ Alfresco Sites ▢ Framework ▢ Weblogic ★ Bookmarks ▢ Java 1.8 ▢ B

{"id":1,"empid":23456,"firstname":"Joel","lastname":"Enage","age":45,"email":"joel@aol.com","birthday":-291196800000,"deptid":361}
{"id":11,"empid":11112,"firstname":"Sherwin","lastname":"Tragura","age":22,"email":"sjctrags@gmail.com","birthday":281203200000,"deptid":359}
{"id":15,"empid":15,"firstname":"John","lastname":"Tragura","age":38,"email":"sjctrags@gmail.com","birthday":281203200000,"deptid":359}
{"id":16,"empid":222222,"firstname":"Johnny","lastname":"Refamonte","age":38,"email":"sjctrags@gmail.com","birthday":427910400000,"deptid":362}
{"id":21,"empid":67876,"firstname":"Jeremy","lastname":"Irons","age":65,"email":"jeremy@aol.com","birthday":null,"deptid":393}
{"id":23,"empid":897654,"firstname":"Owen","lastname":"Estabillo","age":35,"email":"osestabillo@gmail.com","birthday":null,"deptid":389}

There is no need to add `com.fasterxml.jackson.core` dependencies, since Spring Data starter is responsible for the JSON media type parsing.

How it works...

Spring Data JPA has been widely used in the lower versions of Spring Boot because of its easy way of implementing transaction management on CRUD operations. This recipe just proved that, even though Spring Data JPA offers non-reactive repository transactions, it can still be used with Spring 5's reactive and functional web model. Spring Boot 2.0 supports reactive Spring Data repositories, which will be discussed in the next chapters.

Implementing REST services using @RestController and Spring REST

Using `HandlerFunction` and `RouterFunction` in exposing repository data is the major option that is the promoted by this chapter since everything is all about Spring 5. But there are also non-reactive ways of exposing these data using the conventional `@RestController` and **Spring REST** that are still present in **Spring Boot 2.0**, which can be part of building reactive applications and microservices.

Getting started

Open `ch09-flux` and add the following Spring REST support for Spring Boot 2.0.

How to do it...

To implement REST services in Spring 5, follow these steps:

1. To enable Spring REST support, add the following starter POM dependency:

```
<dependency>
    <groupId>org.springframework.boot</groupId>
    <artifactId>spring-boot-starter-data-rest</artifactId>
</dependency>
```

2. All the annotations of `SpringDataConfig` needed to implement Spring Data JPA are also needed here for Spring REST configuration.

3. Inside `org.packt.spring.boot.dao`, create a `DepartmentRepository` that extends `JpaRespository`, which is the same API class used in the previous recipe:

```
@RepositoryRestResource(collectionResourceRel="depts",
        path="depts")
public interface DepartmentRepository
extends JpaRepository<Department, Integer>{

    public List<Department> findByName(@Param("name") String
name);
    public List<Department> findByDeptid(
@Param("deptid")  Integer deptId);
}
```

The optional annotation `@RepositoryRestResource` is present because the requirement wants the REST endpoint name to be shorter as `/depts` than the default, which is `/departments`. Moreover, the `@Param` is required to map the local parameter of the operations to the request parameter value sent by the client.

4. To parse all the JSON request and response, inject the beans concerning JSON converters to `SpringDataConfig` from `RepositoryRestMvcConfiguration` by using `@Import`. Thus, there is no need to add the `com.fasterxml.jackson.core` dependency.

5. However, even without Spring REST, Spring 5's reactive application can expose any data using `@RestController` of Spring MVC components. The usual `@RequestMapping` can still be used to map the handler to the URL with the indicated HTTP method. But the modern way of mapping requests to a URL is through the use of `@GetMapping` and `@PostMapping` annotations:

```
@RestController
public class RestServiceController {
    @Autowired
    private EmployeeService employeeServiceImpl;

    @RequestMapping("/objectSampleRest")
    public String exposeString() {
        return "Hello World";
    }
    @GetMapping("/monoSampleRest")
    public Mono<String> exposeMono() {
        return Mono.just("Hello World");
    }
    @GetMapping("/fluxSampleRest")
    public Flux<String> exposeFlux() {
        List<String> names = Arrays.asList("Anna", "John",
"Lucy");
        return Flux.fromIterable(names)
.map((str) -> str.toUpperCase() + "---");
    }
    @GetMapping("/fluxJpaEmps")
    public Flux<Employee> exposeJpaEmps() {
        return Flux.fromIterable(
employeeServiceImpl.findAllEmps());
    }
    @PostMapping(path = "/fluxAddEmp",
consumes = MediaType.APPLICATION_JSON_VALUE)
    public void addMonoEmp(@RequestBody Mono<Employee>
employee){
```

```
    }
    @PostMapping(path = "/fluxAddListEmps",
consumes = MediaType.APPLICATION_JSON_VALUE)
    public void addFluxEmp(@RequestBody Flux<Employee>
employee){
    }
}
```

6. Save all files. Then `clean` and `deploy` the standalone Spring Boot application. Open a browser and run `http://localhost:8093/ch09-flux/fluxJpaEmps`.

How it works...

The recipe offers two ways to implement REST services using Spring Boot 2.0, and that is through the use of the `@RestController` and Spring REST module. The only difference between the two is that `@RestController` requires Spring MVC setup in order to generate endpoints, while **Spring Data REST** is tied up with Spring Data JPA, so endpoints are generated at the repository configuration.

The `@GetMapping` and `@PostMapping` annotations are new additions to the mapping libraries that can be applied to `@RestController` transactions. If the handler needs to **produce** data objects using the `GET` method, `@GetMapping` is applied. If the request transaction needs to **consume** data objects using the `POST` method, `@PostMapping` is used instead.

Implementing REST services in reactive applications is very important, especially if the main goal is building microservice architecture.

Applying Spring Cache

This final recipe will be about enhancing data retrieval from the data source through Spring Cache. Just like the rest of the recipes, Spring Boot 2.0 provides an auto-configuration when it comes to caching. It supports cache implementations such as `Ehcache`, `Infinispan`, `Caffeine`, `Hazelcast`, and `Redis`. The following is a recipe on how to use two caching types in one reactive application.

Getting started

Open, for the last time, `ch09-flux` and enable `Ehcache` and `Caffeine` caching.

How to do it...

To enable Spring Cache in Spring Boot 2.0 application, follow these steps:

1. Add the starter POM for Spring Boot 2.0 caching:

```
<dependency>
    <groupId>org.springframework.boot</groupId>
    <artifactId>spring-boot-starter-cache</artifactId>
</dependency>
```

2. For `Ehcache` auto-configuration, add the following `Ehcache` provider to the Maven dependencies:

```
<dependency>
    <groupId>net.sf.ehcache</groupId>
    <artifactId>ehcache</artifactId>
    <version>2.9.0</version>
</dependency>
```

3. Also add the following `Caffeine` provider to the Maven dependencies:

```
<dependency>
    <groupId>com.github.ben-manes.caffeine</groupId>
    <artifactId>caffeine</artifactId>
    <version>2.5.2</version>
</dependency>
```

4. For `Ehcache`, copy the `ehcache.xml` of Chapter 5, *Cross-Cutting the MVC*, and modify the cache name and `diskStore` path. Spring Boot's default cache type is `Ehcache` and it always looks for the `ehcache.xml` in the `src/main/resources/` folder by default:

```
<?xml version="1.0" encoding="UTF-8"?>
<ehcache xmlns:xsi="http://www.w3.org/2001/XMLSchema-instance"
    xsi:noNamespaceSchemaLocation="ehcache.xsd"
    updateCheck="true"
    monitoring="autodetect"
    dynamicConfig="true">

    <diskStore path="C://ch09cached" />

    <cache name="departmentCache"
        maxEntriesLocalHeap="10000"
        maxEntriesLocalDisk="1000"
        eternal="false"
        diskSpoolBufferSizeMB="20"
        timeToIdleSeconds="300" timeToLiveSeconds="600"
        memoryStoreEvictionPolicy="LFU"
        transactionalMode="off">
        <persistence strategy="localTempSwap" />
    </cache>
</ehcache>
```

5. To configure `Caffeine` cache manager, open `application.properties` and add the following properties:

```
spring.cache.cache-names=employeeCache
spring.cache.caffeine.spec=maximumSize=500,
expireAfterAccess=30s
```

6. To finally enable caching, create a context definition class in `org.packt.spring.boot.config` with the `@EnableCaching` annotation:

```
@Configuration
@EnableCaching
public class CachingConfig { }
```

7. Open `DepartmentRespository` and apply `Ehcache` cache:

```
@Repository
public interface EmployeeRepository extends
JpaRepository<Employee, Integer> {

    @Cacheable("employeeCache")
    List<Employee> findByDeptid(Integer deptid);
    @Cacheable("employeeCache")
    List<Employee> findByFirstname(String firstname);
    @Cacheable("employeeCache")
    List<Employee> findByLastname(String lastname);
    @Cacheable("employeeCache")
    List<Employee> findByAge(Integer age);
}
```

8. Open `EmployeeRepository` and apply `Caffeine` cache:

```
@Repository
public interface EmployeeRepository extends
        JpaRepository<Employee, Integer> {

    @Cacheable("employeeCache")
    List<Employee> findByDeptid(Integer deptid);
    @Cacheable("employeeCache")
    List<Employee> findByFirstname(String firstname);
    @Cacheable("employeeCache")
    List<Employee> findByLastname(String lastname);
    @Cacheable("employeeCache")
    List<Employee> findByAge(Integer age);
}
```

9. Save all files. Then `clean` and `deploy` the project ch09-flux.

How it works...

Spring Boot 2.0 supports auto-configuration of Spring Cache and can even use multiple cache implementations working altogether during testing, development and deployment stages. Ehcache and JCache are the widely used types in caching huge JPA data to main high performance on CRUD transactions.

10
The Microservices

After the success of **service-oriented architecture (SOA)**, the term **microservice** has been in the enterprise software development for quite a while now and is popular and useful to many experts in building up decomposed services and domain models in many huge applications. Either to be used for small or huge enterprise software development, the purpose of microservice architecture is to break down monolithic software prototypes into independent and granulized service boxes, each having an independent set of objectives and tasks that can be pulled to decorate a needed requirement. Unlike in distributed architecture where each submodule does not necessarily interact with the other at runtime, in microservice design there is always a gray area where these service boxes communicate depending on the modes and approaches of inter-process communication.

But this chapter will not discuss the theoretical concept of microservices per se, rather, it will prove that Spring 5 supports and helps build microservices, either with typical RESTful web services for synchronous transactions or with @Async, Callable<T> and DeferredResult<T> tasks for asynchronous services. Moreover, one of the main highlights also is the newest reactive microservice architecture made up of the Flux<T>, Mono<T> and Publisher<T> data streams generated from Spring Data JPA repositories. Based on the core concepts of a reactive and functional web framework of Chapter 9, *Spring Boot 2.0*, some recipes in this chapter will emphasize building, organizing, and managing reactive RESTful services that will comprise these microservices from different domain responsibilities. Likewise, constructing the client-side application that will consume all the exposed endpoints will also be included.

On the other hand, this chapter will also be about interaction among microservices and how the libraries of **Spring Cloud** work with Spring Boot 2.0.0.M2 in managing the design of these microservices.

In this chapter you will learn:

- Exposing RESTful services in Spring 5
- Using the actuator REST endpoints
- Building a client-side application with RestTemplate, AsyncRestTemplate, and WebClient
- Configuring the Eureka server for service registration
- Implementing the Eureka service discovery and client-side load balancing
- Applying resiliency to client application
- Consuming endpoints using a declarative method
- Using Docker for deployment

Exposing RESTful services in Spring 5

Let us start this chapter with a recipe that will construct, organize, and build microservices based on the `hrs` database. The `login`, `employee`, and `department` domains will have separate and independent microservices catering all the `GET` and `POST` request transactions exposed as blocking, asynchronous and reactive RESTful that **Spring 5** can support. This recipe will require concepts discussed in the previous chapters.

Getting started

Create Maven projects for each domain responsibility and apply synchronous, asynchronous, and reactive implementation of services and controllers.

How to do it...

Let us create our first synchronous, asynchronous and reactive microservices by following these steps:

1. Using **Eclipse STS**, create a Maven project for a Spring Boot application named `ch10-deptservice` that will represent a microservice for the `department` domain. Then, create a **POM** configuration which includes all the needed Spring Boot 2.0.0.M2 starter POM libraries, such as **WebFlux**, **Spring Context**, **JDBC**, **HikariCP** connection pool, **Ehcache**, **JPA**, embedded reactive **Tomcat** container, **Reactor Netty** container, **FreeMarker** and **Thymeleaf**. Also include some required support libraries, such as **MySQL 5.x connector** and **Rx Java 2.0**:

```
<project xmlns="...">
  <modelVersion>4.0.0</modelVersion>
  ....
  <packaging>war</packaging>
  <parent>
    <groupId>org.springframework.boot</groupId>
    <artifactId>spring-boot-starter-parent</artifactId>
    <version>2.0.0.M2</version>
    <relativePath/>
  </parent>
  <properties>
      <project.build.sourceEncoding>
UTF-8</project.build.sourceEncoding>
      <project.reporting.outputEncoding>
UTF-8</project.reporting.outputEncoding>
      <java.version>1.8</java.version>
      <startClass>org.packt.spring.boot.HRDeptBootApplication
</startClass>
  </properties>
  <dependencies>
    <dependency>
        <groupId>org.springframework.boot</groupId>
        <artifactId>spring-boot-starter-jdbc</artifactId>
    </dependency>
    <dependency>
     <groupId>org.springframework.boot</groupId>
     <artifactId>spring-boot-starter-webflux</artifactId>
    </dependency>
    <dependency>
        <groupId>org.springframework.boot</groupId>
        <artifactId>spring-boot-starter-tomcat</artifactId>
    </dependency>
      ...
```

```
    <dependency>
     <groupId>mysql</groupId>
     <artifactId>mysql-connector-java</artifactId>
     <version>5.1.40</version>
     </dependency>
     <dependency>
     <groupId>io.reactivex.rxjava2</groupId>
     <artifactId>rxjava</artifactId>
     <version>2.1.0</version>
     </dependency>
    </dependencies>
    ....
    <build>
     <plugins>
        <plugin>
            <groupId>org.springframework.boot</groupId>
            <artifactId>spring-boot-maven-plugin</artifactId>
        </plugin>
     </plugins>
    <finalName>ch10-dept</finalName>
    </build>
</project>
```

2. Create the core package, `org.packt.microservice.core`, and drop a bootstrap class inside it named as `HRDeptBootApplication`. Update the `<startClass>` property of `pom.xml`:

```
@SpringBootApplication
public class HRDeptBootApplication extends
                        SpringBootServletInitializer  {
    @Override
      protected SpringApplicationBuilder
    configure(SpringApplicationBuilder application) {
            return application.sources(
HRDeptBootApplication.class);
        }
        public static void main(String[] args) throws Exception {
          SpringApplication.run(HRDeptBootApplication.class,
args);
        }
}
```

3. Create another package, `org.packt.microservice.core.config`, for the
reactive `ApplicationContext` configuration details. Drop the following
`@Configuration` classes inside this package:

```
@Configuration
@EnableCaching
public class CachingConfig { // empty }

@Configuration
@EnableJpaRepositories(
basePackages="org.packt.microservice.core.dao")
@Import(RepositoryRestMvcConfiguration.class)
@EnableTransactionManagement
public class SpringDataConfig { // empty  }

@EnableAsync
@Configuration
public class SpringAsynchConfig implements AsyncConfigurer {
  private static Logger logger =
    LoggerFactory.getLogger(SpringAsynchConfig.class);
        @Bean("mvcTaskexecutor")
      @Override
        public Executor getAsyncExecutor() {
          ConcurrentTaskExecutor executor =
new ConcurrentTaskExecutor(
                    Executors.newFixedThreadPool(100));
        executor.setTaskDecorator(new TaskDecorator() {
                @Override
                public Runnable decorate (Runnable runnable) {
                    return () -> {
                        long t = System.currentTimeMillis();
                        runnable.run();
                        logger.info("creating
        ConcurrentTaskExecutor ....");
                        System.out.printf("Thread %s has a
                processing time:  %s%n",
                    Thread.currentThread().getName(),
                            (System.currentTimeMillis() -
t)));
                    };
                }
            });
        return executor;
    }
}

@Configuration
```

```
@EnableWebFlux
public class HttpServerConfig {
  @Bean
  public NettyContext nettyContext(ApplicationContext context)
{
    HttpHandler handler =
      DispatcherHandler.toHttpHandler(context);
    ReactorHttpHandlerAdapter adapter =
new ReactorHttpHandlerAdapter(handler);
    HttpServer httpServer = HttpServer.create("localhost",
        Integer.valueOf("9003"));
    return httpServer.newHandler(adapter).block();
}
}
```

 All of these @Configuration are just the same as the previous chapters.

4. Copy the ehcache.xml and logback.xml configuration files of the previous chapter and drop them to this project's src/main/resources folder. Update the new Ehcache's diskStore and Logger's log file path for this project.

5. Also in src/main/resources, create the required application.properties for the auto-configuration of the embedded reactive Tomcat, JDBC and HikariCP data source setup with JPA and Hibernate 5 data persistency configuration:

```
server.port=8090
server.servlet.context-path=/ch10-dept

spring.datasource.driverClassName=com.mysql.jdbc.Driver
spring.datasource.url=jdbc:mysql://localhost:3306/hrs?autoRecon
nect=true&useSSL=true&serverSslCert=classpath:config/spring5pac
kt.crt
spring.datasource.username=root
spring.datasource.password=spring5mysql
spring.datasource.hikari.connection-timeout=60000

spring.jpa.hibernate.use-new-id-generator-mappings=false
```

6. Building the proper RESTful services starts with the correct JPA entities. Copy and drop the `Department` entity model used in `ch09` to a new package `org.packt.microservice.core.model.data`.

7. Together with the entity models, create an auxiliary **POJO** that will contain aggregate and simple data value such as the *total number of departments* which is a `Long` object type. The main reason behind this is that JSON and XML marshallers do not directly convert wrapper objects (for example, Integer, Double, Float) into **JSON** objects or **XML** entities:

```
public class CountDept implements Serializable{
  private Long count;

  public Long getCount() {
    return count;
  }

  public void setCount(Long count) {
    this.count = count;
  }
}
```

8. Then, implement the `@Repository` class for `DepartmentDao` using **Spring** Data JPA. Apply Ehcache caching to each data retrieval operation. Drop this class inside `org.packt.microservice.core.dao` package:

```
@Repository
public interface DepartmentRepository extends
        JpaRepository<Department, Integer>{

  @Cacheable("departmentCache")
  public List<Department> findByName(String name);
  @Cacheable("departmentCache")
  public List<Department> findByDeptid(Integer deptId);
}
```

9. Next, create a `DepartmentService`, that will compose the RESTful services to be exposed by the microservice. The template includes both asynchronous and synchronous service signatures:

```
public interface DepartmentService {
  public Department findDeptByid(Integer id);
  public List<Department> findAllDepts();
  public List<Department> findDeptsByName(String name);
  public List<Department> findDeptsByDeptId(Integer deptid);
```

```
    public void saveDeptRec(Department dept);

    public CompletableFuture<List<Department>>
readDepartments();
    public Future<Department>  readDepartment(Integer id);
}
```

10. Implement the service class using the preceding DepartmentRepository class.
    The implementations include blocking transactions and non-blocking ones that
    return Future and CompletableFuture tasks. And, since the
    @EnableTransactionManagement has been invoked by the configuration class
    SpringDataConfig, the @Transactional annotation must be applied per
    service implementation class for JPA persistency and commit/rollback
    management:

```
@Service
@Transactional
public class DepartmentServiceImpl implements
DepartmentService{
  @Autowired
  private DepartmentRepository departmentRepository;

  @Override
  public List<Department> findAllDepts() {
    return departmentRepository.findAll();
  }

  @Override
  public List<Department> findDeptsByName(String name) {
    return departmentRepository.findByName(name);
  }

  // refer to sources
  @Override
  public CompletableFuture<List<Department>> readDepartments()
{
    return CompletableFuture.completedFuture(
departmentRepository.findAll());
  }
  @Async
  public Future<Department> readDepartment(Integer id) {
    return new AsyncResult<>(departmentRepository.findById(id)
.orElse(new Department()));
  }
}
```

11. Spring 5's `RouterFunction<?>` has a separate set of *services,* which are written as a handler class. A handler class contains all the `HandlerFunction<?>` implementation that can be mapped later with the corresponding URL. Below is a handler class for this microservice that must be placed inside the `org.packt.microservice.core.handler` package:

```java
@Component
public class DeptDataHandler {
    // refer to sources
    public Mono<ServerResponse> deptList(ServerRequest req) {
    Flux<Department> flux = Flux.fromIterable(
departmentServiceImpl.findAllDepts());
    return ok().contentType(MediaType.APPLICATION_STREAM_JSON)
.body(flux, Department.class);
    }

    public Mono<ServerResponse> chooseDeptById(ServerRequest
req) {
        Scheduler subWorker = Schedulers.newSingle("sub-thread");
        Mono<Department> emp = Mono.defer(() -> Mono.justOrEmpty(
departmentServiceImpl.findDeptByid(
Integer.parseInt(req.pathVariable("id")))))
.subscribeOn(subWorker);
        return ok().contentType(MediaType.APPLICATION_STREAM_JSON)
.body(emp, Department.class)
            .switchIfEmpty(ServerResponse.notFound().build());
    }

    public Mono<ServerResponse> chooseFluxDepts(ServerRequest
req) {
        return ok().contentType(MediaType.APPLICATION_STREAM_JSON)
.body(req.bodyToFlux(Integer.class)
.flatMap((id) -> Mono.justOrEmpty(
departmentServiceImpl.findDeptByid(id))),
        Department.class)
            .switchIfEmpty(ServerResponse.notFound().build());
    }

    public Mono<ServerResponse> saveDepartmentMono(
ServerRequest req) {
        Scheduler subWorker = Schedulers.newSingle("sub-thread");
        Mono<Department> department = req.bodyToMono(
Department.class).doOnNext(
departmentServiceImpl::saveDeptRec)
.subscribeOn(subWorker);
        return ok().contentType(
MediaType.APPLICATION_STREAM_JSON)
```

```
.build(department.then());
  }

  public Mono<ServerResponse> countDepts(ServerRequest req) {
    Mono<Long> count = Flux.fromIterable(departmentServiceImpl
.findAllDepts())   .count();
    CountDept countDept = new CountDept();
    countDept.setCount(count.block());
    Mono<CountDept> monoCntDept = Mono.justOrEmpty(countDept);
    return ok().contentType(
MediaType.APPLICATION_STREAM_JSON)
.body(monoCntDept, CountDept.class)
        .switchIfEmpty(ServerResponse.notFound().build());
  }
}
```

12. At this point, *synchronous*, *asynchronous*, and *reactive* RESTful services can now be implemented to build this microservice for the department domain. Let us start by implementing the GET and POST synchronous REST web services using the `@RestController`, `@GetMapping`, and `@PostMapping` of Spring 5:

```
@RestController
public class DeptBlockingController {
  @Autowired
  private DepartmentService departmentServiceImpl;
  @GetMapping(value="/selectDept/{id}",
produces= MediaType.APPLICATION_JSON_VALUE)
  public Department blockDepartment(
@PathVariable("id") Integer id) {
    return departmentServiceImpl.findDeptByid(id);
  }
  @GetMapping(value="/listDept",
produces= MediaType.APPLICATION_JSON_VALUE)
  public List<Department> blockListDept() {
    return departmentServiceImpl.findAllDepts();
  }
  @PostMapping(value="/saveDeptRec",
consumes= MediaType.APPLICATION_JSON_VALUE)
  public Boolean blockSaveDept(@RequestBody Department dept) {
    try{
      departmentServiceImpl.saveDeptRec(dept);
      return true;
    }catch(Exception e){
      return false;
    }
  }
}
```

13. Now, build the asynchronous REST services that use `WebAsyncTask`, `Callable`, and `DeferredResult` tasks that return the `Future<T>` and `CompletableFuture<T>` objects:

```
@RestController
public class DeptAsyncController {
  @Autowired
  private DepartmentService departmentServiceImpl;
  @GetMapping(value="/webSyncDeptList.json",
produces ="application/json",
headers = {"Accept=text/xml, application/json"})
  public WebAsyncTask<List<Department>> websyncDeptList(){
      Callable<List<Department>> callable =
new Callable<List<Department>>() {
          public List<Department> call() throws Exception {
              return departmentServiceImpl
.readDepartments().get(500, TimeUnit.MILLISECONDS);
          }
      };
      return new WebAsyncTask<List<Department>>(500, callable);
  }
  @GetMapping(value="/deferSelectDept/{id}.json",
produces ="application/json",
headers = {"Accept=text/xml, application/json"})
  public DeferredResult<Department> deferredSelectDept(
@PathVariable("id") Integer id) {
      DeferredResult<Department> deferredResult =
new DeferredResult<>();
      CompletableFuture.supplyAsync(()->{
          try {
          return departmentServiceImpl
.readDepartment(id).get();
          } catch (InterruptedException e) {    }
            catch (ExecutionException e) {    }
      return null;
      }).thenAccept((msg)->{
        deferredResult.setResult(msg);
      });
      return deferredResult;
  }
  @GetMapping(value="/callSelectDept/{id}.json",
      produces ="application/json",
      headers = {"Accept=text/xml, application/json"})
  public Callable<Department> jsonSoloEmployeeCall(
          @PathVariable("id") Integer id){
    Callable<Department> task = new Callable<Department>() {
          @Override
```

```
                    public Department call () throws Exception {
                         Department dept = departmentServiceImpl
    .readDepartment(id).get();
                         return dept;
                    }
              };
         return task;
    }
  }
```

14. The last set of REST services are the reactive ones which can be implemented in two ways: using the typical @RestController and applying the functional and web framework APIs, namely the RouterFunction<T> and HandlerFunction<T> of Spring 5. The following are the reactive services for the department microservice implemented by @RestController:

```
@RestController
public class DeptReactiveController {
   @Autowired
   private DepartmentService departmentServiceImpl;
   @GetMapping("/selectReactDepts")
   public Flux<Department> selectReactDepts() {
      return Flux.fromIterable(
departmentServiceImpl.findAllDepts());
   }
   @GetMapping("/selectReactDept/{id}")
   public Mono<Department> selectReactDept (
@PathVariable("id") Integer id) {
      return Mono.justOrEmpty(
departmentServiceImpl.findDeptByid(id))
         .defaultIfEmpty(new Department());
   }
   @PostMapping("/saveReactDept")
   public Mono<Void> saveReactDept (
@RequestBody Department dept) {
      return Mono.justOrEmpty(dept)
.doOnNext(departmentServiceImpl::saveDeptRec).then();
   }
}
```

15. The following are the reactive REST services built by Spring 5's reactive functional web framework written inside `@Configuration` class:

```
import static
org.springframework.web.reactive.function.server.RequestPredica
tes.GET;
import static
org.springframework.web.reactive.function.server.RequestPredica
tes.POST;
import static
org.springframework.web.reactive.function.server.RouterFunction
s.route;
@Configuration
@EnableWebFlux
public class DeptReactFuncControllers {
    @Autowired
    private DeptDataHandler dataHandler;
    @Bean
    public RouterFunction<ServerResponse>
            departmentServiceBox(){
      return route(GET("/listFluxDepts"),
        dataHandler::deptList)
          .andRoute(GET("/selectDeptById/{id}"),
                dataHandler::chooseDeptById)
          .andRoute(POST("/selectFluxDepts"),
                dataHandler::chooseFluxDepts)
          .andRoute(POST("/saveFluxDept"),
                dataHandler::saveDepartmentMono)
          .andRoute(GET("/countFluxDepts"),
                dataHandler::countDepts);
    }
}
```

16. Save all files. Build and deploy the reactive web project by running the Maven command `clean spring-boot:run -U -e`. Open a browser and execute all the GET services. If no errors and exceptions are found, name this application as the `Department` microservice.

17. Copy the `Login` and `Employee` domains from the previous chapter and perform again all the processes in this recipe to build two more *service boxes* namely the `Employee` microservice as `ch10-empservice` and `Login` microservice as `ch10-loginservice` project.

How it works...

Building microservices has always been a good enterprise solution to break down monolithic applications into functional components that can still interact with each other at runtime, yet have no dependencies on each other when it comes to scalability and code maintenance. Since the first chapter, this book has been using the `hrs` databases consisting of three domain scopes in one application: the `login`, the `employee`, and the `department` domains. It has reached this point where we design and build each domain its own Spring Boot application which caters all the request-response transactions through RESTful services only within the bound of its domain's details.

From the previous huge application, the completion of this recipe will lead us to three applications that depict three service boxes that run side-by-side that can cater the same as the typical single HR application but with more manageable components. This kind of architecture cannot be possible without the use of `@RestController` and its related annotations to expose services that can respond to all user requests to transact with the `hr` data source.

But what is unique with this recipe is the clear proof that the Spring 5 web and functional framework has strong support not only for the usual blocking services, but also for the asynchronous and reactive RESTful service implementation. It gives us an approach to build a service box that can contain any of these types or all of them to satisfy client requirement. Spring Boot 2.0 has provided us the easiest and most straightforward methodology for building reactive microservices. The following diagram will summarize the three microservices after this recipe:

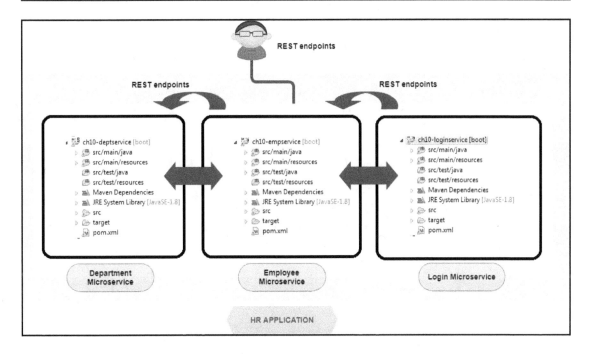

Using the actuator REST endpoints

From one huge reactive web application, the previous recipe built three service boxes which are all **Spring Boot 2.0** applications. As the number of microservices increases, the management and monitoring of each application becomes inconvenient and time-consuming. **Spring Boot 2.0** supports a starter POM that provides audits, metrics, status, management operations, and other analytics that can assist in monitoring each microservice. This dependency is inherited from the repository as the `spring-boot-starter-actuator`.

Getting started

This recipe will need the three Maven projects, `ch10-deptservice`, `ch10-empservice`, and `ch10-loginservice` to contain the **Spring Boot Actuator** in their respective `pom.xml` to view application details and enable shutdown operations to avoid the `java.net.BindException: Address already in use: bind` problem.

How to do it...

Follow these steps to enable Spring Boot Actuator starter POM dependency:

1. Open the `pom.xml` of the three Spring Boot 2.0 applications and add the following POM starter library.

   ```
   <dependency>
       <groupId>org.springframework.boot</groupId>
       <artifactId>spring-boot-starter-actuator</artifactId>
   </dependency>
   ```

2. To avoid conflicts and URL mapping problems, configure the actuator module by adding the following properties to each `application.properties`. Below are the configuration details added to `ch10-deptservice`:

   ```
   management.port=8090
   management.address=localhost
   management.context-path=/appdetails

   endpoints.info.enabled=true
   endpoints.info.sensitive=false
   endpoints.info.id=info
   info.app.description=Department Microservice
   info.app.version=1.0.0

   endpoints.sensitive=false
   endpoints.shutdown.sensitive=false
   endpoints.shutdown.enabled=true
   ```

3. After updating all the `application.properties` to accommodate the *actuator* configuration for `ch10-deptservice`, save all projects and deploy all the microservices. Be sure to have a different `server.port` and `management.port` for each service box to avoid JVM `BindException`.

4. Since the actuator's security management is disabled, actuator REST endpoints are not sensitive and all endpoints are open for access. Execute actuator by running custom actuator endpoint `http:/localhost:xxxx/ch10-xxxx/appdetails` to check the available management services available for each microservice.

5. Open three browsers and try running `/appdetails/info` from each microservice to view the custom **project description** and **version**.

6. Since the actuator's `/shutdown` endpoint service is enabled, we can now shutdown each microservice using the `curl` command. Download `curl` for **Windows** from the site `http://www.paehl.com/open_source/?CURL_7.28.0` and unzip the `curl.exe` file to `C:/Windows/System32`. Afterwards, open a terminal console using the **Administrator**'s account and execute `curl -XPOST http://localhost:xxxx/ch10-xxxx/appdetails/shutdown -k`:

```
C:\>curl -XPOST http://localhost:8090/ch10-dept/appdetails/shutdown -k
{
  "message" : "Shutting down, bye..."
}
C:\>curl -XPOST http://localhost:8092/ch10-emp/appdetails/shutdown -k
{
  "message" : "Shutting down, bye..."
}
C:\>curl -XPOST http://localhost:8094/ch10-login/appdetails/shutdown -k
{
  "message" : "Shutting down, bye..."
}
```

This execution is only applicable to the embedded server auto-configured by the bootstrap. The Reactor Netty server configured in `HttpServerConfig` does not always comply with the `actuator` `/shutdown`.

How it works...

Spring Boot 2.0 offers built-in REST endpoints that can be used by experts to view the information about the microservice application. Some of these endpoints are not available readily or are sensitive and need user credentials, but some are for public use by default. To enable these endpoints, we can just open the `application.properties` and apply the necessary settings just like what the recipe did to `/shutdown` which is disabled by default.

Customizing the actuator module starts at the management endpoint, which is executed through `/actuator` by default but was changed to `/appdetails` in this recipe through `management.context-path` setting. Running this actuator main endpoint will list all the supported endpoints for monitoring the microservice:

```
← → C ⌂   ⓘ localhost:8094/ch10-login/appdetails/

⠿ Apps    Design    Social Tools    Spring    Something    PHP    Data

{
  "links" : [ {
    "rel" : "self",
    "href" : "http://localhost:8094/ch10-login/appdetails"
  }, {
    "rel" : "health",
    "href" : "http://localhost:8094/ch10-login/appdetails/health"
  }, {
    "rel" : "info",
    "href" : "http://localhost:8094/ch10-login/appdetails/info"
  }, {
    "rel" : "mappings",
    "href" : "http://localhost:8094/ch10-login/appdetails/mappings"
  }, {
    "rel" : "metrics",
    "href" : "http://localhost:8094/ch10-login/appdetails/metrics"
  }, {
    "rel" : "beans",
    "href" : "http://localhost:8094/ch10-login/appdetails/beans"
  }, {
    "rel" : "trace",
    "href" : "http://localhost:8094/ch10-login/appdetails/trace"
  }, {
    "rel" : "configprops",
    "href" : "http://localhost:8094/ch10-login/appdetails/configprops"
  }, {
```

One of the widely used endpoints is `/metrics`, which gives the snapshot on the JVM memory space and heap status of the running microservice. Likewise, `/health` is always executed to check if the application is running smoothly or not, and `/mappings` to check all the registered URL request mappings. But above all, it is a necessity to properly shut down each microservice through the `/shutdown` endpoint which can easily be invoked through the `curl` command.

Adding the Spring Boot Actuator module is essential, primarily because we acknowledge the importance of RESTful services, not only in building service boxes but also in establishing an interaction between the application and the software builder.

Building a client-side application with RestTemplate, AsyncRestTemplate and, WebClient

After implementing the RESTful services, let us showcase the procedures on how to consume *synchronous, asynchronous* and *reactive* RESTful services from the three microservices using client APIs offered by Spring 5.

Getting started

Deploy all the error-free `Employee`, `Department` and `Login` microservices. Let us now create a Maven project that will serve as a client application to the exposed web services of these three applications.

How to do it...

Let us build a REST client application by following these steps:

1. Create a `ch10-reports` Maven project and configure `pom.xml` similar to the previous projects. Add the parent POM for **Spring Boot 2.0.0.M2** and all its starter POM dependencies. Just like in the previous recipe, also include the needed support libraries for MySQL connectivity and RxJava 2.0.

2. Copy all the data model classes from `ch09` and place them inside a new `org.packt.microservice.client.model.data` package (such as `AveAge`, `CountDept`, `Employee`, `Department`, and so on).

3. Add a bootstrap class for this project inside a root package: `org.packt.microservice.client`:

```
@Configuration
@ComponentScan("org.packt.microservice.client")
@EnableAutoConfiguration(
    exclude={FreeMarkerAutoConfiguration.class,
    ThymeleafAutoConfiguration.class})
```

```
public class HRClientBootApplication extends
            SpringBootServletInitializer  {
@Override
    protected SpringApplicationBuilder
        configure(SpringApplicationBuilder application) {
            return
application.sources(HRClientBootApplication.class);
    }

    public static void main(String[] args) throws Exception {
        SpringApplication.run(HRClientBootApplication.class,
args);
    }
}
```

 Since I plan to deploy this project to the external Tomcat 9 server as a Spring MVC project, I disabled the `webflux` default auto-configuration for Thymeleaf and FreeMarker view technologies to avoid exceptions.

4. Inside the `src/main/resources` folder, create the `application.properties` and add the following auto-configuration settings in it:

```
server.port=8443
server.servlet.context-path=/ch10-reports
server.ssl.key-store=config/spring5server.keystore
server.ssl.key-store-password=packt@@
server.ssl.keyStoreType=PKCS12
server.ssl.keyAlias=spring5server

spring.datasource.jmx-enabled=false
```

 The data source auto-configuration is disabled in this project.

5. Enable `webflux` components through the following `@Configuration` class to be dropped in the `org.packt.microservice.client.config` package:

```
@Configuration
@EnableWebMvc
public class WebFluxConfig { // empty }
```

6. The class `org.springframework.web.client.RestTemplate` is used to execute all typical and synchronous RESTful web services. To enable its use across the platform, inject `RestTemplate` bean instance into the `WebFluxConfig` container:

```
@Configuration
@EnableWebMvc
public class WebFluxConfig {
    @Bean
        public RestTemplate restTemplate() {
            return new RestTemplate();
        }
}
```

Emphasis is on the `@EnableWebMvc` since this project will be a Spring MVC project.

7. Create a typical `ClientBlockingController` that uses `RestTemplate` to consume REST endpoints of some blocking request transactions exposed from any of the three microservices:

```
@Controller
public class ClientBlockingController {
    @Autowired
    protected RestTemplate restTemplate;
    @RequestMapping("/blockingString")
    @ResponseBody
    public String clientSelectEmps() {
            return restTemplate.getForObject(
"http://localhost:8092/ch10-emp/objectSampleRest",
            String.class);
    }
    @RequestMapping(value="/blockingEmployee/{id}",
produces= MediaType.APPLICATION_JSON_VALUE)
    @ResponseBody
    public Employee clientSelectEmp(
@PathVariable("id") Integer id) {
```

```
        HttpHeaders headers = new HttpHeaders();
        headers.set("Accept", MediaType.APPLICATION_JSON_VALUE);
        HttpEntity<String> entity = new HttpEntity<>(headers);
          ResponseEntity<Employee> response =
    restTemplate.exchange(
    "http://localhost:8092/ch10-emp/selectEmp/{id}" ,
                  HttpMethod.GET, entity, Employee.class, id);
        return response.getBody();
      }
    @RequestMapping(value="/blockingSaveDept",
        method=RequestMethod.POST,
    consumes= MediaType.APPLICATION_JSON_VALUE)
      @ResponseBody
      public String clientSaveDept(
    @RequestBody Department dept){
        try{
          restTemplate.postForObject(
    "http://localhost:8090/ch10-dept/saveDeptRec",
    dept, Department.class);
          return "OK";
        }catch(Exception e){
          return "NOT OK";
        }
      }
    }
```

8. To run asynchronous RESTful endpoints that expose `Callable<T>`,
   `WebAsyncTask<T>` and `DeferredResult<T>` tasks, use the
   `org.springframework.web.client.AsyncRestTemplate`. To enable their
   usage, inject its bean object to `WebFluxConfig` container.

```
    @Bean
      public AsyncRestTemplate asyncRestTemplate(){
        AsyncRestTemplate art = new AsyncRestTemplate();
        return art;
    }
```

9. Create another simple `ClientAsyncController` that will house all client-side
   executions of some asynchronous RESTful services from any of the three
   microservices:

```
    @Controller
    public class ClientAsyncController {
      @Autowired
      private AsyncRestTemplate asyncRestTemplate;
      @RequestMapping(value="/asyncSelectEmp/{id}",
          produces=MediaType.APPLICATION_JSON_VALUE)
```

```
    @ResponseBody
    public Employee asyncSelectEmps(
@PathVariable("id") Integer id){
        String url ="http://localhost:8092/
ch10-emp/callSelectEmp/{id}.json";
        HttpMethod method = HttpMethod.GET;
        HttpHeaders headers = new HttpHeaders();
         headers.set("Accept", MediaType.APPLICATION_JSON_VALUE);
        HttpEntity<String> requestEntity =
new HttpEntity<String>("params", headers);
        ListenableFuture<ResponseEntity<Employee>> future =
          asyncRestTemplate.exchange(url, method, requestEntity,
            Employee.class, id);
        try {
          ResponseEntity<Employee> entity = future.get();
          return entity.getBody();
        } catch (InterruptedException e) {    }
catch (ExecutionException e) {   }
        return null;
    }
}
```

10. To execute the reactive RESTful services, Spring 5 offers a new API `org.springframework.web.reactive.function.client.WebClient` that is available by default in the `webflux` configuration. The `WebClient` executes reactive request transactions either exposed through `@RestController` or `RouterFunction<?>`. Create a typical controller that will consume all reactive services exposed by the embedded reactive Tomcat server and Reactor Netty server:

```
@Controller
public class ClientReactiveController {
  // From Tomcat server
  @RequestMapping("/reactEmps")
   public Flux<Employee> sayFlux() {
            return WebClient.create().method(HttpMethod.GET)
              .uri("http://localhost:8092/
  ch10-emp/selectReactEmps")
                      .contentType(
                  MediaType.APPLICATION_JSON_UTF8)
.retrieve().bodyToFlux(Employee.class);
    }
  @RequestMapping("/reactSelectEmps/{id}")
  public Flux<Employee> sayFlux(@PathVariable("id") Integer id)
{
            return WebClient.create().method(HttpMethod.GET)
              .uri("http://localhost:8092/
```

```
ch10-emp/selectReactEmp/" + id)
                 .contentType(
MediaType.APPLICATION_JSON_UTF8)
.retrieve().bodyToFlux(Employee.class);
    }
  // From Netty Server
  @RequestMapping("/reactFuncEmps")
  public Flux<Employee> sayhandler() {
          return WebClient.create().method(HttpMethod.GET)
              .uri("http://localhost:8902/listFluxEmps")
              .contentType(
MediaType.APPLICATION_JSON_UTF8)
.retrieve().bodyToFlux(Employee.class);
    }
  @RequestMapping("/reactCountDept")
  public Mono<CountDept> count() {
          return WebClient.create().method(HttpMethod.GET)
              .uri("http://localhost:8901/countFluxDepts")
              .contentType(
MediaType.APPLICATION_OCTET_STREAM)
.retrieve().bodyToMono(CountDept.class);
    }
  @RequestMapping(value="/reactSaveEmp",
consumes= MediaType.APPLICATION_JSON_VALUE)
  @ResponseBody
  public String hello(@RequestBody Employee employee){
     Mono<ClientResponse> resp = WebClient.create().post()
.uri("http://localhost:8902/saveEmp")
.accept(MediaType.APPLICATION_JSON)
              .body(BodyInserters.fromObject(employee))
.exchange();
     return resp.block().statusCode().name();
    }
}
```

11. Save all files. Then `clean`, `build`, and `install` the project to our external Tomcat 9.x server. Open a browser and execute all GET REST endpoints.

How it works...

Spring 5 framework provides all the API classes to consume any types of RESTful services. If the web services are synchronous types, the boiler-plated template class `RestTemplate` is used to call, execute, and process the response of any `GET`, `POST`, `HEAD`, `PUT`, `DELETE`, and `OPTIONS` request through its utility methods `getForObject()`, `postForObject()`, `headForHeaders()`, `put()` and `delete()`. It has a specialized method `exchange()` which can work with any HTTP methods, also with or without request parameters. It aims to return `ResponseEntity` that contains the callback headers, status and the body of the response. Since Spring Boot 2.0 has a built in XML marshaller/unmarshaller and JSON encoding/decoding support, `RestTemplate` can now easily produce and consume an individual or list of model objects, except asynchronous and reactive REST web services since it is designed to work with a single-threaded and blocking client model. Although deprecated, Spring 5 still supports `AsyncRestTemplate` that has the core methods of `RestTemplate` but only works with an asynchronous and non-blocking REST client model. Executing endpoints with this class generates `ListenableFuture<T>` tasks which can either wrap a result or be `null` depending on the thread pool executions.

When it comes to reactive REST services, Spring 5 provides a new class `WebClient` that is purely reactive and is composed of reactive operators that can understand Reactor Stream components. This reactive HTTP client is created through its method `create()` and then asks for the type of HTTP `method()` exposed by the endpoint URL indicated in its `uri()` method. Further information, such as the header types, will be needed before it invokes `retrieve()` and converts the response to `Mono<T>` or `Flux<T>`. During POST transactions, WebClient uses `org.springframework.web.reactive.function.BodyInserters` to pass the typical entity model or `Publisher<T>` as form data to the endpoint before it invokes `exchange()` method. All request-response transactions involved in any `WebClient` processing are composed of reactive operators that `RestTemplate` and `AsyncRestTemplate` will not understand.

Configuring the Eureka server for service registration

Another version of building microservices is through **Spring Cloud Finchley** modules that support creating a service registry of microservices with the Spring 5's reactive platform. This recipe will showcase how to build a cloud-based environment that can host instances or nodes of service instances in one server machine.

Getting started

Using the latest Spring Cloud modules for Spring Boot 2.0.0.M2, let us create a **Eureka** server that will be responsible for hosting the `Department`, `Employee`, and `Login` microservices to form one cloud of services that can only be distinguished through their HTTP ports.

How to do it...

Let us create our first Eureka cloud-based services through these steps:

1. First, create a Spring Boot application that will be deployed and run as a Eureka server and nothing else. Name the project `ch10-eureka-hrs`. It should contain only the core starter POM dependencies such as the `spring-boot-starter-webflux` since this will just access the microservices.

2. To enable Spring Cloud Finchley modules, add the following dependency management component inside the `pom.xml`:

```
<dependencyManagement>
    <dependencies>
        <dependency>
            <groupId>org.springframework.cloud</groupId>
            <artifactId>spring-cloud-dependencies</artifactId>
            <version>Finchley.M1</version>
            <type>pom</type>
            <scope>import</scope>
        </dependency>
    </dependencies>
</dependencyManagement>
```

3. Afterwards, add the following Spring Cloud starter POM to the Maven dependencies of our `pom.xml`:

```
<dependency>
    <groupId>org.springframework.cloud</groupId>
    <artifactId>spring-cloud-starter</artifactId>
</dependency>
<dependency>
    <groupId>org.springframework.cloud</groupId>
    <artifactId>spring-cloud-starter-eureka</artifactId>
</dependency>
<dependency>
    <groupId>org.springframework.cloud</groupId>
    <artifactId>spring-cloud-starter-eureka-server</artifactId>
</dependency>
```

4. Also add the `actuator` module and enable the `/shutdown` endpoint to shut down the application:

```
<dependency>
    <groupId>org.springframework.boot</groupId>
    <artifactId>spring-boot-starter-actuator</artifactId>
</dependency>
```

5. Now, create the core package `org.packt.microservice.server` that contains the bootstrap class `HRSEurekaBootApplication` that will purposely load and execute all the needed Eureka management and monitoring commands once deployed. The indicator that it is a Eureka server is the class-level annotation `@EnableEurekaServer` found in the bootstrap:

```
@SpringBootApplication
@EnableEurekaServer
public class HRSEurekaBootApplication {
  public static void main(String[] args) {
      SpringApplication.run(HRSEurekaBootApplication.class,
args);
    }
}
```

6. In `src/main/resources`, add an `application.properties` that will auto-configure this application to become a server only because, by default, Eureka could be both the client and the server which can be a mess when it comes to huge microservice design architecture. Likewise, add all the needed properties for the `actuator` endpoint:

```
eureka.instance.hostname=localhost
spring.application.name=eureka
server.port=5566
eureka.client.register-with-eureka=false
eureka.client.fetch-registry=false

spring.datasource.jmx-enabled=false

management.port=5566
management.address=localhost
management.context-path=/appdetails

endpoints.info.enabled=true
endpoints.info.sensitive=false
endpoints.info.id=info
info.app.description=HRS Eureka Server
info.app.version=1.0.0

endpoints.sensitive=false
endpoints.shutdown.sensitive=false
endpoints.shutdown.enabled=true
```

7. Save all files. Run `clean spring-boot:run -U` to deploy the application. Open a browser and access `http://localhost:5566/`:

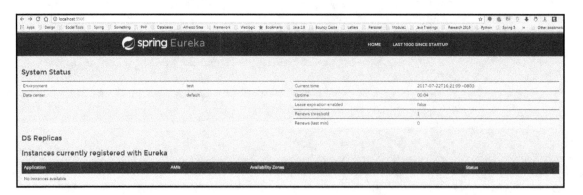

8. Although you can convert the previous `ch10-deptservice`, `ch10-empservice`, and `ch10-loginservice` to become the Eureka clients, this recipe decided to create three separate instances which expose the same RESTful services. To start, create an empty Maven project `ch10-depts-instance` whose `pom.xml` is the same as `ch10-deptservice` with the inclusion of Spring Cloud Finchley dependency management component.

9. Given the `added` plug-in, add the following Spring Cloud starter POM dependencies needed to set up a Eureka client instance:

```
<dependency>
    <groupId>org.springframework.cloud</groupId>
    <artifactId>spring-cloud-starter</artifactId>
</dependency>
<dependency>
    <groupId>org.springframework.cloud</groupId>
    <artifactId>spring-cloud-starter-eureka</artifactId>
</dependency>
```

10. Then, create the core package `org.packt.microservice.instance` with the bootstrap class `DeptInstanceBootApplication`. To enable Eureka server registration of this instance, add the `@EnableDiscoveryClient` or `@EnableEurekaClient` to the bootstrap. These annotations will tell the Eureka server to explicitly discover this instance with its port and register it to its instance store:

```
@SpringBootApplication
@EnableDiscoveryClient
public class DeptInstanceBootApplication {
    public static void main(String[] args) throws Exception {
SpringApplication.run(DeptInstanceBootApplication.class,
        args);
    }
}
```

11. In `src/main/resources`, add an `application.properties` which will contain the same properties in `ch10-deptservice` combined with some Eureka client details for this `Department` microservice instance. Once an exception happens during endpoint execution, Eureka will redirect the execution to `eureka.client.service-url.defaultZone`. Moreover, the server must be allowed to determine the status of the instance, as per `/health` of the actuator module. The Eureka client will only report its health status to Eureka server by enabling `eureka.client.service-url.healthcheck.enabled` property:

```
spring.application.name=depts-service-instance
eureka.client.service-url.defaultZone=
http://localhost:5566/eureka/
eureka.client.service-url.healthcheck.enabled=true
# the rest of the properties from ch10-deptservice
```

12. Copy all the *configuration classes, controllers, handler and route functions, services, JPA repository classes,* and *entity models* from `ch10-deptservice` and drop them to their new packages. Also, be sure to update the **JPA repository base packages** configured in `SpringDataConfig`.

13. Save all files. Run `clean spring-boot:run -U` Maven commands to deploy the Eureka client. Open `http://localhost:5566` again and check that `Department` Eureka instance is declared as part of the service registry.

14. Perform again Steps 8 to 13 to build the `Employee` and `Login` microservice instances. After a long and successful procedure, run the Eureka server again and check if all three instances are registered.

15. Run the following endpoints directly from the Eureka server to validate that all the instances are ready for execution. All the services will run using the IP address of the machine detected by the Eureka server:

   - `http://alibata:8960/selectReactDepts` (from the Department instance)
   - `http://alibata:8965/selectReactEmps` (from the Employee instance)
   - `http://alibata:8970/fluxJpaUsers` (from the Login instance)

16. Observe the status of your Eureka server. Once Eureka's *capacity to renew instances per minute* becomes lower than the *expected renews from its instances*, the message is thrown by the server similar to what is shown below. This occurrence happens when some connection issues are experienced by the Eureka server while some of the instances are expiring due to some *heartbeat* status. To avoid further microservice inter-communication problems, we just leave these instances *preserved* even if some are due for expiration (for example, self-preservation mode).

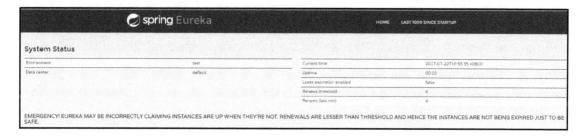

How it works...

Eureka is part of the Spring Cloud Netflix which is some kind of a service box that can be configured to create a registry of microservice instances. It is shown in this recipe that Eureka provides almost the same configuration procedures in building a server and a client instance. In some scenarios, Eureka can be used to build an application that can be both a server and client for some singleton architectures.

Setting up a service registry is similar to building a large online portal with sub-modules independent from the others, but yet interact with each other and come up with one big infrastructure. Spring Cloud, which is the building block of building this design architecture with Spring Boot 2.0 and microservices, provides many solutions, such as Eureka service, that are easy to configure and use. To build a Eureka server only requires building a Spring Boot application that will wrap **Spring Cloud Netflix Eureka** services in its `pom.xml` and enable loading of all the services at bootstrap level using the annotation `@EnableEurekaServer`. Likewise, the same starter POM dependencies are needed to build Eureka clients which are basically the microservices per se. Each microservice just needs to apply the `@EnableDiscoveryClient` annotation in its bootstrap to load all the necessary services needed to automatically register each instance to the Eureka server.

Proper Eureka server and client configurations also depend on the configuration details reflected from their `application.properties` file. As shown by the recipe above, there are Eureka server properties such as `eureka.client.register-with-eureka` and `eureka.client.fetch-registry` that must not be present in any Eureka client configurations. On the other hand, clients must declare some additional necessary settings for the Eureka server to know the exact details of its instances. Just in case, when a client fails to register during its first heartbeat, the server will give a chance to the instance and waits for 30 seconds (`eureka.instance.leaseRenewalIntervalInSeconds`) to explicitly register itself. This property can also be overridden to tell the server to decrease or increase the server waiting time. Likewise, the client needs to override the default property `eureka.instance.leaseRenewalIntervalInSeconds` to quickly declare an instance at dead state. The Eureka server can also add some property, such as disabling `eureka.instance.enableSelfPreservation`, which is not recommended for complex architectures.

To resolve some compatibility issues, the only Spring Cloud release that is built using Spring Boot 2.0 is the `SpringBootFinchley` version.

Implementing the Eureka service discovery and client-side load balancing

Although it is acceptable to call microservice endpoints directly from the Eureka server, explicitly through its machine name and ports, Spring Cloud offers automatic service discovery which makes RESTful service execution free from hardcoding the service URL. When it comes to duplicate instances for backup and recovery purposes, this recipe will define the concept of client-side load balancing wherein an algorithm is used to determine the most viable and healthy instance to utilize in executing the endpoints.

Getting started

Create another Eureka instance that will contain a @Controller, which will consume RESTful services from the Eureka registry applying client-side load balancing built by SpringCloudNetflixRibbon module.

How to do it...

Let us implement *client-side load balancing* by following these steps:

1. First, create a Maven project ch10-eureka-client that contains pom.xml with SpringCloudFinchley dependencies. Just add the core starter POM such as webflux, the actuator and the following SpringCloudNetflixRibbon module dependencies:

   ```
   <dependency>
       <groupId>org.springframework.cloud</groupId>
       <artifactId>spring-cloud-starter-eureka</artifactId>
   </dependency>
   <dependency>
       <groupId>org.springframework.cloud</groupId>
       <artifactId>spring-cloud-starter-ribbon</artifactId>
   </dependency>
   ```

2. Then, create a typical bootstrap class suited for a Eureka client that fetches the registry and automatically registers itself to the Eureka server:

   ```
   @SpringBootApplication
   @EnableDiscoveryClient
   public class HRSEurekaClientBootApplication {
   ```

```
    public static void main(String[] args) {
SpringApplication.run(HRSEurekaClientBootApplication.class,
args);
    }
}
```

3. In its `src/main/resources,` **create the necessary** `application.properties`
   for this Eureka client instance:

```
spring.application.name=hrs-client
eureka.client.service-url.defaultZone=
        http://localhost:5566/eureka/
server.port=8076
# same as the previous recipe
```

4. Create a `webflux` Configuration inside
   `org.packt.microservice.client.config` with the injected `RestTemplate`
   and `AsyncRestTemplate`. To apply Spring Cloud Netflix Ribbon algorithm for
   client-side load balancing, add `@LoadBalanced` annotation to each injected
   `@Bean`:

```
@Configuration
@EnableWebFlux
public class WebFluxConfig {
  @Bean
   @LoadBalanced
   public RestTemplate restTemplate() {
       return new RestTemplate();
   }
  @Bean
   @LoadBalanced
   public AsyncRestTemplate asyncRestTemplate(){
     AsyncRestTemplate art = new AsyncRestTemplate();
     return art;
   }
}
```

5. Copy all the needed entity models from the three microservice projects to the
   package `org.packt.microsrevice.client.model.data` for JSON
   encoding/decoding.

6. Now, create the client controller that will consume any endpoints from these three microservices registered in the Eureka server. This time the service URL (for example, *IP address*, *port*, and so on) does not need to be known, since Ribbon will assist with finding the viable and healthy instances through their declared Eureka service names EMPS-SERVICE-INSTANCE, DEPTS-SERVICE-INSTANCE, and LOGIN-SERVICE-INSTANCE:

```
@Controller
public class AccessRestController {
  private String instanceEmp = "http://EMPS-SERVICE-INSTANCE";
  private String instanceDept =
"http://DEPTS-SERVICE-INSTANCE";
  @Autowired
  protected RestTemplate restTemplate;
  @Autowired
  private AsyncRestTemplate asyncRestTemplate;
  @GetMapping(value="/accessListEmps",
produces= MediaType.APPLICATION_JSON_VALUE)
  @ResponseBody
  public List<Employee> blockListEmp() {
      HttpHeaders headers = new HttpHeaders();
    headers.set("Accept", MediaType.APPLICATION_JSON_VALUE);
    HttpEntity<String> entity = new HttpEntity<>(headers);
    ResponseEntity<List> response = RestTemplate
.exchange(instanceEmp + "/listEmp",
        HttpMethod.GET, entity, List.class);
    return response.getBody();
  }
  @GetMapping(value="/accessListDepts",
produces= MediaType.APPLICATION_JSON_VALUE)
  @ResponseBody
  public List<Employee> blockListDepts() {
    HttpHeaders headers = new HttpHeaders();
    headers.set("Accept", MediaType.APPLICATION_JSON_VALUE);
    HttpEntity<String> entity = new HttpEntity<>(headers);
    ResponseEntity<List> response = restTemplate
.exchange(instanceDept + "/listDept",
HttpMethod.GET, entity, List.class);
    return response.getBody();
  }
  @RequestMapping(value="/asyncSelectEmp/{id}",
      produces=MediaType.APPLICATION_JSON_VALUE)
  @ResponseBody
  public Employee asyncSelectEmps(
@PathVariable("id") Integer id){
    String url = instanceEmp + "/callSelectEmp/{id}.json";
    HttpMethod method = HttpMethod.GET;
```

```
        HttpHeaders headers = new HttpHeaders();
         headers.set("Accept", MediaType.APPLICATION_JSON_VALUE);
        HttpEntity<String> requestEntity =
  new HttpEntity<String>("params", headers);
        ListenableFuture<ResponseEntity<Employee>>
            future = asyncRestTemplate
  .exchange(url, method, requestEntity,
        Employee.class, id);
        try {
          ResponseEntity<Employee> entity = future.get();
          return entity.getBody();
        } catch (InterruptedException e) {
          e.printStackTrace();
        } catch (ExecutionException e) {
          e.printStackTrace();
        }
        return null;
    }
  }
```

7. In the case of consuming reactive REST services, directly inject the
   `LoadBalancerClient` into `AccessRestController` to explicitly search the
   service instance name from any of the healthiest instance of the registry that can
   provide the service URL of the desired reactive endpoint such as
   `/selectReactEmps`:

```
@Autowired
private LoadBalancerClient loadBalancer;

@RequestMapping("/accessReactClients")
public Flux<Employee> sayFlux() {
    ServiceInstance serviceInstance=
loadBalancer.choose("EMPS-SERVICE-INSTANCE");
    String baseUrl=serviceInstance.getUri().toString();
    return WebClient.create().method(HttpMethod.GET)
        .uri(baseUrl + "/selectReactEmps").contentType(
MediaType.APPLICATION_JSON_UTF8).retrieve()
.bodyToFlux(Employee.class);
    }
```

The Ribbon API that executes the client-side load balancing algorithm is `org.springframework.cloud.client.loadbalancer.LoadBalancerClient`. The annotation `@LoadBalanced` configures `RestTemplate` and `AsyncRestTemplate` to become a `LoadBalancerClient` type. The problem arises only when `@LoadBalanced` annotation is directly applied to the new reactive `WebClient` because it generates an exception: `o.s.web.reactive.function.client - java.net.UnknownHostException: EMPS-SERVICE-INSTANCE`

8. Save all files. Run Maven commands `clean spring-boot:run -U` and refresh the Eureka server page. If the `HRS-CLIENT` instance has been registered, run the entire client endpoints indicated in `AccessRestController`.

How it works...

Client-side load balancing is a feature of a client application that decides where to assign the request transactions during traffic and server problems. This solution was formulated when the architectural concepts of SOA and microservices became foundations of software architecture and during the popularity of failover and backup and recovery in the hardware technology. The fusion between the two different techniques provided a way to build a resilient, fault-tolerant, and load sharing microservice architecture.

With or without Eureka service discovery, **Spring Cloud Netflix Ribbon** is always this simple inter-process communication solution that aims to implement client-side load balancing with its set of algorithms. In this recipe, a Eureka client has been used as the specimen in applying Ribbon's `LoadBalancerClient` to choose the healthiest microservice instance without specifying the exact IP address and port. The annotation `@LoadBalanced` has been used also to configure the `RestTemplate` and `AsyncRestTemplate` to apply also the load balancing algorithm. Using Ribbon with a Eureka server is much easier and more straightforward than with the non-Eureka client which requires the addition of the `@RibbonClient(name="custom_service_name")` to the bootstrap class and the registration of all the mapping of this `custom_service_name` to multiple instances to its `application.properties` file:

```
custom_service_name.ribbon.eureka.enabled=false
custom_service_name.ribbon.listOfServers=localhost:8094/ch10-
dept1,localhost:8095/ch10-dept2
```

This Ribbon module of Spring Cloud Finchley dependencies supports synchronous, asynchronous and reactive microservice instances built by Spring Boot 2.0 release.

Applying resiliency to client applications

To apply more effective resilience to endpoint executions, Spring Cloud Netflix Ribbon is sometimes paired with Spring Cloud Netflix Hystrix, which is built through the circuit breaker design pattern whose objective is to rescue client applications from shutting down due to faulty `ResponseEntity` or undefined `Mono<T>` and `Flux<T>` responses.

Getting started

Create a typical Spring Boot 2.0 project named as `ch10-hystrix` that will focus on the independent configuration and setup of `Hystrix`.

How to do it...

Implement recovery transactions by following these steps:

1. Create a new Maven project `ch10-hystrix` and add the core starter POM dependencies of Spring Boot 2.0 such as the `webflux`, embedded Tomcat server and the `actuator`. To import `Hystrix` modules, add first the Spring Cloud Finchley dependency plugin to `pom.xml`.

2. Then, add the **Spring Cloud Netflix Hystrix** dependencies to `pom.xml`:

```
<dependency>
    <groupId>org.springframework.cloud</groupId>
    <artifactId>spring-cloud-starter-hystrix</artifactId>
</dependency>
<dependency>
    <groupId>org.springframework.cloud</groupId>
    <artifactId>spring-cloud-starter-hystrix-dashboard
</artifactId>
</dependency>
Inside the core org.packt.microservice.hystrix package, create
the bootstrap class that enables Hystrix circuit breaker
feature using @EnableCircuitBreaker and @EnableHystrix:
@SpringBootApplication
@EnableCircuitBreaker
@EnableHystrix
public class ConsumeHystrixBootApplication
extends  SpringBootServletInitializer  {
  @Override
    protected SpringApplicationBuilder configure(
SpringApplicationBuilder application) {
```

```
            return application.sources(
ConsumeHystrixBootApplication.class);
        }

        public static void main(String[] args) throws Exception {
SpringApplication.run(ConsumeHystrixBootApplication.class,
            args);
        }
    }
```

3. Inside the core `org.packt.microservice.hystrix` package, now create the bootstrap class that enables `Hystrix` circuit breaker feature using `@EnableCircuitBreaker` and `@EnableHystrix`:

```
@SpringBootApplication
@EnableCircuitBreaker
@EnableHystrix
public class ConsumeHystrixBootApplication
extends  SpringBootServletInitializer  {
    @Override
    protected SpringApplicationBuilder configure(
SpringApplicationBuilder application) {
        return application.sources(
ConsumeHystrixBootApplication.class);
    }

    public static void main(String[] args)
throws Exception {
        SpringApplication.run(
ConsumeHystrixBootApplication.class, args);
    }
}
```

4. Inside `src/main/resources`, create the `application.properties` file that contains the basic Tomcat server deployment properties, just like in the previous recipes.

5. Afterwards, create a package, `org.packt.microservice.hystrix.config`, which contains a `webflux` configuration class with the injected `RestTemplate` and `AsyncRestTemplate`:

```
@Configuration
@EnableWebFlux
public class WebfluxConfig {
    @Bean
    public RestTemplate restTemplate() {
        return new RestTemplate();
```

```
    }
    @Bean
    public AsyncRestTemplate asyncRestTemplate(){
      AsyncRestTemplate art = new AsyncRestTemplate();
      return art;
    }
  }
```

6. Copy and add to a new package,
   `org.packt.microservice.hystrix.model.data`, all the needed entity
   models for JSON encoding/decoding.

7. Now, the essential part of this application is in all the `@Service` found in
   `org.packt.microservice.hystrix.service`; this recipe is after creating
   recovery transactions called fallback methods for each endpoint service. Each
   fallback method is triggered every moment the service method it is assigned to
   reaches its tolerance level and starts emitting exceptions and errors. The
   following is a `DeptHystrixService` that consists of *circuit-aware executions* of
   RESTful services from the DEPARTMENT microservice:

```
@Service
public class DeptHystrixService {
    @HystrixCommand(fallbackMethod = "defaultSelectDept")
    public  Mono<Department> getMonoDept(Integer id) {
        return WebClient.create().method(HttpMethod.GET)
              .uri("http://localhost:8090/
ch10-dept/selectReactDept/" + id)
              .contentType(
      MediaType.APPLICATION_OCTET_STREAM)
    .retrieve().bodyToMono(Department.class);
    }
    private Mono<Department> defaultSelectDept(Integer id) {
      Mono<Department> blankDept =
Mono.justOrEmpty(new Department());
        return blankDept ;
    }
}
```

Not all exceptions and errors will lead to the execution of the
`fallbackMethod`. Since Hystrix supports synchronous, asynchronous
and reactive endpoint calls, the fault tolerance level depends on the type
of endpoint executions. Moreover, `fallbackMethod` is triggered by
unsuccessful execution and not explicitly called.

8. Create also `EmpHystrixService` for Employee microservice based on the
   service methods of its previous recipes.

9. Create also `LoginHystrixService` for `Login` microservice based from the service methods of its previous recipe.

10. To apply all these circuit-aware service methods, create a typical Controller, as shown below:

```
@Controller
public class HystrixClientController {
    @Autowired
    private DeptHystrixService deptHystrixService;
    @Autowired
    private EmpHystrixService empHystrixService;
    @Autowired
    private LoginHystrixService logniHystrixService;
    @RequestMapping("/hystrixUsers")
    @ResponseBody
    public List<UserDetails> hystrixGetUsers(){
       return logniHystrixService.getLoginUsers();
    }
    @RequestMapping("/hystrixGetEmp/{id}")
    @ResponseBody
    public Employee hystrixSelectEmp(
@PathVariable("id") Integer id){
        return empHystrixService.getAsyncEmp(id);
    }
    @RequestMapping("/hystrixGetDept/{id}")
    @ResponseBody
    public Mono<Department> hystrixSelectDept(
@PathVariable("id") Integer id){
        return deptHystrixService.getMonoDept(id);
    }
}
```

11. Save all files. Run `clean spring-boot:run -U` and then open a browser to execute all `HystrixClientController` transactions.

12. `Hystrix` has a built-in dashboard that helps experts in monitoring the closed-open circuit status of each service. To enable this dashboard, just add the following starter POM in the `pom.xml`:

```
<dependency>
    <groupId>org.springframework.cloud</groupId>
    <artifactId>spring-cloud-starter-hystrix-dashboard
</artifactId>
</dependency>
```

Be sure to include a working Spring Boot actuator module in the application.

13. Shut down the application using the `curl` command. Start again and access the `Hystrix` dashboard at
`http://localhost:8790/ch10-hystrix/hystrix.stream`.

14. Insert `http://localhost:8790/ch10-hystrix/hystrix.stream` on the Dashboard and click **Monitor Stream** button to examine all the circuits.

How it works...

The purpose of Spring Cloud Netflix `Hystrix` is to add more resiliency solutions to a client application that aims to execute RESTful services from a set of microservices or from microservice instances registered in a Eureka server. The resiliency applied by `Hystrix` is the execution of a certain recovery method once a RESTful service failed to retrieve a response. `Hystrix` has a `@HystrixCommand` to wire these services to its respective `fallbackMethod` that can only be called given a certain fault tolerance level.

What is best in `Hystrix` is that it can listen to and recognize blocking, non-blocking, and reactive executions given only the restriction that both service method and its `fallbackMethod` must be of the same classification type like a reactive client service execution is wired to a `Mono<T>` or `Flux<T>` `fallbackMethod` type.

Consuming endpoints using a declarative method

Another way of writing client applications for microservices is through the use of `Spring Cloud` Netflix Feign which utilizes a declarative and easy mechanism of writing clients for RESTful endpoints.

Getting started

Create a new Spring Boot application that is an independent specimen on how to enable Feign as the client solution in a client Spring Boot application that aims to consume exposed web services from typical or Eureka-registered microservices.

How to do it...

Apply the Feign client solution to Spring Boot application by the following steps:

1. Create a Maven project `ch10-feign` that contains core starter POM such as `webflux`, actuator, and Tomcat server for **Spring Boot 2.0** with the addition of the needed Spring Cloud dependent management configuration which is Spring Cloud Finchley.

2. Add the following Spring Cloud Netflix Feign dependency in the `pom.xml`.

   ```
   <dependency>
       <groupId>org.springframework.cloud</groupId>
       <artifactId>spring-cloud-starter-feign</artifactId>
   </dependency>
   ```

3. Create a core package, `org.packt.microservice.feign`, and add to it this bootstrap class that enables default Feign configurations:

   ```
   @SpringBootApplication
   @EnableFeignClients
   public class ConsumeFeignBootApplication
   extends  SpringBootServletInitializer  {
     @Override
       protected SpringApplicationBuilder configure(
   SpringApplicationBuilder application) {
           return application.sources(
   ConsumeFeignBootApplication.class);
       }
   ```

```
        public static void main(String[] args) throws Exception {
    SpringApplication.run(ConsumeFeignBootApplication.class,
        args);
    }
}
```

4. In its `src/main/resources`, create a typical `application.properties` that is just needed for a typical RESTful client application. No Feign-related properties are required to be declared in this file.

5. Load all the entity models from the other recipes to a new package `org.packt.microservice.feign.model.data` needed for the converters during the client executions.

6. Now, the core of the client application is found in this `org.packt.microservice.feign.service` package, where all the Feign interfaces are declared and the service URL mappings are processed. Below is a `DeptListClient`, which is a Feign interface needed to implement all the client services together with some required Feign annotations:

```
@FeignClient(name = "department-feign",
url = "http://localhost:8090/ch10-dept")
public interface DeptListClient {
  @RequestMapping(method = RequestMethod.GET,
value = "/selectReactDepts" )
    public Flux<Department> getDepartments();
}
```

7. Create a controller inside the `org.packt.microservice.feign.controller` package that calls the Feign service generated by `@FeignClient`:

```
@RestController
public class DeptFeignController {
  @Autowired
  private DeptListClient deptListClient;
  @RequestMapping(value = "/feignBlockList",
method = RequestMethod.GET, produces = "application/json")
    public List<Department> allBlockingDepts()            {
    List<Department> depts = deptListClient.getListDepts();
    return depts;
    }
}
```

8. Save all files. Deploy the project by running `clean spring-boot:run -U` commands. Open a browser and run `http://localhost:8888/ch10-feign/feignBlockList`.

How it works...

The recipe above highlighted another Spring Cloud module that helps simplify the generation of client application, for microservices. A simple interface with a class-level annotation `@FeignClient` can generate results from RESTful endpoints.

On the other hand, this module has built-in loggers, encoders, and decoders which can process entity models to JSON objects. However, the current version of Feign has no support for asynchronous and reactive web services. Thus, adding and running the following services will give us decoding problems.

```
@RequestMapping(method = RequestMethod.GET,
value = "/selectReactDepts" )
    public Flux<Department> getDepartments();
    @RequestMapping(method = RequestMethod.GET,
value = "/webSyncDeptList.json" )
   public WebAsyncTask<List<Department>> getAsyncListDepts();
```

Despite its limitations, Feign is widely used in interfacing many blocking web services because of its simplicity and robustness in generating client implementation.

Using Docker for deployment

The last recipe will involve deploying our microservices to popular containers such as Docker. This architectural approach to designing an environment of microservices can be more expensive, compared to the Eureka service registry, when it comes to operating system and hardware specification. However, this solution is the best initial big step to building distributed architecture of microservices.

Getting started

Open `ch09-flux` for the last time and enable Ehcache and Caffeine caching.

How to do it...

Let us build a concept of distributed setup for our *Department*, *Employee* and *Login* microservices by following these steps:

1. Before the entire configuration, download and install Docker Toolbox from `https://www.docker.com/products/docker-toolbox` to avoid lots of complicated Docker configurations. The toolbox will provide us a **VirtualBox** and a client to manage our images. Also, it will automatically setup `.dropbox` session details for global access to its CLI commands in the Windows operating system.

2. Install the **Docker Toolbox** and sign up for a free account to create your docker-machine using **Kitematic**:

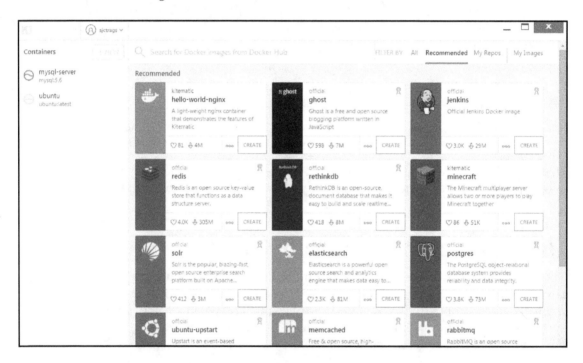

3. Log in to view your Kitematic dashboard. Once online, you can search for free Docker images and install them through your dashboard. Also, your dashboard will keep a list of all installed images in your docker-machine. On the lower left of the dashboard, you will find a button that will invoke the CLI window:

4. Now, go back to Spring Boot development. Modify the `previous ch10-deptservice`, `ch10-empservice`, and `ch10-loginservice` so that these can be *dockerized* into the `docker_machine`. To avoid conflicts, create exact copies of each project with Maven project names `ch10-dept-docker`, `ch10-emp-docker`, and `ch10-login-docker`.

5. Since the microservices use MySQL server, add a `mysql-server` image through the `Kitematic` account and run the following CLI Docker command with the needed database credentials to boot up the MySQL image:

```
docker run --name mysql-server -e
MYSQL_ROOT_PASSWORD=spring5mysql -e MYSQL_DATABASE=hrs -d
mysql:5.6
```

6. Among the three microservices, let us first Dockerized `ch10-dept-docker`. Inside the project, create a folder `src/main/docker`, and drop a Dockerfile. This configuration file is an image structure of the Docker image where the Spring Boot application will be deployed. It has sensitive Docker image information which is found below:

```
FROM java:8
MAINTAINER sjctrags@gmail.com
EXPOSE 8080
CMD java -jar ch10-depty-docker.jar
ADD ch10-depty-docker.jar ch10-depty-docker.jar
ENTRYPOINT ["java","-jar","ch10-depty-docker.jar"]
```

The correct filename must be Dockerfile and without any extension. Changing the case will cause an error during Docker deployment.

7. Afterwards, add the current version of `docker-maven-plugin` to the `<plugins>` of `pom.xml`:

```
<plugin>
     <groupId>com.spotify</groupId>
     <artifactId>docker-maven-plugin</artifactId>
     <version>1.0.0</version>
     <configuration>
<imageName>${docker.image.prefix}/${project.artifactId}
</imageName>
<dockerHost>https://192.168.99.100:2376</dockerHost>
<dockerCertPath>C:/Users/sjctrags/.docker/machine/certs
</dockerCertPath>
          <dockerDirectory>src/main/docker</dockerDirectory>
          <resources>
               <resource>
    <targetPath>/</targetPath>
<directory>${project.build.directory}</directory>
<include>${project.build.finalName}.jar</include>
               </resource>
          </resources>
       </configuration>
     </plugin>
```

To see the host information of your `docker_machine`, open a Docker CLI and run the command docker-machine URL to extract the IP address and the port of the Docker machine. Moreover, Docker machine can be accessed only using HTTPS thus `.pem` certificates found in its repository are needed to be accessed by Maven.

8. Before the deployment, the last configuration is to change `<packaging>war</packaging>` to `<packaging>jar</packaging>`. Docker images are built through JAR files.

9. Finally, run the Maven command `clean package docker:build` to download all the necessary dependencies and execute the **Dockerfile**. The whole process must end with a `BUILD SUCCESS`.

10. Check your Kitematic account; both the **mysql-server** and **ch10-dept-docker** images must now be uploaded:

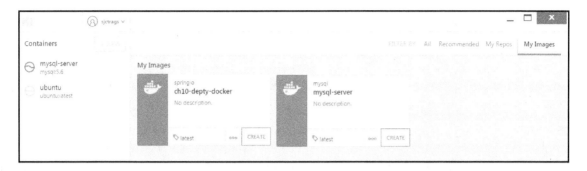

11. Run the image through CLI commands or by clicking the **CREATE** button of the image:

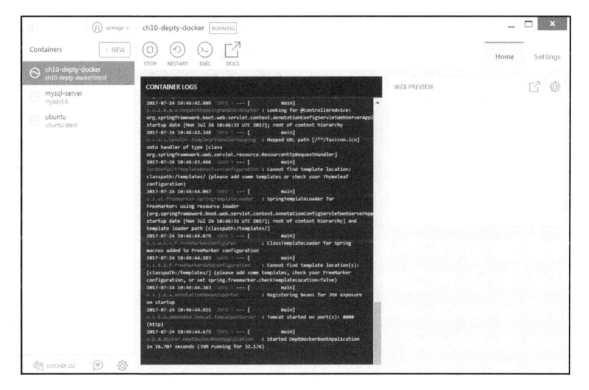

12. Open a browser and run all the controller requests.
13. If the error `https://192.168.99.100:2376: Connection reset by peer: socket write error` is encountered, just try to restart the Docker machine through `docker-machine restart` command.

How it works...

In building microservices in a distributed environment, Docker images are used to implement a totally loosely-coupled design where each application is hosted in one image and can only interact with the others through REST calls and other message-based inter-process communication.

Deploying Spring Boot applications as Docker images does not require any new Maven dependencies to be added or new @Configuration components to be injected, as shown by the recipe. It only takes some changes in the pom.xml and the creation of the **Dockerfile** which is one of the challenges in implementing this recipe. The following information of the **Dockerfile** must be seriously considered before building the image:

- FROM: the image to be created must enable Java 1.8 and above
- MAINTAINER: identification of the image owner
- COPY/ADD: command to copy JAR file to the image
- EXPOSE: the port of the application similar to server port declared in application.properties; the port to be used by the image once the image boots up
- ENTRYPOINT/CMD: the command in JSON format that will be executed by Docker to boot up the image

11
Batch and Message-Driven Processes

The microservices in the previous chapter gave us a clear solution on how to decompose huge applications into independent, scalable, and manageable components that somehow provide the procedure on how to practically apply a loosely coupled architecture design in software development. In applying this loose-coupling approach, the huge `hrs` application built in the previous chapters is now composed of three *service boxes*, each having its own domain-related operations. Some recipes consumed RESTful services from any of these microservices using the **WebClient** or **Spring Cloud** modules, and applied logging, data retrieval, and data persistence to some web services. Other than exposing services through REST, in this chapter, we will explore and scrutinize more features of Spring 5, such as *interprocess communication* among microservices and within a microservice to achieve a scalable and robust Spring 5 application.

The focus will now be on creating synchronous, asynchronous, and reactive *batch processes* and *message-driven communication* that are supported by Spring 5. The inclusion of the broker software called **RabbitMQ** will be showcased to help the implementation of **Advanced Message Queuing Protocol (AMQP)**, which is needed for both direct exchange and message-based communication among microservices. Also, by using the **RabbitMQ** server, **Spring Cloud Stream** will be used to provide a solution for sending the `Object` data and reactive stream from one microservice to another.

On the other hand, the creation of microservices that execute batch process continuously and periodically through **Spring Batch** and **Spring Cloud Task** will also be part of the following recipes. In general, the objective is to venture into Spring 5 modules that support the core concepts of building batch processing and message-driven transactions in a microservice, which are essential in many enterprise solutions.

In this chapter, we will cover the following recipes:

- Building synchronous batch processes
- Implementing batch processes with a database
- Constructing asynchronous batch processes
- Building synchronous interprocess communication using AMQP
- Creating asynchronous send-receive communication
- Creating an event-driven asynchronous communication using AMQP
- Creating stream communication with Spring Cloud Stream
- Implementing batch processes using Spring Cloud Task

Building synchronous batch processes

The first recipe will be about building a simple batch process that transforms data from one rendition type to another. This is a typical solution to bulky, non-interactive, and routine background processes that can be a simple data transformation or a highly computational data mining algorithm that continuously harvests data using either synchronous thread pipes or parallel executors. This recipe highlights the *synchronous* batch process for data conversion.

Getting started

Create a new Maven project that uses `spring-boot-starter-batch` to create a background process that parses an XML file and transfers some filtered content to a text file.

How to do it...

Let's create a standalone application that transforms XML to a text file using the following steps:

1. Using Eclipse STS, create a Maven project, `ch11-batch-sync`, that contains the Spring Boot 2.0.0.M2 *starter* POM dependencies, such as *actuator* and *JDBC*, with some support plugins such as the MySQL connector.

2. Add the starter POM dependency for the latest Spring Batch 4.0:

```
<dependency>
    <groupId>org.springframework.boot</groupId>
    <artifactId>spring-boot-starter-batch</artifactId>
</dependency>
```

3. Since *XML parsing* is involved, add the **Spring OXM** module with its XSTREAM dependency in pom.xml:

```
<dependency>
    <groupId>org.springframework</groupId>
    <artifactId>spring-oxm</artifactId>
</dependency>
<dependency>
    <groupId>com.thoughtworks.xstream</groupId>
    <artifactId>xstream</artifactId>
    <version>1.4.9</version>
</dependency>
```

4. Create a core package, org.packt.process.core, and drop a bootstrap class inside that enables batch processing and task scheduling:

```
@EnableScheduling
@EnableBatchProcessing
@SpringBootApplication
public class SyncBatchBootApplication {
    // refer to sources
}
```

5. Copy logback.xml from the previous project and drop it inside src\main\resources to enable logging.

6. Now, inside src\main\properties, create the application properties with all the server, actuator, and HikariCP datasource autoconfiguration details. Use the newly created batchproc database for the updated spring.datasource.url property. This database will be populated with configuration tables by Spring Batch once the application starts:

```
server.port=9007
server.servlet.context-path=/ch11-batch-sync

spring.datasource.driverClassName=com.mysql.jdbc.Driver
spring.datasource.url=jdbc:mysql://localhost:3306/batchproc?aut
oReconnect=true&useSSL=true&serverSslCert=classpath:config/spri
ng5packt.crt
spring.datasource.username=root
```

```
spring.datasource.password=spring5mysql
spring.datasource.hikari.connection-timeout=60000
spring.jpa.database-platform=org.hibernate.dialect.MySQLDialect

management.port=9007
management.address=localhost
management.context-path=/appdetails

endpoints.info.enabled=true
endpoints.info.sensitive=false
endpoints.info.id=info
info.app.description=Department Microservice
info.app.version=1.0.0

endpoints.sensitive=false
endpoints.shutdown.sensitive=false
endpoints.shutdown.enabled=true
```

7. For the data models, we will utilize the `hrs` data from the previous chapter, so copy the `Department` entity model to the `org.packt.process.core.model.data` package.

8. Since Java Architecture for the **XML Binding (JAXB)** parsing technique will be used in this recipe, apply `@XmlRootElement` and `@XmlElement` to all the domain models to make them JAXB classes:

```
@XmlRootElement(name = "department")
public class Department  implements Serializable{
    private Integer id;
    private Integer deptid;
    private String name;
    @XmlElement
    public Integer getId() {
        return id;
    }
    public void setId(Integer id) {
        this.id = id;
    }
    @XmlElement
    public Integer getDeptid() {
        return deptid;
    }
    public void setDeptid(Integer deptid) {
        this.deptid = deptid;
    }
    @XmlElement
    public String getName() {
        return name;
```

```
    }
    public void setName(String name) {
        this.name = name;
    }
}
```

9. Create an additional JAXB class that will contain all the `Department` elements or records, and place this inside the model package:

```
@XmlRootElement(name="departments")
public class Departments  implements Serializable{
    private List<Department> department;

    public List<Department> getDepartment() {
        return department;
    }

    public void setDepartment(List<Department> department) {
        this.department = department;
    }
}
```

 Do not apply `@XmlElement` to the instance variable since the `Department` class is already a JAXB entity, record, or element. Otherwise, parsing errors will be encountered.

10. Let's now start building the Spring Batch components needed to transform our XML data to a text file. First, it will be easier to start the configuration with the *reader* and *writer* components. Create a package, `org.packt.process.core.reader`, that contains a custom `org.springframework.batch.item.ItemReader<T>` implementation whose `read()` method is executed multiple times to feed the source data into the engine. This method returns `null` once all the data within a given period has been transported:

```
public class DepartmentItemReader
implements ItemReader<Department> {
    private final String filename;
    private ItemReader<Department> delegate;

    public DepartmentItemReader(final String filename) {
        this.filename = filename;
    }

    @Override
```

```
public Department read() throws Exception {
    if (delegate == null) {
        delegate = new IteratorItemReader<>(depts());
    }
    return delegate.read();
}

private List<Department> depts()
throws FileNotFoundException, JAXBException {
    JAXBContext context = JAXBContext.newInstance(
Departments.class, Department.class);
    Unmarshaller unmarshaller =
      context.createUnmarshaller();
    Departments deptList = (Departments) unmarshaller
.unmarshal(new FileInputStream(filename));
    return deptList.getDepartment();
}
}
```

The implementation used *JAXB marshaling* to read all the data from the source file. The *extracted* data will become the *items* of the batch process.

11. Create another package, `org.packt.process.core.writers`, and drop an `org.springframework.batch.item.ItemWriter<T>` implementation in it, which has a `write()` method that is responsible for flushing all items into another file channel. The following is `ItemWriter<T>` that writes all items to a text file but discards writes during rollback:

```
public class DepartmentItemWriter
implements ItemWriter<Department>, Closeable {
    private  PrintWriter writer;

    public DepartmentItemWriter() {
        OutputStream out = null;
        try {
         out = new FileOutputStream("output.txt");
        } catch (FileNotFoundException e) {
            out = System.out;
        } finally{
         this.writer = new PrintWriter(out);
        }
    }

    @Override
    public void write(List<? extends Department> items)
```

```
throws Exception {
        for (Department item : items) {
            writer.println(item.getName() + " "
+ item.getDeptid() );
        }
    }

    @PreDestroy
    @Override
    public void close() throws IOException {
        writer.close();
    }
}
```

 The text file should only contain the department ID and the name of the item.

12. The data transformation or conversion happens only when `org.springframework.batch.item.ItemProcessor<I,O>` interferes in the process by accepting read data from `ItemReader<T>` through its `process()` method. `ItemProcessor` provides the business logic, and a set of rules and constraints for data conversion, and returns an output item to be accessed and collected by `ItemWriter<T>`. The method returns `null` if the input object does not deserve to join the others for writing. Create a new package, `org.packt.process.core.processor`, that contains an `ItemProcess<I,O>` class that processes an input `Department` object with a name length greater than or equal to 5:

```
public class DeptNameProcessor implements
    ItemProcessor<Department, Department> {
    @Override
    public Department process(final Department item)
throws Exception {
        if (item.getName().length() >= 5) {
            return item;
        }
        return null;
    }
}
```

13. To impose validation rules, another processor called
    `org.springframework.batch.item.validator.ValidatingItemProcesso`
    `r` provides additional tasks to filter out unnecessary or unimportant items based
    on the business rules of the requirement. The following class omits a `Department`
    input object that has a department ID lower than 400:

```
public class DeptIDValidProcesor
extends ValidatingItemProcessor<Department> {

    public DeptIDValidProcesor() {
        super(
            item -> {
                if (item.getDeptid() < 400) {
                    throw new ValidationException(
"Customer ID lower than 400...");
                }
            }
        );
        setFilter(true);
    }
}
```

14. At this point, we are now ready to create the `@Configuration` job that requires
    the `DepartmentItemReader`, `DepartmentItemWriter`, `DeptNameProcessor`,
    and `DeptIDValidProcesor` bean objects. The following job configuration class
    implements single-item batch processing. The batch process uses an
    `org.springframework.batch.core.step.tasklet.Tasklet` interface
    whose `execute()` method is repeatedly run until all the source data is
    consumed. Each execution is wrapped in an
    `org.springframework.batch.core.Step` class that contains all the
    information on its attempt to run read-write items. All these step executions will
    not work without the injected `JobBuilderFactory` and `StepBuilderFactory`:

```
@Configuration
@EnableWebFlux
public class BatchConfig {
    @Autowired
    private JobBuilderFactory jobCreators;

    @Autowired
    private StepBuilderFactory stepCreators;

    public Job deptBatchJob() {
        return jobCreators.get("deptReportJob")
            .start(taskletStep())
```

```
            .build();
    }

    @Bean
    public Step taskletStep() {
        return stepCreators.get("taskletStep")
            .tasklet(tasklet())
            .build();
    }

    @Bean
    public Tasklet tasklet() {
        return (contrib, chunkCtx) -> {
            return RepeatStatus.FINISHED;
        };
    }
}
```

15. Our job configuration also implements a bulk batch process by calling the `chunk()` method of `StepBuilderFactory`. This method accepts n number of items, which determines the number of items expected to be rolled out to the reader, the processor, and the writer. The following snippets are added to `BatchConfig`, which will add *bulk batch processing*:

```
@Bean
public Step chunkStep() {
    return stepCreators.get("chunkStep")
        .<Department, Department>chunk(5)
        .build();
}
```

16. Update the following method to execute both *per item* and *per chunk* batch processing:

```
public Job deptBatchJob() {
    return jobCreators.get("deptReportJob")
        .start(taskletStep())
        .next(chunkStep())
        .build();
}
```

17. Now inject all the reader, writer, and processor beans to `BatchConfig`, and ensure that you convert the scopes of these objects from `@Singleton` to `@StepScope`:

```
@StepScope
@Bean
public ItemReader<Department> reader() {
    return new DepartmentItemReader("depts.xml");
  }

@StepScope
@Bean
public ItemProcessor<Department, Department> processor() {
    CompositeItemProcessor<Department, Department>
        processor = new CompositeItemProcessor<>();
    processor.setDelegates(Arrays.asList(
new DeptNameProcessor(), new DeptIDValidProcesor()));
    return processor;
}
    @StepScope
    @Bean
    public ItemWriter<Department> writer() {
        return new DepartmentItemWriter();
    }
```

18. Update the `chunkStep()` method to include the *reader*, `writer`, and `processor`:

```
@Bean
public Step chunkStep() {
    return stepCreators.get("chunkStep")
        .<Department, Department>chunk(5)
        .reader(reader())
            .processor(processor())
        .writer(writer())
        .build();
}
```

19. To complete our job configuration class, inject `JobLauncher` into `BatchConfig` to execute `deptBatchJob()` with a `TimeStamp` job parameter to distinguish one step execution from the other. Create a scheduler to run the `JobLauncher` job every *5,000* milliseconds:

```
@Autowired
private JobLauncher jobLauncher;
```

```
@Scheduled(fixedRate = 5000)
public void startJob() throws Exception {
    JobExecution execution = jobLauncher.run(
      deptBatchJob(), new JobParametersBuilder().addLong(
"procId", System.nanoTime()).toJobParameters());
}
```

20. Create a sample `depts.xml` file and just drop it inside the root project folder:

```
<departments>
   <department>
      <id>111</id>
      <deptid>5656</deptid>
      <name>Human Resources Department</name>
   </department>
   <department>
      <id>1234</id>
      <deptid>6777</deptid>
      <name>Sports and Wellness Department]</name>
   </department>
   <department>
      <id>1456</id>
      <deptid>345</deptid>
      <name>Kiosk</name>
   </department>
   <department>
      <id>1459</id>
      <deptid>23232</deptid>
      <name>Engineering Department</name>
   </department>
   ... ... ...
</departments>
```

21. Save all files. Run Maven `clean spring-boot:run -U` and check the `output.txt` file in the root project folder:

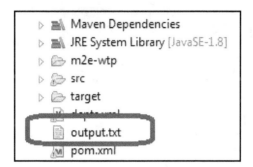

If you encounter any errors related to existing duplicate running job during the launch, disable the `spring.batch.job.enabled` property in `application.properties` and retry running the Maven commands given earlier.

22. Open the MySQL Workbench and check the `batchproc` database after launch:

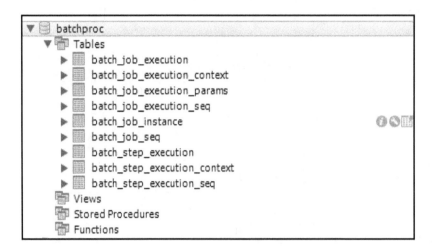

How it works...

There are microservices that are built to run independently in the background, with an objective to capture *real-time, less-biased,* and *optimal results* without user intervention or errors. These kinds of microservices are designed for FTP, data loading, data rendition, report generation, data warehousing, and archive and software auditing.

Spring Batch is not new to Spring; actually, it is still used in many of the current applications requiring data spooling. The preceding recipe shows the step-by-step process to build a complete scheduled batch process. A *scheduled batch process* runs a set of executions continually after a certain period of time. A Spring batch execution is basically all about reading items from a source media and transferring them to another media, with or without any noise or alterations. It has an API class called `ItemReader<T>` that allows the reading of items from a text file, CSV, XML, or database schema. Once injected into the `webflux` container, the singleton `ItemReader<T>` object is converted to `@StepScope`, which asks for a new reader instance and a new set of items to be sifted from the source periodically. This annotation is mandatory, given that these sources are updated in real-time once in a while.

After the `ItemReader<T>` fetches the items, it passes them one at a time or in chunks to the `ItemProcessor<I,O>` and `ValidatingItemProcessor<T>` to filter, scrutinize, and validate these items before it is transferred as the `List<O>` of processed items to `ItemWriter<T>` for the final execution stage. This API class writes to a text file, CSV, XML, or the database schema all the items from `ItemProcessor<I,O>`, and signals the last stage of the execution. Since our implementation is an asynchronous but scheduled batch process, one `Step` execution will be spawned after another to execute the read-process-write again and again. This recipe showed us how to custom implement these readers, writers, and processors.

After establishing the core processes, the next step is to build the steps to be executed using `StepBuilderFactory`; some of these step executions are Tasklet or chunked processes. And, finally, to create the job or task, we design a lineup of step executions using the `JobBuilderFactory` methods, `start()` and `next()`.

To close the implementation and run the microservice, we instantiate `JobExecution` together with the needed job parameters, which are to be launched by a `@Scheduled` method.

Spring Boot 2.0 provides a straightforward and routine solution as long as we invoke `@EnableBatchProcessing` at the `@Configuration` context, and we properly inject all the readers, processors, and writers with `@StepScope`, since the recipe is a scheduled and continuous batch process type.

Each job execution is a live object containing the properties:

```
JobExecution: id=136, version=1, startTime=2017-07-26 14:50:06.0,
endTime=null, lastUpdated=2017-07-26 14:50:06.0, status=STARTED,
exitStatus=exitCode=UNKNOWN;exitDescription=, job=[JobInstance: id=136,
version=0, Job=[deptBatchJob]], jobParameters=[{}].
```

Spring Batch automatically generates its metadata tables for recovery or retry purposes. But this can be disabled by having the `spring.batch.initializer.enabled=false` property in the `application.properties` file.

It will run at the JVM heap until it finishes its algorithm. If the job encounters exceptions and needs to be killed, Spring Batch provides a command-line runner that will execute to stop these jobs.

Implementing batch processes with a database

Some batch processes need to read or write to a database schema, as required per step execution. This recipe will be for a new way of writing a batch process that involves MySQL database transactions.

Getting started

Using the core components of **Spring Batch** 4 of the previous recipe, let's design a short-lived synchronous batch process that reads Employee records from an existing table, and writes some items to another table of the same database and also to an XML file.

How to do it...

Let's now implement a blocking batch transaction that reads data from a database:

1. Create a separate Spring Boot 2.0 application, ch11-batch-db, and add the same starter POM dependencies used in the previous recipe, emphasizing the spring-boot-starter-batch and spring-oxm.

2. Create a bootstrap class inside its core package, org.packt.process.core, that enables batch processing:

```
@SpringBootApplication
@EnableBatchProcessing
public class BatchProcessBootApplication  {
    // refer to sources
}
```

3. Open the MySQL Workbench and create the following reg_employee database schema with the source table, **employee**, and destination table as **permanent**:

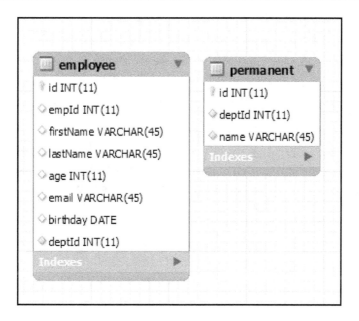

4. Now, create `application.properties` in `src\main\resources` with an emphasis on `reg_employee` as the database source:

```
server.port=9006
server.servlet.context-path=/ch11-batch

spring.datasource.driverClassName=com.mysql.jdbc.Driver
spring.datasource.url=jdbc:mysql://localhost:3306/reg_employee?
autoReconnect=true&useSSL=true&serverSslCert=classpath:config/s
pring5packt.crt
spring.datasource.username=root
spring.datasource.password=spring5mysql
spring.datasource.hikari.connection-timeout=60000
spring.jpa.database-platform=org.hibernate.dialect.MySQLDialect

#spring.batch.job.enabled=false

management.port=9006
management.address=localhost
management.context-path=/appdetails
// refer to sources
```

5. Copy `logback.xml` from the previous project and drop it inside `src\main\resources` to enable logging.

6. Since this recipe requires some data from the previous employee records, copy the Employee entity model from the previous chapter and place it inside `org.packt.process.core.model.data`. Since the input item is an `Employee` record, do not apply `@XmlRootElement` to the model class.

7. Add a custom model, `Permanent`, that will represent the output item of the process. This class must have `@XmlRootElement` since this will be used as a JAXB entity for the XML marshalling.

8. Inside `org.packt.process.core.processor`, create the following `RecordProcessor`, which accepts all items from `ItemReader<T>` and filters only those whose age is greater than 18 for items to be recommended for writing:

```
public class RecordProcessor
implements ItemProcessor<Employee, Permanent> {

    private static final Logger log = LoggerFactory.getLogger(
RecordProcessor.class);

    @Override
    public Permanent process(Employee item) throws Exception {
        if (item.getAge() >= 18) {
            Permanent perm = new Permanent();
            perm.setId(item.getId());
            perm.setDeptid(item.getDeptid());
            perm.setName(item.getFirstname() + " " +
                item.getLastname());
            log.info("empId " + perm.getId() + " passed." );
            return perm;
        }
        return null;
    }
}
```

9. Now let's start building the job `@Configuration` class by injecting `DataSource` and instantiating `JdbcTemplate` to be used by the reader:

```
@Configuration
@EnableWebFlux
public class BatchConfig {
    private DataSource dataSource;
    private JdbcTemplate jdbcTemplate;
    public BatchConfig(DataSource dataSource) {
        this.dataSource = dataSource;
        jdbcTemplate = new JdbcTemplate(dataSource);
    }
}
```

10. Now inject `ItemReader<T>` to `BatchConfig`, which will query records from the employee table of the `reg_employee` database:

```
@Bean
    public ItemReader<Employee> reader(DataSource dataSource) {
        JdbcCursorItemReader<Employee> reader =
new JdbcCursorItemReader<Employee>();
        reader.setSql("select * from employee");
        reader.setDataSource(dataSource);
        reader.setRowMapper(
            (ResultSet resultSet, int rowNum) -> {
                log.info("Retrieving item resultset: {}",
                    resultSet);
                if (!(resultSet.isAfterLast()) &&
                    !(resultSet.isBeforeFirst())) {
                    Employee emp = new Employee();
                    emp.setId(resultSet.getInt("id"));
emp.setEmpid(resultSet.getInt("empId"));
                    emp.setDeptid(resultSet.getInt("deptid"));
                    emp.setFirstname(
resultSet.getString("firstname"));
                        // refer to sources
                        return emp;
                } else {
                    log.info("Returning null item");
                    return null;
                }
            });
        return reader;
}
```

11. In this recipe, we will have two writers, namely the writer that will write to the permanent table and the writer that will generate `emp.xml`. Add these two writers to the following `BatchConfig` class:

```
@Bean("writer1")
public ItemWriter<Permanent> writer() {
    JdbcBatchItemWriter<Permanent> writer =
        new JdbcBatchItemWriter<>();
    writer.setItemPreparedStatementSetter(setter());
    writer.setItemSqlParameterSourceProvider(
new BeanPropertyItemSqlParameterSourceProvider
<Permanent>());
    writer.setDataSource(dataSource);
    writer.setSql("insert into permanent
(id, name, deptid) values (?,?,?)");
    return writer;
```

```
    }
@Bean
public ItemPreparedStatementSetter<Permanent> setter() {
    return (item, ps) -> {
        ps.setInt(1, item.getId());
        ps.setString(2, item.getName());
        ps.setInt(3, item.getDeptid());
    };
  }

@Bean("writer2")
public ItemWriter<Permanent> xmlWriter() {
    StaxEventItemWriter<Permanent> xmlFileWriter =
new StaxEventItemWriter<>();
    String exportFilePath =
        "./src/main/resources/emps.xml";
    xmlFileWriter.setResource(new
        FileSystemResource(exportFilePath));
    xmlFileWriter.setRootTagName("employees");
    Jaxb2Marshaller empMarshaller =
new Jaxb2Marshaller();
    empMarshaller.setClassesToBeBound(Permanent.class);
    xmlFileWriter.setMarshaller(empMarshaller);
    return xmlFileWriter;
}
```

12. Do not forget to inject the custom `RecordProcessor` into the `webflux` container:

```
@Bean
public ItemProcessor<Employee, Permanent> processor() {
    return new RecordProcessor();
}
```

13. Lastly, add the steps and job declaration to complete the configuration details:

```
@Bean
public Job importUserJob(JobBuilderFactory jobs,
Step step1, Step step2, JobExecutionListener
    listener) {
    return jobs.get("importUserJob")
            .incrementer(new RunIdIncrementer())
            .listener(listener)
            .flow(step1)
            .next(step2)
            .end()
            .build();
}
```

```
@Bean("step1")
public Step step1(StepBuilderFactory
        stepBuilderFactory,
    ItemReader<Employee> reader,
     ItemProcessor<Employee, Permanent> processor) {
       return stepBuilderFactory.get("step1")
          .<Employee, Permanent>chunk(5)
          .reader(reader)
          .processor(processor)
          .writer(writer())
          .build();
}
@Bean("step2")
public Step step2(StepBuilderFactory
        stepBuilderFactory,
    ItemReader<Employee> reader,
     ItemProcessor<Employee, Permanent> processor) {
       return stepBuilderFactory.get("step2")
          .<Employee, Permanent>chunk(2)
          .reader(reader)
          .processor(processor)
          .writer(xmlWriter())
          .build();
}
}
```

14. Before we end this recipe, add a listener, `JobExecutionListenerSupport`, inside a new package, `org.packt.process.core.listener`, for verification after a successful batch process execution:

```
@Component
public class OnCompleteJobExecListener
extends JobExecutionListenerSupport {

    private static final Logger log =
        LoggerFactory.getLogger(
OnCompleteJobExecListener.class);

    private DataSource dataSource;
    private JdbcTemplate jdbcTemplate;
    public OnCompleteJobExecListener(DataSource dataSource) {
      this.dataSource = dataSource;
      jdbcTemplate = new JdbcTemplate(dataSource);
    }

    @Override
    public void afterJob(JobExecution jobExecution) {
        if (jobExecution.getStatus() ==
```

```
                              BatchStatus.COMPLETED) {
                              log.info("Short-lived Job Done...");

                              List<Permanent> results = jdbcTemplate
             .query("select * from permanent", (rs, row) -> {
                              Permanent permanent = new Permanent();
                              permanent.setId(rs.getInt("id"));
                              permanent.setDeptid(rs.getInt("deptid"));
                              permanent.setName(rs.getString("name"));
                              return permanent;
                  });

                  for (Permanent permanent : results) {
                              log.info("Data is: " + permanent +
             " in the database.");
                              }
                      }
                  }
              }
```

15. Save all files. Run the `clean spring-boot:run -U` command, check the `emp.xml` file in `src\main\resources`, and check all the output items in permanent table.

How it works...

Comparing this recipe to the previous one, the job configuration of this solution is simpler and without much customization. The only customization created was the `RecordProcessor`, which filters raw `Employee` records with an age greater than 18 and generates the `Permanent` output items. Also, new in this recipe is a callback class, `JobExecutionListenerSupport`, which is executed after a successful or failed execution. This listener class verifies if the processed records are transferred into the `permanent` table.

On the other hand, the job has two steps, namely `step1` and `step2`. The first step, `step1`, calls `ItemReader<T>` to retrieve all the employee records to be processed by `RecordProcessor` before proceeding to `writer1`. The second step, `step2`, calls the same reader to pass database items to the same processor before proceeding to `writer2`. The sole reader uses `JdbcCursorItemReader` to read all the records from the data source using its ResultSet.

The `writer1` writer is implemented using `JdbcBatchItemWriter`, which acts like `NamedParameterJdbcTemplate` when it comes to mapping the properties of each output item using *placeholder notation* (?) before a SQL statement execution performs the writes into the `permanent` table. The other writer, `writer2`, uses `StaxEventItemWriter` to execute a **STAX** parser to generate `emp.xml`, which contains the same records found in the `permanent` table. It is clear that each job can execute multiple steps using varieties of readers, writers, or processors.

Since this is just a one-pipeline batch process, creating a `JobExecution` launcher is not needed since Spring Boot automatically launches the short-lived job with some default job parameters. To disable this configuration, open `application.properties` and disable the `spring.batch.job.enabled` property. Also, since it automatically launches, there is no need to convert reader, writer, and processor beans to the `@StepScope` type.

Constructing asynchronous batch processes

Each step execution can utilize a thread pool to run its readers, writers, and processors. The idea is to implement an asynchronous batch process that can execute independently, instead of each waiting for the previous execution to finish.

Getting started

Create a separate Maven project that will utilize all components of `ch11-batch-sync` with the inclusion of *thread pool generation*.

How to do it...

Let's implement a non-blocking batch process by following these steps:

1. Create a Spring Boot 2.0 project, `ch11-batch-async`, that has the same *starter* POM dependencies with the same MySQL connection pool support and **Spring OXM** module.
2. Create a bootstrap class that enables batch processing and task scheduling:

```
@EnableBatchProcessing
@SpringBootApplication
```

```
@EnableScheduling
public class AsyncBatchBootApplication {
 public static void main(String[] args) throws Exception {
     SpringApplication.run(AsyncBatchBootApplication.class,
 args);
 }
}
```

3. In its `src\main/\resources` directory, create `application.properties` that contain the same configuration as the one in `ch11-batch-sync`. Just modify some server-related configurations.

4. Copy `logback.xml` from the previous project and drop it inside `src\main\resources` to enable logging.

5. Then, copy all the packages from the `ch11-batch-sync` project without any changes.

6. Next, start the asynchronous batch processing configuration and inject the `TaskExecutor` that will generate the *thread pool* into `BatchConfig`:

```
@Bean("mvcTaskexecutor")
    public TaskExecutor getAsyncExecutor() {
        ConcurrentTaskExecutor executor =
new ConcurrentTaskExecutor(
                Executors.newFixedThreadPool(100));
        executor.setTaskDecorator(new TaskDecorator() {
          @Override
          public Runnable decorate (Runnable runnable) {
             return () -> {
                 long t = System.currentTimeMillis();
                 runnable.run();
                 System.out.printf("Thread %s has a
processing time:  %s%n",
                         Thread.currentThread().getName(),
                     (System.currentTimeMillis() - t));
             };
          }
        });
        return executor;
}
```

7. Assign threads to `taskletStep()` and `chunkStep()` by passing the `TaskExecutor` bean to the `taskExecutor()` method of their respective `StepBuildFactory` instances.

8. Save all files. Deploy the application with `clean spring-boot:run` Maven command. Expect random and messy writes to the `output.txt` output file.

How it works...

Creating an asynchronous batch process is supported by **Spring Batch 4.x**, but it may give a different result compared to the synchronous ones. When uncontrolled, all threads will compete to perform read or write on the resources, resulting in an undesirable output. It is advisable to add thread-safe wrapper classes so that the synchronization of these threads can be applied. But, once managed, this solution will provide a faster *reader-processor-writer* transaction compared to its blocking counterpart.

Building synchronous interprocess communication using AMQP

Another important feature of the design architecture in building microservices is studying and analyzing their behavior to each other when it comes to data exchange. Chapter 9, *Spring Boot 2.0*, established the conclusion that *asynchronous*, *reactive*, and *blocking* microservices work by exposing REST services that can be consumed by client applications. Although there is decoupling in the architectural design pattern, a microservice still has direct control over its clients because of the endpoint consumption occurring during the process. This gray area can still be considered to be tightly coupled behavior but to a minor degree. To implement a totally decoupled microservice, this recipe will introduce a new protocol that can initiate microservices to *communicate synchronously* with its clients without any endpoint intervention.

Getting started

Replicate the **EMPLOYEE** and **LOGIN** microservices, and update the projects in order to adopt a new data exchange mechanism using **Advance Message Queuing Protocol (AMQP)**.

How to do it...

Let's build a message-driven communication using the AMQP protocol with these steps:

1. Before doing anything else, download the **Erlang/OTP** and **RabbitMQ** server. Since all recipes here run on Windows, download the **Windows Erlang/OTP** installer from `https://www.erlang.org/downloads`. Likewise, visit `https://www.rabbitmq.com/download.html` and download the Windows installer for the **RabbitMQ** server.

2. Install **Erlang/OTP** first, followed by the **RabbitMQ** server. After a successful installation, open a command-line Terminal, visit the `rabbitmq_server-3.6.10\sbin` folder, and run the `rabbitmq-server start` command to start up the server and the `rabbitmq-server stop` command to shut it down.

3. Inside `rabbitmq_server-3.6.10/sbin`, run the `rabbitmq-plugins enable rabbitmq_management` command to install the *RabbitMQ web management console*. Stop and start the server again. Open a browser to run `http://localhost:15672/` and log in using the default credentials, guest, with the password, guest.

> The RabbitMQ management console uses the `15672` port by default.

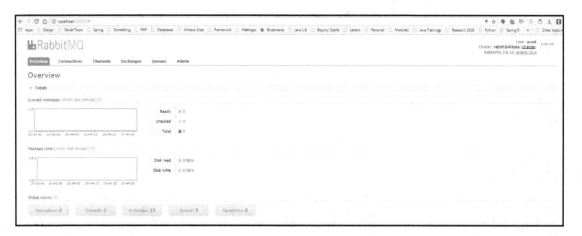

4. Now, return to the STS Eclipse and create a Maven project, `ch11-ipc-emp`. Copy all the packages and the `src\main\resource` files of `ch10-empservice` from the recipes from `Chapter 10`, *The Microservers*.

5. Open `pom.xml` and add the Spring Boot 2.0 starter POM dependency for AMQP support:

```
<dependency>
    <groupId>org.springframework.boot</groupId>
    <artifactId>spring-boot-starter-amqp</artifactId>
</dependency>
```

6. Open `application.properties` and add the following `RabbitMQ`-related details for autoconfiguration purposes:

```
spring.rabbitmq.host=localhost
spring.rabbitmq.port=5672
spring.rabbitmq.username=guest
spring.rabbitmq.password=guest
spring.rabbitmq.requested-heartbeat=60
```

 The default port for the RabbitMQ server is `5672`, while its management console is `15672`.

7. Copy `logback.xml` from the previous project and drop it inside `src\main\resources` to enable logging.

8. Inside its `org.packt.microservice.core.config`, add a `@Configuration` class that enables RabbitMQ components inside the `webflux` container. Since this recipe will implement a *Direct Exchange* style of messaging, wherein a *routing key* or *address* will be used to guide the exchange, add the following bean object to the `webflux` container:

```
@Configuration
@EnableWebFlux
@EnableRabbit
public class RabbitMQConfig {

    @Bean
    public DirectExchange directExchange() {
        return new DirectExchange("login.packt");
    }
}
```

The direct exchange name is `login.packt`.

9. To implement the typical AMQP-based services, create a new package, `org.packt.microservice.core.amqp`, and add a service that is injected into the container as follows:

```
@Service
public class SendRequestLogin {
   @Autowired
   DirectExchange directExchange;
   private RabbitTemplate rabbitTemplate;
   public SendRequestLogin(RabbitTemplate rabbitTemplate) {
      this.rabbitTemplate = rabbitTemplate;
   }
    public LoginDetails send(String content) {
        LoginDetails results =
(LoginDetails) rabbitTemplate
.convertSendAndReceive(
          directExchange.getName(), "packt", content);
       return results;
   }
}
```

The routing key is `packt`, which must be the accept-header address that is common to both the *request sender* (producer) and the *response listener* (consumer) to establish an acknowledgment or handshake.

10. At this point, this *Employee* microservice can now be the *request message producer*, which will establish a direct exchange communication through the routing key. After a successful verification of the routing key, the request will be posted in a `waiting` *queue* where the response service is listening. So, now, inside `org.packt.microservice.core.controller`, add another controller that will send a request to retrieve a `Login` profile when given an employee ID through the AMQP-based service handler:

```
@RestController
public class AmqpController {
   @Autowired
   private SendRequestLogin sendRequestLogin;
   @GetMapping(value="/amqpLoginDetail/{id}",
produces = MediaType.APPLICATION_JSON_VALUE)
```

```
        public LoginDetails exposeGetLoginDetails(
    @PathVariable("id") String id) {
            return sendRequestLogin.send(id);
    }
}
```

11. Save all files.
12. Create another Maven project, ch11-ipc-login, and copy all files of ch10-loginservice from Chapter 10, *The Microservice*. Perform *steps 5* to *8* of this recipe. Update some server-related information to avoid conflicts.
13. Inside the org.packt.microservice.config package, add another @Configuration class for this project to enable the **RabbitMQ** components in its webflux container. This creates the *waiting queue* that the *Employee* microservice utilizes to perform send-reply communication and the *binding* that builds the synchronous exchange-driven style of interaction:

```
@Configuration
@EnableWebFlux
@EnableRabbit
public class RabbitMQConfig {
   @Bean
    public Queue queue() {
        return new Queue("login.packt.retrieval.msg");
    }

    @Bean
    public DirectExchange exchange() {
        return new DirectExchange("login.packt");
    }

    @Bean
    public Binding binding(DirectExchange exchange, Queue
queue) {
        return BindingBuilder.bind(queue)
.to(exchange).with("packt");
    }
}
```

 The routing key indicated by BindingBuilder and the *exchange router name* must be the same as the employee's AMQP details.

14. Now, create the listener class that responds to the request of the *Employee* microservice every time it reaches the queue, `login.packt.retrieval.msg`. Place this class inside another package, `org.packt.microservice.core.amqp`:

```
@Service
@RabbitListener(queues = "login.packt.retrieval.msg")
public class RequestListLogins {
    @Autowired
    private LogindetailsService logindetailsServiceImpl;
    @RabbitHandler
    public LoginDetails process(String content) {
        Integer id = Integer.parseInt(content);
        LoginDetails details =
            logindetailsServiceImpl.findLoginById(id);
        return details ;
    }
}
```

15. Save all files.

16. Deploy both microservices and run the *Employee*'s request. Open `http://localhost:8095/ch11-ipc-emp/amqpLoginDetail/11` in a browser. Open the **RabbitMQ** management console, and observe the behavior of the message exchanges and the queue status for every execution of the URL request.

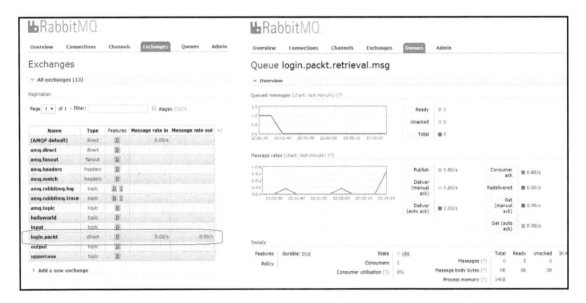

17. Here is some sample data from the **LOGIN Microservice** response.

```
← → C ⌂    🗋 localhost:8095/ch11-ipc-emp/amqpLoginDetail/1

⠿ Apps    Design    Social Tools    Spring    Something    PHP    Dat

{
  "username" : "sjctrags",
  "password" : "sjctrags",
  "encPassword" : "DV5/bhK4AuE1XxbqS6CN6g=="
}
```

How it works...

To achieve a loosely-coupled architecture in an ecosystem of microservices using AMQP synchronous interprocess communication, also called message-driven communication, may be one of the easiest and best solutions that Spring 5 can provide through Spring Boot 2.0. The idea is to replace RESTful web services with AMQP message-based communication to send the message request with some payloads from the *producer* to an exchange router, and deliver the response from the message *consumer* back to the *requester*.

The overall process of the message exchange implemented in this recipe is detailed here:

- The **Login Microservice** sends the message to the queue triggered by its request
- In the **RabbitMQ** server, the message will be verified if its routing key is the same as the routing key of the **Login Microservice** that matches the @RabbitListener service
- Also, the name of the queue, which is login.packt.retrieval.msg, generated in the **Login Microservice** must match
- If the verification is successful, the exchange **login.packt** will pass the message to the **QUEUE**, which will eventually call the @RabbitListener service to process the request
- If the service encounters no exceptions, **Login Microservice** will return to the **login.packt** exchange, the response together with the routing key, which must match the routing key of the request message for the acknowledgment
- Lastly, **Login Microservice** will get the response message from the queue

This recipe is only designed for blocking responses or `Object` from the consumer. If the microservices are required to expose the `Callable<T>`, `DeferredResult<T>`, and `WebAsyncTask<T>` data, the next recipe will guide us on how to properly configure an *asynchronous send-receive communication using the AMQP protocol.*

Creating asynchronous send-receive communication

Spring Boot 2.0 directly supports the asynchronous handling of send and receive messages with asynchronous results. Some microservices purposely implement this kind of exchange mechanism to avoid traffic and blocking problems when several of them send request messages at the same time to an exchange with one routing key. Moreover, this solution is most likely favored due to the presence of client-based callbacks that give microservices resiliency when the `consumer` is down or has crashed.

Getting started

Again, open `ch11-ipc-emp` and `ch11-ipc-login`, and add the following `request` and `reply` queues, `@RabbitListener` response transactions, and client services that will showcase the use of `AsyncRabbitTemplate`.

How to do it...

Let's build non-blocking and message-driven services using the following steps:

1. Let's first modify `consumer` of the message or the source of the response transaction, which is the **Login Microservice**. Add a `@Configuration` class that will create two queues, namely the `request` and `reply` queues. This class will be responsible for creating and binding a new routing key, `packt.async`, which is used for asynchronous messaging:

```
@Configuration
@EnableWebFlux
@EnableRabbit
public class RabbitMQConfigAsync {

@Autowired
    private DirectExchange exchange;
```

```
@Bean
 public Queue requestQueue() {
     return new Queue("msg.request");
 }

 @Bean
 public Queue replyQueue() {
   return new Queue("msg.reply");
 }
 @Bean
 public Binding binding(DirectExchange exchange,
Queue requestQueue) {
     return BindingBuilder.bind(requestQueue)
.to(exchange).with("packt.async");
 }
 }
```

2. The `exchange` router will be the same router used in the previous recipe since there must only be one `exchange` router for the entire application. It is recommended that you have one exchange per application to avoid convoluted and messy bindings that will lead to exceptions or undetected services:

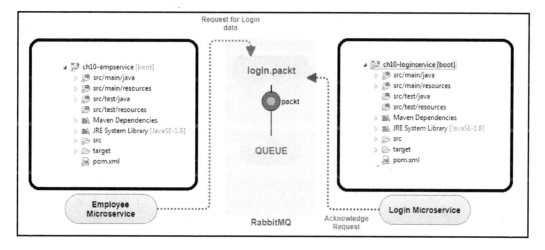

3. Now add another `@RabbitListener` service, which will be executed by the `msg.request` queue with the exchange router's confirmation:

```
@Service
@RabbitListener(queues = "msg.request")
public class RequestAsyncLogins {
    @Autowired
    private LogindetailsService logindetailsServiceImpl;
```

```
        @RabbitHandler
        public LoginDetails process(String content) {
                Integer id = Integer.parseInt(content);
                LoginDetails details =
                    logindetailsServiceImpl.findLoginById(id);
                return details ;

        }
}
```

4. Save all files.
5. Now open `ch11-ipc-emp`, and add another client service that creates `AsyncRestTemplate` and implements a request service handler that when executed will return a `Future<T>` task wrapper:

```
@Service
public class SendAsyncLogin {
    @Autowired
    private DirectExchange exchange;
    private AsyncRabbitTemplate asyncRabbitTemplate;
    public SendAsyncLogin(AsyncRabbitTemplate
            rabbitTemplate) {
        this.asyncRabbitTemplate = rabbitTemplate;
    }
    public DeferredResult<LoginDetails> send(String content) {
        final DeferredResult<LoginDetails> response =
new DeferredResult<>();
        ListenableFuture<LoginDetails> future =
            asyncRabbitTemplate.convertSendAndReceive(
exchange.getName(), "packt.async", content);
        future.addCallback(new
            LoginHandlerResponse(response));
        return response;
    }
    private static class LoginHandlerResponse implements
            ListenableFutureCallback<LoginDetails> {

        private DeferredResult<LoginDetails> result;

        public LoginHandlerResponse (
DeferredResult<LoginDetails> result) {
            this.result = result;
        }

        @Override
        public void onFailure(Throwable throwable) {
            result.setResult(new LoginDetails());
        }
```

```
            @Override
            public void onSuccess(LoginDetails response) {
                result.setResult(response);
            }
        }
    }
```

The `send()` method can also return `Callable<T>` or `WebAsyncTask<T>`, depending on the `asynchronous` model the problem needs.

6. No new AMQP-related configuration classes must be added to the application. Just add injecting the new service in `AmqpController` and add a new request handler method invoking the asynchronous request:

```
@Autowired
private SendAsyncLogin sendAsyncLogin;

@GetMapping(value="/amqpLoginAsync/{id}",
produces = MediaType.APPLICATION_JSON_VALUE)
    public DeferredResult<LoginDetails>
        exposeGetLoginAsync(@PathVariable("id") String id) {
            return sendAsyncLogin.send(id);
}
```

7. Save all files. Deploy both the applications. Open a browser and run `http://localhost:8095/ch10-emp/amqpLoginAsync/1` to have the login profile of an employee with an ID equivalent to 1.

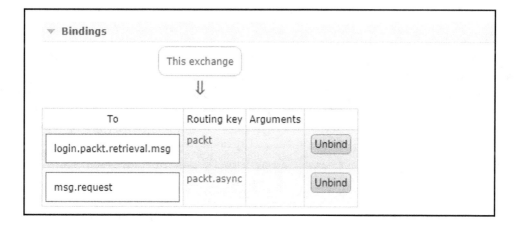

8. Shut down the **Login Microservice** by running `curl -XPOST`
`http://localhost:8094/ch11-ipc-login/appdetails/shutdown -k`. Run
the asynchronous service again and check the result.

```
← → C ⌂    🗋 localhost:8095/ch11-ipc-emp/amqpLoginAsync/1

⣿ Apps    Design    Social Tools    Spring    Something    PHP

{
    "username" : "sjctrags",
    "password" : "sjctrags",
    "encPassword" : "DV5/bhK4AuE1XxbqS6CN6g=="
}
```

How it works...

In Spring Boot 2.0, `AsyncRabbitTemplate` is already autoconfigured and is ready to be
`@Autowired` just like `RabbitTemplate`, its counterpart for the synchronous data exchange.
The main reason why we use this client API is to establish asynchronous requests to the
`request` queue through an exchange router and receive some asynchronous replies from
the `reply` queue. This class uses `SimpleMessageListenerContainer`, which acts like a
broker that fetches the request messages from `requestQueue()` and manages the replies
from `replyQueue()` asynchronously without polling them into only one *queue*, just like we
saw in the previous recipe. The number of requests fetched is based on the `prefetch`
configuration of the RabbitMQ server. All the *send-receive transactions* are still delegated
internally by the `RabbitTemplate` class.

Since it is required that `AsyncRabbitTemplate` implements two queues, `requestQueue()`
and `replyQueue()`, it can delegate send-receive message-based communication based on
the similar methods `sendAndReceive()` and `convertSendAndReceive()`. These
operators send the message requests with some payloads to `requestQueue()` for the *broker*
to fetch it and forward it to `replyQueue()`. Based on the exchange's router key, all the
requests are received and processed by `replyQueue()`, and it later forwards all the
responses to the *exchange* and then to the broker. This returns a `ListenableFuture<T>`, a
special type of a `Future<T>` that wraps and performs some threaded wait operations while
waiting for the response body for *30 seconds* at most, by default. It has
`ListenableFutureCallback<T>` to filter and retrieve the response body during failed or
successful communication. The default waiting time for the replies can be overridden
through its `setReceiveTimeout()` method during auto wiring.

Comparing the two recipes, send-receive communication is faster because of the broker in the middle that returns non-blocking results and provides `ListenableFutureCallback<T>`, which is responsible for providing an immediate resilient solution during communication problems.

To build the simplest asynchronous AMQP communication, the next recipe will highlight the use of event-driven messaging, which scraps the use of router keys.

Creating an event-driven asynchronous communication using AMQP

If we have a totally distributed and *dockerized* setup for microservices, where each has complicated and complex message-driven communication requirements, having multiple exchanges and routing keys might be inappropriate, especially if the expected communication for the distributed ecosystem is for a loosely-coupled design. This recipe will provide a simpler and more adept solution for a loosely-coupled and distributed microservice architecture that uses a *direct reply-to* property without any *exchange-queue* binding.

Getting started

Again, open the `ch11-ipc-emp` and `ch11-ipc-login` microservices, and replace some configuration details that are important in building a totally asynchronous, of the AMQP-based communication for a loosely-coupled setup.

How to do it...

Let's implement a direct reply-to communication using the AMQP protocol by following these steps:

1. Open the first message *consumer*, the **Login Microservice** project. Disable the previous `RabbitMQConfig` for blocking send-receive communication and replace it with `RabbitMQEventConfig` as follows. Obviously, the following class only contains the *queue* and no exchange binding setup:

   ```
   @Configuration
   @EnableWebFlux
   @EnableRabbit
   ```

```
public class RabbitMQEventConfig {
    @Bean
    public Queue queue() {
        return new Queue("login.packt.retrieval.msg");
    }

}
```

2. Then, disable the configuration for the synchronous send-receive and replace it with the following *exchange-queue binding* configuration:

```
@Configuration
@EnableWebFlux
@EnableRabbit
public class RabbitMQEventConfigAsync {
    @Bean
    public Queue requestQueue() {
        return new Queue("msg.request");
    }

    @Bean
    public Queue replyQueue() {
      return new Queue("msg.reply");
    }
}
```

3. Since there will be no additional changes for its `@RabbitListener` services, save all files for deployment later.

4. Go to `ch11-ipc-emp`, the *producer* of the request message, and replace the old blocking AMQP configuration with the following:

```
@Configuration
@EnableWebFlux
@EnableRabbit
public class RabbitMQEventConfig {
    @Bean
    public Queue queue() {
        return new Queue("login.packt.retrieval.msg");
    }
}
```

5. On the asynchronous AMQP send-receive configuration, there will be no changes to be reflected so far.

6. For its blocking client-service implementation, replace `SendRequestLogin` with this `@RepositoryEventHandler` from Spring Data REST, which was purposely created to publish the request message with the payload `content` of `send()` to `queue()` or `requestQueue()`. It has an event handler method annotated with `@HandleAfterCreate` that is triggered to manage the publish once `send()` is called:

```
@Service
@RepositoryEventHandler
public class SendRequestEventLogin {
    private RabbitTemplate rabbitTemplate;
    private Queue queue;
    public SendRequestEventLogin(Queue queue,
RabbitTemplate rabbitTemplate) {
        this.rabbitTemplate = rabbitTemplate;
        this.queue = queue;
    }
    @HandleAfterCreate
    public LoginDetails loginHandler(String content) {
        return send(content);
    }
    public LoginDetails send(String content) {
        System.out.println("send request");
        LoginDetails results = (LoginDetails)
                rabbitTemplate.convertSendAndReceive(
        queue.getName(), content);
        return results;
    }
}
```

7. Also, replace the `SendAsyncLogin` service class with an event handler that filters the parameter content and uses `AsyncRestTemplate` to establish broker-based communication directly with the queue:

```
@Service
@RepositoryEventHandler
public class SendAsyncEventLogin {

    private AsyncRabbitTemplate asyncRabbitTemplate;
    private Queue requestQueue;

    public SendAsyncEventLogin(Queue requestQueue,
            AsyncRabbitTemplate rabbitTemplate) {
        this.asyncRabbitTemplate = rabbitTemplate;
        // rabbitTemplate.setReceiveTimeout(1000);
        this.requestQueue = requestQueue;
```

```
        }

        @HandleAfterCreate
        public DeferredResult<LoginDetails>
loginHandler(String content) {
            return send(content);
        }

        public DeferredResult<LoginDetails> send(String content) {
            System.out.println("send request");
            final DeferredResult<LoginDetails> response =
new DeferredResult<>();
            ListenableFuture<LoginDetails> future =
                asyncRabbitTemplate.convertSendAndReceive(
requestQueue.getName(), content);
            future.addCallback(new
                    LoginHandlerResponse(response));
            return response;
        }
        // refer to sources
        }
```

8. Save all changes in the *Employee* microservice application.

9. Deploy the projects. Run both blocking and asynchronous requests again, and observe how fast their execution is compared to the previous two recipes. No routing keys and exchanges are involved in these processes:

```
← → C ⌂    localhost:8095/ch11-ipc-emp/amqpLoginAsync/1
::: Apps    Design    Social Tools    Spring    Something    PHP    Databa

{
  "username" : null,
  "password" : null,
  "encPassword" : null
}
```

How it works...

Event handlers are the main players in this direct *reply-to* communication among microservices. This recipe uses Spring Data REST's `@RepositoryEventHandler`, registered as the `@Service` to the `webflux` container, which acts like a filter to its service methods. It has filter event methods registered as `@HandlerAfterCreate` that directly publish the request message with or without the payloads included.

Transactions involving event handlers are synchronous by default, but since they are used for AMQP-based communications, they adjust and comply with the asynchronous objectives of the protocol. At this point of this chapter, a loosely-coupled architecture has been established using only a few simple steps.

Creating stream communication with Spring Cloud Stream

Event-driven communication is one of the best initiatives for building distributed architecture for microservices. Spring Cloud Stream offers distributed and streaming data pipelines that can be used to provide data channels to message consumers, producers, and listener classes through the queues and brokers provided by a binding platform such as RabbitMQ. With **Spring Cloud Stream**, Spring Boot 2.0 can build any pluggable components that will implement the *topic-exchange* style of message communication, which is the highlight of this recipe. This also will include reactive streams such as `Flux<T>` data streams, which are not yet supported by the previous recipes.

Getting started

Let's create three Spring Boot 2.0 applications that will represent the *producer*, *processor*, and *consumer* components of the Spring Cloud Stream that has a binding to our RabbitMQ server setup.

How to do it...

Let's create a *reactive stream communication* with the Spring Cloud Stream module by performing the following steps:

1. First, let's create the message **producer,** which is technically referred to as the **SOURCE** in the **Spring Cloud Stream** terminology. Create a **Spring Boot 2.0** application with all the core *starter* POM dependencies, such as webflux, actuator, Thymeleaf, and FreeMarker. Since this project will be for Spring Cloud libraries and plugins for Spring Boot 2.0, add the following Spring Cloud Finchley dependency configuration into the `pom.xml` file:

```
<dependencyManagement>
    <dependencies>
        <dependency>
            <groupId>org.springframework.cloud</groupId>
            <artifactId>spring-cloud-dependencies
</artifactId>
            <version>Finchley.M1</version>
            <type>pom</type>
            <scope>import</scope>
        </dependency>
    </dependencies>
</dependencyManagement>
```

2. Add the following *starter* POM, which is required to implement the reactive **Spring Cloud Stream**:

```
<dependency>
        <groupId>org.springframework.cloud</groupId>
        <artifactId>spring-cloud-stream-reactive</artifactId>
    </dependency>
```

3. Since we will be using a RabbitMQ broker for the message exchange, verify that you have the server installed on the machine. Also, add the following Spring Cloud Stream module for RabbitMQ transactions:

```
<dependency>
  <groupId>org.springframework.cloud</groupId>
  <artifactId>spring-cloud-starter-stream-rabbit
  </artifactId>
</dependency>
```

4. Inside the core package, `org.packt.process.core`, create the bootstrap class for this **SOURCE** application with an `@EnableBinding` annotation, together with an interface argument that identifies the channel connection with which it registers to the RabbitMQ exchange broker. For this application, the default `Source` interface will be used:

```
@SpringBootApplication
@EnableBinding(Source.class)
public class SourceMsgBootApplication
extends  SpringBootServletInitializer  {
    // refer to sources
}
```

5. Inside its `src\main\properties` directory, create `application.properties` that contain the same Tomcat server-related and connectivity details for the `hrs` database. Moreover, add the following new details that pertain to the *source message channel* and the *type of source message* that this channel will retrieve during the process. Also include the **RabbitMQ** server details that will host the messaging:

```
spring.rabbitmq.host=localhost
spring.rabbitmq.port=5672
spring.rabbitmq.username=guest
spring.rabbitmq.password=guest
spring.rabbitmq.requested-heartbeat=60

spring.cloud.stream.bindings.output.destination=packt.cloud
spring.cloud.stream.bindings.output.content-
type=application/json
```

6. Create `@Controller` that will contain two request handlers --one that will send the request with an employee ID for the verification of its profile and one that will send a `Department` payload object to the consumer for saving. Both triggers and event send the request messages to its consumer:

```
@Controller
public class MessageController {

@Autowired
private Source source;

@RequestMapping(method = RequestMethod.GET,
value = "/selectDept/{id}")
@ResponseBody
public String verifyEmployee(@PathVariable("id")
```

```
String id) {
Message<String> result =
MessageBuilder.withPayload(id).build();
source.output().send(result);
return result.getPayload();
}

@RequestMapping(method = RequestMethod.GET,
value = "/addDept/{id}/{deptid}/{name}/")
@ResponseBody
public Department addEmployee(@PathVariable("id")
    Integer id, @PathVariable("deptid") Integer deptid,
        @PathVariable("name") String name) {

Department dept = new Department();
dept.setId(id);
dept.setDeptid(deptid);
dept.setName(name);
Message<Department> result =
        MessageBuilder.withPayload(dept).build();
source.output().send(result);
return result.getPayload();
}
}
```

7. Save all files.

8. Since we are done with the producer, let's now create the message *consumer* or the **SINK** application. Create a Spring Boot 2.0 application, ch11-ipc-sink, with all the core starter POM dependencies similar to those for the *producer* application. Add the JDBC and JPA starter POM for database transactions. Above all, add the **Spring Cloud Finchley** Maven dependency configuration to pom.xml.

9. Now create a core page for the consumer named org.packt.process.core and drop the following bootstrap class that enables message binding using the **SINK** definition:

```
@SpringBootApplication
@EnableBinding(Sink.class)
public class SinkMsgBootApplication
extends  SpringBootServletInitializer  {
    // refer to sources
}
```

10. In its `src\main\resources`, add `application.properties` that contain the RabbitMQ *server details*, the *input exchange channel*, and the *type of message to be consumed*. Also disable `spring.jpa.hibernate.use-new-id-generator-mappings` to follow the MySQL auto-increment procedure for primary key generation:

```
spring.jpa.hibernate.use-new-id-generator-mappings=false
spring.cloud.stream.bindings.input.destination=packt.cloud
spring.cloud.stream.bindings.input.content-
type=application/json

spring.rabbitmq.host=localhost
spring.rabbitmq.port=5672
spring.rabbitmq.username=guest
spring.rabbitmq.password=guest
spring.rabbitmq.requested-heartbeat=60
// see the sources
```

The *consumer* and *producer* exchange channel must be one and the same, which is `packt.cloud`, in order for the exchange to happen.

11. Copy the JPA repository, service, and entity models from the `ch10-empservice` application. Drop them into this project, and apply the needed package refactoring and some syntax changes.

12. Create an event handler class that contains events that will be executed every time the request reaches the `input` queue. For Spring Cloud to detect this bean class, it must have the `@Component` annotation:

```
@Component
public class VerifyEmployeeService {
    @Autowired
    private DepartmentService departmentServiceImpl;
    private static final Logger log =
        LoggerFactory.getLogger(
VerifyEmployeeService.class);
    @ServiceActivator(inputChannel=Sink.INPUT)
    public void validateEmployee(Integer deptId) {
        Department dept = null;
        try{
            dept = departmentServiceImpl.findDeptByid(deptId);
        }catch(Exception e){
            dept = new Department();
            dept.setName("Non-existent");
```

```
    }
      log.info("{}", dept.getName());
    }
    @ServiceActivator(inputChannel=Sink.INPUT)
    public void addDepartment(Department dept) {
      try{
          departmentServiceImpl.saveDeptRec(dept);
      }catch(Exception e){
          log.info("{}", e.getMessage());
      }
        log.info("{}", dept.getName());
    }
  }
```

 Spring Cloud Stream has a built-in object *converter* and *mapper,* which is the only reason why **SINK** can easily access employee ID as an `int` object from the input channel. Object payloads are automatically converted into JSON without adding Jackson mapper plugins.

13. Save all files. Assuming that the RabbitMQ server is running, deploy the **SOURCE** and **SINK** projects. Run both `http://localhost:9004/ch11-ipc-source/addDept/777/3433/Psycholo gy/` and `http://localhost:9004/ch11-ipc-source/selectDept/395`, and check the logs. Also, check the `department` table if the *Psychology* record has been inserted.

14. An optional component of **Spring Cloud Stream,** which is called a **PROCESSOR** can be added to this recipe to act like a filter to the incoming stream that matches an event. These events can forward reactive stream data to SINK. Let's create a new Spring Boot 2.0 application that will pose as the **PROCESSOR** for the preceding message exchange. Add the same core starter POM and **Spring Cloud Finchley** dependencies to `pom.xml`.

15. Inside its core package `org.packt.process.core`, create a bootstrap class that enables message binding using the default class definition of the `Processor` interface:

```
@EnableBinding(Processor.class)
@SpringBootApplication
public class ProcessorMsgBootApplication
extends  SpringBootServletInitializer  {
    // refer to sources
}
```

16. Inside the `org.packt.process.core.config` package, create this listener class that will filter the employee ID payload from the *producer* message, validate if it's convertible to an `int` object, and return 0 if the employee ID is not convertible to an integer value:

```
@Configuration
public class EmpIdConverterConverter {
    @StreamListener(Processor.INPUT)
    @SendTo(Processor.OUTPUT)
    public Integer verifyEmpString(String message) {
        System.out.println("first");
        Integer empid = null;
        try{
            empid = Integer.parseInt(message);
        } catch(Exception e){
            empid = 0;
        }
        return empid;
    }
}
```

 This implementation processes and forwards a blocking stream.

17. Save all files. Deploy the **SOURCE**, **SINK**, and **PROCESSOR** applications. Open a browser and run `http://localhost:9004/ch11-ipc-source/selectDept/39` again. Send an invalid employee ID and observe the logs.

18. Unlike in the previous recipe, Spring Cloud Stream is a messaging framework design for long-lived interprocess communication. To create a **PROCESSOR** that will manage a *hot stream* or continuous flow of message requests, the reactor-based event handlers wherein outgoing and incoming message requests will all be in `Flux<T>` stream. Then try once again replacing the previous blocking `verifyEmpString()` with the following reactive handler:

```
@StreamListener
@Output(Processor.OUTPUT)
public Flux<String> verifyEmpString(
@Input(Processor.INPUT) Flux<String> id) {
        System.out.println("first");
        id.delayElements(Duration.ofMillis(2))
           .log();
        return id;
}
```

19. Save all files. Deploy all three applications. Rerun `http://localhost:9004/ch11-ipc-source/selectDept/39`, and observe the broker exchange between the input and output queues:

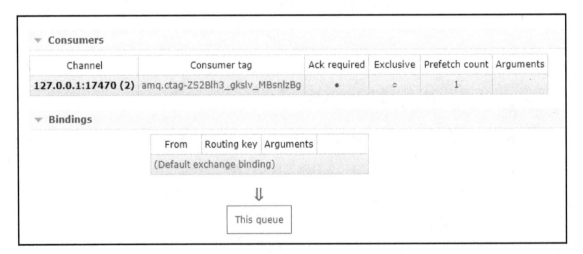

How it works...

Spring Cloud Stream is a framework composed of **Spring Integration** and **Spring Boot 2.0**, which is purposely used to establish broker-based communication among microservices that produce and consume messages at a high rate. Though not shown in this recipe, Spring Cloud Stream can establish groups or clusters in order to maintain scalability despite high stream traffic.

All configuration classes and components are considered to be event handler classes or filters, wherein each of its event methods has an annotation, `@StreamListener`, an indicator that these methods are listeners, and sensitive to incoming and outgoing events. What types of events they are considering depends on the class interfaces defined in their `@EnableBinding` bootstrap class configuration. These interfaces contain queue names and channel definitions. If they follow the **SOURCE** channel definition, then events of that application respond to the sending of messages either through REST endpoints or typical `@Controller` requests. If the application binds with the **SINK** messaging definition, then the application will respond to inputs from incoming requests with their payloads. The **PROCESSOR** types are special listeners that add validation or transformation to incoming messages before they are forwarded to the **SINK** events. If there are custom queues and definitions, these interfaces can be customized like **SINK** and **SOURCE**:

```
public interface Sink {
  String INPUT = "packt.input";
  @Input(Sink.INPUT)
  SubscribableChannel input();
}
public interface Source {
    String OUTPUT = "output";
  @Output(Source.OUTPUT)
    MessageChannel output();
}
```

Custom application gateways can also be defined through a custom interface like the following, which defines two output and one input channels:

```
public interface PaymentGateway {
    @Input
    SubscribableChannel payment();
    @Output
    MessageChannel order();
    @Output
    MessageChannel shipping();
}
```

The @Output annotation inside these interfaces defines an output channel through which the request messages are being pushed by the output events. The @Input annotation, on the other hand, defines an input channel through which the SINK applications, for instance, retrieve the requests. The default queue channel SOURCE is output and for SINK it is input.

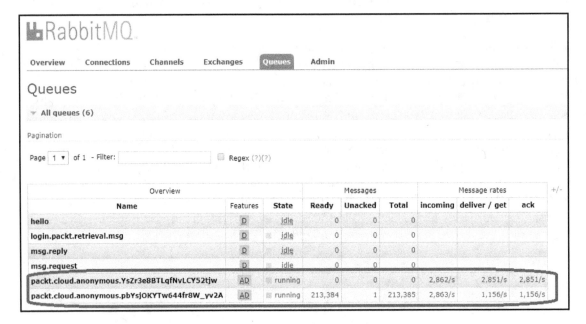

When it comes to the **PROCESSOR**, @Input supports the Reactor type Flux<T>, which produces a continuous flow of data streams that can capture either payloads or the entire messages.

Implementing batch processes using Spring Cloud Task

All of the microservices implemented here are designed for long-lived communication. There are service boxes that are written just to trigger auditing, transfer files through FTP, convert Excel sheets to PDF, and complete file compression and decompression. Spring Cloud Task is part of the Spring Cloud project that offers implementation for short-lived microservices, which will be showcased by this last recipe.

Getting started

This application is a simple microservice template that will guide us on how to build and execute tasks that run only within a short period of time.

How to do it...

Let's implement a simple event using Spring Cloud Task:

1. Create a Spring Boot 2.0 project, `ch11-batch-task`, that contains the core *starter* POM such as webflux, actuator, and the Tomcat server for Spring Boot 2.0, with the addition of the needed Spring Cloud dependent management configuration, which is **Spring Cloud Finchley**.

2. Add the following **Spring Cloud Task** dependency into the `pom.xml` file:

```
<dependency>
  <groupId>org.springframework.cloud</groupId>
  <artifactId>spring-cloud-task-core</artifactId>
</dependency>
```

3. Create a core package `org.packt.process.core` and create a bootstrap class that enables Spring Cloud Task through the `@EnableTask` annotation:

```
@SpringBootApplication
@EnableTask
public class TaskBootApplication extends
          SpringBootServletInitializer  {
     // refer to sources
}
```

4. Inside its `srcmain\resources` folder, create `application.properties` similar to the previous recipes. Just create a blank database named `springcloudtask` that is mapped solely to this application.

5. Copy the `logback.xml` file from the previous chapters and place this file in `src\main\resources` with some updates.

6. Inside a new package, `org.packt.process.core.config`, create a configuration for the task to be executed by implementing the **Spring Cloud Task** core interface, `org.springframework.boot.CommandLineRunner`. This class simply logs a dummy message:

```
@Configuration
public class MonitorTask implements CommandLineRunner {

    private final Logger log =
    LoggerFactory.getLogger(MonitorTask.class);

    @Override
    public void run(String... args) throws Exception {
        log.info("running task");
    }
}
```

7. Save all files. Deploy the project. Check the log file and open a MySQL Workbench to check the `springcloudtask` schema:

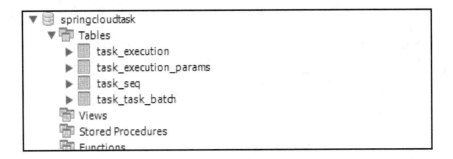

How it works...

Spring Cloud Task is used for a short cycle of transaction executed by `org.springframework.boot.ApplicationRunner` and `org.springframework.boot.CommandLineRunner`. With only the `@EnableTask` annotation, the processes wrapped by these interfaces will be executed once without a restart. Better utilization and execution of Spring Cloud Task can be achieved whenever it is deployed to the **Spring Cloud Data Flow** server.

12
Other Spring 5 Features

From the installation and configuration of HTTP/2 down to Spring 5 microservices using Spring Boot 2.0 development, this book has listed a lot of old modules and showed that Spring 5 still supports them through some successful recipes. Likewise, half of the chapters also dropped some how-tos on the new set of foundation classes and interfaces needed to build asynchronous and reactive web solutions.

This book will not be complete without these features, that may or may not be familiar to some but are within the realms of the Spring 5 platform. These features may belong to the Spring MVC and Spring WebFlux modules but can be useful in general to solve some future problems involving Spring 5 web development.

In this chapter, we will cover the following topics:

- Using Hibernate 5 object-relational mapping
- Applying Hazelcast distributed caching
- Building client-server communications with WebSocket
- Implementing Reactive WebSocket communication
- Implementing asynchronous Spring Data JPA properties
- Implementing Reactive Spring Data JPA repositories
- Using Spring Data MongoDB
- Building applications for big data storage
- Building a Spring 5 application using Kotlin

Using Hibernate 5 object-relational mapping

When it comes to **object-relational mapping (ORM)**, this Spring 5 framework supports **Hibernate 5** with easy configuration through the context of **Spring Boot 2.0** methodologies. This first recipe will be about applying Hibernate object-relational mapping to a MySQL data source using the **HikariCP** data pooling mechanism.

Getting ready

Create a new Maven project, ch12-hiber, and integrate the **Hibernate 5** ORM framework.

How to do it...

Let us integrate Hibernate 5 to the Spring 5 application using the following steps:

1. Convert the Maven project ch12-hiber to a Spring Boot application by adding the following Spring Boot 2.0.0.M2 starter POM dependencies, such as webflux, actuator, and JDBC, with some support plugins such as the MySQL connector.

2. Hibernate 5 has no dedicated starter POM in Spring Boot 2.0, but it is by default contained in the Spring Data JPA starter POM. Since adding the ORM framework is covered by the Spring MVC module, it is mandatory to include the Spring MVC starter POM in the Maven configuration, as follows:

```
<dependency>
        <groupId>org.springframework.boot</groupId>
         <artifactId>spring-boot-starter-data-jpa</artifactId>
</dependency>
<dependency>
     <groupId>org.springframework.boot</groupId>
     <artifactId>spring-boot-starter-web</artifactId>
</dependency>
```

3. Inside a new org.packt.hiber.core package, add a Bootstrap class that disables the JPA autoconfiguration process, because JPA is bound with Hibernate 5 in Spring Boot, making it impossible to use Hibernate 5 as a standalone solution. Even without JPA, still ensure that the @EnableTransactionManagement annotation is applied to the Bootstrap class:

```
@SpringBootApplication(exclude =
          JpaRepositoriesAutoConfiguration.class)
@EnableTransactionManagement
```

```
public class HiberBootApplication
extends SpringBootServletInitializer  {
     // refer to sources
}
```

4. Inside its src\main\resources directory, create an application.properties
   file that contains the same server-related and database properties. Also, include
   the actuator endpoint details for project monitoring and deployment. Most
   importantly, add in here all the needed Hibernate details to be fetched by some
   API classes in @Configuration later:

```
server.port=8087
server.servlet.context-path=/ch12-hiber

spring.datasource.driverClassName=com.mysql.jdbc.Driver
spring.datasource.url=jdbc:mysql://localhost:3306/hrs?autoRecon
nect=true&useSSL=true&serverSslCert=classpath:config/spring5pac
kt.crt
spring.datasource.username=root
spring.datasource.password=spring5mysql
spring.datasource.hikari.connection-timeout=60000

management.port=8087
management.address=localhost
management.context-path=/appdetails

// refer to sources

#Hibernate 5 Details
hibernate.dialect=org.hibernate.dialect.MySQL5InnoDBDialect
hibernate.show_sql=true
hibernate.format_sql=true
```

5. Also, include logback.xml and the config folder in the src\main\resources
   directory, from the previous projects.
6. Copy the entity model Department from the previous Spring JPA project.

7. Before implementing the Hibernate transactions inside the `org.packt.hiber.core.config` package, add the following configuration class which builds the `org.springframework.orm.hibernate5.LocalSessionFactoryBean`, `org.springframework.orm.hibernate5.HibernateTransactionManager`, and `org.springframework.orm.hibernate5.HibernateTemplate` packages and injects these beans in to the container. The Hibernate properties from the `application.properties` file are fetched by these APIs through the property placeholder variant `org.springframework.core.env.Environment`, as follows:

```
@Configuration
@EnableWebFlux
public class HiberConfig {
        @Autowired
        private Environment environment;
        @Bean
        public Properties hibernateProperties() {
            Properties properties = new Properties();
            properties.put("hibernate.dialect",
environment.getRequiredProperty("hibernate.dialect"));
            properties.put("hibernate.show_sql",
environment.getRequiredProperty("hibernate.show_sql"));
            properties.put("hibernate.format_sql",
environment.getRequiredProperty("hibernate.show_sql"));
            return properties;
        }
    }
    @Bean("sessionFactory")
    public LocalSessionFactoryBean localSessionFactory(
DataSource dataSource, Properties hibernateProperties) {
            LocalSessionFactoryBean sessionFactory =
new LocalSessionFactoryBean();
            sessionFactory.setDataSource(dataSource);
            sessionFactory.setPackagesToScan(
                "org.packt.hiber.core.model.data");
sessionFactory.setHibernateProperties(hibernateProperties);
            return sessionFactory;
        }
    @Bean
    public HibernateTransactionManager db1TransactionManager(
DataSource dataSource,
        LocalSessionFactoryBean localSessionFactory) {
            HibernateTransactionManager txManager =
new HibernateTransactionManager();
            txManager.setSessionFactory(
localSessionFactory.getObject());
```

```
            txManager.setDataSource(dataSource);
            return txManager;
      }
      @Bean
      public HibernateTemplate hibernateTemplate(
    SessionFactory sessionFactory) {
                return new HibernateTemplate(sessionFactory);
      }
}
```

8. Let's now build a Hibernate transaction manager for the `department` table schema of the `hrs` database. The following are the template methods for the department `@Repository` transactions found in the `org.packt.hiber.core.dao` package:

```
public interface DepartmentDao {

    public List<Department> getAllDepts();
    public List<Department> getDeptsByName(String name);
    public List<Department> getDeptsByDeptid(Integer
        deptid);
    public Department getDeptById(Integer id);
    public void saveDept(Department dept);
}
```

9. Implement the preceding template methods using the generated `org.hibernate.SessionFactory` package and its `createQuery()` method. Drop this implementation class inside the `org.packt.hiber.core.dao.impl` package as follows:

```
@Repository
public class DepartmentDaoImpl implements DepartmentDao{
    @Autowired
    private SessionFactory sessionFactory;

    @Override
    public List<Department> getAllDepts() {
        return sessionFactory.openSession()
.createQuery("select d from Department d",
            Department.class).getResultList();
    }

    @Override
    public List<Department> getDeptsByName(String name) {
        return sessionFactory.openSession()
.createQuery("select d from Department d
where d.name LIKE '%:name%'", Department.class)
```

```
.setParameter("name", name).getResultList();
    }

    @Override
    public List<Department> getDeptsByDeptid(Integer deptid) {
        return sessionFactory.openSession()
.createQuery("select d from Department d
where d.deptid = :deptid", Department.class)
                    .setParameter("deptid",
                        deptid).getResultList();
    }

    @Override
    public Department getDeptById(Integer id) {
        return sessionFactory.openSession()
.createQuery("select d from Department d
where d.id = :id", Department.class)
.setParameter("id", id).getSingleResult();
    }

    @Override
    public void saveDept(Department dept) {
        sessionFactory.openSession().persist(dept);
    }
}
```

10. Now, implement the service layer by having a set of services found in the `org.packt.hiber.core.service` package, as follows:

```
public interface DepartmentService {

    public List<Department> getAllDeptList();
    public List<Department> getDeptsByName(String name);
    public List<Department> getDeptsByDeptid(Integer
        deptid);
    public Department getDeptById(Integer id);
    public void saveDept(Department dept);
}
```

11. Inside the `org.packt.hiber.core.service.impl` package, implement the preceding service methods using the `DepartmentDao` repository transactions, as follows:

```
@Service
public class DepartmentServiceImpl implements
        DepartmentService{
    @Autowired
```

```
    private DepartmentDao departmentDaoImpl;

    @Override
    public List<Department> getAllDeptList() {
        return departmentDaoImpl.getAllDepts();
    }

    @Override
    public List<Department> getDeptsByName(String name) {
        return departmentDaoImpl.getDeptsByName(name);
    }
}

// refer to sources
}
```

 Avoid using the @Transaction annotation since Hibernate transaction management has been enabled by @EnableTransactionManagement during Bootstrap. The @Transaction annotation is appropriate for JPA transactions only.

12. To test Hibernate services, implement the following RESTful services through HiberController in the org.packt.hiber.core.controller package, as follows:

```
@RestController
public class HiberController {
    @Autowired
    private DepartmentService departmentServiceImpl;
    @GetMapping(value="/listDepts",
produces= MediaType.APPLICATION_JSON_VALUE)
    public List<Department> listDepts() {
        return departmentServiceImpl.getAllDeptList();
    }
    @GetMapping(value="/selectDept/{id}",
produces= MediaType.APPLICATION_JSON_VALUE)
    public Department selectDept(@PathVariable("id") Integer id)
{
        return departmentServiceImpl.getDeptById(id);
    }
    @GetMapping(value="/selectDeptByDeptid/{deptid}",
produces= MediaType.APPLICATION_JSON_VALUE)
    public List<Department>selectDeptByDeptid(
@PathVariable("deptid") Integer deptid) {
        return
            departmentServiceImpl.getDeptsByDeptid(deptid);
    }
}
```

13. Save all files.
14. Build and deploy the project with the `clean spring-boot:run -U` command.
15. Finally, open a browser and execute a sample RESTful service, as shown in the following screenshot:

How it works...

This recipe is obviously under the Spring MVC module which is concerned with the implementation and performance of DAO layers in an application. Spring 5 totally supports the Hibernate ORM framework, but only version 5.x. There is no means for Spring 5 to inject `SessionFactory` and the transaction manager like in the previous Hibernate versions.

To successfully use Hibernate 5, it is advisable to turn off `JpaRepositoriesAutoConfiguration` since it is part of the JPA autoconfiguration process during Bootstrap. This allows us to implement transaction management from Hibernate 5 when applying the `@Repository` annotation instead of the default JPA framework of Spring Boot 2.0.

Since the autoconfiguration for JPA is required to be disabled, the bean objects of these Hibernate 5 APIs, namely `HibernateTransactionManager`, `HibernateTemplate`, and `LocalSessionFactoryBean`, must be explicitly injected to the container. Together with the Hibernate properties declared in the `application.properties` file, these beans will be consumed in order to configure the `SessionFactory` needed to build and execute the **Hibernate Query Language (HQL)**.

Applying Hazelcast distributed caching

In Chapter 9, *Spring Boot 2.0*, we introduced a recipe that highlighted Ehcache configuration with the Spring Boot 2.0 development. However, Ehcache works fine with applications deployed to a single-node deployment environment only. Once this simple architecture starts to adapt the distributed or clustered microservices set up, a new object caching mechanism that fits in a distributed environment must also be used, replacing the old caching. Unfortunately, Ehcache is not scalable when it comes to infrastructure changes like this. This recipe will show us a procedure that will implement a distributed caching mechanism suitable for a loosely-coupled architecture.

Getting ready

Utilize again the Hibernate project ch12-hiber in order to show the step-by-step process of how to apply Hazelcast distributed caching.

How to do it...

Let us assume that there is a distributed setup of microservices, which can dockerized or not, just for us to apply the following steps in building **Hazelcast** caching:

1. Open the pom.xml file of the ch12-hiber project and add the following Spring Cache starter POM dependency, as follows:

```
<dependency>
        <groupId>org.springframework.boot</groupId>
        <artifactId>spring-boot-starter-cache</artifactId>
</dependency>
```

2. Then, add the Spring Boot 2.0 starter POM for Hazelcast support. Also, include the updated and stable version of the **Hazelcast-Spring** external libraries needed to configure the **Hazelcast cache manager** for the Spring 5 application, as follows:

```
<dependency>
        <groupId>com.hazelcast</groupId>
        <artifactId>hazelcast</artifactId>
</dependency>
<dependency>
        <groupId>com.hazelcast</groupId>
        <artifactId>hazelcast-spring</artifactId>
        <version>3.8.3</version>
</dependency>
```

3. For the serialization of `ArrayList<T>` and data models, add the following supplementary cache libraries that can help avoid Hazelcast serialization-related exceptions:

```
<dependency>
    <groupId>javax.cache</groupId>
    <artifactId>cache-api</artifactId>
</dependency>
```

4. Check whether all data models in the `org.packt.hiber.core.model.data` package implement `java.io.Serializable`. All entity models must be serializable, and that is a requirement for Hazelcast caching.

5. Now, it is time to build the caching configuration class. Inside the `org.packt.hiber.core.config`, package and add the `CachingConfig` class that builds the cache manager with the Hazelcast instance and some properties. Do not forget to apply the `@EnableCaching` class-level annotation:

```
@Configuration
@EnableCaching
public class CachingConfig {
    @Bean
    public Config hazelCastConfig() {
        Config config = new Config();
        config.setInstanceName("hazelcast-packt-cache");
        config.setProperty("hazelcast.jmx", "true");
        MapConfig deptCache = new MapConfig();
        deptCache.setTimeToLiveSeconds(20);
        deptCache.setEvictionPolicy(EvictionPolicy.LFU);
        config.getMapConfigs().put("hazeldept",deptCache);
        return config;
    }
    @Bean
    public HazelcastInstance hazelcastInstance(
Config hazelCastConfig) {
        return
          Hazelcast.newHazelcastInstance(hazelCastConfig);
    }
    @Bean
    public CacheManager cacheManager(
HazelcastInstance hazelcastInstance) {
        return new
          HazelcastCacheManager(hazelcastInstance);
    }
}
```

6. To apply Hazelcast caching, open `DepartmentDaoImpl` and attach `@Cacheable` to the data retrieval operations:

```
@Repository
public class DepartmentDaoImpl implements DepartmentDao{
    @Autowired
    private SessionFactory sessionFactory;

    @Cacheable("hazeldept")
    @Override
    public List<Department> getAllDepts() {
        return sessionFactory.openSession()
.createQuery("select d from Department d",
            Department.class).getResultList();
    }

    @Cacheable("hazeldept")
    @Override
    public List<Department> getDeptsByName(String name) {
        return sessionFactory.openSession()
.createQuery("select d from Department d
where d.name LIKE '%:name%'", Department.class)
.setParameter("name", name).getResultList();
    }
    // refer to sources
    }
```

7. Save all files. Deploy the project and check the log file:

```
15:45:22.591 [main] INFO  com.hazelcast.system -
[192.168.56.1]:5701 [dev]
[3.8.2] Hazelcast 3.8.2 (20170518 - a60f944) starting at
[192.168.56.1]:5701
15:45:22.591 [main] INFO  com.hazelcast.system -
[192.168.56.1]:5701 [dev]
[3.8.2] Copyright (c) 2008-2016, Hazelcast, Inc. All Rights
Reserved.
15:45:22.591 [main] INFO  com.hazelcast.system -
[192.168.56.1]:5701 [dev]
[3.8.2] Configured Hazelcast Serialization version : 1
15:45:22.820 [main] INFO  c.h.s.i.o.impl.BackpressureRegulator
-
[192.168.56.1]:5701 [dev] [3.8.2] Backpressure is disabled
15:45:23.702 [main] INFO  com.hazelcast.instance.Node -
[192.168.56.1]:5701
[dev] [3.8.2] Creating MulticastJoiner
15:45:23.871 [main] INFO  c.h.s.i.o.impl.OperationExecutorImpl
-
```

```
[192.168.56.1]:5701 [dev] [3.8.2] Starting 8 partition threads
15:45:23.871 [main] INFO  c.h.s.i.o.impl.OperationExecutorImpl
-
[192.168.56.1]:5701 [dev] [3.8.2] Starting 5 generic threads (1
dedicated for priority tasks)
15:45:23.871 [main] INFO  com.hazelcast.core.LifecycleService -
[192.168.56.1]:5701 [dev] [3.8.2] [192.168.56.1]:5701 is
STARTING
15:45:26.435 [main] INFO  com.hazelcast.system -
[192.168.56.1]:5701 [dev]
[3.8.2] Cluster version set to 3.8
15:45:26.437 [main] INFO  c.h.i.cluster.impl.MulticastJoiner -
[192.168.56.1]:5701
[dev] [3.8.2]
Members [1] {
   Member [192.168.56.1]:5701 - 3b7936c6-9eda-479a-
ba21-02552e3b24b1
   this
}
15:45:26.477 [main] INFO  c.h.internal.jmx.ManagementService -
[192.168.56.1]:5701 [dev] [3.8.2] Hazelcast JMX agent enabled.
15:45:26.501 [main] INFO  com.hazelcast.core.LifecycleService -
[192.168.56.1]:5701 [dev] [3.8.2] [192.168.56.1]:5701 is
STARTED
```

8. Again, run the same application but with a different port. Observe the following log file:

```
15:54:54.784 [main] INFO  c.h.i.cluster.impl.MulticastJoiner -
[192.168.56.1]:5702
[dev] [3.8.2] Trying to join to discovered node:
[192.168.56.1]:5701
15:54:54.786 [hz.hazelcast-packt-cache.cached.thread-2] INFO
c.h.nio.tcp.InitConnectionTask - [192.168.56.1]:5702 [dev]
[3.8.2] Connecting to /192.168.56.1:5701, timeout: 0, bind-any:
true
15:54:54.796 [hz.hazelcast-packt-cache.IO.thread-Acceptor] INFO
c.h.nio.tcp.SocketAcceptorThread - [192.168.56.1]:5701 [dev]
[3.8.2]
Accepting socket connection from /192.168.56.1:31400
15:54:54.806 [hz.hazelcast-packt-cache.cached.thread-2] INFO
c.h.nio.tcp.TcpIpConnectionManager - [192.168.56.1]:5702 [dev]
[3.8.2]
Established socket connection between /192.168.56.1:31400 and
/192.168.56.1:5701
15:54:54.806 [hz.hazelcast-packt-cache.cached.thread-3] INFO
c.h.nio.tcp.TcpIpConnectionManager - [192.168.56.1]:5701 [dev]
[3.8.2]
```

```
Established socket connection between /192.168.56.1:5701 and
/192.168.56.1:31400
```

How it works...

Most of the time, distributed database architecture is an option to optimize monolithic databases in a clustered enterprise ecosystem. With this setup, some servers, which can house microservices, may share data through their own models of data communication. Now, this recipe provides another solution for optimizing data operations by setting up a distributed data caching, instead of distributed databases in a distributed ecosystem of microservices.

Spring Boot 2.0 offers a built-in `HazelcastAutoConfiguration` class, which does not require a separate caching server just to establish the nodes of Hazelcast cache instances. Once applications or microservices that have Hazelcast caches are deployed, their instances will autodiscover each other and will form a cluster. Instead of connecting to the dedicated data source, a cluster can just provide a reference to the Hazelcast node of another service box to retrieve data in that cache.

As we all know, Hazelcast is a popular distributed in-memory tool popular for any grid project when it comes to caching. Its most important API, which is `com.hazelcast.core.HazelcastInstance`, can be configured either by using an XML file or a Java Configuration class just like in this recipe. If XML configuration is used, drop the file in `src\main\resources` and register its location in `application.properties` through the `spring.hazelcast.config` property.

If there is no plan for building, distributed applications or microservices, using Ehcache is already a perfect data caching solution to optimize huge data retrieval.

Building client-server communications with WebSocket

Just like its predecessors, Spring 5 supports a high-frequency but low-latency data exchange between a client and a server using a `websocket` protocol. This recipe will just provide a step-by-step procedure on how to implement raw and real-time WebSocket messaging without using any third-party brokers.

Getting ready

Create a new Maven project, `ch12-websocket`, that will implement the simple and non-reactive `TextSocketWebHandler` to entertain complaints from clients.

How to do it...

Let us create a simple messenger by performing the following steps:

1. First, convert `ch12-websocket` to the Spring Boot 2.0 application by to `pom.xml` the Spring Boot 2.0.0.M2 starter POM dependencies, such as Spring WebFlux for Reactive components and Spring Boot actuator for project status monitoring and management.

2. To add support for the `websocket` protocol, add the following starter POM dependency in `pom.xml`:

```
<dependency>
    <groupId>org.springframework.boot</groupId>
    <artifactId>spring-boot-starter-websocket</artifactId>
</dependency>
```

3. To convert message payloads in JSON format to Java objects, add the following additional Maven dependency:

```
<dependency>
        <groupId>com.google.code.gson</groupId>
        <artifactId>gson</artifactId>
</dependency>
```

4. Inside the core package `org.packt.messaging.core`, add the following typical Bootstrap class:

```
@SpringBootApplication
public class ChatBootApplication {
  public static void main(String[] args) throws Exception {
      SpringApplication.run(ChatBootApplication.class,
          args);
    }
}
```

5. Inside `src\main\resources`, create an `application.properties` file that contains basic autoconfiguration details similar to the previous projects. No special properties for WebSocket support are needed to be registered here.

6. Copy the `config` folder and `logback.xml` from the previous projects. Update the logger information of the `logback.xml` file.

7. To manage the incoming payloads and outgoing messages, implement a custom handler inside the `org.packt.messaging.core.config` package through the `org.springframework.web.socket.handler.TextWebSocketHandler` API. This handler will utilize the `Gson()` utility to convert JSON payloads from the client to valid Java String objects. Moreover, this is the only `@Component` annotation where sessions are established per message received:

```
@Component
public class HotlineSocketHandler extends TextWebSocketHandler
{
    List<WebSocketSession> sessions = new
CopyOnWriteArrayList<>();

    @Override
    public void handleTextMessage(WebSocketSession session,
            TextMessage message)
        throws InterruptedException, IOException {
      for(WebSocketSession webSocketSession : sessions) {
        Map value = new
            Gson().fromJson(message.getPayload(),
              Map.class);
        String[] data =
            value.get("data").toString().split(",");
        webSocketSession.sendMessage(
new TextMessage("Dear " +
        data[0] + ", you complaint is now ..."));
      }
    }

    @Override
    public void afterConnectionEstablished(
WebSocketSession session) throws Exception {
        sessions.add(session);
    }
}
```

8. This WebSocket messaging needs an endpoint that a client can be used to open message the communication channels. This endpoint is a unique URL mapped to one custom handler by the `org.springframework.web.socket.config.annotation.WebSocketConfigurer` class. This `@Configuration` class must enable WebSocket support in Spring Boot by applying the class-level annotation `@EnableWebSocket`:

```
@Configuration
@EnableWebSocket
public class ChatSocketConfig implements WebSocketConfigurer {

    public void registerWebSocketHandlers(
WebSocketHandlerRegistry registry) {
        registry.addHandler(new HotlineSocketHandler(),
            "/data");
    }

}
```

9. At this point, we are finished configuring the server side of this application. It is time to set up the client side of the application by creating the required static resources needed to face the users. All these HTML, CSS, and JS files must be dropped inside a `static` folder, `src/main/resources`, in order for Spring Boot to auto recognize them:

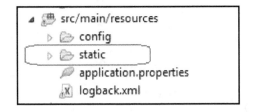

10. Now, inside the `static` folder, drop some HTML Bootstrap files (for example, `bootstrap.min.css`) for response web design, and jQuery JS files (for example, `jquery-xxxx-min.js`) for client-side socket implementation. Another option is to import these files from `https://cdnjs.com/libraries/jquery/`.

11. Create an HTML 5 page, `hotline.html`, which will serve as the client of the application. It will contain form data needed to be sent through the WebSocket channels:

```
<!DOCTYPE html>
<html>
<head>
    <title>Chapter 12</title>
```

```
        <link href="./bootstrap.min.css" rel="stylesheet">
        <link href="./main.css" rel="stylesheet">
        <script src="./jquery-1.10.2.min.js"></script>
</head>
<body>
        <div class="col-md-6">
            <form id="complaintForm" class="form-inline">
                <div class="form-group">
                    <label for="name">What is your name?
</label>
                    <input type="text" id="name"
class="form-control"
placeholder="Your name here...">
                    <label for="complaint">
What is your complaint?
 </label>
                    <input type="text" id="complaint"
                        class="form-control"
placeholder="Your complaint here...">
                </div>
                <button id="send"
class="btn btn-success"
                    type="submit">Send</button>
            </form>
        </div>
        <div class="row">
          <div class="col-md-12">
            <table id="helpdesk" class="table table-hover">
                <thead>
                <tr>
                    <th>Customer Service</th>
                </tr>
                </thead>
                <tbody id="feedbacks">
                </tbody>
            </table>
        </div>
    </div>
</body>
</html>
```

Assign the necessary element ID to each of the form components.

12. All the client-side WebSocket connections and transactions happen inside a JavaScript file. Using the jQuery API, create the following `socketapp.js` file, which implements some event handlers such as `connect()`, `disconnect()`, and `sendFormData()`:

```javascript
var ws;
function setConnected(connected) {
    $("#connect").prop("disabled", connected);
    $("#disconnect").prop("disabled", !connected);
    if (connected) {
        $("#helpdesk").show();
    }
    else {
        $("#helpdesk").hide();
    }
    $("#feedbacks").html("");
}

function connect() {
    ws = new WebSocket('ws://localhost:8085/
ch12-websocket/data');
    ws.onmessage = function(data){
        showFeedbacks(data.data);
    }
     setConnected(true);
}

function disconnect() {
    if (ws != null) {
        ws.close();
    }
    setConnected(false);
    console.log("Disconnected");
}

function sendFormData() {
    var data = JSON.stringify({'data': $("#name").val() +
        "," + $("#complaint").val()})
    ws.send(data);
}

function showFeedbacks (message) {
    $("#feedbacks").append("<tr><td><em> " + message +
        "</em></td></tr>");
}

$(function () {
```

```
$("form").on('submit', function (e) {
    e.preventDefault();
});
$( "#connect" ).click(function() { connect(); });
$( "#disconnect" ).click(function() { disconnect(); });
$( "#send" ).click(function() { sendFormData(); });
});
```

13. Import `socketapps.js` inside `hotline.html` using the `<script>` tag.

14. Save all files. `Clean`, `build`, and `deploy` the Spring Boot application. Open a browser and execute
`http://localhost:8085/ch12-websocket/hotline.html`:

How it works...

One of the popular solutions nowadays in building web-based real-time communication is WebSocket, which utilizes a TCP connection in establishing client-server communication. This communication strategy allows saving client sessions at the server side, which enhances bi-directional communication between the client and the server. Lots of payload converters and serializers are available nowadays that can help scrutinize and persist messages for security and audit purposes. Moreover, communication using WebSocket is lighter than the usual HTTP-based strategy, since the header information involved during the process is less. In the WebSocket client and in server exchange, the transfer of data per frame is at least 2 bytes compared to HTTP-based communications, which can take at least 8 Kb per frame. Some requirements may not apply low-latency communication, which will always need an HTTP header exchange.

Implementing Reactive WebSocket communication

It is only with Spring 5 that APIs for Reactive WebSocket communication are available to build an ideal, resilient, optimized, and real-time client-server messaging without too many complicated configurations. Part of the additional Reactive modules added to Spring Boot 2.0 are the classes and interfaces ready to build WebSocket communications that utilize the `Flux<T>` and `Mono<T>` stream payloads, with backpressure operators applied during bi-directional stream processing.

Getting ready

Create another Maven project, `ch12-messenger`, needed to implement a mini-chat room based on the Reactive WebSocket APIs.

How to do it...

Let us build a fast and asynchronous messenger using Reactive WebSocket by performing the following steps:

1. Just like in the previous recipe, convert `ch12-messenger` to a Spring Boot 2.0 application by adding the Spring Boot 2.0.0.M2 starter POM dependencies, like `webflux`, `actuator` for project status monitoring and management, and the `websocket` protocol we recently used.

 There is no Reactive counterpart for the POM starter WebSocket.

2. Inside the core package `org.packt.messenger.core`, add the following Bootstrap class:

```
@SpringBootApplication
public class ChatBootApplication {
    public static void main(String[] args) throws Exception {
        SpringApplication.run(ChatBootApplication.class,
            args);
    }
}
```

3. The `application.properties` file inside the `src/main/resources` directory will be just the same as in the previous recipe.

4. Enable logging using logback and SLF4J.

5. Implement `org.springframework.web.reactive.socket.WebSocketHandler`, which is the appropriate custom handler for incoming Reactive sessions wrapped in an `org.springframework.web.reactive.socket.WebSocketSession`. It has a `handle()` method that manages the communication between the client and server by retrieving the message payloads in the form of the `Flux<WebSocketMessage>` streams that no converters or serializers can process, but only through a reactor server. Drop `@Component` inside `org.packt.messaging.core.handler`:

```
@Component
public class MessageWebSocketHandler implements
WebSocketHandler {
    @Override
    public Mono<Void> handle(WebSocketSession session) {
        return session.send(session.receive()
        .map(str -> str.getPayloadAsText())
        .map(str -> "Howdy, " + str
+ "? Welcome to the Portal!")
        .map(session::textMessage))
        .delayElement(Duration.ofMillis(2)).log();
    }
}
```

In `WebSocketHandler`, it is mandatory for a server to broadcast its reply in the form of a `textMessage()` method. Also, it is essential to always include the `delayElement()` backpressure operator during simultaneous `Flux<WebSocketMessage>` exchanges to avoid server-related exceptions.

6. To enable WebSocket support and to build an entry point for each custom handler, implement the following WebSocket configuration inside the `org.packt.messaging.core.config` package. Unlike the non-reactive version, this configuration requires three beans to be injected into the container, namely the `org.springframework.web.reactive.HandlerMapping`, `org.springframework.web.reactive.socket.server.support.WebSocketHandlerAdapter`, and `org.springframework.web.reactive.socket.server.WebSocketService` packages. The `WebSocketHandlerAdapter` and `WebSocketService` methods automatically check and detect any container-specific `RequestUpgradeStrategy` that is needed to implement Reactive WebSocket handshakes through the endpoints:

```
@Configuration
@EnableWebSocket
public class ReactiveChatSocketConfig {

    @Autowired
    private WebSocketHandler messageWebSocketHandler;

    @Bean
    public HandlerMapping webSocketMapping() {
        Map<String, WebSocketHandler> map = new HashMap<>();
        map.put("/react", messageWebSocketHandler);
        SimpleUrlHandlerMapping mapping =
new SimpleUrlHandlerMapping();
        mapping.setOrder(10);
        mapping.setUrlMap(map);
        return mapping;
    }

    @Bean
    public WebSocketHandlerAdapter handlerAdapter() {
        return new WebSocketHandlerAdapter(
webSocketService());
    }

    @Bean
    public WebSocketService webSocketService() {
        return new HandshakeWebSocketService(
new ReactorNettyRequestUpgradeStrategy());
    }
}
```

7. In order to create a Reactive WebSocket handshake, which will eventually transfer `Flux<WebSocketMessage>` from client to server and vice versa, a server-specific strategy used to initiate the WebSocket exchange is required. The embedded Tomcat does not have this so called `RequestUpgradeStrategy`, but the **Reactor Netty server** has. Drop this Reactor Netty configuration class, used in the previous chapters, in order to run our reactive chatroom:

```
@Configuration
@EnableWebFlux
public class HttpServerConfig implements WebFluxConfigurer{
    @Bean
    public NettyContext nettyContext(ApplicationContext context)
{
        HttpHandler handler =
            DispatcherHandler.toHttpHandler(context);
        ReactorHttpHandlerAdapter adapter =
new ReactorHttpHandlerAdapter(handler);
        HttpServer httpServer =
HttpServer.create("localhost",
    Integer.valueOf("8908"));
        return httpServer.newHandler(adapter).block();
    }
}
```

8. At this point, we are finished building the server side aspect of this Reactive WebSocket project. Let's start building the client side by having an HTML 5 `client.html` page inside the `src/main/resources/static` folder of the application:

```
<!DOCTYPE html>
<html>
<head>
    <title>Chapter 12</title>
    <link href="./bootstrap.min.css" rel="stylesheet">
    <link href="./main.css" rel="stylesheet">
    <script src="./jquery-1.10.2.min.js"></script>
</head>
<body>
<div id="main-content" class="container">
    <div class="row">
        <H2>GreetMe Portal</H2>
        <div class="col-md-12">
            <form class="form-inline">
                <div id="greetForm" class="form-group">
                    <label for="name">What is your name?
    </label>
```

```
                        <input type="text" id="name"
class="form-control"
placeholder="Your name here...">
                        <label for="greet">Say your greetings?
 </label>
                        <input type="text" id="greet"
class="form-control"
placeholder="Your greeting here...">
                        <button id="send"
class="btn btn-success"
                                type="submit">Send</button>
                </div>
            </form>
        </div>
    </div>
    <div class="row">
        <div class="col-md-12">
            <table id="greetings" class="table
table-hover">
                <thead>
                <tr>
                    <th>Conversation with Portal</th>
                </tr>
                </thead>
                <tbody id="conversations">
                </tbody>
            </table>
        </div>
    </div>
</div>
</body>
</html>
```

Ensure that you assign the element tag ID to the form components.

9. Now, implement the WebSocket client event handlers, namely `onopen()` and `onmessage()`. Drop the `reactivesocketapp.js` file as a static resource inside the `static` folder:

```
$(document).ready(function () {
        var socket = new
WebSocket("ws://localhost:8908/react");
        socket.onopen = function (event) {
            var newMessage = document.createElement('p');
            newMessage.textContent =
"--- CONVERSATION READY";
            document.getElementById('conversations')
.appendChild(newMessage);
            socket.onmessage = function (e) {
                var newMessage =
                    document.createElement('p');
                newMessage.textContent =
"--- PORTAL: " + e.data;
                document.getElementById('conversations')
.appendChild(newMessage);
            }
            $("#send").click(function (e) {
                e.preventDefault();
                var message = $("#name").val();
                socket.send(message);
                var newMessage =
                    document.createElement('p');
                newMessage.textContent =
"--- GUEST: " + message;
                document.getElementById('conversations')
.appendChild(newMessage);
            });
        }
});
```

The IP address and port of the Reactor Netty server must be the details used in establishing a Reactive WebSocket connection.

10. Import `reactivesocketapps.js` inside `client.html` using the `<script>` tag.
11. Save all files. `Clean`, `build`, and `deploy` the Spring Boot application.

12. Open a browser and go to
    `http://localhost:8085/ch12-messenger/client.html`:

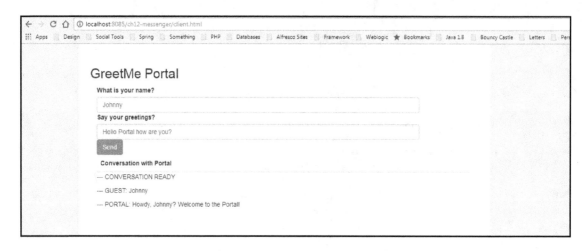

How it works...

The reactive approach to WebSocket is necessary when the requirement for client-server messaging involves an unbounded number of request streams and event subscriptions. The request handler instances can be instantiated infinitely, wherein each is being managed by an assigned thread. Then, these instances can be shared among existing WebSocket connections triggered by the client. To confirm this behavior, open the `ch12-messenger.log` project and study this audit from the request handler created in the preceding recipe:

```
18:14:27.878 [reactor-http-nio-2] INFO   reactor.Mono.DelayElement.1 -
    onSubscribe([Fuseable] MonoDelayElement.DelayElementSubscriber)
18:14:27.879 [reactor-http-nio-2] INFO   reactor.Mono.DelayElement.1 -
    request(unbounded)
```

The reactive data exchange should be managed by a reactive application server that supports the `RequestUpgradeStrategy` component, which is a kind of container needed for the Reactive WebSocket handshake. Unfortunately, Tomcat 9.x does not support `RequestUpgradeStrategy` by default, which means it is not capable of recognizing Reactive sessions with `Flux<WebSocketMessage>` as payloads.

Implementing asynchronous Spring Data JPA properties

Previously, we had lots of recipes and snippets regarding how to build repositories using the Spring Data JPA module through Spring Boot 2.0. All the repository properties created earlier were mostly non-blocking that return typical collections of model data. This recipe will focus on asynchronous `JpaRepository` properties that retrieve `Future<T>`, `CompletableFuture<T>`, and `ListenableFuture<T>`.

Getting ready

Create a new Maven project, `ch12-asyncjpa`, that will implement the Spring Data JPA with asynchronous properties.

How to do it...

Let us now explore the asynchronous side of Spring Data JPA module:

1. Convert `ch12-asyncjpa` to a Spring Boot 2.0 application by adding the Spring Boot 2.0.0.M2*starter* POM dependencies, such as `webflux`, `actuator` for project status monitoring and management, Spring JDBC, and MYSQL connector.

2. Since there is no dedicated Spring Data JPA module for asynchronous repository transactions, add the same starter POM dependencies for Spring Data JPA to `pom.xml`:

```
<dependency>
        <groupId>org.springframework.boot</groupId>
        <artifactId>spring-boot-starter-data-jpa</artifactId>
</dependency>
```

3. Inside the core package, `org.packt.microservice.core`, add the following Bootstrap class:

```
@SpringBootApplication
public class HRDeptBootApplication
extends  SpringBootServletInitializer  {
   // refer to sources
}
```

4. Copy the `config` folder and `logback.xml` from the previous project to `src/main/resources`. Update the log file details of `logback.xml`.

5. Inside the `src/main/resources` directory, add `application.properties` that contains the same details as the previous Spring Data JPA project. Since we will rely on the auto-increment feature of MySQL for object ID generation, always set `spring.jpa.hibernate.use-new-id-generator-mappings` to `false` to allow data persistence.

6. To configure the Spring Data JPA module, add the following configuration class inside `org.packt.microservice.core.config`, which will enable JPA transaction management:

```
@Configuration
@EnableJpaRepositories(
        basePackages="org.packt.microservice.core.dao")
@EnableTransactionManagement
public class SpringDataConfig { }
```

7. Enable asynchronous features though this configuration class that also generates thread pools through `Executor`:

```
@EnableAsync
@Configuration
public class SpringAsynchConfig implements AsyncConfigurer {
    private static Logger logger =
        LoggerFactory.getLogger(SpringAsynchConfig.class);
        @Bean("mvcTaskexecutor")
        @Override
        public Executor getAsyncExecutor() {
          ConcurrentTaskExecutor executor =
            new ConcurrentTaskExecutor(
                    Executors.newFixedThreadPool(100));
          executor.setTaskDecorator(new TaskDecorator() {
            @Override
            public Runnable decorate (Runnable
            runnable) {
                return () -> {
                    long t =
                      System.currentTimeMillis();
                    runnable.run();
                    logger.info("creating thread
                      pool....");
                    System.out.printf("Thread %s has a
                    processing time:  %s%n",
Thread.currentThread().getName(),
(System.currentTimeMillis() - t));
```

```
                    };
                }
            });
            return executor;
        }
    }
```

8. Copy the JPA `Department` entity model from the previous project to the
   `org.packt.microservice.core.model.data` package.

9. Now, create the `DepartmentRepository` interface using `JpaRepository`,
   showcasing the implementation of asynchronous properties as follows:

```
@Repository
public interface DepartmentRepository
extends JpaRepository<Department, Integer>{
    @Async
    public Future<List<Department>>
findAllByDeptid(Integer deptid);
    @Async
    public CompletableFuture<Department>
      findIgnoreCaseByName(String name);
    @Async
    public ListenableFuture<Department>
      findDeptById(Integer id);

}
```

10. Then, create a `DepartmentService` interface that has the following services.
    Drop this file inside the `org.packt.microservice.core.service` package:

```
public interface DepartmentService {
    public List<Department> findAllDeptList();
    public Department findAllDeptById(Integer id);
    public List<Department> findAllByDeptName(String name);
    public Future<List<Department>>
findAllByDeptId(Integer deptId);
    public CompletableFuture<Department>
        findAllFirstByNameIgnoreCase(String name);
    public ListenableFuture<Department>
findAllFirstById(Integer id);
}
```

11. To implement the services, just apply the asynchronous properties from
    `DepartmentRepository`:

```
@Service
public class DepartmentServiceImpl implements
DepartmentService{
    @Autowired
    private DepartmentRepository departmentRepository;

    @Override
    public Future<List<Department>>
findAllByDeptId(Integer deptId) {
        return departmentRepository.findAllByDeptid(deptId);
    }

    @Override
    public CompletableFuture<Department>
                findAllFirstByNameIgnoreCase(String name) {
        return departmentRepository
.findIgnoreCaseByName(name);
    }

    @Override
    public ListenableFuture<Department>
findAllFirstById(Integer id) {
        return departmentRepository.findDeptById(id);
}

    // refer to sources

}
```

12. We have come to the highlight of this recipe, which is the implementation of the
    request handlers given the asynchronous data retrieval from
    `DepartmentRepository`. These request handlers just reuse the concepts
    discussed in the previous chapters on how to build callbacks which retrieve the
    exact data from `Future<T>`, `CompletableFuture<T>`, and
    `ListenableFuture<T>`.

13. Create `@Controller`, bearing all these request methods inside
    `org.packt.microservice.core.controller`:

```
@RestController
public class DeptAsyncController {
    @Autowired
    private DepartmentService departmentServiceImpl;
    private Department result = new Department();
    @GetMapping(value="/webSyncDept/{id}.json",
```

```
         produces ="application/json",
         headers = {"Accept=text/xml, application/json"})
            public WebAsyncTask<Department> websyncDeptList(
                        @PathVariable("id") Integer id){
                Callable<Department> callable =
                        new Callable<Department>() {
                    public Department call() throws Exception {
                        ListenableFuture<Department> listenFuture =
                          departmentServiceImpl.findAllFirstById(id);
                        listenFuture.addCallback(
         new ListenableFutureCallback<Department>(){

                          @Override
                          public void onSuccess(Department dept) {
                            result = dept;
                          }

                          @Override
                          public void onFailure(Throwable arg0) {
                            result = new Department();
                          }
                      });
                    return result;
                    }
            };
            return new WebAsyncTask<Department>(500, callable);
        }
    @GetMapping(value="/deferSelectDept/{name}.json",
    produces ="application/json",
    headers = {"Accept=text/xml, application/json"})
        public DeferredResult<Department> deferredSelectDept(
            @PathVariable("name") String name) {
            DeferredResult<Department> deferredResult =
                    new DeferredResult<>();
            CompletableFuture.supplyAsync(()->{
              try {
                return departmentServiceImpl
                  .findAllFirstByNameIgnoreCase(name)
                  .get(500, TimeUnit.MILLISECONDS);
              } catch (InterruptedException e) {
                e.printStackTrace();
              } catch (ExecutionException e) {
                e.printStackTrace();
              } catch (TimeoutException e) {
                // TODO Auto-generated catch block
                e.printStackTrace();
              }
              return null;
```

```
        }).thenAccept((msg)->{
          deferredResult.setResult(msg);
        });
        return deferredResult;
    }
    // refer to sources
}
```

14. Save all files. Then `clean`, `build`, and `deploy` the microservice.

How it works...

Although this asynchronous JPA feature appears in its previous version, Spring 5 still supports the `@Async` repository transactions to enhance multiple and simultaneous CRUD transactions. At the DAO layer, these asynchronous JPA properties promote resiliency among the request handlers just by providing them the necessary callback handlers through which the data processing will be managed, not only during success but also when failure happens along the way. Also, these kinds of DAO transactions give requests time delays to process the response within a specific and practical time frame.

Implementing Reactive Spring Data JPA repositories

After the synchronous repository methods, this recipe will showcase the Spring 5 support for Reactive Spring Data JPA repositories. If you are expecting that this recipe will be used for relational databases, this Reactive Spring Data JPA is feasible only for NoSQL databases such as MongoDB and Couchbase, and not with MySQL and other relational databases.

Getting ready

Create another Maven project, `ch12-mongodb`, that will be used to implement the Reactive Spring Data JPA with a MongoDB database.

How to do it...

Let us utilize Reactive Spring Data JPA by performing the following steps:

1. Convert `ch12-mongodb` to a Spring Boot 2.0 application by adding the Spring Boot 2.0.0.M2 starter POM dependencies, such as `webflux`, `actuator` for project status monitoring and management, Spring JDBC, MySQL connector, and the Spring Data JPA starter POM that we just used.

 There is no reactive counterpart for the Spring Data JPA's `CrudRepository` and `JpaRepository`.

2. Before anything else, verify that you have installed the recent binary for the MongoDB server in your system. If not, go back to Chapter 1, *Getting Started with Spring*, and follow the procedure on how to install the MongoDB server.

3. To turn on the MongoDB server, open a command-line terminal and run the server using the `\bin\mongod` command.

4. Open another terminal and open the server shell through `\bin\mongo`. Using MongoDB tutorials from https://docs.mongodb.com/manual/tutorial/, we are now ready to administer and manage a MongoDB database.

5. Create a `hrs` database by running the `use hrs` command.

6. Create an `employee` collection and insert a record in it using the following command:

```
db.employee.insert({ "id":23456, "firstName": "Sherwin John",
"lastName": "Tragura", "age":39, "email":"sjctrags@gmail.com",
"birthday":"10-30-1978", "deptid":359})
```

7. Add more document records to `employee` and then view all `Collections` using the `db.employee.find()` command.

NoSQL databases, such as MongoDB, leverage **JSON** as the core data model. Thus, use data types that are recognizable only to JSON documents such as `Long`, `Double`, `String`, `Boolean`, and other JSON objects defined by MongoDB.

8. After the entire MongoDB server configuration and database setup, let's create the Bootstrap class for our Spring Boot application inside a core package, `org.packt.nosql.mongo.core`:

```
@SpringBootApplication
public class MongoBootApplication
extends  SpringBootServletInitializer  {
    // refer to sources
}
```

9. Copy the `config` folder and `logback.xml` from the previous recipe. Update the log file details correctly to enable logging for this application.

10. Create an `application.properties` file for this project containing all the server-related and MySQL database-related information for JPA autoconfiguration. The only irony here is that we will not be using any MySQL features in this recipe. We just need to comply with the JPA autoconfiguration process for the implementation of its transaction management beans.

11. Inside `org.packt.nosql.mongo.core.config`, add a Reactive Spring Data configuration class that looks similar to the one from previous recipes:

```
@Configuration
@EnableJpaRepositories(
basePackages="org.packt.nosql.mongo.core.dao")
@EnableTransactionManagement
public class ReactiveDataConfig { }
```

12. Since the base storage unit of MongoDB is an entity called `document`, create an entity model needed for persisting the `Employee` documents into the Mongo database. Drop this document object inside the `org.packt.nosql.mongo.core.model.data` package:

```
@Document(collection="employee")
public class Employee   {
    private BigInteger _id;
    @Id
    private Long id;
    private Long empid;
    private String firstname;
    private String lastname;
```

```
            private Long age;
            private String email;
            private Date birthday;
            private Long deptid;
            @PersistenceConstructor
            public Employee(Long id, BigInteger _id, Long empid,
        String firstname, String lastname, Long age,
        String email, Date birthday, Long deptid) {
                super();
                this.id = id;
                this._id = _id;
                this.empid = empid;
                this.firstname = firstname;
                this.lastname = lastname;
                this.age = age;
                this.email = email;
                this.birthday = birthday;
                this.deptid = deptid;
        }
        // getters and setters
        }
```

 We declared the custom **employee** id as the primary @Id of the entity
model and not BigInteger _id, which is the default object ID assigned
to each document by the Mongo server. Likewise, there is a shift from
Integer to Long data types in this entity model due to the data type
constraints of JSON.

13. Inside org.packt.nosql.mongo.core.dao, create a custom
EmployeeRepository interface that will highlight the Reactive API class
org.springframework.data.repository.reactive.ReactiveCrudReposi
tory:

```
@Repository
public interface EmployeeRepository
extends ReactiveCrudRepository<Employee, Long>{
    public Flux<Employee> findAllById(Flux<Long> ids);
    public Flux<Employee> findAllByFirstname(String fname);
    public Flux<Employee> findAllByLastname(String lname);
}
```

14. Create an Employee service class that will consist of the following template
methods:

```
public interface EmployeeService {
    public Flux<Employee> getAllEmps();
```

```
        public Flux<Employee> getAllEmps(Flux<Long> ids);
        public Mono<Employee> getEmpByid(Long id);
        public Flux<Employee> getEmpsByFname(String fname);
        public Flux<Employee> getEmpsByLname(String lname);
        public void saveEmp(Employee emp);
        public void saveEmps(Flux<Employee> emps);
    }
```

15. Implement the preceding service class using the reactive `EmployeeRepository` class:

```
@Service
public class EmployeeServiceImpl implements EmployeeService{
    @Autowired
    private EmployeeRepository employeeRepository;

    @Override
    public Flux<Employee> getAllEmps() {
        return employeeRepository.findAll();
    }

    @Override
    public Flux<Employee> getAllEmps(Flux<Long> ids) {
        return employeeRepository.findAllById(ids);
    }

    @Override
    public Mono<Employee> getEmpByid(Long id) {
        return employeeRepository.findById(id);
    }
}
// refer to sources
}
```

16. Inside `org.packt.nosql.mongo.core.controller`, create `EmReactiveController`, which will execute the Reactive services implemented:

```
@RestController
public class EmpReactiveController {
    @Autowired
    private EmployeeService employeeServiceImpl;
    @GetMapping("/selectReactEmps")
    public Flux<Employee> selectReactDepts() {
        return employeeServiceImpl.getAllEmps();
    }
    @GetMapping("/selectReactEmp/{id}")
    public Mono<Employee> selectReactDept(
@PathVariable("id") Long id) {
```

```
                    return employeeServiceImpl.getEmpByid(id);
            }
        }
```

17. Save all files. Then `clean`, `build`, and `deploy` the application.

18. Open a browser and run one of the REST services:

How it works...

Currently, Spring Boot has dedicated support for **MongoDB**, **Apache Cassandra**, **Couchbase**, and **Redis** when it comes to reactive repository transactions. Any document-based database can be used to store, retrieve, update, and delete data using Reactive streams operations as long as Spring Data JPA can detect their server configurations. Currently, there is still no reactive support for relational databases like MySQL, but we can write asynchronous repository transactions as discussed in the previous recipe.

Using Spring Data MongoDB

Spring Framework has been supporting MongoDB, Apache Cassandra, and Redis when it comes to NoSQL data transactions. Each data repository has its own Spring Data module that developers can use without much effort on the configuration side. Spring 5, with the help of Spring Boot 2.0, can still provide support to MongoDB, and both non-blocking and Reactive repository transactions. But this recipe is all about implementing **Reactive Spring Data MongoDB** repository properties.

Getting ready

Again, open `ch12-mongodb` without removing previous **Spring Data JPA** reactive components.

How to do it...

Let us not use the dedicated Spring Data MongoDB to implement Reactive repository transactions:

1. Add the following Reactive Spring Data MongoDB dependency in the `pom.xml` file:

```
<dependency>
    <groupId>org.springframework.boot</groupId>
    <artifactId>spring-boot-starter-data-mongodb-reactive
</artifactId>
</dependency>
```

2. Open the `application.properties` file and add the following MongoDB server configuration details:

```
spring.data.mongodb.host=localhost
spring.data.mongodb.port=27017
spring.data.mongodb.database=app1
```

3. Before we proceed, create another `Collections` in the `hrs` database, but this time composed of the `Department` records. Insert a few documents using the Mongo commands mentioned in the previous recipe.

4. Go back again to the Spring Eclipse STS. Create a `Department` model, which will be used by the application to transact with the Mongo database. Drop this file inside the `org.packt.nosql.mongo.core.model.data` package:

```
@Document(collection="department")
public class Department {
    private BigInteger _id;
    @Id
    private Long id;
    private Long deptid;
    private String name;
    @PersistenceConstructor
    public Department(BigInteger _id, Long id, Long deptid,
String name) {
        super();
        this._id = _id;
        this.id = id;
        this.deptid = deptid;
        this.name = name;
    }
// setters and getters
}
```

5. Create a configuration class inside `org.packt.nosql.mongo.core.config`, which will enable MongoDB transaction management. This class must inherit `org.springframework.data.mongodb.config.AbstractReactiveMongoConfiguration` to inject some beans needed to establish Reactive MongoDB CRUD transactions, such as `ReactiveMongoTemplate`:

```
@Configuration
@EnableReactiveMongoRepositories(
basePackages="org.packt.nosql.mongo.core.dao")
@EnableWebFlux
public class MongoConfig
extends AbstractReactiveMongoConfiguration {

    @Override
    public MongoClient mongoClient() {
        return MongoClients.create();
    }

    @Override
    protected String getDatabaseName() {
        return "hrs";
    }
    @Bean
    public ReactiveMongoTemplate reactiveMongoTemplate() {
        return new ReactiveMongoTemplate(
mongoClient(), getDatabaseName());
    }
}
```

6. Now, let's create a MongoDB Reactive repository class inside `org.packt.nosql.mongo.core.dao` using its own Spring Data MongoDB module:

```
@Repository
public interface DepartmentRepository
extends ReactiveMongoRepository<Department, Long>{
    public Flux<Department> findAllById(Flux<Long> ids);
    public Flux<Department> findAllByName(String name);
}
```

7. Create a `Department` service class that consists of all Reactive services:

```
public interface DepartmentService {
    public Flux<Department> getAllDepts();
    public Flux<Department> getAllDepts(Flux<Long> ids);
    public Mono<Department> getDeptById(Long id);
```

```
        public void saveDept(Department dept);
        public void saveDepts(Flux<Department> depts);
    }
```

8. Implement all the services in `DepartmentService` using
   `DepartmentRepository`:

```
@Service
public class DepartmentServiceImpl implements
    DepartmentService {
    @Autowired
    private DepartmentRepository departmentRepository;

    @Override
    public Flux<Department> getAllDepts() {
        return departmentRepository.findAll();
    }

    @Override
    public Flux<Department> getAllDepts(Flux<Long> ids) {
        return departmentRepository.findAllById(ids);
    }

    @Override
    public Mono<Department> getDeptByid(Long id) {
        return departmentRepository.findById(id);
    }
    // refer to sources
}
```

9. Create REST services to use the following Reactive services. Save all files. Then
   `clean`, `build`, and `deploy` the application.

How it works...

This recipe illustrated how Spring 5 supports MongoDB when it comes to both typical and
Reactive Spring Data JPA. If an application needs non-blocking data repository
transactions, the typical `spring-boot-starter-data-mongodb` starter POM dependency
needs to be added in `pom.xml`. If the application is more of the resilient type, then the
`spring-boot-starter-data-mongodb-reactive` starter must be of the required
dependency. This kind of support is also true for Apache Cassandra and Redis.

Reactive Spring Data MongoDB is a module of Spring Data that provides support starting from entity models down to MongoDB reactive repositories, providing data from derived queries wrapped in a `Flux<T>` or `Mono<T>` stream. The module has both `ReactiveMongoRepository` and `ReactiveCrudRepository`, which can be used synonymously without any difference in performance, since the former is derived from the latter. The only matter here is the use of `ReactiveMongoTemplate`, which can make reference to Mongo databases with the help of `ReactiveMongoRepository` but not with `ReactiveCrudRepository`.

Since MongoDB is a document-based NoSQL database, it requires its entity model to be annotated with `@Document` to hold all the binary JSON (BSON) data to be persisted into its collections. The idea of `Collections` depicts the concept of a relation containing all Mongo unstructured documents. MongoDB is an unstructured database, so it has no concept of relational models such as databases and table schema.

The `@Id` annotation is associated with the primary key of the document and is mapped to the `Object` `_id` of `Collections` by default. To retrieve the `_id` per `Document`, include it inside the entity model as a `BigInteger` object, not to be confused with `Long id`, which is the custom data assigned per `Department` record.

To successfully retrieve data from `Collections`, each entity model must have a constructor with all the injected fields as parameters and a `@PersistenceConstructor` annotation mapped to it.

Building applications for big data storage

NoSQL databases have become popular nowadays in building big data storage. Spring has provided support for some of the most popular big data technologies like Hadoop. However, this recipe aims to implement an application that can persist and retrieve data from big data storage technology that is scalable, easy to configure and set up, and simple when it comes to sharding, replications, and CRUD transactions. Before this chapter ends, here is an implementation of Spring Boot 2.0 that connects to Apache CouchDB with fewer configuration details.

Getting ready

Create a new Maven project, `ch12-couch`, that will implement data persistence and retrieval from the CouchDB storage.

How to do it...

Let us build a Spring 5 application that uses Apache CouchDB for big data storage by performing the following steps:

1. First download the recent version of the **Apache CouchDB** installer from http://couchdb.apache.org/. Follow the installation procedure from their technical documentation at http://docs.couchdb.org/en/2.1.0/.

2. After a successful installation, open a browser and run `http://127.0.0.1:5984/_utils/`. This will launch **CouchDB Fauxton**, which is a web-based administration console for CouchDB. Verify the installation and create a root account using the console.

3. Then, click on the **Databases** setup option and **Log In** using your specified root account:

4. In the **Databases** dashboard, create a database named `hrs`:

5. Click on the newly created database so that you can view all the records or `DesignDocuments` in table, metadata, or JSON format:

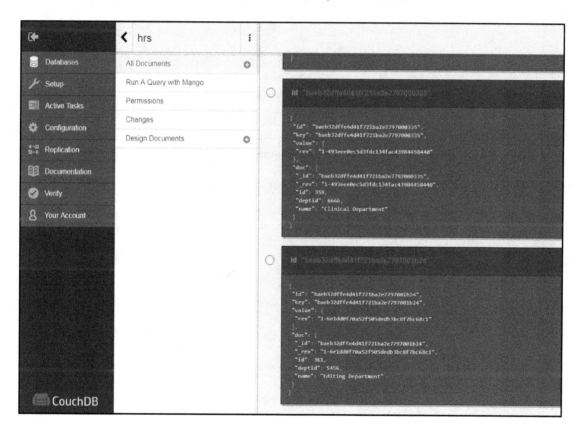

6. For the time being, that is all for CouchDB configuration and database setup. Let's shift to Spring STS Eclipse and convert `ch12-couchdb` into a Spring Boot 2.0 application. Just like in the previous recipes, add `webflux`, `actuator`, and a Spring MVC module for the `@RestController` implementation.

7. The simplest way to connect to CouchDB or Cloudant is to add this starter POM dependency inside `pom.xml`:

```
<dependency>
        <groupId>com.clianz</groupId>
        <artifactId>cloudant-spring-boot-starter</artifactId>
        <version>0.9.5</version>
</dependency>
```

8. Inside the core package `org.packt.nosql.couch.core`, add the following Bootstrap class:

```
@SpringBootApplication
public class CouchBootApplication
extends SpringBootServletInitializer  {
    // refer to sources
}
```

9. Copy the `config` folder and `logback.xml` from the other recipes and drop them in to `src/main/resources`. Edit logging details in `logback.xml` to enable logging correctly.

10. Create `application.properties` inside `src/main/resources` and register the actuator properties, server information, and database-related details needed for autoconfiguration. Also add the following CouchDB server details:

```
server.port=8090
server.servlet.context-path=/ch12-couch

// refer to sources
cloudant.username=packt
cloudant.password=spring5server
cloudant.url=http://localhost:5984
```

11. Add the following `@Configuration` annotation inside `org.packt.nosql.couch.core.config`, which injects the CouchDB databases required to connect. In our case, our big data infrastructure only has one database from one node address, and that is `hrs`:

```
@Configuration
public class CouchDbConfig {
    @Bean
    public Database hrsDb(CloudantClient cloudant) {
        return cloudant.database("hrs", true);
    }
}
```

12. Due to its simplicity, CouchDB and Cloudant only require a typical POJO with setters, getters, and a constructor in order to implement data persistence and retrieval. Create the `Department` POJO and drop this inside the `org.packt.nosql.couch.core.model.data` package:

```
public class Department {
    private Long id;
    private Long deptid;
    private String name;

    public Department(Long id, Long deptid, String name) {
        this.id = id;
        this.deptid = deptid;
        this.name = name;
    }
    // setters and getters
}
```

13. Inside `org.packt.nosql.couch.core.controller`, create the following REST service that retrieves all the current databases based on the Cloudant configuration, lists all `DesignDocuments` which are JSON-based `Department` records from `hrs`, and Couchbase database, and saves the `Department` document record as `DesignDocument`:

```
@RestController
public class CouchController {

    @Autowired
    private Database hrsDb;

    @Autowired
    private CloudantClient cloudant;
```

```
@GetMapping("/alldbs")
public List<String> checkdbs(){
    return cloudant.getAllDbs();
}

@GetMapping("/listDepts")
public List<Department> listDepts() throws IOException{
    return hrsDb.getAllDocsRequestBuilder()
    .includeDocs(true).build().getResponse()
    .getDocsAs(Department.class);
}

@GetMapping("/save/{id}/{deptid}/{name}")
public String saver(@PathVariable("id") Long id,
@PathVariable("deptid") Long deptid,
@PathVariable("name") String name) {
    Response resp = hrsDb.save(
    new Department(id, deptid, name));
    return resp.getReason();
}

}
```

14. Save all files. Then `clean`, `build`, and `deploy` the project.

How it works...

MongoDB and CouchDB are two different NoSQL databases when it comes to goals and objectives. MongoDB always promotes data integrity and consistency to all of its clients, while CouchDB applies map reduction to merge redundant data. As with building huge and distributed data storage, choosing CouchDB as the storage will consume less time in configuration than MongoDB, since the latter requires us to consider more details. Although CouchDB lacks SQL-like transactions and familiarity of data transactions, the implementation of its data persistency and retrieval requires less code and time. All its foundation objects are derived from its `com.cloudant.client.api.CloudantClient`, which carries all transactions, from retrieving all databases to data retrieval using map reductions.

Building a Spring 5 application using Kotlin

The last recipe of this chapter will be about a new feature integrated into the new platform of Spring 5, Kotlin. This is a JVM language created by **JetBrains** that can work with some Java APIs. This Kotlin extension is another powerful and concise option for writing a Spring 5 application that is at par with the Java-based style when it comes to performance and quality. Its short and readable language makes developers focus more on high-level requirements rather than the complex programming how-tos. This recipe will illustrate how to create Spring 5 applications with Reactive services using Kotlin.

Getting ready

Create the last Maven project for this chapter, `ch12-kot`, which will provide with us a microservice written in Kotlin.

How to do it...

Let us build a Spring 5 reactive web project using Kotlin by performing the following steps:

1. Convert the `ch12-kot` project to Spring Boot 2.0 by adding the parent starter POM of Spring Boot 2.0.0M2, including some major dependencies such as `webflux`, `actuator`, Spring JDBC, Spring Data JPA, and the MySQL connector plugin.

2. Inside the `<properties>` tag of `pom.xml`, add these lines specific to Kotlin plugins:

```
<kotlin.compiler.incremental>true
</kotlin.compiler.incremental>
        <kotlin.version>1.1.3-2</kotlin.version>
    <project.build.sourceEncoding>UTF-8
</project.build.sourceEncoding>
        <project.reporting.outputEncoding>UTF-8
</project.reporting.outputEncoding>
        <java.version>1.8</java.version>
        <startClass>
    org.packt.microservice.kotlin.KotlinBootApplication
    </startClass>
```

3. With the properties inserted, add the following `JetBrains` plugins for Kotlin dependencies:

```
<dependency>
        <groupId>org.jetbrains.kotlin</groupId>
        <artifactId>kotlin-stdlib-jre8</artifactId>
        <version>${kotlin.version}</version>
    </dependency>
    <dependency>
        <groupId>org.jetbrains.kotlin</groupId>
        <artifactId>kotlin-reflect</artifactId>
        <version>${kotlin.version}</version>
</dependency>
```

4. Maven will not compile Kotlin components without this Kotlin Maven plugin added to the `<plugins>` tag of the `pom.xml` file:

```
<plugin>
        <artifactId>kotlin-maven-plugin</artifactId>
        <groupId>org.jetbrains.kotlin</groupId>
        <version>${kotlin.version}</version>
        <configuration>
            <compilerPlugins>
                    <plugin>spring</plugin>
                    <plugin>jpa</plugin>
            </compilerPlugins>
            <jvmTarget>1.8</jvmTarget>
        </configuration>
        <executions>
            <execution>
                <id>compile</id>
                <phase>compile</phase>
                <goals>
                    <goal>compile</goal>
                </goals>
            </execution>
            <execution>
                <id>test-compile</id>
                <phase>test-compile</phase>
                <goals>
                    <goal>test-compile</goal>
                </goals>
            </execution>
        </executions>
        <dependencies>
            <dependency>
                <groupId>org.jetbrains.kotlin</groupId>
```

```
            <artifactId>kotlin-maven-allopen
</artifactId>
            <version>${kotlin.version}</version>
        </dependency>
        <dependency>
            <groupId>org.jetbrains.kotlin
</groupId>
            <artifactId>kotlin-maven-noarg
</artifactId>
            <version>${kotlin.version}</version>
        </dependency>
    </dependencies>
</plugin>
```

Always use the current Kotlin release and its compatible Java version. This recipe only covers Kotlin executed by Java 1.8 at runtime.

5. We are now ready to build the application. Inside a new package, `org.packt.microservice.kotlin`, create a file, `KotlinBootApplication.kt`, that contains the Bootstrap class:

```
@SpringBootApplication
open class KotlinBootApplication {
    companion object {
        @JvmStatic
        fun main(args: Array<String>) {
            SpringApplication.run(
KotlinBootApplication::class.java, *args)
        }
    }
}
```

There is no concept of `static` objects in Kotlin, so always wrap your object with `companion object {}` with the annotation `@JvmStatic` to convert it to static.

6. Copy the `config` folder and `logback.xml` from the previous recipe. Update the log file details correctly to enable logging for this application.

7. Create an `application.properties` file for this project, containing all the server-related and MySQL database-related information for JPA autoconfiguration.

8. Now, let's generate the JPA entity models in Kotlin. Here is a file, `Department.kt`, that contains an entity model, `Department`. Drop this class inside the `org.packt.microservice.kotlin.model.data` package:

```
@Entity
class Department {
    lateinit var id : Integer
    lateinit var name: String
    @Id @GeneratedValue(strategy = GenerationType.AUTO)
    lateinit var deptid: Integer
     constructor(
         id: Integer,
         name: String,
         deptid: Integer) {
             this.id = id
             this.name = name
             this.deptid = deptid
     }
}
```

9. Let's now create the JPA repository in the Kotlin language. Here is a Kotlin class that implements `CrudRepository<K, T>` to generate the blocking JPA properties:

```
interface DepartmentRepository :
CrudRepository<Department, Integer>{
    fun findByName(name: String): Iterable<Department>
    fun findByDeptid(deptid: Integer): Iterable<Department>
}
```

10. Lastly, create a Kotlin `@RestController` annotation inside `org.packt.microservice.kotlin.controller`, which contains a service that produces the `List<Department>` and `Flux<Department>` stream results:

```
@RestController
public class DepartmentController {
    @Autowired
     private lateinit var repository:DepartmentRepository

    @GetMapping("/listdepts")
    fun findAll() = repository.findAll()
```

```
@GetMapping("/listdepts/{name}")
fun findByName(@PathVariable name:String) =
    repository.findByName(name)
@GetMapping("/fluxdepts")
fun fluxDepts() = Flux.just(repository.findAll())
}
```

11. Save all files. Then `clean`, `build`, and `deploy` the Kotlin microservice.

How it works...

As you can see from the processes involved in this recipe, there is great similarity between Kotlin and Java-based styles of writing Spring 5 applications using Spring Boot 2.0. The only reason for this is that Kotlin provides strong interoperability behavior with libraries compiled in Java 1.8, unlike Groovy.

Groovy is a dynamically-typed and object-oriented language which is considered a popular JVM-based language. Its codes are compiled using static Java compilers to generate bytecodes faster than Java compilation. Its edge is some string and numerical operations which are heavy if executed multiple times in Java. But Groovy fails to execute a majority of Java APIs, unlike Kotlin, which can import almost all of them. Kotlin is also a JVM-based language, but written as an improvement to Java and not to Groovy and other JVM-based languages.

The strength of Kotlin over Java is the clarity and simplicity of its coding convention, which allows developers to focus on the high-level specification of the project. Everything that we have done, from `Chapter 2`, *Learning Dependency Injection (DI)* up to this chapter, can be done by Kotlin with less code. Currently, Kotlin can be used to implement Android-based applications because of its shorter and lighter bytecodes. You can learn more about Kotlin through the documentation at `https://kotlinlang.org/docs/tutorials/`.

13
Testing Spring 5 Components

It has been a long way getting to know the features and modules of Spring 5 Framework, through details of every ground-up implementation or through the Spring Boot 2.0 way of developing each of its components. We had categorized, scrutinized, and examined several Spring 5 major components already such services, `@Repository` transactions, view resolvers, and request handlers through sets of recipes we performed in the earlier chapters. We had arrived at several conclusions and recommendations already as to when, where, and how to use this newest installment of the Spring Framework to solve any real-world problems, be it in some experimental sample problem or for enterprise software solution.

This book will not end without providing the knowledge of how to perform different kind of tests to all recipes before deploying them to the production servers. This last chapter will enumerate the core concepts of context-dependent and standalone testing of Spring MVC and the Spring WebFlux components of Spring 5. It will also highlight some new **Spring Test Framework APIs** that are needed to test some reactive RESTful services, Spring Cloud module implementations; Kotlin-written components, and microservices built using Spring Boot 2.0.

It is time to use the Spring Test starter POM of Spring Boot 2.0 in building unit and integration test cases for some major MVC functionalities especially the functional and reactive web framework, reactive JPA repositories, asynchronous `@Controller`, and non-blocking services.

In this chapter, you will learn the following topics:

- Creating tests for Spring MVC components
- Building standalone controller tests
- Creating tests for DAO and service layers
- Creating tests on secured applications
- Creating tests using Spring Boot 2.0

- Creating tests for Spring Data JPA
- Building tests for blocking asynchronous and reactive RESTful services
- Building tests for Kotlin components

Creating tests for Spring MVC components

This first recipe is about writing unit tests for a general Spring 5 web application. This will highlight the basic steps on how to start integration testing with **Spring TestContext framework** by validating and verifying that all the beans injected into the container are @Autowired correctly in order to build the required MVC application. This framework can be used not only for testing, but also for test-driven development methodology.

Getting ready

Open the previous Maven Spring ch03 and add the following MVC test cases.

How to do it...

Let us perform Spring core testing with JUnit 4, Mockito 2.x, and Spring TestContext framework:

1. Before we start the configuration, ensure that you have the spring-context module in pom.xml. Then, add the following Spring Test, and now the JUnit 4.x and Mockito 2.x Maven dependencies to your pom.xml:

```
<dependency>
        <groupId>org.springframework</groupId>
        <artifactId>spring-test</artifactId>
        <version>${spring.version}</version>
        <scope>test</scope>
</dependency>
    <dependency>
        <groupId>junit</groupId>
        <artifactId>junit</artifactId>
        <version>4.12</version>
        <scope>test</scope>
        <exclusions>
            <exclusion>
                <groupId>org.hamcrest</groupId>
                <artifactId>hamcrest-core</artifactId>
```

```
            </exclusion>
          </exclusions>
        </dependency>
        <dependency>
            <groupId>org.hamcrest</groupId>
            <artifactId>hamcrest-library</artifactId>
            <version>1.3</version>
            <scope>test</scope>
        </dependency>
        <dependency>
            <groupId>org.mockito</groupId>
          <artifactId>mockito-core</artifactId>
            <version>2.8.47</version>
            <scope>test</scope>
      </dependency>
```

The `hamcrest-library` framework is optional. The given `hamcrest-core` framework of the JUnit 4.x dependency can still be utilized instead.

2. Inside the project's `src/test/java` folder, create a core package `org.packt.dissect.mvc.test` and add a Spring TextContext test class to it with the proper configuration details. This test class will load all the beans injected inside the container into the Test Framework for integration testing:

```
import static org.springframework.test.web.servlet.request
.MockMvcRequestBuilders.get;
import static org.springframework.test.web.servlet.request.
MockMvcRequestBuilders.post;
import static org.springframework.test.web.servlet.result.
MockMvcResultHandlers.print;
import static org.springframework.test.web.servlet.result.
MockMvcResultMatchers.status;
import static org.springframework.test.web.servlet.result.
MockMvcResultMatchers.view;
@RunWith(SpringJUnit4ClassRunner.class)
@WebAppConfiguration
@ContextConfiguration(classes = { SpringWebinitializer.class,
    SpringDispatcherConfig.class , SpringContextConfig.class})
public class TestContextConfiguration {

@Autowired
    private WebApplicationContext ctx;

}
```

The `ctx` object has been defined by the `@WebApplicaConfiguration` annotation as the container of the Spring TestContext is loaded and configured by the application's contexts defined in `@ContextConfiguration`.

3. To proceed with MVC testing, `ctx` must be injected into a specialized class called `org.springframework.test.web.servlet.MockMvc`, which will provide all the needed utilities to run integrated testing. Add the following lines inside `TestContextConfiguration`:

```
private MockMvc mockMvc;
@Before
public void setUp() {
this.mockMvc = MockMvcBuilders.webAppContextSetup(ctx)
.build();
}
```

4. Let's now create our first test case, which is to check whether all the beans are `@Autowired` correctly into the application container:

```
@Test
public void testApplicaticatonContextBeans() {
        ServletContext servletContext = ctx.getServletContext();
        Assert.assertNotNull(servletContext);
}
```

5. Running the program gave me an exception because a validator was not correctly injected into the container. Any errors or exceptions on the bean autowiring must be fixed, otherwise all test cases will fail to run:

```
Caused by: org.springframework.beans.factory.NoSuchBeanDefinitionException: No qualifying bean of type 'org.packt.dissect.mvc.validator.EmployeeValidator' available:
    at org.springframework.beans.factory.support.DefaultListableBeanFactory.raiseNoMatchingBeanFound(DefaultListableBeanFactory.java:1486)
    at org.springframework.beans.factory.support.DefaultListableBeanFactory.doResolveDependency(DefaultListableBeanFactory.java:1097)
    at org.springframework.beans.factory.support.DefaultListableBeanFactory.resolveDependency(DefaultListableBeanFactory.java:1058)
    at org.springframework.beans.factory.annotation.AutowiredAnnotationBeanPostProcessor$AutowiredFieldElement.inject(AutowiredAnnotationBeanPostProcessor.java:5(
... 43 more
```

6. After fixing any errors, modify the test case and add the following lines to it in order to check whether certain controllers exist inside the container:

```
@Test
public void testApplicaticatonContextBeans() {
        ServletContext servletContext = ctx.getServletContext();
        Assert.assertNotNull(servletContext);
        Assert.assertNotNull(ctx.getBean("helloController"));
        Assert.assertNotNull(ctx.getBean("formController"));
}
```

7. Now, add a test case that will test a GET handler request and print the details of its execution:

```
@Test
public void testSimpleGet() throws Exception {
    mockMvc.perform(get("/simple.html")).andDo(print())
    .andExpect(view().name("get"));
}
```

8. Look at the following test case that checks whether there is a form model attribute mapped to the form page and verifies the class type of the model attribute:

```
@Test
public void testFormViewPage() throws Exception {
    mockMvc.perform(get("/employee_form.html"))
    .andDo(print())
    .andExpect(status().isOk())
    .andExpect(view().name("form_page"))
    .andExpect(model()
    .attributeExists("employeeForm"))
    .andExpect(model().attribute("employeeForm",
    any(EmployeeForm.class)));
}
```

9. Here is a test case that executes a POST request handler with a sample form data that will undergo EmployeeValidator and some custom property editors mapped to the form model attribute:

```
@Test
public void testFormSubmitPage() throws Exception {
    mockMvc.perform(post("/employee_form.html")
    .contentType(MediaType.APPLICATION_FORM_URLENCODED)
    .param("firstName", "Emma")
    .param("lastName", "Yoda")
    .param("position", "Project Manager")
    .param("age", "22")
    .param("birthday", "October 30, 2001")
    .param("email", "xxccyy@yahoo.com")
    .accept(MediaType.APPLICATION_FORM_URLENCODED))
    .andExpect(view().name("success_page"))
    .andDo(print())
    .andExpect(status().isOk());
}
```

10. Since the application's `EmployeeValidator` does not allow any employee profile with an age greater than 65, the following is a test case that proves that the test data is erroneous and will just send it back to `form_page` to ask for some other data:

```
@Test
public void testFormSubmitPageErrors() throws Exception {
        mockMvc.perform(post("/employee_form.html")
        .contentType(MediaType.APPLICATION_FORM_URLENCODED)
        .param("firstName", "Emma")
        .param("lastName", "Yoda")
        .param("position", "Project Manager")
        .param("age", "80")
        .param("birthday", "October 30, 2001")
        .param("email", "sjctrags@yahoo.com")
        .accept(MediaType.APPLICATION_FORM_URLENCODED))
        .andExpect(view().name("form_page"))
        .andDo(print())
        .andExpect(status().isOk())
        .andExpect(model()
        .attributeHasFieldErrors("employeeForm", "age"));
}
```

11. Save all files.

How it works...

Spring MVC testing is a method of integration testing provided by the Spring TestContext framework. The framework starts with calling the JUnit 4 runner `org.junit.runner.RunWith`, which is an annotation used for executing the JUnit 4 tests. The `org.springframework.test.context.junit4.SpringJUnit4ClassRunner` annotation of the framework is applied to the test class in order to load the `ApplicationContext` container to the test suite. Let us not forget that all beans involved in testing are `@Autowired` to the `ApplicationContext` container.

Aside from the runner, the framework has other annotations namely `@WebAppConfiguration` and `@ContextConfiguration` which help load and expose the `WebAplicationContext` beans to the framework's `MockMvc`, the provider of all the test utilities for integration testing. One of the useful methods of `MockMvc` is `perform()`, which executes a request URI to return a failure or success.

No matter how complete and correct the `Spring TestContext` configuration is, if the loaded `WebApplicationContext` beans contains autowiring errors, the whole framework will not work.

Building standalone controller tests

There are times when individual controller testing is preferable to loading the whole context into the Spring TestContext framework. This mechanism is only applicable to controllers that have fewer dependencies on other beans of the container, which makes them easy to test individually.

Getting ready

Once again, open the Maven `ch03` project and add the following standalone controller test cases.

How to do it...

Let us test some existing controllers in `ch03` by performing the following steps:

1. Create another test class inside `org.packt.dissect.mvc.test` without loading `WebApplicationContext` and configure `MockMvc` to test only `SimpleController` of this project:

```
import static org.springframework.test.web.servlet.request.
MockMvcRequestBuilders.get;
import static org.springframework.test.web.servlet.request.
MockMvcRequestBuilders.post;
import static     org.springframework.test.web.servlet.result.
MockMvcResultHandlers.print;
import static org.springframework.test.web.servlet.result.
MockMvcResultMatchers.status;
import static org.springframework.test.web.servlet.result.
MockMvcResultMatchers.view;
@RunWith(MockitoJUnitRunner.class)
public class TestControllerConfiguration {
    private MockMvc mockMvc;
    @Before
public void setUp() {
        this.mockMvc = MockMvcBuilders.standaloneSetup(new
```

```
                    SimpleController()).build();
    }
}
```

2. Add some test cases on the controller's GET and POST request handlers:

```
@Test
    public void testGetPage() throws Exception {
mockMvc.perform(get("/simple.html")).andDo(print())
            .andExpect(status().isOk())
            .andExpect(view().name("get"));
    }
@Test
    public void testPostPage() throws Exception {
            mockMvc.perform(post("/simple.html"))
            .andExpect(view().name("post"))
            .andDo(print())
            .andExpect(status().isOk());
    }
```

3. Add another test case that will test a non-existent component or a handler request that is not found inside SimpleController.

```
@Test
    public void testOtherRequest() throws Exception {
        mockMvc.perform(get("/login.html")).andDo(print())
            .andExpect(view().name("login"));
    }
```

4. Run the test method and observe what happens.

How it works...

This recipe is about building a unit test for a controller through the use of the Spring TestContext framework. The use of @MockitoJUnitRunner is to load the controller to the SpringContext container for testing. This Mockito injection only loads the controller to the Test framework including its validators, view resolvers, and message handlers. After this procedure, MockMvcBuilders offers some utility methods that will instantiate the controller and mock its request handlers.

This type of testing focuses more on the properties of each controller, making the tests more refined and focused on the behavior of each component. This is also an effective and convenient way of determining what causes some bugs during its actual execution.

Creating tests for DAO and service layers

Integration testing is also needed to validate and verify the results of each repository and service method. All repository transactions are dependent on the `java.sql.DataSource` package configured by one of the context definitions. Likewise, the services will not be working without the repository beans injected into the container. Although it needs the full configuration of Spring TestContext, this recipe does not need the creation of `MockMvc` just to execute these test cases.

Getting ready

Open the Maven project `ch03-jdbc` and add the following unit test cases for service and DAO layers.

How to do it...

Let us test the service and DAO layers by performing the following steps:

1. Add the Spring Test module, JUnit 4, and Mockito Maven dependencies into the project's `pom.xml` file.

2. Inside `src/test/java`, create the `org.packt.dissect.mvc.test` package and add inside it a Spring TestContext class:

```
import static org.junit.Assert.*;
@RunWith(SpringJUnit4ClassRunner.class)
@WebAppConfiguration
@ContextConfiguration(classes = { SpringDbConfig.class,
    SpringDispatcherConfig.class })
public class TestDepartmentDao { }
```

3. Add the following test cases that execute the actual `DepartmentDao` repository transactions using `JdbcTemplate` and evaluate the results using the `Assert` methods of JUnit:

```
@Autowired
private DepartmentDao departmentDaoImpl;

@Test
    public void testGetDepartment(){
        Department dept = departmentDaoImpl.getDepartmentData(8);
        assertNotNull(dept);
```

```
    }
    @Test
    public void testUpdateDepartment(){
        Department rec1 = new Department();
        rec1.setId(9);
        rec1.setDeptId(555555);
        rec1.setName("Accounting Department");
        departmentDaoImpl.updateDepartment(rec1);
        Department dept = departmentDaoImpl.getDepartmentData(9);
        assertSame("Accounting Department",dept.getName());
    }
    @Test
    public void testDeleteDepartment(){
        departmentDaoImpl.delDepartment(1);
        List<Department> depts = departmentDaoImpl.getDepartments();
        assertTrue(depts.size() > 0);
    }
    @Test
    public void testReadDepartmentRecords(){
        List<Department> depts = departmentDaoImpl.getDepartments();
        assertNotNull(depts);
        for(Department d : depts){
            System.out.println(d.getName());
        }
    }
}
```

4. Create another test class that uses mocking to test the `DepartmentService` methods:

```
@RunWith(SpringJUnit4ClassRunner.class)
@WebAppConfiguration
@ContextConfiguration(classes = { SpringWebinitializer.class,
  SpringDbConfig.class, SpringDispatcherConfig.class })
public class TestEmployeeService{
    @InjectMocks
    private EmployeeServiceImpl employeeServiceImpl;
    @Mock
    private EmployeeDaoImpl employeeDaoImpl;
    @Before
    public void setUp(){
        MockitoAnnotations.initMocks(this);
    }
    @Test
    public void testService(){
        List<Employee> emps = new ArrayList<>();
        Employee rec1 = new Employee();
        rec1.setId(22);
        rec1.setEmpId(3673);
```

```
        rec1.setAge(22);
        rec1.setBirthday(new Date(101,11,1));
        rec1.setDeptId(555);
        rec1.setFirstName("Joanna");
        rec1.setLastName("Kiko");
        emps.add(rec1);
        given(employeeDaoImpl.getEmployees()).willReturn(emps);
        System.out.println(employeeServiceImpl.readEmployees());
    }
}
```

How it works...

It is ideal to run tests against all repositories and service methods before applying them to any request-response transactions. To test all these components, we need to load all the necessary context definitions to Spring TestContext in order to access every autowiring detail of each bean. To test the correctness and effectiveness of each method, we have to execute the actual methods or perform isolated testing using mocking.

Although quite risky, TestDepartmentDao executes the actual repository transactions that deal with the actual database schema. This can be effective, as long as the data involved is not live. On the other hand, TestDepartmentService prefers to use the @Mock objects to be injected into some @InjectMock objects for testing. To avoid using the actual data, the test class mocked DepartmentDao and substituted some dummy lists of departments instead into the service transaction readEmployees() to check whether the process of retrieval does not encounter any exceptions or performance problems. This can be effective, especially if the resources are not readily available to provide some test data to service layer.

Creating tests on secured applications

Spring TestContext can also provide ways to test methods and controllers that need login credentials, which many applications with Spring Security integration require. This recipe builds MockMvc to the ApplicationContext container secured by the **Spring Security 4.x** module.

Getting ready

Open the Maven project ch04 and add test classes to test secured methods.

How to do it...

Let us apply security model to some service methods and test them using Spring TestContext:

1. Add the Spring Test module, JUnit 4, and Mockito Maven dependencies to the project's pom.xml file.

2. Add a specialized Spring Security Test dependency to the pom.xml file:

```xml
<dependency>
    <groupId>org.springframework.security</groupId>
    <artifactId>spring-security-test</artifactId>
    <version>4.2.2.BUILD-SNAPSHOT</version>
    <scope>test</scope>
</dependency>
```

3. Inside src/test/java, create a org.packt.mvc.secured.test package and drop inside it a test class that builds MockMvc from a secured WebApplicationContext method. Also, it tests controllers by providing some Spring Security details such as the username and password:

```java
import static
org.springframework.security.test.web.servlet.setup.SecurityMockMvcConfigur
ers.
        springSecurity;
        @RunWith(SpringJUnit4ClassRunner.class)
        @WebAppConfiguration
        @ContextConfiguration(classes = { SpringWebinitializer.class,
            SpringDispatcherConfig.class , SpringContextConfig.class})
        public class TestSecuredControllers {
            @Autowired
            private WebApplicationContext ctx;
            private MockMvc mockMvc;
            @Before
            public void setUp() {
                this.mockMvc = MockMvcBuilders.webAppContextSetup(ctx)
                .apply(springSecurity()).build();
            }
            @Test
            public void testApplicaticatonContextBeans() {
                ServletContext servletContext = ctx.getServletContext();
                Assert.assertNotNull(servletContext);
            }
            @Test
             public void adminCanCreateOrganization()
        throws Exception {
```

```
this.mockMvc.perform(get("/deptform.html").with(user("sjctrags")
                .password("sjctrags").roles("USER"))
                .contentType(MediaType.APPLICATION_FORM_URLENCODED)
                .accept(MediaType.APPLICATION_FORM_URLENCODED))
                .andDo(print())
                .andExpect(status().isOk());
    }
}
```

4. Using invalid credentials, the execution of
   `adminCanCreateOrganization()` will lead to `HTTP 302`:

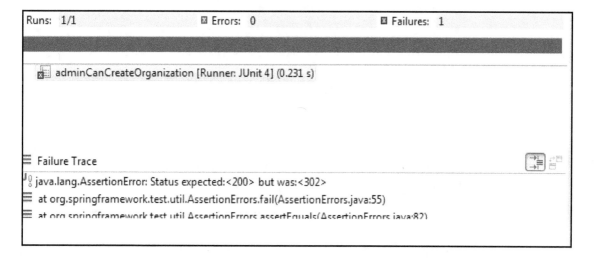

5. Create another test class that tests a secured method using the correct login
   credentials and role. Recall from Chapter 4, *Applying Aspect-Oriented
   Programming*, that three roles were created for the entire application, namely
   ROLE_USER, ROLE_ADMIN, and ROLE_HR, and each is assigned to different
   `DepartmentService` methods. Accessing the `readDepartments()` method
   requires a ROLE_USER role:

```
import static org.springframework.security.test.web.servlet.setup.
    SecurityMockMvcConfigurers.springSecurity;
import static org.junit.Assert.*;
@RunWith(SpringJUnit4ClassRunner.class)
@WebAppConfiguration
@ContextConfiguration(classes = { SpringWebinitializer.class,
SpringDispatcherConfig.class, SpringContextConfig.class})
public class TestSecuredServices {
    @Autowired
    private DepartmentService departmentServiceImpl;
```

```
        @Autowired
        private WebApplicationContext ctx;
        private MockMvc mockMvc;
        @Before
        public void setUp() {
            this.mockMvc = MockMvcBuilders.webAppContextSetup(ctx)
            .apply(springSecurity()).build();
        }
        @Test
         @WithMockUser(roles="USER")
        public void testListDepts(){
            SecurityContextHolder.getContext()
            .setAuthentication(new UsernamePasswordAuthenticationToken(
            "sjctrags", "sjctrags"));
            List<Department> depts =
departmentServiceImpl.readDepartments();
            assertNotNull(depts);
            for(Department dept : depts){
               System.out.println(dept.getDeptId());
             }
        }
    }
```

6. Running the test method `testListDepts()` with the wrong credentials and role will lead to the following exception:

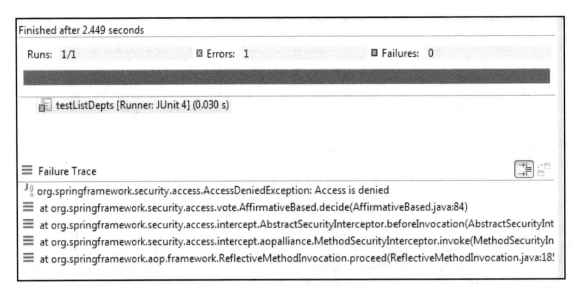

How it works...

In order to test controllers and methods from an application secured by Spring Security 4.x, it is required to build a Spring TestContext that employs Spring Security into the test suite. One way is to instantiate `MockMvc` with `WebApplicationText` by applying the `springSecurity()` mock method from `SecurityMockMvcConfigurers`.

Using the application from Chapter 4, *Applying Aspect-Oriented Programming*, we tested `/deptform.html` bypassing `/login.html`, which results in using the appropriate user credentials and role to successfully run the request. On the other hand, the `@WithMockUser` annotation from the Spring Security Test module that provides utilities to mock secured methods. The test will be successful only given the proper login credentials which must be provided to, `SecurityContextHolder.getContext().setAuthentication(new UsernamePasswordAuthenticationToken("admin", "admin"));`. This authentication API must always be the first line to be executed in any test cases involving secured methods.

Creating tests using Spring Boot 2.0

At this point, we are done with creating test classes using the Spring 5 framework from the ground up. This recipe will highlight how to build test classes using Spring Boot 2.0 `spring-boot-starter-test`.

Getting ready

Open the Spring Boot `ch09` project and implement some test cases using Spring Boot 2.0.

How to do it...

Let us implement test cases in Spring Boot 2.0 projects by performing the following steps:

1. First, add the Spring Test starter POM in the `pom.xml` file:

```
<dependency>
    <groupId>org.springframework.boot</groupId>
    <artifactId>spring-boot-starter-test</artifactId>
    <scope>test</scope>
</dependency>
```

2. This application is secured by Spring Security, so add the following Spring Security Test module to the application in order to utilize some mock-related annotations useful during testing:

```
<dependency>
    <groupId>org.springframework.security</groupId>
    <artifactId>spring-security-test</artifactId>
    <version>4.2.2.BUILD-SNAPSHOT</version>
    <scope>test</scope>
</dependency>
```

3. To test the Spring Boot 2.0 controller methods, add the following SpringTestContext class inside `org.packt.secured.mvc.test` of `src/test/java` with an emphasis on the new annotations, `@SpringBootTest` and `@AutoConfigureMockMvc`:

```
import static
org.springframework.security.test.web.servlet.request.
SecurityMockMvcRequestPostProcessors.user;
import static org.springframework.test.web.servlet.request.
MockMvcRequestBuilders.get;
import static org.springframework.test.web.servlet.result.
MockMvcResultHandlers.print;
import static org.springframework.test.web.servlet.result.
MockMvcResultMatchers.status;
@RunWith(SpringRunner.class)
@SpringBootTest
@AutoConfigureMockMvc
@ContextConfiguration(classes={ HRBootApplication.class,
    SpringContextConfig.class, SpringAsynchConfig.class })
public class TestControllers {
    @Autowired
    private MockMvc mvc;
    @Test
    public void callEmpFormReq()  throws Exception {
        mvc.perform(get("/react/empform.html")
        .with(user("sjctrags")
        .password("sjctrags").roles("USER")))
        .andDo(print())
        .andExpect(status().isOk());
    }
}
```

4. To simply test the JDBC, DAO, and service layers, add the following
   `@SpringBootTest` class inside the same `org.packt.spring.boot.test`
   package:

```
import static org.junit.Assert.*;
@RunWith(SpringRunner.class)
@SpringBootTest
@ContextConfiguration(classes={ HRBootApplication.class,
    SpringContextConfig.class, SpringAsynchConfig.class })
public class TestDaoLayer {

@Autowired
private DepartmentDao departmentDaoImpl;
@Test
public void testDeptDao(){
assertNotNull(departmentDaoImpl.getDepartments());
System.out.println(
departmentDaoImpl.getDepartments());
}
}
```

How it works...

Similar to the previous recipe, Spring Boot test classes always start with a call to the
`@RunWith` annotation with a `SpringRunner` parameter that tells JUnit to run all test cases
within the context of the Spring TestContext framework. The `SpringRunner` parameter is a
newer and shorter name for `SpringJUnit4ClassRunner`. The `@SpringBootTest`
annotation, on the other hand, can be used to bootstrap the entire container in preparation
for the integration testing. All beans are loaded into the Test framework to build `MockMvc`
through the `@AutoConfigureMockMvc` annotation.

The unit test for request handler in Spring Boot 2.0 uses `@WebMvcTest` instead of
`@SpringBootTest`, which is limited only to a single controller and can only execute with
all the needed `@MockBean` annotation to provide mock implementations for the controller's
required autowired beans. Mocking services and repository components are needed since
not all beans are loaded into the Test framework.

Creating tests for Spring Data JPA

Spring Boot offers a convenient way of writing test classes to run Spring Data JPA
transactions.

Getting ready

Open the Spring Boot `ch09-flux` project and add the following test classes for Spring Data JPA repository transactions.

How to do it...

Perform the following steps in creating test cases for Spring Data JPA repository layer:

1. Just like in the previous recipe, add the required Spring Test starter POM dependency in the project's `pom.xml` file.

2. Inside `src/test/java`, create an `org.packt.spring.boot.test` package and add inside a test class with a new annotation, `@DataJpaTest`, inside it:

```
@RunWith(SpringRunner.class)
@DataJpaTest
@ContextConfiguration(classes={ HRBootApplication.class,
    CachingConfig.class, SpringDataConfig.class,
WebFluxConfig.class})
@AutoConfigureTestDatabase(replace=Replace.NONE)
public class EmployeeRepositoryTest {
    @Autowired
     private TestEntityManager entityManager;
    @Autowired
    private EmployeeRepository employeeRepository;
    @Test
    public void testLoadGames() {
       List<Employee> deptTest =
          employeeRepository.findAll();
       assertNotNull(deptTest);
       System.out.println(deptTest.size());

    }
}
```

3. Save all files. Execute the test class.

How it works...

A Spring Boot test class dedicated to testing Spring Data JPA transactions has a distinct annotation, @DataJpaTest, that configures testing on the JPA persistence layer. It automatically searches for an in-memory database with Hibernate and the Spring Data JPA setup and recognizes JPA entity classes involved in the transactions management. It has an option to use the current DataSource configuration instead of default in-memory database, just by adding @AutoConfigureTestDatabase(replace=Replace.NONE) on the test class. The @DataJpaTest annotation always enables SQL log, thus, running the preceding test method will generate the following output:

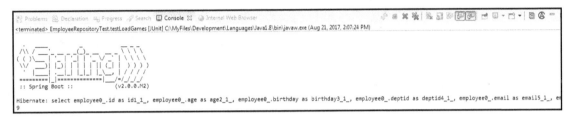

Building tests for blocking, asynchronous and reactive RESTful services

If testing Spring Data JPA transactions is easier with Spring Boot, then the following recipe that involves testing RESTful services is also quite straightforward and convenient as compared to the usual MockMvc style.

Getting ready

Again, open the DEPARTMENT microservices project, which is ch10-deptservice, and add the following test classes that will validate the results of each RESTful service.

How to do it...

Let us implement test cases for each RESTful service of a microservice by performing the following steps:

1. Just like in the previous recipe, add the needed Spring Test starter POM dependency in the project's pom.xml file.

2. Inside `src/test/java`, create an `org.packt.microservice.core.test` package and drop a test class that executes blocking RESTful services using `org.springframework.boot.test.web.client.TestRestTemplate`:

```
import static org.assertj.core.api.Assertions.assertThat;
@RunWith(SpringRunner.class)
@SpringBootTest(webEnvironment = WebEnvironment.RANDOM_PORT)
@ContextConfiguration(classes={ HRDeptBootApplication.class,
    CacheConfig.class, SpringDataConfig.class,
    SpringAsynchConfig.class })
public class TestRestService {
    @Autowired
    private TestRestTemplate restTemplate;

    @Test
    public void exampleTest() {
        String body = this.restTemplate.getForObject(
"/objectSampleRest", String.class);
        assertThat(body).isEqualTo("Hello World");
    }
    @Test
    public void exampleTestList() {
        String body = this.restTemplate.getForObject(
"/objectSampleRest", String.class);
        assertThat(body).isEqualTo("Hello World");
    }
    @Test
    public void exampleTestListAll() {
        List<Department> body =
            this.restTemplate.getForObject(
"/listDept", List.class);
        assertNotNull(body);
System.out.println(body);
    }
}
```

3. Add another test class that scrutinizes asynchronous services that return the `Callable<T>`, `DeferredResult<T>`, and `WebAsyncTask<T>` tasks:

```
import static
org.springframework.test.web.servlet.request.MockMvcRequestBuil
ders.asyncDispatch;
import static
org.springframework.test.web.servlet.request.MockMvcRequestBuil
ders.get;
import static
org.springframework.test.web.servlet.result.MockMvcResultMatche
```

```
rs.header;
import static
org.springframework.test.web.servlet.result.MockMvcResultMatche
rs.request;
import static
org.springframework.test.web.servlet.result.MockMvcResultMatche
rs.status;
@RunWith(SpringRunner.class)
@AutoConfigureMockMvc
@SpringBootTest(webEnvironment = WebEnvironment.RANDOM_PORT)
@ContextConfiguration(classes={ HRDeptBootApplication.class,
   CacheConfig.class, SpringDataConfig.class,
   SpringAsynchConfig.class })
public class TestAsyncService {
   @Autowired
    private MockMvc mockMvc;
    @Test
    public void testController () throws Exception {
        MvcResult result = mockMvc.perform(
get("/callSelectDept/359.json"))
        .andExpect(request().asyncStarted())
        .andReturn();
        result.getRequest().getAsyncContext()
.setTimeout(5000);
        result.getAsyncResult();
        result= mockMvc.perform(asyncDispatch(result))
            .andExpect(status().isOk())
            .andExpect(header().string("Content-Type",
MediaType.APPLICATION_JSON_UTF8_VALUE))
            .andReturn();
        System.out.println(result.getResponse()
.getContentAsString());
    }
}
```

 Although there is `AsyncRestTemplate`, there is no corresponding test API for this as of the moment.

4. Lastly, add a Spring TestContext class that evaluates reactive RESTful services exposed through either the `@RestController` or `HandlerRouter<T>` implementation. This test class uses the new API `org.springframework.test.web.reactive.server.WebTestClient` from Spring 5:

```
import static org.junit.Assert.assertEquals;
@RunWith(SpringRunner.class)
@AutoConfigureMockMvc
@SpringBootTest(webEnvironment = WebEnvironment.RANDOM_PORT)
@ContextConfiguration(classes={ HRDeptBootApplication.class,
    HttpServerConfig.class, SpringDataConfig.class,
    SpringAsynchConfig.class })
public class TestReactService {

    @Autowired
    private WebTestClient webTestClient;
     @Test
     public void testDeptById(){
         FluxExchangeResult<Department> result =
             webTestClient.get()
.uri("http://localhost:8090/ch10-
             dept/selectReactDept/359")
.accept(MediaType.APPLICATION_JSON_UTF8)
             .exchange().returnResult(Department.class);
             assertEquals( result.getStatus().value(), 200);
             Department dept =
                 result.getResponseBody().blockFirst();
             System.out.println(dept.getName());
         }
     @Test
     public void testDeptByIdRouter(){
         FluxExchangeResult<Department> result =
             webTestClient.get()
.uri("http://localhost:8901/selectDeptById/359")
.accept(MediaType.APPLICATION_JSON_UTF8)
             .exchange().returnResult(Department.class);
             assertEquals( result.getStatus().value(), 200);
Department dept =
    result.getResponseBody().blockFirst();
             System.out.println(dept.getName());
         }
    }
```

How it works...

To test RESTful services, aside from using the typical MockMvc, Spring Framework provides a utility class named TestRestTemplate, which is a convenient alternative to Spring REST integration tests. Together with the simulated random ports given by WebEnvironment.RANDOM_PORT of @SpingBootTest, TestRestTemplate can easily be injected into the test class without much configuration and can then proceed executing the REST endpoints through its methods such as exchange(), getForObject(), postForObject(), delete(), and put().

Since there is no utility test class for asynchronous or non-blocking REST services, it is recommended to use MockMvc with some asynchronous mocking events such as asyncStarted() and asyncDispatch(). Although not pretty straightforward as the blocking counterpart, the first request execution of the perform() method of MockMvc with the service URL must execute the asyncStarted() method, which flags the start of asynchronous processing. Then create another request execution triggered by asyncDispatch(), which handles the continuation of the previous request processing. If the test method always returns a null result, set a time delay to the first MvcResult before the second perform() method starts to execute.

Reactive REST services can be tested through WebTestClient, which was discussed in the previous chapter. It is a variant of WebClient that is used to run services that return the Flux<T>, Mono<T>, or Publisher<T> stream data. It is also used to save a stream of data into the repository. The REST endpoint generated by HandlerRouter<T> and HandlerFunction<T> can also be tested using WebTestClient.

Building tests for Kotlin components

Spring Boot 2.0 supports writing test classes for Kotlin component testing. This recipe will highlight how to test a RESTful service written in the Kotlin language.

Getting ready

Open the Spring Boot ch12-kotlin project and add a Kotlin test class.

How to do it...

Using Kotlin language, perform the following steps in implementing test cases for Kotlin request handlers:

1. First, add the Kotlin-JUnit Maven dependency into the `pom.xml` file:

```
<dependency>
    <groupId>org.jetbrains.kotlin</groupId>
    <artifactId>kotlin-test-junit</artifactId>
    <version>${kotlin.version}</version>
    <scope>test</scope>
</dependency>
```

2. Add a JUnit 4 plugin.
3. Inside `src/test/kotlin`, create an `org.packt.microservice.kotlin.test` package and add inside it a Kotlin test class that will test one of the Kotlin REST endpoints:

```
import org.junit.Assert.*;
@RunWith(SpringRunner::class)
@SpringBootTest(webEnvironment =
    SpringBootTest.WebEnvironment.RANDOM_PORT)
public class DepartmentControllerTest {
    @Autowired
    lateinit var restTemplate: TestRestTemplate
    @Test
    fun testRestData() {
        val listDepts = restTemplate.getForObject(
"/listdepts", List::class.java)
        assertTrue(listdepts.size > 0)
    }
}
```

 Avoid using `static import` because Kotlin does not support the `static` keyword.

4. Save all files. Run the test class through the Maven command, `test`.

How it works...

Kotlin test classes are slimmer versions of Java-based test classes. To run the test classes, the Maven command `test` must be executed, either through command line or the Eclipse Maven plugin. Other than its condensed syntax, the rest of the APIs are derived from the Spring 5 framework components, which makes it easier to use.

Index

S

www.ingramcontent.com/pod-product-compliance
Lightning Source LLC
LaVergne TN
LVHW081505050326
832903LV00025B/1394